All God's Creatures

DAILY DEVOTIONS
for ANIMAL LOVERS

2021

Guideposts
Danbury, Connecticut

All God's Creatures 2021

100 Reserve Road, Suite E200
Danbury, CT 06810
Guideposts.org

Acknowledgments

Every attempt has been made to credit the sources of copyrighted material used in this book. If any such acknowledgment has been inadvertently omitted or miscredited, receipt of such information would be appreciated.

Cover and interior design by Müllerhaus
Cover photos by Shutterstock
Monthly page opener photos by Shutterstock
Indexed by Maria A. Sullivan
Typeset by Aptara, Inc.

Photos on pages 378–389 are courtesy of the authors.

Printed and bound in the United States of America
10 9 8 7 6 5 4 3 2 1

Who teacheth us more than the beasts of the earth,
and maketh us wiser than the fowls of heaven?

—Job 35:11

Introduction

Every day when I arrive home, the first things I see through the beveled-glass panels of my front door are the eager faces of my golden retrievers, waiting to greet me. Senior golden Ernest sits calmly. But youngster Pete wiggles his whole body, and he always has at least one shoe in his mouth. One day I was returning home along with my adult son, who had come for a visit. When I opened the door, there was Ernest sitting patiently. And of course, there was Pete with my leather loafer dangling from his teeth.

"Thank you, Pete," I said, hugging his furry neck.

Seeing this, my son shook his head, laughing. "Why do you say 'thank you' when he's misbehaving? He shouldn't chew your shoes."

"He's not misbehaving," I said. "When I return, he runs to find something he thinks I value and brings it to me. It's a gift."

God has given me a love for critters of all kinds. Throughout the years, He's blessed me with many pets, including dogs, cats, rabbits, guinea pigs, turtles, and more. All my life I've received their gifts of companionship, comfort, and humor. And yes, even the gift of slightly slobbery footwear.

God has also shown me the gifts that I can give to animals, such as compassion, nurturing, and, in the wild, conservation of their environment. And He gave my husband and me hearts for adopting senior dogs. At first, I'd hesitated. Loving and losing would not be easy. Looking into those old, wise, and sometimes cataract-covered eyes, however, I clearly saw that it wasn't only about what dogs could give us. It was about what we could give them, as well—good food, a soft bed, and a loving forever home to live out their golden years.

That joyous exchange of love is one way God uses animals to point us toward Him and His love, but anyone who spends time with animals knows that there are so many others. And that's what *All God's Creatures* is all about.

Turn the pages of this book and you'll find daily faith-filled devotions about our bond with pets who love, comfort, and make us happy, as well as encounters with other creatures that give us unexpected insights into our relationship with God and others. You'll also meet people like you who care for, respect, and nurture animals, and discover the "visiting miracles," as one author describes them, in a dragonfly, a spider, or a honeybee. These little lessons strengthen our connections with all God's amazing creatures and draw us ever closer to our Creator.

—**Peggy Frezon**,
contributing editor of *All Creatures* magazine,
author of books about the human-animal bond,
and mom to rescue dogs Pete and Ernest

January

JANUARY 1

God's Better Plan

For as the heavens are higher than the earth, so are My ways higher than your ways, and My thoughts than your thoughts.

—Isaiah 55:9 (NKJV)

IT WAS THE first day of the new year, and I was feeling out of shape. "This year, I am going to start walking at the mall every morning," I pledged, "no matter what."

Later the same day, my neighbor Jean called. "Would you mind feeding and walking Amy, my little Pomeranian, every morning and afternoon for one week?"

"My pleasure" was my reply.

The first morning of my walking duties was bitter cold. I regretted telling Jean "my pleasure." The truth was, no matter how much I love animals, it would still be "my inconvenience."

When I arrived at Amy's house, a fluffy, dancing ball of orange fur with sparkly polished-stone brown eyes greeted me. She finished her hello by licking my leg, leaving a trail of dripping doggy drool. I pulled back. Then I took another look—and came face to face with the earnest gaze of a Pomeranian, inviting me to be her friend. As an exclamation point, she made sure to slurp my pant leg again.

The two of us headed outside into the frigid morning. The more we walked, the more I felt a warmth coming from my little companion—from her little Pom heart to mine. Back at the house, after her meal and water, she curled into a ball, using my foot as her pillow, and fell asleep. I closed my eyes for a bit . . . revived in a way that a walk at the mall could never make me feel.

My early mornings with Amy were not an unpleasant chore at all. They were a New Year's gift from God, whose mysterious ways brought me an adorable Pom filled with love.

Walk of Faith: *The Lord is ready at any time to revive your life, but are you ready? Be open to how He may do it through one of His creatures.*

—Sandra Clifton

JANUARY 2

Over Fences

Therefore, since we are surrounded by such a great cloud of witnesses, let us throw off everything that hinders and the sin that so easily entangles. And let us run with perseverance.

—HEBREWS 12:1–2 (NIV)

MY MOM'S FAMILY did not have the financial resources to send her to horseback-riding camp when she was a girl, but she found a way to get there anyway: she worked at the camp. Working in the kitchen was a small offering for the opportunity to ride horses. Her first lessons were on a small rust-colored horse named Rusty. "He was push-button," she said. "I didn't have to do much—he knew what to do."

Her passion to ride took a back seat to raising a family of five children. But much later in life, when my sister got married and left her horse, Cricket, at home, Mom decided to take up riding again. By then, my sister's quarter horse was also a push-button horse, so Mom made a goal: she would go over fences by the time she turned sixty-five. And sure enough, she did—on her sixty-fifth birthday. She set up the jumps behind the house and told Cricket, "You know what to do." Over the short fences they went.

My mom's sweet adventures with Cricket remind me that perseverance is a hallmark of those who consistently meet personal goals. After I determine my goals, plans with action steps will help me reach them. Instead of becoming complacent with intermittent progress, I need to keep the end goal in mind.

For example, because I made a goal of becoming closer to God this year, I created a plan to read the Bible each day. Part of my plan includes a reading time and a place. One day at a time—persevering each day—will add up to hours invested in my relationship with God.

Lord, I do want to spend more time with You this year. Help me stay focused so I can persevere in my plan to learn more about You each day. Amen.

—Janet Holm McHenry

JANUARY 3

Learning from Lizards

I wait for the Lord, my whole being waits, and in his word, I put my hope.

—Psalm 130:5 (NIV)

I SPENT A YEAR as a zookeeper of sorts. My friends would tease me, saying that was when I had three young boys at home, but the boys were more like mayhem makers than zoo animals. No, I actually took care of animals at a residential school for children waiting for foster homes. Since this was a temporary home for the children, they were allowed to have pets. The pets, however, had to be housed in a separate facility, hence the need for caretakers.

Bunnies and birds were great. But when I took the job, I didn't realize I would also be working with . . . lizards? What kind of pet was that? A popular one with boys, as it turns out. Taking care of the lizards included feeding them live crickets. That skill was not on my bucket list. It wasn't pretty, but I soon learned it was doable.

The lizards learned too. They soon realized I was their lunch date. When they saw me enter the area, they would climb up on their individual perches and wait. I was pretty sure they were smiling. Until that point in my life, I had not realized how intelligent and trusting lizards are. They had the faith and hope that I would provide meals for them. They would graciously wait until I prepared their food and then humbly accept it.

God asks me to wait patiently with trust like those lizards did. They had it down pat. I, however, often get impatient with God's timing. I was blessed with human intelligence, but I learned quite a bit about waiting, hoping, and trusting from lizards.

Father, may I, like a lizard, wait, trust, and hope. Amen.

—Linda Bartlett

JANUARY 4

The Crows

Look at the birds of the air, for they neither sow nor reap nor gather into barns; yet your heavenly Father feeds them. Are you not of more value than they?

—MATTHEW 6:26 (NKJV)

ONE DAY, I watched the birds as I enjoyed a snack on my outdoor swing. A crow perched on a nearby branch was doing the same thing, only it was watching me! I tossed a couple of potato chips into the yard and went inside to watch what it would do. It cautiously picked up the chips in its beak and flew off.

After I repeated the routine a few times, several crows began showing up each morning. Before long I couldn't sleep in because of the racket they made demanding their breakfast. They even learned to eat off a paper plate.

Crows are intelligent birds, and these crows seemed to recognize me as I took walks around the neighborhood. As my route circled back home, they would notify the other crows that I was coming through a series of caws that echoed down the block. Several of them would be waiting for me (and their food) when I arrived at my front door.

The crows always kept a distance of about thirty feet from me, and only once did one of them come any closer. However, we all seemed to enjoy our relationship. I fed them plenty of bird food, and they gave me great joy. I looked forward to their early-morning cacophony and delighted to see their swooping flight into my yard.

Jesus compared our heavenly Father's care and concern for creatures like these birds to His immensely greater care for me. Based on my humble experience feeding the birds, I think our Father also delights in watching us draw near to enjoy the gifts He has carefully chosen and prepared for us.

[The fowls of heaven] trust your Father's providence, and will not you trust it? In dependence upon that, they are careless for the morrow; and being so, they live the merriest lives of all creatures; they sing among the branches. . . . —Matthew Henry

—Randy Benedetto

JANUARY 5

God Is in the Details

For we are God's handiwork, created in Christ Jesus to do good works, which God prepared in advance for us to do.

—EPHESIANS 2:10 (NIV)

I SLOWLY ROCKED in my hammock, listening to the sounds of Lake Superior. We were spending the weekend camping with friends in Michigan's scenic Upper Peninsula. I was relishing the quiet moment when my friend Amber interrupted my dozing with an excited voice, "Twila, come see the buck I found!" Puzzled, I quickly followed her.

Amber explained that while she was picking up firewood, she'd sensed a presence. When she looked up, she was surprised to see a large male deer fairly close to her. Feeling uneasy, she kept her eye on him while backing away down the trail.

As we quietly returned, I didn't see him at first. Then he took a step, and I smiled. Light from the afternoon sun was shining on him through the trees. He wasn't bothered by the intrusion and continued on with dinner.

This was a rare treat, indeed, to be close to a buck in the wild. He blended with the woods, mysteriously disappearing or reappearing, depending on where he stood. The points on his rack, his soft eyes, and his beautiful brown fur were created especially for him by a Creator to allow him to hide in plain sight in the forest. Every detail was planned.

Remembering my encounter with the deer, I am reminded that God describes us as His handiwork. My Creator made my green eyes that change color, every freckle on my face, and my loud laugh. He created my caring spirit and gave me the ability to sing. As He created the deer for the woods, so my loving Father delightfully created every detail of me for my particular role on earth.

Thank You for creating me exactly as I am, Father.
Every single part of me is Yours. Amen.

—Twila Bennett

JANUARY 6

Holding Fast

It is the Lord your God you must follow, and him you must revere. Keep his commands and obey him; serve him and hold fast to him.

—Deuteronomy 13:4 (NIV)

BABY WAS AN orphaned piglet I met during a recent mission trip to Brazil.

She was a wild boar, only a few weeks old when a farmer in the Amazon found her near her dead mother. The tiny pig squealed and struggled to get away from the farmer. But someone told him to carry the beast under his arm as he walked home, so the pig could feel his heartbeat and bond with him.

As instructed, he put the piglet under his shirt, and she immediately calmed down. As the man began to care for the animal, she quickly became a pet. Baby followed the farmer wherever he went, allowing only a foot or two between herself and the farmer. Often, she would sit between his feet or fall asleep in his arms. When the heat and humidity of the rain forest became too much, Baby would rest in the farmer's shadow, rolling over to beg for a tummy rub.

Each day when the farmer left, Baby wandered the property calling for him until he returned. She was completely dependent upon the farmer to provide food, shelter, and safety. There was no mistaking that she needed him to survive. It brought the farmer, and all of us who observed their interaction, great joy.

Baby reminds me of the relationship God desires to have with me. How I long to be like that sweet little piglet—to cry for the Master when I need His touch, to rest in His arms, to follow Him anywhere.

I will always remember Baby and her desperate need for relationship with her master. I pray my walk with Christ models that as well.

Heavenly Father, thank You for adopting me when I was lost and alone. Teach me to depend on You completely—to follow You everywhere and never leave Your side. Amen.

—Tez Brooks

JANUARY 7

Being Seen

The Lord will watch over your coming and going both now and forevermore.

—Psalm 121:8 (NIV)

I'VE BEEN PRACTICING using my new camera by taking pictures of flowers in my garden. I particularly like using the macro setting. It zooms in close to capture God's glorious design and detail better than a regular shot could do. After taking dozens of pictures, I download them onto my computer and carefully look them over, then "spot fix" the prettiest pictures to share with family and friends.

While examining one particularly lovely photo of a cluster of pink tea roses, taking out any blemishes that detracted from the overall effect, my attention was drawn to an unusual "spot" in the photo I was about to fix. But I zoomed in further and, to my surprise, I was looking at a tiny insect. I don't know what kind of insect I saw, but it was so very small that I hadn't noticed it when I took the picture and even nearly missed it as I looked the picture over on my computer. This minuscule living creature, hunkered down between the petals of a rose, was something I'd never have noticed without my camera. And then I thought, *God knew it was there. And He didn't even need a macro lens!*

I had to smile at the thought. Sometimes I feel like that tiny bug—hidden away, unnoticed. But God knew it was there, just as He knows my coming and my going. God is everywhere I go, watching over me. He knows me. He sees me and loves me, and He is always around me. I was moved to praise when I thought about that tiny bug and the great big infinite God who knew of its tiny existence and knows of mine as well.

We may ignore, but we can nowhere evade the presence of God.
The world is crowded with Him. He walks everywhere incognito.
—C.S. Lewis

—Marianne Campbell

JANUARY 8

Great Blue Stillness

He says, "Be still, and know that I am God; I will be exalted among the nations, I will be exalted in the earth."

—PSALM 46:10 (NIV)

THE FLAPPING OF wings broke the silence of the woods. To my left, a massive span of feathers spread in midair, long legs gliding behind. Spurring myself faster, I approached the small pond, anxious to get a look at the grand bird I had inadvertently frightened.

Across the pond, it landed in a tree, and I stood, leaning against a rock, determined to wait for it to leave its perch so I could better glimpse its grandeur. I stood still, staring at the great blue heron with it staring back at me. Minutes ticked by. Somewhere in the back of my mind, I knew I couldn't stay there indefinitely—that quite possibly the crane had more tenacity at this waiting game than I did. I had edits due the next day, laundry to be folded, grocery list to be made, and supper to prepare. I thrived on getting things done and getting things done well.

But that morning, something about staring across the blue pond at the majestic bird, listening to the chorus of insects and birds making beautiful music around me, compelled me to lay aside my to-do list. A soothing yet unexplainable peace stirred my heart. In this waiting time, I felt that this bird—now my friend—was teaching me something. *Be still.*

Here, dwelling on this verse I had long ago memorized, staring across the pond at the crane that would no doubt win this being-still contest, the best thing was apparent. And it wasn't found in striving, fearing, or checking off to-do lists. It was found in quieting my heart, in marinating not in what *I* had to get done, but in what *God* had already done for me.

Heavenly Father, You are the great I Am, our strength, and our Savior. May we take time to rest not in our to-do lists, but in the majesty of who You are. Amen.

—Heidi Chiavaroli

JANUARY 9

A Sunny Outlook

I have learned how to be content with whatever I have. I know how to live on almost nothing or with everything. I have learned the secret of living in every situation. . . . For I can do everything through Christ, who gives me strength.

—PHILIPPIANS 4:11–13 (NLT)

THE STRAY KITTY, a beautiful calico, appeared on my street, hungry and expecting. Since childhood, I've wanted to take in every animal I found, but this time, I couldn't handle any more due to my recovery from major shoulder surgery. Thankfully, my neighbor took in Mama Kitty, who soon gave birth to four wiggly kittens.

The litter included two more calico females, a tuxedo male, and a rare calico male. I was struggling to manage postoperative pain and faced possible permanent disability as a result. But each time I watched the kitties chase one another around our quiet street, I had to smile.

Suddenly, the male calico went missing. Weeks later, when I saw him again, he was missing a back leg. My neighbor, such a sweet soul, explained through tears that the now-teenage kitten had survived an accident that may have cost him his leg but didn't slow him down one bit. I thanked her for saving the little guy. "I've named him Sunny," she said. The cat promptly raced circles around our legs.

Sunny doesn't seem to care that he's a leg short or that it's unfair. His exuberant take on life reminds me that although I haven't been miraculously delivered out of my troubles, I don't have to adopt an attitude of doom and gloom. Sunny teaches me that I can choose to do the best I can with what I've got. Even in the tough times, I can flash the world a "Sunny" smile.

God, give me an outlook that finds contentment and peace in every situation, every day, rain or shine. Amen.

—Linda S. Clare

JANUARY 10

Prayer in Action

For we are God's masterpiece. He has created us anew in Christ Jesus, so we can do the good things he planned for us long ago.

—EPHESIANS 2:10 (NLT)

HAVING DECIDED TO go out for lunch, my husband and I were about to enter a restaurant when we noticed a small bird having trouble flying. We watched the bird for a little while but didn't know what to do. I was so concerned I began to pray God would send *someone* to help. Surely, God had someone more equipped than I at His disposal!

We went inside to eat, planning to check on the bird after our meal. We reasoned that it may have flown into something and just needed a bit of time to recover from the disorientation. But when we came back outside, we found the little bird still flapping its wings, still unable to fly. The superhero bird rescuer I had made up in my prayer hadn't materialized. So I got on the phone with the animal sanctuary. We asked the restaurant for an old towel to catch the bird—a harder feat than you might expect, even with an injured bird—and transported it in a cardboard box to the sanctuary.

When we arrived, a volunteer took the box from me. "Oh, a sparrow," she said. She assured me the bird looked as if it had simply flown into an object and said she was confident they could give it the care it would need to recover. She also told us that if we hadn't stopped to help, a predator would have most likely caught and killed the little bird.

And that's when it hit me—God had answered my prayer by sending *me*.

I continued to call and check on my little sparrow, and the sanctuary released it, fully recovered, about a week later. But the lesson stayed with me far longer. Sometimes God sends a cavalry to help, but other times He uses my heart and ability and sends me.

Prayer in action is love, love in action is service. —Mother Teresa

—Ashley Clark

JANUARY 11

What's Yours Is . . . Mine

For where you have envy and selfish ambition, there you find disorder and every evil practice.

—JAMES 3:16 (NIV)

MISHA IS A Siamese cat that owns my house, all the food in every bowl, and me. Or at least that is how she lives her life. I love her deeply, but she is not an only cat, despite her apparent belief to the contrary. In the world of animal rescue, learning to share is part of socialization. Learning to share helps foster animals get forever homes when there are other animals and children in the house.

When the food bowls are put down for supper, dogs and cats each have their own area for eating. But Misha will go to each and every bowl. And if not stopped, she will growl and then box the noses of the dogs and cats, chasing them away from their bowls as if she were the only one being served dinner and they were taking something that was hers.

Misha gets fed in her own space now, alone, so others at the rescue ranch can eat in peace. There is always plenty to go around, but with any group, there is always at least one that gets greedy and territorial. It happens with people too.

We've all seen it. In the office, someone gets a higher position, and another begins whispers of discontent because he or she did not get that promotion. At home, a sibling starts a fight because another sibling got a gift and the first sibling did not receive one.

Selfishness and greed are never satisfied. They are ravenous and insatiable, and, unchecked, they eat into relationships and peace until they are gone. It is only in living in gratitude and faith in God's provision that we will truly find joy.

God, help me remember that just because someone has more does not mean I ever have less. Amen.

—Devon O'Day

JANUARY 12

Rest Assured

And my God shall supply all your need according to His riches in glory by Christ Jesus.

—PHILIPPIANS 4:19 (NKJV)

IT'S THE MIDDLE of the night, and I am wide awake and walking through the silent house. I can't seem to break these predawn ramblings since coming home from cancer surgery. Although the operation was successful and I have a good prognosis, I struggle with middle-of-the-night worries: what is ahead for me healthwise or financially?

As I go from room to room, I see my dear wife, Sandra, and our family cats sound asleep. One of them is Mr. Barnie, our orphan rescue from the streets. When we took him home, he was so tiny, thin, and weak that the vet gave him very little chance of survival. He has proven the doctor wrong and lived eighteen years beyond his original diagnosis. He is curled up on the sofa in the moonlit living room as if he were in the lap of luxury. And I suppose he is, compared to what we rescued him from years ago. What strikes me, in the early first light, is his posture of deep rest, born of trust—an instinctual reliance on his master's love and care that will provide for all his needs.

I should take a hint from Barnie. Our rescue cat has a deep trust in me, his loving provider. I need to start trusting and resting in God, my eternal provider. I give Barnie a gentle pat on the head and walk back to the bedroom—this time, to sleep in my Master's love.

You have made us for Yourself, and our hearts are restless until they rest in You. —Saint Augustine of Hippo

—Terry Clifton

JANUARY 13

God's Jealousy Flows from Love

Do not worship any other god, for the LORD, whose name is Jealous, is a jealous God.

—EXODUS 34:14 (NIV)

WE HAD ARRIVED at Safari West, a world-class wildlife preserve in Northern California, and my husband carried our son, Xavier, in his arms as we walked toward the tour Jeep. While our guide reviewed the rules, a large male ostrich stood in front of me. He spread his wings, shook his black and white feathers, and bobbed his head.

The guide chuckled. "He's trying to woo you into mating."

Our group laughed as we climbed into the open back of the Jeep. The ostrich continued his love dance, stepping close, then backing away.

My husband placed Xavier in a seat, then turned to help me into the vehicle. The ostrich ruffled his feathers and pecked him . . . hard. The guide waved the ostrich away and helped me into my seat, but the jealous bird returned and chased us for a few feet as we drove away.

Xavier's eyes widened as he grinned. "That bird really loves you, Mom," he said.

His comment triggered a sober reminder about Moses's description of God—the jealous God. After destroying the first stone tablets when he caught the Israelites worshipping a golden calf, Moses carved out two new tablets and went up Mount Sinai. The Lord affirmed His covenant with His beloved people, who would receive His loving grace and just discipline.

The ostrich reminded me that God's jealousy flows from love. My human frailty and sin can cause me to take jealousy and love to unhealthy levels. But God's love is perfect. With immeasurable grace, He helps me follow His commands, which are designed to protect me and draw me closer to His heart.

Father God, please help me remember everything You do flows from Your limitless love for us. Amen.

—Xochitl E. Dixon

My Partridge Family

If you really fulfill the royal law according to the Scripture, "You shall love your neighbor as yourself," you are doing well.

—JAMES 2:8 (ESV)

WHEN I WAS a young girl, my daddy found a lone partridge chick, apparently orphaned. Not wanting to leave it defenseless on the golf course, he brought it home for me to tend.

Soft as a kitten, the chick was covered with light gray feathers. Since my artist mom painted portraits, I imagined the dark marks on its wings as dabs of paint. Cupped in my hands, it trembled, settled down, then settled in. I loved it right away.

Daddy found a large box, cut off the top, and fashioned a square of wire over the opening. Then he lined the bottom with newspaper. I helped him add some grass flooring, and we cushioned one corner with a velvety towel. Water and birdseed completed the impromptu suite. When I lowered the bird into the box, it hopped around, exploring.

The next morning, I released my chick into the front yard, delighted as it hopped behind me, as if I were Mama. There was joyful pecking, too, and tiny tweets. My partridge seemed to feel at home.

Soon, it had grown a good deal, and the tweets turned into loud cheeps. When we would go for walks, the chick didn't always follow me. And Daddy said it was time to take it back to the golf course to find its family. Released where it was first found, the partridge disappeared into the foliage. Home again, I missed my little partridge, but I was glad God trusted me to look after the partridge for a time, then send it on its way, stronger than before.

Looking back, I remember the childhood confidence that equipped me to help this small creature. May I have the same confidence now that God still entrusts me, with His help, to make a difference in others' lives, just as I did then.

You are not too small. No one is ever too small to offer help. —Emlyn Chand

—Cathy Elliott

JANUARY 15

A Mighty, Small Reminder

Commit to the LORD whatever you do, and he will establish your plans.

—PROVERBS 16:3 (NIV)

THERE HE IS again," my husband, Mike, said.

A large green insect waited in the grass near our front door. It had buggy green eyes, antennae, and leaf-like wings. Its long front legs were bent and raised toward its face. "It looks like it's holding something," I said. "I wonder what it is."

"A Bible," Mike answered. "That insect is a praying mantis, after all."

Our praying mantis appeared every day, just outside the house. Once I spotted it on the slate walkway as I carried in groceries. Another time, it sat beneath the boxwood as we left to visit friends. Sometimes it perched on the bottom of the creaky front steps.

Each time I encountered the insect, with its hands folded so reverently, it reminded me of the importance of taking time in my busy day to pray. I began to pause right then and there and turn whatever lay ahead over to God. "Dear Father, please be with me and guide me in the ways I'm to go," I would whisper, nodding at the worshipful little fellow. Sometimes, if I was in a rush, I would get the false sense of having everything in control myself. Then I would see the insect in my path and remember to pray.

My little green friend became something of a marker—I would walk out the door, see it, and lift up my day to my Father in heaven, turning every thought over to Him in prayer. Yes, even a mighty small creature can remind me of the awesome power of the One who is all-seeing, all-knowing, and all-powerful.

Dear Lord, thank You for the way you direct my path, always bringing to mind the things I need to remember and placing before me the things I need to see. In Jesus's name. Amen.

—Peggy Frezon

JANUARY 16

Every Trick in the Book

Search me, God, and know my heart; test me and know my anxious thoughts. See if there is any offensive way in me, and lead me in the way everlasting.

—Psalm 139:23–24 (NIV)

WHEN I WAS in college, my family got a black cocker spaniel named Dancer. He was full grown but not too old to learn tricks, so we taught him to sit, lie down, play dead, roll over, shake hands, and high-five. Dancer quickly caught on that doing tricks got him treats, so he made a routine of giving me and my sisters pitiful looks when we were eating, hoping we'd say "Dancer, sit" and toss him something when he obeyed. If his sad eyes didn't move us, he would sit, then lie down, and then roll over. Sometimes he frantically went through his entire repertoire until my sisters and I cracked up and one of us tossed him a treat.

Dancer came to mind recently. While waiting impatiently for God to answer a request that I must admit was selfish, I had written a series of prayers in my journal, each one getting more desperate. I had tried everything: pouring out my heart, being specific in Jesus's name, finding a scripture that supported my noncritical need, and so on. When God finally came through, I composed a prayer of thanks. Then I remembered those other pages in my journal and wondered if I had come across like Dancer, trying every trick in the book until God gave me what I wanted.

My journals are filled with evidence of my tendency to beg instead of trusting that God heard me the first time and knows what's best for me. His kindness in granting even some of my frivolous desires testifies to His patience. Today, it also motivates me to try not to behave like a whimpering puppy so often.

Heavenly Father, I can be such a baby sometimes. Forgive me. Thank You for hearing me, whether my requests are critical or self-centered. Help me to recognize the difference as I learn to trust You to know my needs. Amen.

—Jeanette Hanscome

JANUARY 17

Remembering Toby

But do not overlook this one fact, beloved, that with the Lord one day is as a thousand years, and a thousand years as one day.

—2 PETER 3:8 (ESV)

IF YOU WERE a kid in the 1960s, living in or around Saint Paul, Minnesota, then you probably found yourself astride the back of a Galápagos tortoise named Toby whenever you visited the Como Zoo. You weren't looking for a fast ride. Toby could only get up to around a thousand feet per hour. But those rides were unforgettable.

My first recollection of Toby was when I was about five years old. He seemed to exude a sense of the ancient, to be an embodiment of wisdom. He made no sound, but patiently plodded, hour after hour, while myriad children waited their turn to have a ride on this exotic creature. Just after my high school graduation, Toby was relocated to the Honolulu Zoo, where he still lives today and is well into his eighties.

A new generation of Saint Paul children has come to love Toby in a different way. He has been commemorated in a life-size bronze sculpture on display just inside the zoo entrance. He presents a favorite photo opportunity and climbing experience, a means by which many of today's parents can relive their memories vicariously through their young ones.

I often wish I had a photo album with pictures reminding me of God's presence throughout my life. He rescued me from death on the first day of my life. He drew me to Himself and delighted when I gave my heart to Him as a young child. He protected my spirit, soul, and body as I waited to meet the man I would marry. He knew from the beginning all that I would encounter throughout my life. And the ride has been unforgettable.

Father, You have always been and always will be. My memories of years gone by are but a moment to You. You understand my limitations. The joy that You continue to pour into me will carry me through my life. Amen.

—Liz Kimmel

JANUARY 18

Called by Name

Do not fear, for I have redeemed you; I have called you by name; you are Mine!

—ISAIAH 43:1 (NASB)

MOM, I SEE a falcon!" my four-year-old's voice burst with excitement. I looked out to the backyard to find a large bird perched on our garden shed; it was not quite a falcon, and unlike any bird I had seen before. We reached for our bird book to identify our visitor.

"A northern goshawk," my husband announced. Outside, the goshawk turned toward us, and we admired its brown-and-white plumage and piercing yellow eyes. Around us, the world went on. The goshawk watched our neighbors working in their yards, unaware of its presence. We watched, steady and unmoving, for the next five minutes until it flew off.

Our boys still speak about our visitor that day, in part because we found its name. After it flew away, we wrote "Northern Goshawk" and the date on our bird-spotting chalkboard that hangs in our kitchen. Through the act of identifying birds and learning an interesting fact or two about them, we remember them and appreciate their uniqueness. Attaching a name has a way of etching someone into our memory.

All throughout God's Word, there is a sacredness to the act of giving someone a name. I find assurance as I dwell on the names God has given me: *redeemed, beloved, cherished, righteous, pure, delightful, strong, gifted, brave, His child.* As I spend time thinking on these names, I become more secure in my identity in Christ. Just like our northern goshawk friend, these names and promises are inscribed upon my memory. In the moment when I need them most, God reminds me who I am in Him.

Walk of Faith: *Take time to sit and write a list of what is true of you in Christ. If you need some inspiration to get started, read the short book of Colossians, especially chapter 3, verses 1–17.*

—Eryn Lynum

JANUARY 19

Nest Outside, Snake Inside

But the Lord is faithful, who will establish you and guard you from the evil one.

—2 THESSALONIANS 3:3 (NKJV)

"I DON'T KNOW HOW to handle this." My husband had gone to see what made the noise in our kitchen at midnight. Crawling from bed, I followed him and looked in the flashlight's beam.

A rope-like black item hung down several inches from inside our top cabinets. Kevin opened the door. A snake lay draped over dinner plates and dessert bowls.

"How do I get it out of there?" I envisioned dishes scattering and breaking. Thinking fast, I handed Kevin a pair of tongs. He grabbed the snake behind its head, cringing as it wound its body around the tongs close to his hands. Opening the screen door, he tossed the intruder out.

Several nights later, the snake returned, this time balancing itself on curtain holders above the kitchen window, inches from its previous hiding place. We wondered what it wanted in our cabinets. We had mice sometimes but never in the upper cabinets. I suggested taking it down the road where it wouldn't find its way back in again.

In the daylight, I noticed the proximity of its hiding places to the wrens' nest on the other side of the window screen, the nest with babies growing where the parents thought they were safe. I felt sure those fledglings were the snake's intended meal. We'll never know why the snake felt a need to come inside our house to get at a nest on the outside, but we're glad it stayed confined to the kitchen.

Our unusual visitor reminded me that I, like the baby wrens, often don't know danger is lurking nearby. I'm glad God's angels guard me and my family as that window screen guarded the birds.

The enemy prowls like lions and slithers like snakes.
Our God watches over us; a shield He makes. —C.M.

—Cathy Mayfield

JANUARY 20

The Perfect Foot Warmer

Comfort, comfort my people, says your God.

—Isaiah 40:1 (NIV)

WHY IS IT that the heat never goes out until the temperatures drop below freezing? It's like a rule that when we really need our heating system to work, in the middle of a cold night is the time for it to fail.

I was cuddled up and covered up trying to stay warm. All my fur babies were in the room with me. Sleep came, and somewhere in the middle of the night, I woke to the most amazing feeling of comfortable warmth around my feet. I had tucked them into my fuzzy travel blanket that had a little pocket for my feet. But this warmth was from more than just a blanket.

As my mind cleared from sleep, I realized the warmth was from Molly, my sweet gray kitty. She had climbed in that pocket, wrapped herself around my feet, and was purring loudly. It was like a gentle, warm, soft massage and made the cold night suddenly euphoric. It's the little things that help us get through the uncomfortable situations, and God stops at nothing to send us love notes and constant reassurance that we are the most important thing to Him.

Something as small as a kitten keeping my feet warm is suddenly not such a small thing when I look at it as a special gift from our Creator, who cares about my comfort, my peace, and my joy. When it comes to taking care of His children, no details are too small for God. I discovered that even after my heat got fixed, a cat wrapped around my feet is still a wonderful way to get a comfy night's sleep!

God, thank You for caring even about my comfort in Your busy days and nights. Amen.

—Devon O'Day

JANUARY 21

Gentle Ben

Never be lacking in zeal, but keep your spiritual fervor, serving the Lord.

—ROMANS 12:11 (NIV)

THE HAPPIEST FELLOW I ever met was Gentle Ben, my sister Nancy's dog, a Caucasian shepherd. The first time I saw Ben, I thought he was a bear—he was that big. But I quickly learned he was mostly fluff.

Ben loved everything and everyone, but he had two favorites. The first was Walmart. Nancy would say, "Ben, do you want to go to Walmart?"

His eyes would sparkle, and he would wag his tail, waiting for instructions.

Then Nancy would say, "Let's go!"

And Ben would do his best to scoot his big body up the plank into her pickup bed.

Ben was not a service dog, so that meant his job was the unofficial parking-lot greeter, and he did his duty faithfully.

His favorite time of year, though, was Halloween. Ben did not need a disguise, because with his bushy mane around his face, he was already in costume as Lion Bear. But he was the official trick-or-treat greeter with his happy smile and wagging tail.

Ben's love for life and its simple pleasures taught me to embrace the ordinariness of days with their simple routines. I can thank God each morning. I can embrace household chores and call them "exercise." Instead of saying, "I have to go to the store," I can say, "I get to be the greeter today," and then look for an opportunity to say a kind word to a stranger. A teddy bear of a dog showed me that embracing the ordinary makes it extraordinary.

Walk of Faith: *Life is a gift. We can choose to put it in the back of the closet, still tightly wrapped, or open it up and share it with others. How will you share a life gift today?*

—Janet Holm McHenry

JANUARY 22

The Hospitality Pig

Now you are the body of Christ, and each of you is a part of it.

—1 CORINTHIANS 12:27 (NIV)

WHEN WE WERE given the opportunity to add a pig to our homestead, the first question we asked ourselves was, *What will its job be?*

You see, homesteading is all about self-sustainability, so everything has to play a role. The garden provides food for both animals and people, the animals provide fertilizer for the garden and more food, both provide products we can sell to support the homestead. The goal is that everything produces something that benefits the whole.

For a pig, the obvious answer is that it will produce meat. However, that answer presented a problem: this was the cutest pig we had ever met.

Penelope was a mini-pig, complete with a storybook look and an endearing personality. There was no way we could raise a pig like that for bacon. Yet, we still had to answer the question, *What role could a pig like Penelope play on our homestead?*

And then it hit us: hospitality.

You see, we are constantly hosting people out at the homestead, and Penelope's personality could add incredible value to the way we do that. Her charm would add an unforgettably unique aspect to the experience of visitors to our home. She would endear herself to everyone around her. So, although it may not be a traditional job for a pig, it was perfect for her.

I was reminded that, in the same way, I have a role to play in the body of Christ. I was created with unique gifts in order to bless and support those around me. Sometimes my roles and gifts may not be traditional, as was the case with Penelope, but they are perfect for me and for God's purpose for me.

Each of you should use whatever gift you have received to serve others, as faithful stewards of God's grace in its various forms. —1 Peter 4:10 (NIV)

—Joy Pitner

JANUARY 23

Tiger, Tiger, Burning Bright

Like newborn babies, crave pure spiritual milk, so that by it you may grow up in your salvation.

—1 PETER 2:2 (NIV)

GOING TO AUNT Sandy's house is always an adventure. My youngsters never know what sort of critter they might find curled up on her sofa or safely caged in the yard. As an experienced wildlife rehabber, my sister cares for injured fawns and foxes, crippled ducks, and even an ailing wolf. One summer, she took in three tiger cubs. One had been injured by its father at a small zoo and needed medical attention. The others had been taken from their mother at six weeks old to be bottle-fed, so they could get used to human contact. They would be used for educational purposes at schools and other venues.

What fun it was to cuddle on the couch with a tiger cub or romp with the cubs in the yard! Enthusiastic eaters, the cubs latched on to their bottles filled with formula. How cute they were with milk dribbling down their chins. Watching them feed so eagerly brought to my mind the Bible verse urging believers to crave spiritual milk. I paused to consider my own appetite. Did I read my Bible every day with enthusiasm? My sister would never have fed those growing cubs potato chips and other junk food, expecting them to thrive. Why would any of us think our spiritual lives could thrive without being properly nourished too?

I want to grow strong in my faith, so I need to fill myself with God's Word. Sandy's cubs drained their bottles and eagerly looked forward to their next meal. I want to be like that, too, when it comes to feasting on God's Word.

Jesus answered, "It is written: 'Man shall not live on bread alone, but on every word that comes from the mouth of God.'" —Matthew 4:4 (NIV)

—Shirley Raye Redmond

Seek and Rejoice

But may all who seek you rejoice and be glad in you; may those who long for your saving help always say, "The Lord is great!"

—Psalm 40:16 (NIV)

THE CAPTAIN MADE an announcement over the intercom as we boarded the ferry for a forty-five-minute trip to an island in the Gulf of Mexico. "Be sure to look out for dolphins. They love to play in the wake of the boat. Feel free to get up and walk around so you can see them better."

My family scanned the water for a while, then gave up looking. Soon, we saw groups of people jumping up and pointing. We joined the crowd and saw several dolphins jumping across the waves near the boat. We had a front-row seat to their joyful play.

I've come to realize that God has given me a front-row seat to His work in the world around us. Yet I often miss His work as I get caught up in busyness, problems, or the rut of my days. It takes effort to look at the world around me through eyes focused on God. One day, we had an unexpected car repair we didn't have money for. The next day, I received payment for a writing job. I nearly cashed the check without thought, but something made me pause. Then I said to my husband, "This check is the exact amount of that car bill. God timed this to meet our needs!" When we stopped to recognize God's help in the situation, we were filled with deep joy. It wasn't just a check to pay a bill. It was God's provision to pay a bill He knew we would have long before we did.

Just as we enjoyed our ride to the island so much more as we watched the play of the dolphins that day, I've learned that when I look for God's work in my life, He fills me with joy.

Lord, show me a glimpse of Yourself today. Help me see and take delight in the ways You are working in and around me. Amen.

—Amelia Rhodes

JANUARY 25

Devoured

But if you bite and devour one another, beware
lest you be consumed by one another!

—GALATIANS 5:15 (NKJV)

MOJO IS MY daughter's dog, a rescued husky-corgi that shared my home when Hannah was in college. He's also my canine soul mate.

Mojo was wounded by a previous owner and still bears the scars of a chain/collar that had once become embedded under his neck. Once he learned to trust that we are kind, he was a love who enjoyed cuddling and lying still for hours. I adored that about him. When I was writing, he never bothered me to take him for walks, and when I rested, he was content to lie beside me. A perfectly calm companion for this sedentary author.

Which is why I was distraught the night Hannah called from the farm she and her husband now own to tell me the news. Their Flemish giant rabbits had finally had an adorable brood, but the latch failed on their cage, and some of the babies had escaped. Hannah rescued most, but her Australian shepherd, Obi, and Mojo had made hasty snacks of two bunnies.

Hannah was unfazed—that's life on a farm. I, however, was bothered for days at the thought that my once-peaceful canine companion had, in a wild moment, participated in coney carnage! I loved the big galoot but had already bonded with the fresh, fuzzy brood.

The bunny massacre gave me a deeper appreciation for God's heart when His children, whom He loves, fail to love one another. Paul warns that when I complain, quarrel, and insist on my own way, I risk devouring others. Nature takes its course in animals, but I trust that in Jesus I can rise above my nature and choose love over consumption!

Walk of Faith: *I've made a habit of designating one week a month to pay special attention to how I speak about others. If I've fallen into the habit of griping, sniping, or complaining, I repent and ask God to change my heart.*

—Lori Stanley Roeleveld

A Loving Dialogue

I am the gate; whoever enters through me will be saved.
They will come in and go out, and find pasture.

—JOHN 10:9 (NIV)

MY SON AND his family live in a rural area and lease their pasture to a farmer. Recently, I played on their deck with my grandsons and watched a Holstein calf gallop on the other side of the fence, mooing, while three deer ran in front of it. Within a moment, a Holstein cow sprinted behind the calf, mooing in a loud voice. I was awestruck. I had never seen a cow gallop before.

I wondered if the cow and her calf were running from a coyote or frolicking with the deer—and was the baby calling the mother until she came close enough for it to feel secure? Both cow and calf trotted into the woods and out to pasture again.

In just moments, I witnessed the strong but tender bond of a mama cow and her calf.

Using detailed acoustics, researchers in Nottingham, England, studied two herds of free-range cattle and discovered two distinct maternal calls and one calf call. When cows were close to their calves, they mooed at a low frequency, but when they were out of visual contact, they mooed louder at a higher frequency. Calves used a third call to let their mothers know they needed to nurse. Researchers say it is possible to identify each cow and her calf by the dialogue between them.

My experience bids me to think about the still, small voice I hear in my heart when I'm alone with God; but when I run or wander away, He may need to speak louder to get my attention. My call to God is my cry for spiritual nourishment. And there is no greater joy than a loving dialogue with God in the pasture of life.

Dear Creator of pastures and fields and gentle creatures who roam there, thank You for revealing Your glory in unexpected places. Amen.

—Kathleen Ruckman

JANUARY 27

Evidence of His Presence

This is how we know that we belong to the truth and how we set our hearts at rest in his presence: If our hearts condemn us, we know that God is greater than our hearts, and he knows everything.

—1 JOHN 3:19–20 (NIV)

I HAD A BLACK sweater that wrapped around me like a warm hug. It's the sweater I wore when I sat in my chair to read God's Word with my parrot, Lorito, sitting on my shoulder. I had received comments about the pieces of fuzz on my shoulders because his small white feathers stayed with me long after Lorito returned to his cage.

One Saturday, my husband asked how soon I would be ready to leave for lunch. I told him I still needed to have my quiet time, adding, "It's worth the wait because I'm nicer after my time with Jesus."

"No, you're not."

Ouch! He's right. My quiet time brings tranquility to my heart and refreshes me. I read and journal and play music that soothes my soul. God's presence wraps around me like the warm hug of my sweater. Lorito reminds me to linger in that sweet space.

Then I walk out to find a bouncing dog that needs a walk and a hungry husband. Lorito screams to add his voice to the noise. They jolt me from the peace-filled presence of God into their stress-filled chaos.

But shouldn't I carry evidence of being with Jesus the same way I carry Lorito's feathers on my shoulders? Shouldn't remnants of His peace in me overcome the noise around me? When my heart is filled with stress, I can turn to God, who is greater, and walk in His patience that overcomes my agitation and fills me with His peace.

Lord, remind me that You abide in me. When my heart is filled with stress, replace it with Your peace. Amen.

—Crystal Storms

JANUARY 28

Bone-Deep Sense of Home

We've been given a glimpse of the real thing, our true home, our resurrection bodies! The Spirit of God whets our appetite by giving us a taste of what's ahead. He puts a little of heaven in our hearts so that we'll never settle for less.

—2 CORINTHIANS 5:1–5 (MSG)

WHAT REMINDS YOU of home? For me, it's a cardinal, the state bird of Kentucky, where I was born and raised. Whenever I see a bright-red male cardinal or a lovely brown female cardinal with red highlights in the bushes outside our kitchen window, or in the tree near our deck, I long for home. Considering I've lived in Georgia for the last thirty-five-plus years, it might sound odd to say that.

Yet when I recently returned to my home state for a funeral for the last of my dad's siblings, the scenery pulled at my heartstrings just like the birds do on a daily basis. The mountains, rolling hills, and horse farms call out to me in a way no other landscape does. It's like I have the love of Kentucky embedded in my DNA. Spending time with family I don't get to see often also sparked that longing for connection.

Anytime I see a beautiful cardinal flitting around my backyard, I'll long for my home in Kentucky, sure. But I also want to be reminded of my ultimate home, my heavenly home. When I feel that bone-deep longing for connection, it's a longing only God can fill.

All things must come to the soul from its roots, from where it is planted.
—Saint Teresa of Ávila

—Missy Tippens

JANUARY 29

Millie the Service Hero

Then, because so many people were coming and going that they did not even have a chance to eat, he said to them, "Come with me by yourselves to a quiet place and get some rest."

—MARK 6:31 (NIV)

I'VE BEEN SPENDING time with a new friend, Millie the service dog. But I've dubbed her "service hero," my own version of a caped defender with dual personalities. When Millie is on duty, she is able to sit for long periods of time, brace herself to support her handler's weight, and ignore distractions (well . . . they're still working on that).

Millie's owner, Brenda, started training Millie when the pup was just six weeks old. They started with relationship building and crate training. After Millie turned three months old, Brenda became her handler—and that was the beginning of the service training.

Millie's best skill is picking up items, so Brenda doesn't have to bend over. She retrieves keys and leash on command. She scoops up anything her handler needs, including receipts.

But Millie is an everyday dog too. She loves to play fetch, and she soaks up all the belly rubs we give her when she's off duty. She has learned the command "make friends" and naps with the best of them.

I've learned from Millie that while it's great for me to serve others and attempt amazing things, I'm not going to get it 100 percent right all the time, and I need to rest once in a while. I'm okay with that. I need to put my to-do list off duty every so often and focus on making friends and self-care. Just as Superman is also Clark Kent and service hero Millie is also playmate Millie, I can take off my cape and be simply Kathy.

Father, I trust You to handle my business for me, so I know when it's time to work and when it's time to play or rest. Amen.

—Kathy Carlton Willis

JANUARY 30

Milo's in a Pickle . . . Again

I call out to the Lord, and he answers me from his holy mountain.

—Psalm 3:4 (NIV)

THE MOTHER CAT showed up a few weeks after I moved into my farm. She was so skinny you couldn't even tell she was pregnant. Then one morning, I heard the tiny mews of five kittens born to a mother who wouldn't let me touch her but stayed because I fed her.

I was allowed to reach into the small pet igloo where the litter was and pick up each kitten and handle it. All . . . except one. I named him Milo. He hissed and tried to scratch and bite anytime I tried to pick him up. Finally, I had enough and just picked him up anyway. He immediately began to purr.

The loudest and meanest turned out to be the most loving of the litter and also the most prone to getting caught in odd places. I found him in the heating ducts and had to cut him out. I found him lost inside the pillowcase of a pillow, unable to get out until I came to rescue him. If there is a cabinet or a container that can be entered, Milo is drawn to it. Unfortunately, he knows how to get in anywhere. Getting out is not in his wheelhouse.

So Milo calls to me with an identifiable scream I follow till I find him and get him out of whatever pickle he is in.

God rescues us from pickles we get into and have no way of getting out of as well. Sometimes the fight to get out of something "quicksands" us deeper. Calling and waiting for love to find us is always better than struggling when we are lost.

God, please find me in all my lost moments when I call out to You. Amen.

—Devon O'Day

Faded Memory, Vivid Reminder

He will rejoice over you with gladness, He will quiet you with His love, He will rejoice over you with singing.

—ZEPHANIAH 3:17 (NKJV)

I HAVE BEEN A city girl from the day of my birth. I've grown up learning how to navigate metropolitan freeways and tangled city streets. My mode of transportation has always been a car, a bus, or a bike. But I do have some vivid memories from my early years of actually riding on a horse. My mom was raised in southern Minnesota and still had friends who lived on farms.

Recently, I found a faded black-and-white Polaroid photo from my childhood that I'd nearly forgotten. In it I'm perched on the back of a jet-black pony. My eyes are wide open in elation, and I'm hanging on to the reins for dear life as the pony breaks into trot.

I'm so thankful I rediscovered this memory. The photo reminded me not only of the joy and amazement my young city-girl heart felt back then, but also of something much more important that is every bit as true today.

I'm still a city girl, and my experiences on horseback are now relegated to cherished childhood recollections. But those memories remind me that, every once in a while, in the middle of my everyday routine, God drops an extraordinary occurrence into my life that reaffirms for me how much He delights in bringing me moments of pure joy. A sailboat ride, sledding with the grandkids, watching as my grandson shoots the winning basket in his game. And—of course—remembering the lovely pony rides from my childhood.

Heavenly Father, You delight in seeing Your children experience delight. Thank You for all the times in my life that You surprise me with joy beyond my imagination. I know You are laughing right alongside me! In Jesus's name. Amen.

—Liz Kimmel

February

FEBRUARY 1

Full Assurance of Hope

And we desire that each one of you show the same diligence to the full assurance of hope until the end, that you do not become sluggish, but imitate those who through faith and patience inherit the promises.

—HEBREWS 6:11–14 (NKJV)

SOMETIMES, THE GREATEST teachers are the smallest beings. Terrence the turtle taught me the importance of perseverance.

Terrence didn't talk a lot, or ever, but he excelled as a great listener. After I'd had a full day, he listened attentively as I shared my life's melodramas.

I took him out of his terrarium and placed him at the other end of the couch. He slowly made his way in my direction. Terrence's determination felt palpable as he crossed each small divide between the seat cushions. Ever onward, my terrapin would not be denied. He crawled with his tiny legs in my direction.

The turtle didn't work so hard solely for the joy of reaching me. His reward included a large leafy green of some sort. He showed the same dogged determination about eating his treat. With a munch here and there, he eventually ingested the whole leaf.

My tales of difficulties with traffic, hurried lunches, and rude customers didn't faze Terrence. He never seemed bored, or at least if he was, he didn't say so. Terrence remained a stoic figure and good friend after work.

Although slow, my terrapin friend never dawdled. He set his jaw and marched single-mindedly forward, always looking ahead.

When the preacher at church mentioned perseverance, I thought of Terrence. Although not fast, he usually accomplished what he had a mind to do. Whether traversing a long couch or munching a plant in his glass home, he kept going until he succeeded. God wants me to remain just as diligent in my spiritual journey. With faith and patience, I can inherit those rewards God promises in His Word.

What we hope ever to do with ease, we must learn first to do with diligence. —Samuel Johnson

—David L. Winters

FEBRUARY 2

Prayers for Alex

Praise be to the LORD, for he has heard my cry for mercy. The LORD is my strength and my shield; my heart trusts in him, and he helps me.

—PSALM 28:6–7 (NIV)

WHEN YOU VOLUNTEER at a dog shelter, you meet all kinds of personalities in the canine world. My favorite dogs were the "bad boys." Alex was not a bad boy, but he was stuck in the kennel with them because of his accommodating ways. He could get along with anyone, even the bad boys. He could put up with their partying and food hoarding, and he wasn't big enough or mean enough to change their behavior. With such a lovable disposition, he should have been adopted immediately, but like many black dogs in shelters, he remained unnoticed.

We took Alex to local pet stores on adoption days. He would cuddle, allow people to take his picture, and be a perfect gentleman, but still no one took him home. I felt sure he had begun to dread going back to his kennel at the end of the day, but I had no choice. Sometimes love hurts.

I spent as much time with Alex as I could, but I would soon be going north for the summer. I hated to think of Alex alone, but I couldn't take him with me. So I said many prayers. Surely, God did not mean for Alex to be homeless.

Then, a miracle. An older newly married couple wanted a small dog. The wife was used to cats, and the husband remembered the black Lab he'd had while growing up. That was Alex! He looked exactly like a small Lab, and, of course, his personality was perfect.

Set against all the big issues in life and in the world, my prayers for Alex probably seem insignificant to others, but to me his quality of life was important. Apparently, God thought so too. Once again, I was reminded: God is merciful to all His creatures. Like Alex, I matter to Him.

Father, thank You for the wonderful experience of loving
Alex and for the gift of his forever home.
You never cease to show mercy. Amen.

—Linda Bartlett

The Guardian

The highway of the upright avoids evil; those who guard their ways preserve their lives.

—PROVERBS 16:17 (NIV)

THE SCRAWNY-LEGGED BIRD ran directly toward my SUV as I pulled into the driveway at work. I saw it at the last second and stopped quickly when it didn't fly off.

Hoping that I hadn't hit the bird, I looked around. There it was, running back to its starting point. Turning around, it charged toward me as if it were a bull. I decided to wait it out, hoping this silly bird would fly away or at least move to the grass. Instead, it repeated the process. This was beginning to seem like a high-stakes game of cat and mouse.

Dramatically dropping one wing to the ground, it dragged the appendage and fluttered around as if it were injured. Either this bird was aiming for an Academy Award, or it didn't want me driving on that road. It hobbled backward again, this time moving toward the opposite side of the driveway.

I felt ridiculous that this bird was controlling my day. Since I was running late for a meeting, I decided to back out of the driveway and use another entrance. *You win, little bird.*

I discovered later that the bird was a female killdeer. Oddly, killdeer lay their eggs in gravel alongside roads; the eggs are camouflaged to look exactly like the ground beneath them. No wonder this avian mother was showing such aggressive behavior. She didn't want me to run over her babies.

Do I guard myself from temptation with that much intensity? Scripture says that if I do, it will save my life. I need to assume the posture of a protective mama bird, going to any length to protect against anything that threatens my relationship with God.

Father, I always assume that I can resist temptation, but I simply cannot do it on my own. Help me guard my heart and keep me in close connection to You. Amen.

—Twila Bennett

FEBRUARY 4

Strength in Numbers

Just as a body, though one, has many parts, but all its many parts form one body, so it is with Christ. For we were all baptized by one Spirit so as to form one body—whether Jews or Gentiles, slave or free—and we were all given the one Spirit to drink. Even so the body is not made up of one part but of many.

—1 CORINTHIANS 12:12–14 (NIV)

MEERKATS ARE FUNNY little mammals known for sticking together. At home on the African savanna, several families may live together in a large clan—each member with a different role.

One meerkat may act as a babysitter while another may serve as a lookout by standing on its hind legs. A critical role within the meerkat community is the teacher, who shows the pups how to hunt.

Even when a meerkat is digging a burrow, other meerkats come and assist, forming a lineup. The team passes the loose soil upward, toward the opening. There, another meerkat builds a mound of dirt so the guard can stand and keep watch.

Although each has a particular job, they unite for many jobs. The entire group works together against danger. Following the directions of the leader, meerkats defend their homes and stand up to dangerous predators, like snakes. If a lone meerkat attempted to defend itself, it would fail.

Community is important for meerkats. We need community too. Being alone is dangerous. One of the most important teams is our local church. This is where we find strength in numbers, using our varying gifts to serve one another.

Scripture reminds us how desperately we need others to live and grow as Christians. Although each of us has special gifts and skills, none of us can say we don't need anyone else. Together, we can encourage and defend one another and accomplish so much more for God's kingdom.

Walk of Faith: *Write down three things you are both good at and enjoy doing. Then think of a way to share each one in your church, community, or neighborhood this week.*

—Tez Brooks

Watchful Eyes

Therefore keep watch, because you do not know on what day your Lord will come.

—MATTHEW 24:42 (NIV)

WHEN MY FAMILY heard there were river otters at Skaggs Island in the nearby San Pablo Bay National Wildlife Refuge, we jumped in the car and made a day trip out of it. After pulling into the wetlands, we eagerly walked along the waterways, eyes peeled for otters. We were certain we would see one at any moment. But an hour went by, and we didn't see anything except a few common ducks. Disappointed, we turned back toward our car. On the walk back, we doggedly continued to scan the surface of the water for signs of otter life. Then . . .

"I see one!"

I whirled around and saw my husband pointing.

"Where?" my daughter and I cried.

"It's right there!"

All I saw were a few bubbles breaking on the water's surface. I had missed it.

We redoubled our watch. Surely, it would surface again. As we watched and waited, we dubbed my husband "The Official Family Otter Spotter." I really hoped his sharp eyes would spot another otter before it was time to leave, but it was the only sighting we had that day.

Our eagerness to spot an otter made me think of how I and other believers eagerly watch for Jesus's return. How watchful am I? Mind you, being watchful doesn't mean I'm fearful or anxious. It means being observant and attentive. In that way, I'll be ready when He comes back and leads me and all believers safely to heaven. Until that day arrives, though, He wants me to be vigilant in prayer and show His love to others.

Dear Jesus, help me to eagerly, faithfully, and fearlessly watch for Your return, and to share the good news of Your gift of salvation until that day. Amen.

—Marianne Campbell

The Beauty of a . . . Skunk?

He has made everything beautiful in its time.

—ECCLESIASTES 3:11 (NIV)

THE PARK WAS almost eerily empty as my family and I rounded a corner alongside the river. That's when we spotted a glistening ball of black and white—a skunk making its way toward a stone wall.

Surprisingly, my first thought wasn't to run in the opposite direction (though that was my very close second!). The first impression I had of this creature was not one of fear but one of awe. I hadn't had many close encounters with living skunks, and I was struck by the beauty of this animal—the clean white stripes running between shining black along its back. The fur that looked soft . . . and definitely *not* smelly.

Because we knew better than to chase after skunks—even beautiful, clean-smelling ones—we made a wide circle, hoping to catch a glimpse of this skunk on the other side of the stone wall. But it was nowhere in sight, probably just as wary of us as we were of the little creature.

As we walked toward our car, I thought of the many nuances and often surprising beauty of God's creation, of how if I could but look with eyes not previously disposed to judgment, I might find so much more beauty. I thought of a bee that doesn't just sting but makes honey and is gorgeous in its own right, a spider with the ability to weave delicate webs, or a skunk with a brilliant black-and-white coat that glorifies our Lord.

I wonder—if I were better able to see God's creation in this light, would I see humanity better as well? Could I learn to appreciate the gifts of my fellow human beings instead of being so quick to jump to judgment? I think of that skunk often—a gift in the most unexpected of creatures.

Father, give us eyes to look for beauty and grace instead of judgment and cynicism. May You be glorified. Amen.

—Heidi Chiavaroli

FEBRUARY 7

Fishing for Smiles

Be strong and courageous. Do not be afraid or terrified because of them, for the Lord *your God goes with you; he will never leave you nor forsake you.*

—Deuteronomy 31:6 (NIV)

CRANKY WAS THE most unusual male cat I had ever adopted—half Siamese, half Manx. He was gorgeous, with long back legs, short fur, and no tail. His markings and crystal-blue eyes were all Siamese, but his attitude was 100 percent cranky. Thinking I could cheer him up, I put him on a leash for a walk outside.

What a scaredy-cat. Even the breeze spooked him. He hissed, and if he'd had a tail, it would have puffed out. Back indoors, I trashed the leash, but he still growled. To help Cranky adjust, I gave him extra treats and lots of attention. But at the slightest noise, he bolted under my bed. Cranky seemed afraid of life itself.

One day, I tied a toy mouse to the end of a fishing pole and stood in the yard casting. Cranky eyed the moving target, wiggling his cute tailless rear end in readiness. As the line sailed out, Cranky leaped at least five feet into the air and nabbed the mouse on the first try. And the second and third tries. Over the next weeks, Cranky's crabbiness faded. He stopped hissing and delighted me with his loud purr. Every afternoon, he would stand by the door, eager for another round of catfishing.

It made me think of all the times I've grumped my way through life. Usually, my crankiness stems from fear—fear I'm not good enough, fear that others will hurt me, fear I won't make it. Although I try not to hiss at anyone, I smile more when I remember that God loves me and will never abandon me. These days, if Cranky Cat gets grumpy, we still go outside for a little catfishing. Before you know it, we're both in better moods.

Don't be pushed around by the fears in your mind.
Be led by the dreams in your heart. —Roy T. Bennett

—Linda S. Clare

FEBRUARY 8

Casting a Big Shadow

In him was life, and that life was the light of all mankind.

—JOHN 1:4 (NIV)

THE OTHER EVENING, I was folding clothes when I noticed a large blur of movement from the corner of my eye. *What was that?* I wondered. I hoped some kind of wasp or bee hadn't made its way into the house, and my imagination began to run away with me. You see, I'm terrified of stinging bugs. We are talking arms-flailing, heart-racing, scared-senseless terrified. I couldn't see the mystery bug, but its effect was substantial. I was just sure a hornet had climbed on my sweater, hitched a ride inside my house, and was lying in wait for my defenses to be down. Humor aside, I was about to call my husband for bug assistance when I discovered the culprit.

It wasn't a wasp or a bee, not even a beetle or June bug, but a gnat—a tiny, little gnat, perfectly aligned with the light so that the scope and size of its shadow was intensified. I smiled to myself as I considered how I am like that gnat—tiny in the grand scheme of the universe. So small that, left to my own devices, I may go unnoticed, seemingly inconsequential in comparison to the grand scope of creation. And yet as Scripture says, Christ is the light of the world. When I align myself with His light, something amazing happens. The scope of my influence, the size of my shadow, multiplies dramatically. Some days, I may feel my contribution is small, but even on those days, God is working beyond me to reach places I could never affect on my own accord. I simply have to intentionally align myself with Him and His purpose. It's the light, not the wings, that travels far beyond.

Father, my own efforts to better the world are limited, at best—but Your work within me is great and lasting. Give me eyes to see and a heart to trust all You are doing through and beyond me. Amen.

—Ashley Clark

FEBRUARY 9

Life-Extension Coach

Blessed be the Lord, who daily loads us with benefits.

—PSALM 68:19 (NKJV)

COCK-A-DOODLE-DOOOOO TO YOU toooo!" I whined, putting the pillow over my head, at the shrill sound of the pesky rooster named Richard. My husband, Terry, and I had just moved into our rural neighborhood. Richard was a neighbor's pet, well known for getting the residents "up and at 'em" with his persistent predawn crow. As charmingly romantic as the scene might seem, I didn't consider Richard to be at all a delight. He was the enemy of my deep and restful sleep.

Richard the rooster reminded me of when Terry and I lived with my folks while taking care of them. They, too, had an especially loud two-legged, winged alarm clock in their neighborhood. My late stepdad, Dale, a lieutenant colonel in the US Army, looked upon their neighborhood rooster as his own personal military revelry. It was just the thing to get him up, giving him extra time in his day. "He's sort of like a life-extension coach," Dale would tell me. "With the rooster, I'm getting up earlier and gaining more productive hours to my life."

So I decided to adopt Dale's attitude about the rooster. He would *not* be my enemy—but my own personal life-extension coach, training me to rise up and make the most of my bonus morning hours.

Richard's morning alarm had such a positive effect on me that I began to see where God surely was in this. Early one morning, I found I had more time to pray and establish myself in God for a better day. "Having my very own feathered life-extension coach," I told Terry, "is something to crow about!"

Walk of Faith: *Why not add hours to your life, and with it, quality—by getting up a bit earlier to pray in the new day. Then get ready to see all that God has for you!*

—Sandra Clifton

FEBRUARY 10

Suppertime at the Farm

They found rich, good pasture, and the land was spacious, peaceful and quiet.

—1 CHRONICLES 4:40 (NIV)

THERE IS SOMETHING so sweet about suppertime at the farm. There is routine and ritual about it. It's at roughly the same time each night, and there is a certain sequence to how it is done. The horses get fed first in the same order each night. The cats are next. Then the dogs line up and wait for supper to be made. Kibble, warm broth, and some kind of meat in six bowls. Cold kibble alone is just not good enough.

It's as much about the preparation as the food. The horses, cats, and dogs all wait until they get their bowls, and the sound that follows is one of my favorites. Slurping and crunching with such satisfaction just fills the end of my day with peace. It sets everything back in order. No matter how bad or stressful the day goes, that sound of something as simple as supper works better than any other relaxation tool.

There is a rhythm to the way our pets eat or graze. Watching my bull lie out in the sun and chew his cud slows my heartbeat, and my pulse evens with this strange feeling of sweetness that settles in. When life gets so busy and deadlines become heavy, taking the time to focus on the program of feeding our pets can be something we look forward to and count on. Having something routine keeps us grounded, and with that grounding, we become tethered amid the chaos that always threatens our peace. When life runs us, let us take back the reins one peaceful moment at a time. By focusing on the simple, we can disconnect from the complicated and begin enjoying all the good gifts God has for us.

Dear God, please help me focus on the simple gifts
You reserve daily for me, like peace and joy. Amen.

—Devon O'Day

Koi Story

He makes me lie down in green pastures, he leads me beside quiet waters, he refreshes my soul.

—PSALM 23:2–3 (NIV)

WHENEVER WE PLAY cards at Jan's house, someone is bound to ask about her koi in the backyard pond. She always updates us on how the fish are doing, especially her favorite, Big Boy.

Though he isn't the prettiest of her koi, Big Boy is her baby. And the most beloved of all because he was the first to live in the pond, the first of the fish family, and he's still first in Jan's affections. Whenever she approaches the teeming pool, Big Boy swims over like an obedient puppy and tarries at the edge, allowing her to stroke him.

Jan says the best thing about having koi is their calming effect. When she's had a stressful day, she sits by the sparkling pond, interacts with her fish, and then watches them swim. The sight brings down her blood pressure, putting her into something of a meditative state. For Jan, contemplating the koi is restful, even therapeutic.

It is no accident that God created such a beautiful world and populated it with His animals as a special gift to us. He provided them as blessings to His beloved children. They comfort us when we are unhappy, give us joy when the time is right, and encourage us as we journey through life. In their company, we experience His grace.

The best remedy for those who are afraid, lonely, or unhappy is to go outside, somewhere where they can be quite alone with the heavens, nature, and God. Because only then does one feel that all is as it should be and that God wishes to see people happy, amidst the simple beauty of nature. —Anne Frank

—Cathy Elliott

FEBRUARY 12

Baby Girl

Praise be to the God and Father of our Lord Jesus Christ, the Father of compassion and the God of all comfort, who comforts us in all our troubles, so that we can comfort those in any trouble with the comfort we ourselves receive from God.

—2 CORINTHIANS 1:3–4 (NIV)

DURING A RECENT visit with my friend Susy, I was introduced to their many animals, including a beautiful calico named Baby Girl.

"You won't see much of her," Susy's husband, Robert, told me.

Susy added that they had rescued the calico from an animal hoarder and the cat avoided everyone except their daughter.

Then Baby Girl slinked over. I've always been a cat lover, so I couldn't resist kneeling down to say hello, prepared for her to ignore me. She brushed against my hand.

"Wow," Robert said. "That never happens."

All week long, I felt drawn to Baby Girl. I remembered what it felt like to be suspicious of people while recovering from some traumatic experiences. The friends I treasured most had patiently drawn me out of my cocoon. I tried to do the same with Baby Girl, greeting her in the morning and whenever I saw her outside, letting her come and go on her terms. One day, while sitting on the porch, I felt her paw on my leg. I reached down and touched her head. "Hey, Baby Girl." She stretched both paws up to my knee, then she hopped on to my lap, curled up, and started to purr. My heart melted as I stroked her.

My bond with Baby Girl felt like God's way of pointing out a gift I had gained from painful experience: the ability to give others what I had once needed—friendship, affection, and patience. It was one more reminder to never forget the comfort God provides so I can pass it on to someone else.

Walk of Faith: *Think of someone who needs extra patience right now. Ask God to show you one act of kindness that you can do for that person this week.*

—Jeanette Hanscome

FEBRUARY 13

Otter-ly Adorable

A cheerful heart is good medicine, but a crushed spirit dries up the bones.

—Proverbs 17:22 (NIV)

ONE OF MY favorite exhibits at the zoo is the sea otter habitat. I love to watch the playful mammals frolic. But life for the otters isn't all fun and games. Because the zoo seeks to maintain the wild state of the animals as much as possible, most don't receive their food handed to them on a plate. They have to hunt for it.

One day, I arrived at the exhibit just in time for feeding. The zookeeper tossed clams into the pond, then left. The otters raced to the edge of the water, then dove to the bottom like heat-seeking missiles. When they spotted their breakfast, they homed in on it, grabbed the shellfish, and churned toward the surface. There they floated on their backs, cracked the shellfish open on their chests, and ate the soft meat inside. I swear I saw whiskery smiles on their faces before they dove beneath the surface again.

Although the otters were working for their dinner, they approached the task with flair and fun. They could have lumbered to the side of the pond and moseyed into the water. Instead, they launched themselves like little torpedoes. They could have carried their clams to the side of the pond to crack. Instead, they floated on their backs like they were relaxing in a swimming pool. Their lighthearted, fun-loving spirit infused the mundane routine of their lives and made those around them smile.

I learned a lesson from the otters that day. Much of my life is also routine, but it doesn't have to be boring. With a little creativity, I, too, can add some flair and fun to my ordinary day. A lighthearted approach will make my life happier. And who knows? It might just bring a smile to someone who's watching me.

Father, show me creative ways to infuse fun
and laughter into my days. Amen.

—Lori Hatcher

FEBRUARY 14

Lily the Sphynx

For the Lord does not see as man sees; for man looks at the outward appearance, but the Lord looks at the heart.

—1 Samuel 16:7 (NKJV)

WHEN I THINK of a kitten, most often my mind's eye imagines a short-legged, round-faced, fluffy bundle of fur. My niece Katie has always wanted a different breed of cat in her life. And her husband, James, gave her the delight of her heart one Valentine's Day. Her gift was Lily, a sphynx, also known as a hairless cat. Her triangular head, huge ears, wide-set eyes, and sleek, muscular body endeared her to the family in no time at all.

Some cat breeds hold themselves aloof from their humans, but sphynx are friendly, almost doglike in their attraction to people. They are sweet and smart, and Lily is no exception. But what Lily knows, perhaps better than anything else, is how precious she is to the family. Katie and James's daughter, Elizabeth, adores her, and while the gift was for Katie, the cat has become Elizabeth's baby. Elizabeth is convinced that Lily is the cutest thing ever and is shocked to think that some people may feel otherwise.

To be honest, I think hairless cats are pretty funny looking (maybe not *ugly,* but funny). And to be even more honest, I am not all that pleased with the way I look. It is in my old nature to be very critical of the view as I look into a mirror. My hair is too fine, my face is too round . . . But what God sees when He looks at me is His precious, beloved daughter. He knows me inside and out. He loves me with an everlasting love. And that love is shaping me into a beautiful reflection of my heavenly Father.

Thank You, Father, that You see every part of us and love us as no one else can. Help me to stop striving for outer beauty. I trust that You will pour Your beautiful nature into and through me, that I might bless those I interact with daily. Amen.

—Liz Kimmel

FEBRUARY 15

Hoo-Hoo Are You?

The wild animals honor me, the jackals and the owls, because I provide water in the wilderness and streams in the wasteland, to give drink to my people, my chosen, the people I formed for myself that they may proclaim my praise.

—ISAIAH 43:20–21 (NIV)

MY ADULT DAUGHTER does professional family photography. Her favorite setting for photographs is a park with a gazebo and a variety of trees where she can consistently get perfect shots. As my daughter works, my job is to keep my grandson busy. One day, as we were exploring the park, we heard the distinct *hoo-hoo* of a great horned owl. It was well camouflaged, but my grandson eventually pointed up to a branch where the majestic owl gazed down upon us with wise eyes.

This was the closest we had ever been to an owl, and we were excited to take a closer look. As we examined the raptor, my grandson noticed the owl's two ears were different sizes. He wondered if God had made an error in creation or if only this owl had mismatched ears.

Once home, my voracious learner hopped online and discovered we had actually been looking at feathery tufts, not ears, which aid the owl in camouflage and communication. However, owls *do* have asymmetrical ears that give them radar-like hearing. The right ear is slightly higher and receives sound a split second before the left ear does. The owls turn their heads until their eyes home in on what they've already heard.

The great horned owl uses what may appear to be an error in its creation to its advantage. As with the owl, I may not look or feel the same as those around me. I sometimes struggle with self-image issues and lack of confidence. Yet like the owl, I am made by God to be exactly the way He wants me to be.

Dear Lord, thank You for the reminder that You don't make mistakes. Help me understand that my differences are actually gifts I can use in a special way to serve You and others. Amen.

—Deb Kastner

FEBRUARY 16

Keeping Track of Time

Teach us to number our days, that we may gain a heart of wisdom.

—PSALM 90:12 (NIV)

WE WEREN'T QUITE sure what to expect as we pulled up to the cabin. It was nestled in a patch of wild grasses in the middle of nowhere. As my husband and I unloaded bags for our weeklong stay, our three young boys scooted rocking chairs up to the large windows facing the ravine out back. And then they waited.

Their patience paid off as, one by one, hummingbirds arrived to feast at the feeders hanging outside each window. Throughout our vacation, this was where I was certain to find our sons. They studied those birds, welcoming them each morning as they sat at the windows and enjoyed their breakfast while watching the birds gather theirs.

I observed my sons admiring their newfound friends as they darted from one feeder to the next, hovering at times right in front of my boys' widened eyes. The birds seemed motionless but were in fact flapping their wings up to seventy times each second. Just as the hands of a clock seem to gather minutes, these birds collect time with their movement. *How many wingbeats have carried this bird through its day?* I wondered. With each beat they count time, just as I do with my children. Every breath is counted a blessing, and each dawn carries with it new mercies.

When I stop, just as my boys did that week, to measure the moments carried on the wings of a bird, I see it so much more clearly. I count time and collect memories. With each rotation of the earth, every pull of the moon on the tides, and every breath that greets the day, may I count the gifts that God has placed all around me. May I stop to count time and make time count.

Walk of Faith: *Practice "counting time" today by writing down one blessing you see every hour. Set a timer to remind you to stop what you're doing and look around for one of God's gifts to record on paper.*

—Eryn Lynum

Things Above

Since, then, you have been raised with Christ, set your hearts on things above, where Christ is, seated at the right hand of God. Set your minds on things above, not on earthly things.

—COLOSSIANS 3:1–2 (NIV)

I CRESTED THE HILL of my usual morning run before slowing to a walk. My neck and upper shoulders burned—not from the run, but from stress. Looming deadlines and a spine that seemed permanently curled over a keyboard had sent me in desperate search of help.

I could still hear the chiropractor's words from the day before. "We aren't meant to be hunched over, focusing on our computers, phones, problems. Our body works best when it's stretched open—when we take time to look up."

I took his advice, resisting the pain in my neck to glimpse the cerulean blue of the sky. At that moment, a single bird—a robin—sailed overhead, its small wings spread in effortless flight, its rust-colored belly facing downward.

I stopped walking, in awe of the bird and of the message God had given me, first through my chiropractor and, in that moment, through one of His tiny creatures. That robin's flight looked effortless—wings open, belly thrust out, tiny muscles of its neck elongated. It didn't appear to have a stressful agenda. It was simply busy doing what the Lord had created it to do.

How I needed this message. God had created my heart for things above. He created me for Jesus. Yet how often do I get weighted down by the stresses of this world, my fears, and my own inadequacy?

Whenever I feel that old, familiar pain in my neck, I think of my friend the robin. It inspires me to do what I was created to do—look up. It inspires me to set my mind on things above and to fly free.

Jesus, You made our hearts for heaven, but You also encourage us to do Your work on earth. Help us better glimpse Your grandeur and majesty before we focus on things of this world. Amen.

—Heidi Chiavaroli

FEBRUARY 18

When Love Casts Out Fear

That you, being rooted and grounded in love, may have strength to comprehend with all the saints what is the breadth and length and height and depth, and to know the love of Christ that surpasses knowledge, that you may be filled with all the fullness of God.

—EPHESIANS 3:17–19 (ESV)

SHE'S TOO FERAL." The humane shelter employee went on to inform me that the cat I had captured would be euthanized if I left her.

I blinked back tears as I hefted the carrier that housed the frightened feline and trudged to my car. Were death or a life of danger in the wild the only options for this beautiful calico?

But an experienced source almost begged, "Don't return her to the wild." She assured me feral cats can be rehabilitated. I grabbed at the hope. I wanted this precious cat to be free from a life of fear.

I was careful not to rush the rehabilitation process, though eager to show her how much I loved her. One day, I reached a finger through the bars of her large crate and touched her soft fur. She didn't startle. Instead, she stayed near, and I extended a few more fingers to pet her.

Breakthrough. She leaned into the petting, and her life changed. My touch had shattered the wall of fear surrounding her. After that day, I could help her confront anything frightening simply by stroking her, as if my love flowed into her and came out as courage.

When I look at my rescued cat, I see a reflection of myself. How many times have I relied on fear instead of God to keep me safe? How often have I tried to conquer my fears without God's help? I often let fear drive me away from God, but He's waiting for me to draw close so He can show me just how much He loves me.

Lord, when I am afraid, remind me to draw near to You. Touch me with Your love. Let it flow through me and come out as courage. Amen.

—Jerusha Agen

FEBRUARY 19

The Midnight Prowler

Fear not, for I am with you; be not dismayed, for I am your God; I will strengthen you, I will help you, I will uphold you with my righteous right hand.

—Isaiah 41:10 (ESV)

THE PHONE RANG late one night, waking me from a sound sleep. I squinted at the red numbers of the alarm clock. It was 11:38 p.m.

"There's a bear on my back porch," my mother hissed. "It's eating peanuts out of my feeder, and it's huge! Oh, it's leaving. It might be headed your way." I could hear anxiety tinged with excitement in her voice.

We live in the foothills of the Rockies, so bear visitors are not uncommon. Our newspapers print articles reminding us to observe bear-encounter safety tips. Folks post bear sightings on Facebook. The hardware store sells bear bells and bear repellent.

Bears don't worry me as much as other dangers. I fret about con artists scamming my elderly neighbors out of their life savings. I worry about an armed shooter wreaking havoc at my grandson's school. I fear the danger of drunk drivers on the roads.

Reminding myself to trust the Lord, I climbed out of bed, staggering sleepily to the kitchen to peer out the window. Sure enough, the streetlight's glow revealed a black bear loping across the small grassy knoll that separates our home from Mom's. The bear raised its nose, then headed in the opposite direction. I watched until it disappeared from view before returning to bed with the blessed assurance that God has the whole world in His hands.

Fear is a reaction. Courage is a decision.
—often attributed to Winston Churchill

—Shirley Raye Redmond

FEBRUARY 20

Wings of Power

You yourselves have seen what I did to Egypt, and how I carried you on eagles' wings and brought you to myself.

—EXODUS 19:4 (NIV)

I PADDLED MY KAYAK down river, enjoying the quiet until I heard the sound of an engine approaching behind me. I turned my head, expecting to see a small boat. Instead, a swan flew past. Each powerful flap of its wings beating the air produced a roaring sound. Its neck outstretched, the bird's body formed a straight line. I paddled faster to follow it, but the bird moved with speed I could never match in my kayak. I watched as the swan became a white speck on the horizon, the strength of its wings leaving an impression on me.

The Lord reminded His people how He brought them out of slavery in Egypt by describing His power as like that of a bird's wings. When His people were too weary to fight, He whisked them to safety. When they were powerless to defend themselves, He destroyed their enemy. He brought them out of their troubles on the safety of His wings.

I've learned God does the same for me. I find strength to endure when I turn my attention away from my problems and focus on His power. I recall the ways I've seen His power in Scripture—parting the Red Sea, defeating death through Jesus, and performing countless miracles. Then I remember the stories of His power in my life: rescuing me from the darkness of anxiety, providing peace in the midst of health trials, granting wisdom when I worried over a child, helping with friction in a friendship, paving a path through addiction.

The power in that swan's wings gave me but a glimpse of the power and strength of its Creator, the same power that lives within me through His Spirit. When I'm too weary to fight, He stands ready to lift me up on His wings and bring me to Himself.

With the power of God within us, we need never fear the powers around us. —Woodrow Kroll

—Amelia Rhodes

What the Pigs Are Having

Do not fret because of evildoers, nor be envious of the workers of iniquity.

—PSALM 37:1 (NKJV)

MOJO STARED AT the pigs. He knew not to approach the electric fence, but he was as close as he could get without feeling the shock. His tongue hung out, and the look in his eyes was mesmerized longing. On the other side of the fence, my daughter's two pigs devoured the table scraps she had tossed over to fatten them.

Mojo is her beloved rescue dog (and one of my favorite dogs in the world). He lives inside her house. He sleeps on or beside Hannah's bed. He's pampered, petted, and provided the best dog food and treats available.

The pigs aren't even given names because soon they will meet their intended fate. They sleep in a wooden shelter outdoors and aren't free to roam the yard the way Mojo does. They rummage in the ground, eat their swill, and enjoy the occasional gift of scraps.

But Mojo envied their lot.

For the first time, I understood how ridiculous it looks to God when I envy the pleasures enjoyed by those outside His family. But even from my secure place inside God's family, I occasionally envy them the worldly feast in which they indulge.

God showed me my own heart as I watched Mojo, and I felt a new level of humility impress my spirit. I belong to the very family of God and have a place at His table. Whatever makes me sometimes long for more?

Walk of Faith: *When I feel tempted to envy the worldly pleasures enjoyed by someone who rejects Jesus, I'll remember I reside in the house of God. I'll list the joys that are mine because God counts me a member of His household.*

—Lori Stanley Roeleveld

FEBRUARY 22

Betta Beauty

And God said, "Let the water teem with living creatures."

—GENESIS 1:20 (NIV)

MY FOUR-YEAR-OLD GRANDSON and I walked through the aisle of the pet store. His wide, curious eyes gazed at species of fish. His betta fish had recently died, and he missed the little creature, so I promised I would buy him a new fish.

"I want another betta," he told me, making his decision after several minutes. He picked an aqua-colored fish with a deeper-turquoise feathery tail.

I had just attended a performance at his preschool, where he and his buddies sang the words, "All things, all things, God has created." I found a renewed sense of wonder, like the child at my side, and I couldn't wait to learn more about betta fish.

Because of their beauty, bettas, which originated in Thailand, have been called the jewels of the Orient. They prefer to be alone and are named after the Bettah, an ancient clan of warriors. Most bettas live up to three to five years in captivity, but some have lived twice that long.

This adaptable fish can breathe oxygen from the air and through its gills. If a betta stays moist, it can survive for short periods out of water. It also prefers small aquariums.

Suddenly, my heart awakened to what this unique fish can teach me. It's okay to be alone sometimes, and I need to be more adaptable too. I shouldn't strive for the biggest and best but be content with small and simple blessings. And if God has given me any gift, I should not be proud—like the betta with its elegant tail that isn't aware of the beauty we see in it.

As my grandson gets older, I will remind him how his special fish, created for the glory of God, inspired his grandmother.

Dear God, help me to be adaptable, to cherish my time alone,
and if I'm a warrior, let it be for a good cause. Help me
to stay humble and live for Your glory. Amen.

—Kathleen Ruckman

FEBRUARY 23

Single-Minded Devotion

So now Israel, what do you think God expects from you? Just this: Live in his presence in holy reverence, follow the road he sets out for you, love him, serve God, your God, with everything you have in you, obey the commandments and regulations of God that I'm commanding you today—live a good life.

—Deuteronomy 10:12–13 (MSG)

I HAVE ENJOYED WATCHING the giant pandas at Zoo Atlanta as well as on panda cams online. I love how they sit leaned back against a log or a wall as if lounging while they eat their bamboo. If they get tired of sitting in one position, they'll just flop over on their side and keep eating. Then they may nap for a while. But soon, they'll be eating once again, because they have to eat twenty to forty pounds of bamboo a day, which means they're looking for food or eating for ten to sixteen hours a day.

I wish I had that kind of single-minded devotion. I recently began reading a series on obedience because it's something I struggle with, and I've also wondered how I can possibly love God well. A verse in the second epistle of John has really helped me understand that one way I can love God is by walking in obedience to His commands.

The pandas rolling around in the single-minded pursuit of filling their stomachs with bamboo remind me that I want to stay focused on God's Word to guide me in the life God has planned for me. I want to live with single-minded devotion to Him, obeying His commands and living a life of love.

And this is love: that we walk in obedience to his commands. As you have heard from the beginning, his command is that you walk in love. —2 John 6 (NIV)

—Missy Tippens

Call and Response

I say to you, though he will not rise and give to him because he is his friend, yet because of his persistence he will rise and give him as many as he needs.

—LUKE 11:8 (NKJV)

OUR HOUSE BUZZED with activity as everyone grew excited about a new resident. Perry, the lovebird, would soon arrive to find his permanent place in our home. Perry was a foster that needed a forever home, and we were eager to provide it.

Once he was in our home, I let him fly around a bit, then coaxed him back to his cage with fresh water and food. He ate a bite and settled on one of his perches. The beautiful, mostly blue-and-white lovebird peered at me quizzically. Over the next few hours, he played with his toys and observed us watching television. At bedtime, I wished him good night and turned out the lights.

Later that night, I woke from a sound sleep at about 2:30 a.m. to loud chirping. After ten minutes of trying to ignore his various whistles, tweets, and beeps, I donned my bathrobe and made my way downstairs. Perry sat comfortably on his perch, shaking his head affirmatively in my direction.

"You just wanted some more attention, right, Perry?" I asked. "Well, we have to get up for work in a few hours. So you need to relax and get some sleep. I know it's a new house to you, but it's safe. Go to sleep now, little bird."

Although I hadn't wanted to get out of bed, Perry's determined calls had required a response. As I headed back to dreamland, a story Jesus told about a persistent, middle-of-the-night request came to mind. Jesus followed this story with the assurance that God is a good father. I know that if I keep asking, He will respond.

Heavenly Father, thank You for your constant care. Your love as expressed in answered prayer encourages my faith and bolsters trust. Help me to frame my requests thoughtfully and always take time to listen for Your response. Amen.

—David L. Winters

FEBRUARY 25

I Know What I Saw

Now faith is confidence in what we hope for and assurance about what we do not see.

—HEBREWS 11:1 (NIV)

I HAVE A HISTORY of seeing wild animals in strange places. My family has a history of not believing me. Like the time I saw a mountain lion outside my tent in Big Bend National Park, Texas, or when I saw a panther on a golf green. They didn't see what I saw, so they would say, "You're imagining things."

They always made me doubt my experience until I saw the jaguarundi. We were fishing on the southern Texas coast. As the sun rose, my husband waded off after a redfish. Half-awake, I gazed at the shore. A primitive-looking big cat scooted through the tall grass. Its back sloped down toward a small flat head, and its thick tail waved powerfully over the brush. What was it?

"A coyote," my husband said when I told him about it. I insisted that it was a primitive cat. "Okay, maybe a bobcat," he said. No. I knew what I had seen, and it was a very special creature.

I described it to the old-timers at the tackle store. "Sounds like a jaguarundi," they said. They got excited and told us about this endangered creature that moves like a weasel, swims, and leaps from trees to capture prey. Jaguarundi are considered extinct in Texas, but we agreed: I wasn't imagining it.

The old-timers had seen them in the past. Even though no one had encountered one here recently, I had seen a jaguarundi. Their faith helped me trust that my experience was real. Others may doubt my encounters, but when I talk with those who understand, I am strengthened. I have felt God's presence in my life. I have seen a jaguarundi. It doesn't matter what anyone else thinks. I know what I saw.

Dear Lord, help us to know You and recognize Your presence in our lives. Provide us with friends who can help us hold on to our faith, even when others doubt. Amen.

—Lucy H. Chambers

FEBRUARY 26

Everyone's a Critic

We want to avoid any criticism of the way we administer this liberal gift.

—2 CORINTHIANS 8:20 (NIV)

AFTER A FERAL kitty chose my carport as the safe place to give birth to a litter of kittens, I didn't think that anyone would find fault with my posting pictures of them on social media when it was time to find their forever homes.

Who would have a problem with pictures of kittens? Apparently, with social media, there is always someone who finds fault, no matter what you do. If you give time to animals, someone will complain you don't work with children. If you work with children, there are complaints you don't help the veterans. Basically, when people are given a keyboard to voice their opinions, they can become both brave and cruel.

When I posted pictures of these kittens, there was an onslaught of people who criticized me for not spaying and neutering. They did not seem to care the feral mother was untouchable and wild as could be. Those who left negative comments didn't even try to be kind when they posted their thoughts on my page. It hurt me deeply that with their mean comments they could tear apart my life's work in caring for animals. These were people who called themselves my friends, but their words were anything but friendly.

When my best intentions are met with hurtful words, I have to let go of how those words affect me. I cannot stop the good I do because someone slings mud at my gift. I want to use my life and my social media for good, and, when someone hurts me with a post, learn to use the delete button.

Dear God, help me seek approval from You rather than from strangers on social media. Amen.

—Devon O'Day

Escape Artist

A person's wisdom yields patience; it is to one's glory to overlook an offense.

—PROVERBS 19:11 (NIV)

COWBOY WAS A favorite dog of mine at the no-kill shelter where I volunteered. He was what you call a party in a bottle, always full of energy and joyful. Cowboy liked everyone and everything—except horses. I found that out when I took him as my partner in a parade. Imagine someone named Cowboy who didn't like horses. Oh, the irony! I thought he would make the perfect pet for my son's family. My son agreed to adopt him, so we sent him from Florida north to Minnesota.

Turns out Cowboy had quite an adjustment period. He had a bad case of separation anxiety. When my son's family was gone for school and work, Cowboy ate doorknobs, jumped out a second-story window, trashed the trash, and generally let the family know how much he missed them. I tried to help by providing an outdoor pen, but Cowboy dug out of it in five minutes. Once loose from the pen, he would just sit on the doorstep and wait for someone to come home. There was no containing him.

There was a bit of poetic justice in this situation because this was the son who was the most difficult of my sons growing up. I did feel a bit bad, though, to have saddled my son with such a tough task. I asked if he wanted to give up and send Cowboy back.

"No, we love him and don't want him to leave," was the answer.

It took months, yet eventually Cowboy became used to his new routine. He never became the perfect pet, but he became the perfect pet for this imperfect family.

God never gives up on us either. His patience is amazing. He sees us through our doorknob-eating, trash-spilling episodes and loves us anyway.

Dear Father, I know I must try Your patience at times. I want to do better. Please give me the skill and the will to be the person You want me to be. Amen.

—Linda Bartlett

FEBRUARY 28

The Catbird's Call

Trust in the Lord with all your heart and lean not on your own understanding; in all your ways submit to him, and he will make your paths straight.

—Proverbs 3:5–6 (NIV)

WE HAD GOTTEN used to the mewing of the birds in our backyard. That's right—mewing! Catbirds, including the ones that nested in our bushes, imitate the calls of other birds and even animals to create their own unique songs. Male and female catbirds then sing their strange melodies together. My wife and I had enjoyed listening to the catbirds' tunes and watching their long tail feathers rustle in the breeze during the more than forty years that we had lived in this home. The nearby stream and thicket provided perfect habitation for both catbirds and couples raising their families.

However, our hearts were being pulled from this charming home in Ohio to be closer to our children and grandchildren in Colorado. As we prayed about this over the years, God slammed many doors shut to confirm His will. It was heartbreaking, as we longed to be with our family, but we learned to trust God's goodness and timing. Our hearts were happy to follow His footsteps instead of making our own path.

Then we sensed doors opening. One confirmation was that our dear friends and next-door neighbors moved away to be near their children. The couple who bought our home were relocating to be near their children, and we were finally on our way to be near our children too! And the catbirds did not return to nest in our backyard that year.

I cannot see the road ahead, nor the direction where I'm led.
Trusting God to go before, I wait for Him to open doors. —R.B.

—Randy Benedetto

March

MARCH 1

Inhaling the Goodness of God

Let them give thanks to the LORD for his unfailing love and his wonderful deeds for mankind, for he satisfies the thirsty and fills the hungry with good things.

—PSALM 107:8–9 (NIV)

YOU CAN FEED this fawn because she's our Wild One," said the zoo-keeper from Deer Tracks Junction in Cedar Springs, Michigan. "She likes her bottles."

Eight fawns shyly stood to the side of the large pen. I wasn't sure what to expect as the keeper handed me an oversized bottle of milk. Instantly, one young doe made a beeline for the drink. Wild One had found me. This precious creature had light brown fur and white spots covering her tiny back. She seemed innocent enough at first glance. Wild One was hungry, though, and manners went by the wayside.

I turned to ask the keeper a quick question, then felt something on my leg. Hooves pushed against me. Looking down, I saw long eyelashes, an inquisitive nose, and those front hooves, which were now climbing my chest. I backed away in order to kneel down. The fawn quickly latched onto the bottle and began gulping down the milk.

I patiently waited for Wild One while she made sure the bottle was empty. Then, speaking quietly, I let her smell my hand before I petted her. As I was trying to take a picture, she put her nose up to my phone. I turned the camera to selfie mode, and she began sniffing my hair. In a flash, she licked my cheek. One more thank-you kiss came, and then she ran away.

Speechless with joy, I grinned the rest of the day. I recalled times when I have been physically or spiritually thirsty. God always satisfied me. That deer couldn't gulp down the goodness fast enough! When God meets my needs, do I inhale His goodness the same way?

What shall I return to the LORD for all his goodness to me?
—Psalm 116:12 (NIV)

—Twila Bennett

MARCH 2

Freedom

It is for freedom that Christ has set us free. Stand firm, then, and do not let yourselves be burdened again by a yoke of slavery.

—GALATIANS 5:1 (NIV)

OSCAR THE DUCK gave me great comfort after the loss of my dog. He was only a few weeks old when he was orphaned and found wandering the halls of a local school. But his calming nature and friendly disposition brought me hours of joy as I watched him swim and hunt for bugs in the grass.

Even with a child's plastic pool filled with water and soft hay for his bed, Oscar's large pen was not enough. His wild nature could not be caged. I knew the young drake wasn't happy. Sometimes I would catch him staring earnestly out toward the back of our yard, no doubt longing for something more.

As his feathers replaced the fluffy yellow down he'd sported all spring, he would raise his wings and quack, testing his lift. Eventually, I could no longer deny Oscar his liberty. Once he learned to fly, I released him. Oscar waddled out of the yard. Then he flapped and lifted skyward, quacking happily. His freedom ended up bringing me more joy than I could have found if I had kept him imprisoned.

Oscar's emancipation caused me to reflect on my own pardon. Until I accepted Christ as my Lord, I, too, was in captivity—trapped in a cage of sin and hopelessness. Jesus set me free, and only then was I able to fly above the bondage that held me earthbound. I am so grateful that Jesus made a way for me to fly to the Father's arms and experience real freedom.

Now the Lord is the Spirit, and where the Spirit of the Lord is, there is freedom. —2 Corinthians 3:17 (NIV)

—Tez Brooks

MARCH 3

Love Lessons from Zoe

Dear children, let us not love with words or speech but with actions and in truth.

—1 JOHN 3:18 (NIV)

MY CAT, ZOE, loves me. How do I know? She told me so! Obviously, Zoe can't use words. She makes it clear using her actions. She purrs, trills, rubs against me, and butts her head on mine. Sometimes she even stretches her little gray paw to pet me. She may express herself in primitive ways, but her sentiments are perfectly clear. Zoe loves me, and I should be more like her.

Speaking from a human standpoint, kind and uplifting words are very important, but I'm the first to admit I could do a better job loving others using actions rather than words. Specifically, the "action" of keeping my mouth shut! It's a challenge for a type-A personality like me to listen attentively without judgment, comment, or trying to "fix" anything. But I'm learning that just sitting with someone or listening over the phone, being there, taking time, is often the kindest, most loving action I can take. I know I appreciate it when family and friends take time with me.

So Zoe has reminded me that words are not necessary when showing love, and I can best demonstrate my love for others through attentive kindness. It means I may have to put aside whatever I'm doing and take time to listen or simply be present, but my temporary inconvenience is nothing compared to the opportunity I'm provided to, perhaps, be a blessing to someone else.

Simple, sincere people seldom speak much of their piety. It shows itself in acts rather than words, and has more influence than homilies or protestations. —Louisa May Alcott

—Marianne Campbell

MARCH 4

Unmerited Favor

For it is by grace you have been saved, through faith—and this is not from yourselves, it is the gift of God—not by works, so that no one can boast.

—EPHESIANS 2:8–9 (NIV)

THE PIG WAS black and huge. It lay down and poked its pink snout in fresh hay, searching for something in the dirt below. Rolls of fat took up the space of its belly. It seemed totally oblivious to the fairgoers, the scents of popcorn and fried dough, the fellow pig in the next pen . . . and the seven-year-old boy who gave it the most caring brush down I had ever seen.

I watched as the boy tenderly stroked the pig's bristly hair with a brush, making it gleam.

I couldn't help but think of the loving grace that God bestows on His children. Like this hefty pig, I've done nothing to deserve favor. I have no great works to boast about, no efforts of unusual worth. Many times, I search in the dirt instead of looking up to the treasure of heaven. But God, in His infinite mercy, lavishes favor on me nonetheless.

What a beautiful love He has shown me, and yet how often do I begrudge the same care and love to others? How often do I catch myself resentful of waking early to make my children's lunches? How often would I rather be doing what *I* want to do rather than taking the time to visit an elderly relative or neighbor or lend a listening ear to a troubled friend? I think if I can more often remind myself of how God treats *me*, if I can let it sink in and sit and then dwell on all that's been accomplished on my behalf, then these tasks of love and caregiving—even to the ungrateful—might become more natural. Like this little boy's love for his pig, our acts of love will always glorify our Father.

Heavenly Father, thank You for showing us unmerited favor. May we bask in this truth, then in turn show the world Your love. Amen.

—Heidi Chiavaroli

MARCH 5

A Quail of a Team

But who can discern their own errors? Forgive my hidden faults.

—PSALM 19:12 (NIV)

THAT MORNING, I stared out at the desert around Scottsdale, Arizona, feeling lost even in the place where I had grown up. Moments before, my ex-marine husband and I had argued, and in the heat of the moment, I had stomped across the desert landscape, emotional and confused but hoping to hear God's voice. Instead, birdsong stopped me. Under nearby bushes, a pair of quail sat perched on a rock, nuzzling each other's neck while their brood of youngsters scratched for insects.

I smiled. With their chubby gray bodies, black-and-white masks, and signature plumes of feathers drooping over their eyes, quail run instead of flying across the desert. I watched as the adults foraged for seeds and vegetation much like free-range chickens, those quail plumes bobbing along comically.

"Silly birds," I whispered to no one. But even as I chuckled, the quails' devotion to each other reached into my conflicted heart. God seemed to whisper what I already knew: despite a harsh life in the desert, quail are monogamous and mate for life. My husband's severe PTSD often left him rigid and unbending in that jarhead way only military families know. Could I be the first to forgive?

Just then, my husband walked toward me, hands in his pockets, as if to say, "Let's pretend it never happened." I pointed to the covey of quail and hugged my marine, whispering, "I'm sorry too." Like the quail, we had promised always to be there for one another, in sickness and in health, even with the challenges of PTSD. Embracing, we laughed at these funny little round birds that reminded us of why we had fallen in love and showed us the path to forgiveness.

When you forgive, you in no way change the past, but you sure do change the future. —Bernard Meltzer

—Linda S. Clare

MARCH 6

Holding Ducklings

The Lord will keep you from all harm—he will watch over your life; the Lord will watch over your coming and going both now and forevermore.

—Psalm 121:7–8 (NIV)

MY FAMILY RECENTLY attended a seasonal festival that included a petting zoo full of goats, ducks, and even donkeys for children to ride. I think I was even more excited than my four-year-old to discover the baby pool full of tiny ducklings. The young woman in charge of the ducks asked if we would like to hold a duckling—to which we responded enthusiastically—then explained to my son how to cradle it in one hand and gently cover its wings with the other.

He was elated. He so carefully followed the instructions she gave and laughed with glee as the little duckling flapped its wings. Meanwhile, I covered his own hands with my own. One by one, he held them, and one by one, I made sure the baby ducks stayed safe from harm.

It occurred to me later that's exactly what God does with us. Like my son holding those ducklings, I often fear I'm at risk of destroying the good work of God if I don't get the sacred, special things in life perfect. I think I'm in control or that I have the responsibility to work out God's plan. But the truth is, God does not gift me with skills, desires, and opportunities, then step away. He gives me these things so I can be used by Him, experiencing them relationally alongside Him. It's not up to me to do it all. As we hold our little corner of the world—new life and dreams and callings and even burdens—His own hands are always working to cover our own.

Walk of Faith: *What areas of my life am I attempting to "hold" on my own, outside God's hand? How has my firm grasp failed, and how can I take intentional steps to release these areas to the God who has kept and sustained me all along?*

—Ashley Clark

MARCH 7

The Uninvited Guest

Rejoice the soul of Your servant, for to You, O Lord, I lift up my soul.

—PSALM 86:4 (NKJV)

I SAT IN THE living room, looking out through the steamy windows at our neglected backyard. After three days of nonstop rain, it looked like a swamp. It was 3:30 a.m., and I couldn't sleep. My freelance design work was nonexistent, and this was straining our finances. "Lord, what do I do?" I prayed, "I feel stuck." My gaze dropped to the floor, where three black sticks lay on the carpet. Are those sticks moving? I turned on a lamp. "Ugh, earthworms," I moaned. "What next, Lord?"

I had to devise a quick plan to move these intruders outside. After a trip to the garage, I settled on using a garden hoe as a makeshift earthworm lift. I scooped up and carried each one to the backyard.

I later phoned Rodney at our nursery to solve the mystery of why the worms were in our house. "Earthworms absorb oxygen through their moist skin," he told me. "After heavy rains, oxygen in too-wet soil may run out, and the worms have to come up to the surface to breathe. Sometimes they get disoriented and stranded. In your case, it was in your living room."

"You're a hero," added Rodney, "for rescuing them, but those little guys are the unsung and, normally, unseen heroes in your yard. They keep the soil healthy."

Earlier that day, I had felt helpless about getting our finances on a firm footing. I had doubted that I could be lifted out of my situation. Thanks to my squiggly visitors' need for help, I turned to the always helpful presence of my loving heavenly Father who, I now realized, would gently lift and carry me to safer ground.

Walk of Faith: *When you are going through a seemingly hopeless or challenging situation with no obvious solution, know that your Creator is at your side. He's always there to lift you up and carry any burden you may be experiencing.*

—Terry Clifton

MARCH 8

Confirm the Work of Our Hands

Let the favor of the Lord our God be upon us; and confirm for us the work of our hands.

—PSALM 90:17 (NASB)

YOU HAVE TO go see this."

There was urgency in my husband's voice. Excitement shone in his eyes as he handed me the car keys. He and our older boys remained at our picnic spot by the river as I drove with our youngest toward the place they had described for us: "Drive a mile down the road. She's across the river."

My eyes narrowed, focusing on the adjacent shore, and then—there! Just as they had described, a bear poked its paw into the pooling water in the trees. Later the national park's ranger would confirm for us, "Oh, yes! That's our cinnamon black bear. Were her babies with her also?"

Although we didn't glimpse her offspring, the mama bear's actions struck a deep familial feeling within me. We watched her plunge into the water and come up with a trout in her mouth. On mission, she lunged into the woods and up the mountain to feed her young. With three children of our own, I was humbled to witness this fellow mama's workday.

How often I can doubt the work of my own hands. I can question my purpose, worth, and abilities. Yet everything God has called me to He has provided for. He equips me for my calling. Watching that cinnamon black bear show up at the water ready to work and seeing how God provides what she and her young need, I am reassured that He will do the same for me and my family. The psalmist uses the word *confirm* to mean "establish, direct, or provide." God calls us to great purposes, and He confirms the work of our hands.

Dear Lord, when I find myself doubting my purpose or abilities, assure me of the work You have called me to. Help me to not depend on my own skills or to try and control the outcome, but simply trust that, as I show up with hands ready to work, You will establish my efforts and provide for my needs. Amen.

—Eryn Lynum

MARCH 9

Healing Words

Gracious words are a honeycomb, sweet to the soul and healing to the bones.

—PROVERBS 16:24 (NIV)

MY MOM ADOPTED a chunky miniature rat terrier named Roxy. The dog had suffered years of abuse by her previous owners. She barked whenever anyone came to the front door. She shied away from people, cowering under furniture when my parents had company. She wouldn't even let my mom get too close when she first arrived in her new home.

As a dog lover, I grew determined to help Roxy feel safe around me. I gave her treats and spoke to her in a soft tone. Still, she flinched, whined, and skittered out of my reach when I moved my hand toward her. My heart broke for this fearful little pup that didn't know how to receive the love I offered her.

I continued showering Roxy with affirming words and assuring her of my love until she grew to trust me enough to let me scratch her back. One day, Roxy greeted me at the door with a full-body wiggle. She hopped onto my lap, placed her paws on my chest, and welcomed me with a few minutes of tail wagging and kisses. "Good girl, Roxy," I said. "I love you too."

Like Roxy, I've been wounded by people I trusted. I flinched at the thought of allowing people to get close emotionally. My fears and mistrust led me to believe I didn't deserve to be loved by others . . . or by God.

God used the gracious words of Scripture as a healing balm to my hurting heart. As I grew more confident in His love and learned to trust Him, He helped me love others genuinely and graciously receive love from Him and others.

Father God, please give us compassion for those who have been hurt. Help us speak life-giving words of encouragement and affirming love as we grow closer to You and others. Amen.

—Xochitl E. Dixon

MARCH 10

Claws Gets His Way

Jesus answered, "It is written: 'Man shall not live on bread alone, but on every word that comes from the mouth of God.'"

—MATTHEW 4:4 (NIV)

I HEARD ABOUT CLAWS from my "grandgem," Nicholas. He caught a little lizard and put it inside a glass jar. Nicholas named it Claws and fashioned a soft nest of grass and leaves for it. Then he laid a piece of fresh lettuce inside the jar, right near its nose, for breakfast. In the boy's young mind, it seemed the critter had everything it needed. But there was a problem.

It wouldn't eat—not lettuce, no matter how crispy, nor any other vegetable offered. Nothing. Apparently, Claws was on a hunger strike.

Nicholas tempted it with some ants. It ate one. But that was it. Nicholas checked often, keeping the jar stocked with lettuce and ants. Still, the lizard didn't eat. Without food, Claws seemed weaker every day. Nicholas feared it was dying. Finally, he and his mom made a hard decision. They took Claws outside and shook it out of the jar onto the ground, near some ants.

They had hoped it would celebrate with an ant feast and then, refreshed, scamper about. But Claws just sat there for a long time, not moving. A few ants strolled by, and it snapped one up. Only one. No feeding frenzy. Eventually, Nicholas smiled as Claws crawled away.

Claws's refusal to eat diminished his strength. Observing Claws reminded me of times I neglected to nourish my soul with God's Word and the weakness of spirit that resulted. God gives me His Word, the Bible, to nurture my inner person. May I eagerly take it in so I can experience total health and thrive.

Father, let me recognize the hunger that only You can satisfy and always partake of the spiritual nourishment you offer us in Your Word. Amen.

—Cathy Elliott

MARCH 11

The Spotted Cow

You shall not covet your neighbor's house. You shall not covet your neighbor's wife, or his male or female servant, his ox or donkey, or anything that belongs to your neighbor.

—EXODUS 20:17 (NIV)

WE HAD REACHED my favorite stretch of the trip—miles of long, straight road in rural Vermont, with lush green pastures flanking both sides. It was my favorite part because of the cows that lined up against the fences by the road. I have always had a fondness for cows.

My husband and I were on our way to visit dear friends. "I suppose their new house is gorgeous," I said. "And they'll have stunning pictures of their latest vacation." I immediately regretted the jealous tone in my voice.

To divert my focus, I turned my attention out the window, to the cows. A group of them were stretching their necks, squeezing their noses under a low fence wire, straining for the grass just beyond their reach. As the adage goes, it must have seemed greener on the other side. But several yards back, a white cow covered in black spots stood all alone. She quietly munched all the fresh green grass she could ever want. While the others competed for mere mouthfuls of vegetation, she had her fill. As she looked up at me with her big brown eyes, she seemed to send me a message. I smiled.

Sometimes friends may possess something we don't. They may have a nicer house or more money or better opportunities. But God plants us right where we are for a reason. He surrounds us with everything we need. We are not pleasing Him when we compare ourselves and desire things others have.

I reminded myself as we drove on down the road: be the spotted cow.

Dear Lord, how wonderful is the life You have planned for me. How glorious are the riches You have in store. Thank You for my home, my family, my job, and especially for Your Son, our Lord. Amen.

—Peggy Frezon

Serving the Kingdom

For we are God's handiwork, created in Christ Jesus to do good works, which God prepared in advance for us to do.

—EPHESIANS 2:10 (NIV)

DURING OUR TRIP to England, my friend Julie and I went to the Tower of London and immediately noticed the well-fed ravens. We got some great close-ups of one and read the sign about their diet. Julie pointed out one that was sorting through the contents of a rubbish bin, but we were more interested in exploring the ancient fortress than asking about the ravens. It wasn't until I got home and looked them up that I learned what a big deal the tower ravens are. Legend says that six ravens (plus a spare in case one flies the coop) must be at the tower at all times to protect the Crown. According to the legend, if the ravens leave, the kingdom of Britain will fall. They are cared for by the Ravenmaster, who must have at least twenty-two years of military service and is ultimately chosen by the ravens. The ravens can even be fired for unbecoming behavior.

I looked at a close-up I had taken. The raven looked almost regal, as if he knew the queen needed him. The Ravenmaster took his role seriously too. I found it moving that, though it was obvious everyone involved knew the six ravens didn't really protect the kingdom, those birds were cared for as if their presence in the tower made a difference. They had been chosen for a purpose, just as God chooses each of us to play a part in His kingdom and then provides the nurturing and spiritual nourishment that we need to fulfill our role. But unlike the tower ravens, whose role is based on legend and superstition, our service is vital and valued by the Lord who created us for it.

Walk of Faith: *Whose ministry or special giftedness has made a difference in your life? In what specific way (or ways) did God use that ministry or giftedness? Write a note of appreciation to that person.*

—Jeanette Hanscome

MARCH 13

Why Do We Flee?

So the LORD must wait for you to come to him so he can show you his love and compassion. For the LORD is a faithful God. Blessed are those who wait for his help. . . . He will surely respond to the sound of your cries.

—ISAIAH 30:18–19 (NLT)

MY FRIEND MARGIE had just opened the drain on her algae-filled swimming pool when she noticed movement on the water's surface. Curious, she stepped closer.

She was accustomed to scooping out snakes, frogs, and the occasional lizard. Once she had even fished out a squirrel. But she had never seen anything like this. The water was teeming with hundreds of baby frogs. Eyeing the steadily emptying pool, she knew they would be sucked into the drain if she didn't rescue them. She grabbed the net and extended it toward the frogs.

Instead of welcoming her attempts to save them, however, the terrified creatures swam away. To them, her looming shadow looked like a predator poised to swoop down and devour them. Her net, instead of a means of deliverance, looked like an instrument of capture.

"No, no, no," Margie said as they swam away from her. "Come back. I want to help you. I'm your friend."

Hearing her story, I realized that frogs and I have a lot in common. Apart from God, I face certain destruction. Left to myself, I am hopeless and helpless. But God, in His mercy, sent a Savior who is eager to save me. He wants to lift me out of the mire and set my feet on solid ground.

Why do I sometimes resist His helping hands? Why do I flee from His saving net and distrust His pure motives? Why do I close my ears to His whisper? I want to run toward His loving arms—always.

Walk of Faith: *If you're experiencing a situation that only God can rescue you from, I encourage you to turn toward Him today. He loves you. He wants to help you. He is your friend.*

—Lori Hatcher

MARCH 14

Remember the Turtles

Let the morning bring me word of your unfailing love, for I have put my trust in you. Show me the way I should go, for to you I entrust my life.

—PSALM 143:8 (NIV)

ON OUR LAST beach vacation, I left my still-sleeping family and headed out on a sunrise walk. As the sky warmed to pink and gold, I smiled in wonder at the unmistakable tracks of leatherback sea turtles crisscrossing the sand to lay their eggs in the dunes. Ahead of me, a small crowd circled around a nest. At their center, the sand splashed and stirred as a baby turtle fought its way to the surface and immediately began paddling through the sand toward the sea.

Although the hatchling was born to become a giant, the long journey ahead was daunting. The turtle tumbled into each footprint as if it were a crater, only to fight its way up the other side. It didn't stop to consider its size or the obstacles in its way, only the call of the sea.

As I watched the struggle, a tear slid down my cheek. I knew God was speaking to my heart. How many times have the footprints of others become my stumbling block? How many times have I questioned why my journey mattered when others have done it bigger or better? How many times have my small beginnings deterred me from a giant future?

Fourteen minutes later, the little champion slipped into the sea and swam away, and conviction settled in me. It was time for me to be brave. One day, I might be a giant turtle. I might leave my own trail in the sand if only I have the courage to fight through the footprints of others and follow my own heart.

Lord, help me not to be intimidated by the successes and failures of those who have gone before me. Thank You that their footsteps don't lead to my destiny. Help me to remember the turtles and press on. In Jesus's name. Amen.

—Tracy Joy Jones

The Milk of the Word

In fact, though by this time you ought to be teachers, you need someone to teach you the elementary truths of God's word all over again. You need milk, not solid food!

—HEBREWS 5:12 (NIV)

WE RECENTLY HAD the blessing of seeing a baby giraffe being born. Through my tears of joy, I watched as the baby made that perilous drop to the ground. How was that even possible without the giraffe being hurt from the fall?

In the wild, it's extremely important for the baby giraffe to get on its feet right away and start nursing. Otherwise, it's vulnerable to predators. My family and I waited with bated breath as the baby giraffe tried, with little success, to stand. Again and again it tried, but those long legs wobbled and knocked together, and it couldn't find its balance.

Finally, when we were beginning to despair, the baby giraffe wobbled to its feet and took a couple of steps. Everyone cheered as the young one nuzzled its mother and started nursing. It was just exactly what was needed to help this baby grow to be a healthy, hearty adult giraffe.

Just as the baby giraffe needs its mother's milk, I need the precious milk of the Word of God, eventually transitioning to the meat of Scripture as I grow in Christ. Without this milk, I, too, am open to "predators," vulnerable to temptation that threatens to draw me away from my heavenly Father. May I always, like this baby giraffe, find my footing and seek out the milk that will help me grow.

Like newborn babies, crave pure spiritual milk, so that by it you may grow up in your salvation. —1 Peter 2:2 (NIV)

—Deb Kastner

MARCH 16

Equipped for the Journey

His divine power has granted to us everything pertaining to life and godliness . . .

—2 PETER 1:3 (NASB)

WE'D LEFT THE tree line behind over an hour before. Our pace had slowed as we worked to steady our breathing and maintain our heart rate. Up here, at nearly thirteen thousand feet of elevation, the air was thin. On we hiked, one foot in front of the other, toward the summit of Mount Audubon in Colorado.

As we rounded a switchback, my husband motioned for me to stop. "Did you hear that? Look, there." He pointed twenty feet ahead of me on the trail. From out of the tundra brush, the figure of a bird emerged. "It's a ptarmigan," my husband told me. In all our mountain adventures, I had never seen one. I walked forward, waiting for the ptarmigan to dart away from the trail, but it remained. As I drew closer, I realized why. Two chicks eagerly foraged in the brush behind the mama bird.

The preceding four hours of hiking had taken us through pine trees, aspen, and wildflowers to the high-altitude tundra, and I was astounded at how much life we discovered near the summit. God designed and equipped that mama ptarmigan and her young for these harsh climates. He gave her camouflaging plumage for protection, thick, feathered feet to keep her warm in the harsh winter terrain, and black lines around her eyes to shield her from the sunlight at high elevations. In the same way, He has equipped me for wherever He might lead me in my own journey. When my surroundings feel harsh, daunting, or barren, He provides exactly what I need for life and godliness.

Walk of Faith: *Make a list of difficult circumstances you have faced over the past year. Afterward, make a list of specific ways you see God equipping you for the journey He has given to you. Record blessings, skills, talents, encouragement, and miracles you have seen.*

—Eryn Lynum

MARCH 17

Terror in the Night

Fear not, for I am with you.

—ISAIAH 41:10 (NKJV)

MIDNIGHT HAD PASSED. Together with my brother Bill and his wife, my husband and I sat around the long table of the vacation cabin. The children slept while we enjoyed adult conversation that was not about potty chairs and teething rings.

Before retiring, my brother took the first turn to the outhouse. An unexpected scream split the air, echoed by a second. Fearing something horrendous happening, we ran for the door just as Bill burst inside.

The screams continued, reverberating through the hollow beside the cabin. No one knew what they could be. Fear of the unknown built. Our imaginations filled our minds with images that ranged from a cougar about to leap through the door to a deranged person. Bill and Kevin tried using the spotlight in Bill's truck to identify what was causing the screams, but with no success.

For almost an hour, we huddled. The screams filled the cabin, sometimes coming from behind it, sometimes racing through the trees overhead.

When quiet returned, we went to bed, but no one slept. The next day, we learned from a park ranger that we had heard a bobcat. Another vacationer's sighting of one near the cabin the following week verified it. We laughed about our fear of something as small as a bobcat but never forgot that night.

Throughout our lives, fears will attack us. This world can be a scary place. Things known and unknown bring fear and doubts. But our God knew we would experience this and told us more than three hundred times in the Bible not to be afraid, that He would be with us. We can surely trust a promise given enough times that we can read one almost every day of the year.

When fear has caught us in its spell,
we can trust Him; all is well. —C.M.

—Cathy Mayfield

MARCH 18

Nice Catch

Therefore, as God's chosen people, holy and dearly loved, clothe yourselves with compassion, kindness, humility, gentleness and patience.

—COLOSSIANS 3:12 (NIV)

MY GRANDDAUGHTER FAITH is not your ordinary girl. She loves the creepy, crawly things of life—particularly reptiles. Years ago, I had a pocket-size reptile identification book that she loved to pore over, hours on end—learning the different kinds of snakes, turtles, lizards, chameleons, and geckos.

At home, she would catch the creatures, keep them for a day, and then release them. This went on for years with geckos, lizards, garter snakes, a rubber boa, and a black water snake, until her parents finally let her keep one she found in the backyard as a pet: a garter snake with brown spots, yellow eyes, and a pink tongue.

Faith used a plastic storage box with a lid to make a terrarium, adding dirt, sticks, and a container for water. But its inside existence was short lived when friends who were feeding the family pets decided it was poisonous and let it go. She has since resigned herself to a catch-and-release policy—just keeping the creatures in her hands long enough to study them. She's a tenderhearted soul who sees the best in all creatures—the creepy, crawly types and even human ones.

God would have me demonstrate kindness to those around me. It's not that hard to write a card to someone who has lost a loved one or call a family member on her birthday. When I make a big meal, like lasagna, it's not that much more work to make a second casserole for a young family. Love works best when I have a catch-and-release policy just as Faith has with her critters: God freely hands love over to me, and I release it to others.

God, You created us all and love us. Help me see others as You see them, and nudge me to be kind to those in need by offering a kind word or help that will make a difference with the challenges they have. Amen.

—Janet Holm McHenry

MARCH 19

The First Egg

But encourage one another daily.

—HEBREWS 3:13 (NIV)

DID YOU KNOW that chickens talk to one another? They make certain sounds and clucks to say good morning, to warn of danger, to say they found food, to say good night, and so on.

One of these sounds is a particular song hens sing when they lay an egg. The hen will come strutting out of the coop, clucking at the top of her lungs. Then the other hens join in, singing along. It doesn't matter that they lay eggs every single day. From a chicken's perspective, the eggs are worth singing about every time.

You would think that as they got older, their enthusiasm would diminish . . . but, no. From the day they lay that first egg until the day they lay their last, these girls celebrate every egg.

One day, as I was working in the garden, I heard one of our young chickens sing her song for the first time. Our sweet Daisy-Girl had laid her first egg, and she was beside herself with excitement. She paraded back and forth, calling out to all the other hens to come see what she had done. Then, true to form, they joined in and delighted with her in that first tiny light-brown egg . . . and every single egg she has laid since.

That day as I stood and watched the cacophony of celebration, it dawned on me that this is what I am called to do for others as part of the body of Christ. I'm called to encourage others, not just in the big things but in the little things, in the day-to-day strivings to live for Christ, in the mundane and ordinary, and those daily choices will become the legacy I leave behind for the kingdom of God.

Walk of Faith: *As a community of believers, we are stronger when we encourage one another daily, singing encouragement to each other . . . just like the chickens. Whom can you encourage today?*

—Joy Pitner

MARCH 20

Provision

They shall mount up with wings like eagles.

—Isaiah 40:31 (NKJV)

IT WAS THE first week of spring. My husband, Terry, and I had gone to a lake resort to do some walking. To our dismay, an unseasonable snowstorm with heavy winds hit the area, and we were forced to stay indoors.

As I gazed out the lodge window, I noticed a young boy attempting to launch a kite. Unfortunately, the rough, icy winds didn't cooperate. The boy's paper kite was being whipped about, tearing in various places.

I watched the fragile kite twisting to the left, then to the right, and down into a fluttering crash onto the snow-covered parking lot. I had felt just like that kite the previous winter—tossed about in every direction by my emotions as I gave care to my beloved Terry, who was struggling through chemo. No matter how hard I tried, I was just like that paper kite, fighting the wind, about to crash.

My attention was suddenly drawn to something moving far above the doomed kite. It was a brown-and-white bald eagle. The same turbulent wind was hitting at the eagle, but it overcame the wind's current by tucking its massive wings under its chest. Once through it, the eagle soared upward, then glided ahead, full speed to its destination.

I stood at the window, aware that only God could create such a creature, endowing the eagle with the miraculous abilities to survive such resistance. I realized this same God had endowed me with my own human provision to survive—*my faith in God*—that would not only move me through life's turbulent spots but also lift me . . . to soar like an eagle.

God has dealt to each one a measure of faith. —Romans 12:3 (NKJV)

—Sandra Clifton

MARCH 21

Live and Learn

Get wisdom, get understanding; do not forget my words or turn away from them.

—PROVERBS 4:5 (NIV)

SUGARFOOT HAD LOST his snap. My rabbit—a picture-perfect Easter-card bunny that I had purchased on a whim—didn't want to eat. His bright eyes and silky white coat appeared dull. I couldn't figure out what was wrong with him. One day after work, I hopped the bus to the pet store where I had purchased Sugarfoot and explained my problem to the clerk.

"What have you been feeding him?" he asked.

"Carrots, lettuce, that sort of thing," I replied.

He frowned. "Rabbits need something more substantial." His tone clearly indicated his disapproval of my lack of knowledge. He plucked a bag of rabbit food from one of the shelves. The contents proved to be a mixture of alfalfa pellets, rolled oats, seeds, and ground rice. I had assumed rabbits ate only garden veggies, like Peter Rabbit in the children's story. Apparently not.

Sheepishly, I paid for the feed. Later, when I put a full dish in front of my listless pet, Sugarfoot didn't budge. With a bit of coaxing, he finally began to nibble. I sighed with relief. Eventually, Sugarfoot returned to his happy, healthy self.

Looking back on that incident, I realize that my carelessness could have cost Sugarfoot his life. I had purchased him thoughtlessly without considering how to care for him. I have made other impulsive choices, too, but I am learning to slow down and count the cost, to pray for God's guidance, and to seek advice from those more experienced than I am. It's the wise thing to do.

Lord, help me not to be wise in my own eyes. I want to make responsible choices. Thank You for always being there for me. Amen.

—Shirley Raye Redmond

MARCH 22

The Watchful Mama Bird

The L*ORD* *will keep you from all harm—he will watch over your life; the* L*ORD* *will watch over your coming and going both now and forevermore.*

—PSALM 121:7–8 (NIV)

A HOUSE FINCH NESTED in the hanging basket on my porch. I didn't realize she had taken up residence until she flew out of the basket and over my head one evening while I watered the plants. I gently took the basket down and saw a tightly woven nest filled with small bright-blue eggs. Mama bird sat in the tree next to the porch, chirping her displeasure at the disruption to her home. Each evening for the next few weeks, I carefully took the basket down and watered around the nest. Each time, mama bird sat nearby, scolding me.

Her careful attention, protection, and loud annoyance at the hint of danger to her babies gave me a glimpse of my Lord. Like the mama bird keeping watch over her nest, He pays careful attention to every detail of my life. He never sleeps on the job. He watches over me as I come and go. He will not abandon me or get distracted with other cares. Sometimes I see His care in the well-timed encouraging text from a friend. Often, He brings just the right Scripture to mind in a moment of discouragement. Sometimes I feel His watchful eye during a heart-pounding near accident.

When I am tempted to think He doesn't see or care about my life, I remember the mama bird chirping in the tree, scolding me when I came too close. I recognize that even when I cannot see or hear Him and I wonder where God is, He is there, working even in the unseen. He has tightly woven my life into His. I may not see His hand today, but I trust that He holds my life in His hands and He will not let go.

A God wise enough to create me and the world I live in is wise enough to watch out for me. —Philip Yancey

—Amelia Rhodes

MARCH 23

The Master's Voice

My sheep listen to my voice; I know them, and they follow me.

—JOHN 10:27 (NIV)

MY DAUGHTER AND her husband and their dog, Tuck, live on the property adjacent to us in the Rocky Mountains. Trees separate our cabins, so it's quite private, although we're only a few yards apart. Tuck can hear us calling him from each cabin, and he goes back and forth all day long. He has a cozy bed and steady supply of treats at his grandparents' place!

One day when Tuck was visiting me, he heard my daughter's voice calling him, so he jumped up and ran down the path toward home. I waited until he was almost out of sight before I summoned him with a duck call I had found in my camping supplies. He spun around and raced to our cabin, only to have his master call him back again. Tuck skidded to a stop, quickly reversed, and ran the other way—kicking up a storm of dust in his wake! We played this game a couple of times before rewarding him with an extra treat.

Tuck might be tempted by the artificial sounds of a fake duck, but he has been listening to his master closely. He comes when she calls because he truly loves her, and he trusts the safety and security of the home his family has created for him.

Jesus likened Himself to a shepherd whose sheep follow Him when they recognize His voice. The key words for sheep like me are *listening* and *following*. It's one thing for me to hear God's call; it's quite another to recognize the advantage of His instruction and actually go along with it. Everything He has ever asked me to do has turned out for my good, although sometimes it takes me a few wrong turns before I put myself on the narrow path toward home.

Most of us possess a formidable amount of factual information on what the Master expects of us. Precious few have either the will, intention, or determination to act on it and comply with His instructions.

—W. Phillip Keller

—Randy Benedetto

MARCH 24

Highway in the Sky

You led your people like a flock by the hand of Moses and Aaron.

—PSALM 77:20 (NIV)

YOU HAVE A highway in the sky, Kathy," Papa told me as we stood on my front porch listening to a loud honking sound. "I've been watching the geese follow this route every time I visit Oregon." I wondered if the V formation reminded Dad of the fighter jets in World War II that flew with purpose and honor when he was a soldier on the European front.

I have always thought of geese as a bit elegant, but messy and noisy. That day, I thanked God for this miracle in nature, right above my roof, that I had taken for granted.

When geese flap their wings, they create an uplift for the birds that follow. By flying in a V formation, the whole flock gains 71 percent greater flying range than if one bird flew alone.

When geese lose their place, they instantly feel the resistance and get back into formation. If the leader gets tired, it rotates back and another bird flies at the point position. The geese from behind honk as if to encourage those up front to keep their speed.

When geese get sick or wounded, a few other birds in the flock will land with the ailing bird to help. The tending birds stay until the fallen one can fly or until it dies, and then they join another flock or catch up with the original one.

These migratory birds teach us about teamwork, loyalty, and aiming at our goals. They inspire us to spur one another on and to stop with compassion when another is wounded, dying, or in need.

Papa is in heaven now, and I still watch for the V in the sky that reminds me of my soldier father and VE Day. It is also symbolic to us as Christians. Our victory is in Christ, as we unite with one accord and soar to heaven.

Dear Lord, lead us like a flock, in unity with other believers, compassionate and strong. In Jesus's name. Amen.

—Kathleen Ruckman

MARCH 25

Minnie's Sticky Situation

He lifted me out of the slimy pit, out of the mud and mire; he set my feet on a rock and gave me a firm place to stand.

—PSALM 40:2 (NIV)

ONE SPRING AFTERNOON, I took Minnie for a walk along the side of our house. We headed toward the back but stopped before we got to the field. The weeds were nearly as tall as my almost-six-pound Yorkie. Time to mow.

We turned around to go inside when Minnie spotted a lizard. She chased it under the hammock and through the weeds. The lizard ran up a palm tree where it found freedom just beyond Minnie's reach.

Since Minnie hasn't learned to climb trees, I convinced her to continue her pursuit another day, and we went inside.

I undid her leash at the entryway and walked to the kitchen. Minnie wouldn't budge. She sat on the rug and waited.

I turned back to see why Minnie wasn't at my feet. Little green teardrop-shaped prickly pods clung to her hair from the bottom of her chin to the tips of her toes. They stuck to her like glue and didn't allow her much room to move.

But Minnie knew just what to do. She waited for me to rescue her. She reminded me that no matter the circumstance I find myself in, Jesus is always right there with me. He is my Rescuer.

I painstakingly combed through Minnie's hair to remove the prickly pods. But it took a shower to remove their sticky remnants.

I'm thankful God not only cleanses the sin from my life but also removes the sticky remnants from my heart. All I have to do is ask.

Lord, thank You for being my Rescuer. Your grace keeps my foot from slipping, and in You I have a firm place to stand. Amen.

—Crystal Storms

MARCH 26

Living in Real Life

I'm ready, God, so ready, ready from head to toe. Ready to sing, ready to raise a God-song: "Wake, soul! Wake, lute! Wake up, you sleepyhead sun!"

—PSALM 108:1–2 (MSG)

HOW MANY TIMES have we missed out by being on our phones or computers or tablets? How often have we missed out on living in the moment while trying to get just the perfect photo of that moment?

I have done this over and over. And God brought this to my mind while I was at the Tennessee Aquarium in Chattanooga with my husband at the habitat for the river otters. Oh, how fun they were to watch, so playful and cute as they zoomed through the water and did flips. I grabbed my phone to take photos and short videos from different angles, never stopping, because I didn't want to miss the perfect otter trick!

I don't know how long I was there, but when I finally put my phone back in my pocket, I realized I had become separated from my husband. I had no idea when I had lost him. I couldn't be sure how much time had passed. While I was so zoomed in on trying to capture individual otter antics, I had missed enjoying watching the whole group together.

I had gotten so focused on capturing the perfect photo or video to share later with the rest of our family or on social media that I had missed watching the otters playing together with my own eyes. Instead, I had watched them only through a screen. And worse, I had missed the opportunity to share the experience with my husband.

God has given me a beautiful world to enjoy and special people who can share that joy with me. I want to be sure to wake up, put my electronic devices away occasionally, and live real life in each and every moment.

Enjoy the little things in life, for one day you may look back and realize they were the big things. —Robert Breault

—Missy Tippens

MARCH 27

Seek the Son

So that they should seek the Lord, in the hope that they might grope for Him and find Him, though He is not far from each one of us.

—ACTS 17:27 (NKJV)

I NEVER KNEW DOGS were natural heat seekers! At just fourteen weeks old, Mijo the Boston terrier taught me a valuable life lesson.

Mijo [*MEE-hoe]* learned what time of day the sun shone through our front door. Every day, like clockwork, he stopped whatever he was doing to get to his sunny spot. There he enjoyed leisurely naps wrapped in the warmth of the sunbeams.

One day, he spent the early hours playing outdoors. Suddenly, even though he was having a good time, he urgently wanted to go inside. Once I opened the door, he darted past me. Curious to see where he went, I followed him through the house. Wouldn't you know that Mijo had already found his place in the sun, and his snores sounded like a chainsaw!

By simply replacing the word *sun* with *Son*, I pondered several lessons. It is good to get in the habit of seeking the Son. The warmth of Jesus's embrace is all I need. I grow closer to Jesus when I seek the Son early and daily, like clockwork. I can develop this habit, just as Mijo did. It is second nature for him to look for the sun. Is it second nature for me to daily look for the Son?

Not only does the Son provide warm, welcoming intimacy; He also gives me rest when I come to Him. Mijo fell asleep right away when he hunkered down in the warmth of the sunbeams. I can find that same instant rest in Jesus. And not just physically, but emotionally, mentally, and spiritually, as well. When I rest in Jesus, I can put all other thoughts to rest. No more doing or striving, just being—all found in the Son.

There is greater rest and solace to be found in the presence of God for one hour, than in an eternity of the presence of man.
—Robert Murray McCheyne

—Kathy Carlton Willis

MARCH 28

A Not-So-Stubborn Donkey

Behold, your king is coming to you; He is just and endowed with salvation, humble, and mounted on a donkey, Even on a colt, the foal of a donkey.

—ZECHARIAH 9:9 (NASB)

DONKEYS HAVE A reputation for stubbornness, though those who keep them will often tell you that they are intelligent creatures and that if a donkey is being stubborn, it might just be for good reason. Researchers have learned that donkeys do well in cognitive tests, scoring higher than either mules or horses, and are less inclined than their equine cousins to panic.

Author Isabel George tells the story of a donkey named Murphy who was a true hero in World War I. Acting as an ambulance for stretcher bearer Jack Simpson, Murphy calmly carried wounded soldiers over the rough terrain of Gallipoli, Turkey, to a field hospital, even as shells and bullets hailed down around him.

Scripture tells us of another donkey—one whose name is never mentioned—that played a brief but crucial role in an epic story. Jesus's disciples borrowed this unassuming donkey with its owner's permission, and it carried Jesus into Jerusalem, where, just a few days later, He would be crucified.

On this Palm Sunday, we remember a day that saw crowds laying down palms before Jesus, in recognition of the royalty He was, and calling Him the King who comes in the name of the Lord. May we remember Him as the humble, gentle King bringing us salvation as He rode into Jerusalem on the back of a donkey.

"Hosanna in the highest!" That ancient song we sing,
for Christ is our Redeemer, the Lord of heaven, our King.
—Jennette Threlfall

—The Editors of Guideposts

MARCH 29

The Chick at Baby Animals Day

Therefore, if anyone is in Christ, the new creation has come: The old has gone, the new is here!

—2 CORINTHIANS 5:17 (NIV)

SPRING FELT VERY far away. Late into March, it was still cold and snowy, and I was feeling as empty and dark as the bare branches outside. I was sick of the chill, but at least I had something good to hold on to—Baby Animals Day at a nearby farm, held each spring around Easter. I don't know who was more excited—me or my young granddaughters. "Ten more sleeps until baby animals," I told them one day after preschool. They counted on their fingers every day, just as I counted on my calendar.

Finally, the day arrived, and Grace, Lily, and I rushed into the barn to meet the animals. I leaned over a tidy pen. There in the hay was a muddle of tiny yellow chicks. Their soft feathers puffed over stubby orange legs. "They just hatched," the farmhand said. "They're only ten days old." One of the chicks scuttled over my way, chirping cheerfully. I used one finger to stroke its downy back. *Peep! Peep!* It jumped into my palm, and I cradled it close to my chest. This brand-new life, from within its hay-strewn pen, lifted the heaviness I had been carrying and brought me joy.

Ten days ago, this chick was safely tucked inside its brown speckled egg. Ten days ago, I was empty and discouraged. I couldn't see the beautiful new life that was waiting. But it was there. I don't know why I forget, but every spring I'm reminded—some days seem dark and dreary, but if I'm patient, I will see everything renewed as I celebrate the light of Christ.

Dear Father, in the spring, in baby chicks, and in our eternity with You in heaven, thank You for Your miracle of new life. Amen.

—Peggy Frezon

MARCH 30

Trust in the Valley

I trust in the steadfast love of God forever and ever.
I will thank you forever, because you have done it.

—PSALM 52:8–9 (ESV)

CANCER. I HAD expected something minor, something treatable. Instead, I was told my beloved dog, Norway, had a cancer that would kill him in three to four months. He was only five years old—too young to die.

The diagnosis hit hard and painfully chipped at my heart, preparing it to shatter when the end would come, far sooner than I had expected. The apparent injustice of the diagnosis strangled me. Norway was healthy and happy. He should have had more years to enjoy life.

Fear clawed at the back of my grief. How would I face this? I couldn't watch him suffer, couldn't see him be destroyed by the disease that would take him from me. The pain felt too intense for me to bear.

But then the Holy Spirit prompted me to remember to trust God. Did I trust Him only with unimportant things? Or did I trust Him with what I loved most? Through tears, I handed my fears over.

Two years later, my sweet dog, Norway, was still with us, living his life to the fullest while we savored every moment we had with him. The cancer specialists were astounded. Some disbelieved that the impossible could have happened.

But I hold up this testimony as a witness, against my own doubts and the doubts of others, that I can trust in the steadfast love of God. He is the giver of good gifts who can and *will* bring about His plan. I can trust Him even with my precious ones.

Father, thank You that in the darkest times, I can trust You with the people and things dearest to me because You love me and are more than able to work all things for good. Amen.

—Jerusha Agen

MARCH 31

Sky High

God made the wild animals according to their kinds, the livestock according to their kinds, and all the creatures that move along the ground according to their kinds. And God saw that it was good.

—GENESIS 1:25 (NIV)

I LEANED BACK AND looked up into the kindest eyes I have ever seen. The sky above was brilliant blue, contrasting with the rust-colored spots on Tucker, a reticulated male giraffe at Boulder Ridge Wild Animal Park in Grand Rapids, Michigan. Tears came to my eyes. This was a dream come true. Both of the previous times I was at a zoo that had feeding stations for giraffes, the exhibit was closed. At age forty-nine, I was finally getting to feed one.

Wanting to look at the giraffe more closely, I stared in wonder, grinning from ear to ear. He had long, fluttering eyelashes and a knob on his head. Funny little ears stuck out sideways. His eighteen-foot height took my breath away. He leaned down to look at me, and I could see the whiskers on his face.

Standing on tiptoes, I raised a carrot above my head. Immediately, a long black tongue shot out of his mouth. I gasped as his tongue twirled in a perfect curlicue around the carrot. As Tucker gently pulled my offering into his mouth, I imagined the carrot's long descent to his stomach. The giraffe's neck was taller than my entire body! I wanted to see his tongue spiral again, so I offered a piece of lettuce. Instinctively, I reached to pet him with my other hand, but Tucker shyly grabbed the leaf and lifted his head just out of my reach.

The intricate detail in this one animal is brilliant, but imagine it multiplied over and over in all other creatures. Interacting with Tucker deepened my awe of that amazing sixth day of creation when God created them.

Whence comes this idea that if what we are doing is fun, it can't be God's will? The God who made giraffes . . . has a sense of humor. Make no mistake about that. —Catherine Marshall.

—Twila Bennett

April

APRIL 1

Rocky the Encourager

Therefore encourage one another and build each other up, just as in fact you are doing.

—1 THESSALONIANS 5:11 (NIV)

ROCKY IS THE friendliest horse in the rescue-ranch herd. He is the first to welcome a new equine, nuzzle a barn cat, or guide our blind steer to the water trough. He is the first to step up to get his fly spray so he can show the others it's not a bad thing. When another horse is upset, he finds a way to comfort it. He is truly Mr. Congeniality.

He also has issues that brought him to a rescue ranch rather than to a farm where he would be ridden regularly. Nerve damage to one of his legs makes an adult rider very painful for him, so he had been overlooked by horse buyers. When a horse is not rideable, his value drops for most people who have horses. At that point, they become pasture ornaments, and many end up at auction.

For me, a horse's value has never been based on its ability to carry me on its back, to win a race, or to work a field. The value of a horse is in its healing qualities, and in this category, Rocky was over the top. He could sense when I'd had a bad day and help bring me out of it. It was his way with every creature on the farm. This big red horse has taught me to value within myself the things that cannot ever be lessened. Encouragement is a choice and a gift we can always give to others. That gift far surpasses anything that time can erode, and the more we practice it, the stronger it becomes.

God, please give me words of encouragement for those You place in my path, and let me never be afraid to offer a spirit lift to anyone. Amen.

—Devon O'Day

APRIL 2

Crackers

"But I will restore you to health and heal your wounds," declares the Lord, *"because you are called an outcast, Zion for whom no one cares."*

—Jeremiah 30:17 (NIV)

IN MIAMI, A wild parrot we named Crackers found his way into the yard of my friend Lorna. Crackers had somehow broken his wing so, using his beak and feet, he crawled up the trunk of a palm tree to heal.

Other parrots deserted Crackers, so he was alone and in pain. When Lorna noticed the little green bird, she stepped up to the challenge of helping Crackers survive.

Each day, he was waiting for her in the same tree. Lorna would set out fruit and other food he might be used to eating. When her cats were around, she shooed them away, so Crackers wouldn't have to climb to safety so often.

Soon, Crackers began to attach himself to Lorna. She noticed he was learning how to mimic her voice, too, repeating words like *Hello, Crackers* and *Good morning.*

Before long, the parrot's wing healed, and he began to fly. But with such a loving provider, Crackers never went far. Although the other birds accepted him back, he remained loyal to Lorna.

When I consider the relationship between Lorna and Crackers, I'm reminded of my own Savior, who was wounded for my transgressions. I, too, was broken and wounded—an outcast looking for shelter. Aren't we all? But Christ has made a way to restore us, providing healing for us from His own wounds.

But he was pierced for our transgressions, he was crushed for our iniquities; the punishment that brought us peace was on him, and by his wounds we are healed. —Isaiah 53:5 (NIV)

—Tez Brooks

APRIL 3

A Deer in the Woods

If you need wisdom, ask our generous God, and he will give it to you. He will not rebuke you for asking.

—JAMES 1:5 (NLT)

FROM THE WOODED path, I saw a buck in the distance. His head was low, grazing on tender green plants. His long, graceful legs supported a sturdy body, with a flickering white tail. He didn't see or hear me. It was a treat to watch him in his natural environment, so I stood as still as possible.

Then, despite my efforts to be quiet, my weight shifted, and a twig snapped. The deer lifted his head, and our gazes connected. His large ears pointed my way, and his nostrils flared. As he studied my presence, I imagined he was deciding, *Should I stay, or should I run away?*

So many times, I've been faced with a decision that has left me paralyzed with fear. I don't know what to do, so I stop in my tracks. But unlike the deer, I often let panic take over. The worst part is when I start to worry, *What if? What if?* I become stuck in fear.

There is only one way to dispel the fear, and that is to turn to God and ask for His guidance. Not only does God know the future; He has it perfectly orchestrated. All He asks is that I trust in Him. When I'm in doubt and in panic, God has all things under control. I may not know what lies ahead, but God does.

The deer sized me up and decided that I wasn't a threat. He lowered his head and returned to grazing. I left him in peace and moved on down the path.

Walk of Faith: *When you feel anxious about a decision, close your eyes and imagine yourself on a peaceful woodland path. Feel yourself handing your decision over to God. Then confidently continue on that beautiful path, knowing that He walks with you and will give you the wisdom you need.*

—Peggy Frezon

APRIL 4

The Reptile Road of Salvation

He saved us, not because of righteous things we had done, but because of his mercy.

—TITUS 3:5 (NIV)

MY HUSBAND AND I were sitting at the dining-room table when a movement caught my eye. Running outside, we discovered a turtle trying to get to the pond behind our property. It had apparently wandered away and gotten lost. Now, it was trying to scale the fence that stood between it and home. Let me tell you, a turtle trying to climb a chain-link fence is a pitiful sight. Home was calling, but there was no way it could get there.

In compassion, my husband reached down, picked up the creature, which was muddy and a bit smelly, and lifted it over the fence. After setting it down gently, he pointed it in the direction of the pond. "Go home, Mr. Turtle. You're free. And don't come back."

I could empathize with the turtle because I've been there. As a young adult, I had wandered far from my heavenly home. I was lost. My sin stood as an impenetrable wall between me and my Creator. I did my best to scale the barrier. I tried morality and good works. I tried success and accomplishments. Even going to church wasn't enough to lift me over the top.

Then one day, Jesus lifted me over the sin barrier and pointed me toward heaven. He ignored the dirt and stench that clung to my soul and reached out to me with compassion and forgiveness.

My life changed forever that day. The power of Jesus's death and resurrection enabled me to overcome my sin barrier and secured for me abundant life now and eternal life one day in heaven.

I am the resurrection, and the life: he that believeth in me, though he were dead, yet shall he live. —John 11:25 (KJV)

—Lori Hatcher

APRIL 5

The Bee Collects Honey

God blessed them and said to them, "Be fruitful and increase in number; fill the earth and subdue it. Rule over the fish in the sea and the birds in the sky and over every living creature that moves on the ground."

—GENESIS 1:28 (NIV)

ONE OF MY favorite things to do in the springtime in Colorado is visit the Rocky Mountains to enjoy the newly opening wildflowers. Grassy fields teem with a variety of shapes, colors, and aromas.

Amid all this teeming majesty, I hear the buzzing of honeybees, busily moving from flower to flower as they seek the nectar the flowers produce. Honeybees are wonderful conservationists. Not only do they not harm the flowers as they take the nectar they need to survive and thrive, but they give as well as take, pollinating the flowers as they go. Future fields of wildflowers depend on their buzzing friends.

God has given me—like the honeybees—the responsibility of caring for the earth He has provided. I need to be sure I'm not harming the earth without giving back. My life is not all about me but also about how I can help others.

Heavenly Father, thank You for offering me the creation You have made for my use. May I always be aware of how my actions affect Your creation. When I eat, may I plant. When I pick, may I grow. May I watch where I tread. Like the honeybee, may I give when I take.

The bee is more honored than other animals, not because she labors, but because she labors for others. —Saint John Chrysostom

—Deb Kastner

APRIL 6

Jump In! The Water Is Safe

For I, the LORD your God, will hold your right hand,
saying to you, "Fear not, I will help you."

—ISAIAH 41:13 (NKJV)

ONE LONE PENGUIN waddled along the side of the pool at the zoo. The others in the habitat had jumped into the water and were happily swimming and diving. But that one stayed on dry land, following the group as they did laps back and forth. Why didn't it dive in too?

I had a flashback to a picture I had found of myself at about age thirteen, standing at the edge of a swimming pool in my swimsuit while my sisters and cousins played in the water. I had always hated that picture, which captured one moment of a lifelong fear of the water I still battled. Judging from my damp hair, I had been able to enjoy myself for a while, only to get spooked and hop out.

I caught myself feeling sad for the penguin, even though I knew it was unlikely that it was afraid to swim. Something was holding it back. Then I heard one of its friends calling. The penguin waddled to the edge of the pool, paused, and leaped in.

I remembered that penguin when I decided it was time to get to the root of my fear of the water and overcome it. I made a routine of picturing Jesus with me, promising, "The water is safe. I'm here." Each time, I felt more relaxed and stayed in a little longer. He provided what I had needed as a frightened girl—what we all need when we're afraid or just hesitant like the penguin—a loving voice giving assurance that it's safe to jump in.

Walk of Faith: *What are you afraid of? How does that fear hold you back? This week, ask at least one friend to pray for you as you challenge yourself to take a step toward conquering that fear.*

—Jeanette Hanscome

APRIL 7

Apple Bees

For God's gift and his call are irrevocable.

—ROMANS 11:29 (NIV)

DURING MY FIRST year at my rescue ranch, I was thrilled when the apple trees were heavy with blossoms. My neighbor informed me that the trees gave the sweetest apples in the world, and I would have all the apples I wanted if he were allowed to spray my tree with pesticide.

I told him I would carefully consider his offer. And I did, as I watched bees cover the apple blossoms, garnering nourishment as if they were starving. I walked around those trees for days, watching the fuzzy honeybees do their job before returning to a hive somewhere to make honey. And as they worked, they pollinated gardens, including my neighbor's, along the way.

There was no way I would feel comfortable covering a tree in poisons that might affect these little food makers. Deciding to sacrifice apples if it meant bees might live, I did not give my neighbor the go-ahead to spray my tree with poison. However, when it was time for fruit, the branches were so heavy with apples, my horses thought they had hit the mother lode of treats. My neighbor's garden was green and growing with tons of vegetables.

Now, whenever the chill leaves the air and the first blossoms spring out—even dandelions that dot our front yards—I take that as a sign the bees are waking up to God's call to get to work. The blossoms of early spring also remind me to ask myself if I'm doing the job God has called me to do. Just as bees are on task to keep our food supply fruitful, we are given the job of spreading good news with just as much urgency. Every time we bless God's garden of humanity with goodness, the harvest is bountiful and continues on, just as the work of the bees continues to create beauty wherever they've been.

God, please awaken Your call on my life and thank You for protecting it from theft by those who are threatened by its use. Amen.

—Devon O'Day

APRIL 8

Dead Seas and Babbling Brooks

Moses said to the LORD, "Pardon your servant, Lord. I have never been eloquent, neither in the past nor since you have spoken to your servant. I am slow of speech and tongue."

—EXODUS 4:10 (NIV)

AS I SAT outdoors early one morning, a tiny bird fluttered onto the porch beside me. It sported the spikey feathers of a fledgling and looked like a teenager with a bad case of bedhead. Instead of flying away when it caught sight of me, it opened its beak and started squawking.

It would hop a few feet, squawk a bit, hop another few feet, and squawk some more. Carolina wrens are known for their raspy voices, and this little fella had the characteristic call down perfectly. Soon after it arrived, another wren fluttered to the porch. A fledgling from the same clutch, this bird was as quiet as the first was noisy. It kept its eye on its companion and hopped silently along behind, content to follow its sibling's lead.

The pair of opposites reminded me of what Dr. Gary Chapman calls "Dead Sea" and "babbling brook" communicators. In his book *Things I Wish I'd Known before We Got Married,* he contrasts those who verbalize every thought and those who use their words sparingly. Neither approach is wrong, he points out. They are just different.

The front-porch wrens reminded me how important it is to recognize the strengths of varying personalities and celebrate them. Instead of criticizing and complaining about those who aren't like me, I need to remember that God created each of us with a unique approach to communication. When we learn to work together, as Moses and Aaron did during the Exodus (see Exodus 4:10–14), God can use us to accomplish amazing things.

Walk of Faith: *Are you a babbling brook or a Dead Sea communicator? What about the people around you? Take time today to thank God for the way He created each of you for His good purposes.*

—Lori Hatcher

APRIL 9

Bethany's Bat

Have I not commanded you? Be strong and courageous. Do not be afraid; do not be discouraged, for the LORD your God will be with you wherever you go.

—JOSHUA 1:9 (NIV)

BATS HAVE GOTTEN a pretty bad rap because of so many misconceptions about them. They are often found in scary movies. They're not the kind of creature you'd want to cuddle or have as a pet. But they do a great job keeping the mosquito population in check, among other duties.

We don't see much of them in the city where I live, but we do occasionally notice evidence of their presence in the eaves of our homes. My family had recently moved, and our five-year-old daughter was trying to accustom herself to new sights and sounds, especially at night. We had all settled into our beds for the night when she raced across the hallway and pushed her way into our room, hollering, "Dad! There's a duck in the attic!"

Her bedroom at the front of the house had an attic-access stairway. When she heard a scratching noise coming from behind the door, she inched it open and peeked inside. She saw what she thought was a webbed foot nestled among blankets in a laundry basket. I'm so thankful that fear was not her first response. She felt safe, even in an unfamiliar setting. She was more startled than scared and ran to tell us the news.

I have not personally had any potentially frightening experiences with scary animals (though a gerbil did bite my finger once). But I have had plenty of other opportunities to feel afraid: driving on Minnesota roads in the winter, concern about finances, health challenges, and more. The best thing I can do in those times is to remember that I am never alone, no matter the situation.

God, it is so good to know that we are secure in Your presence. Though we live in a fallen world, we know that Your arms of protection are always around us. Thanks for staying on watch, even in the dark of the night. Amen.

—Liz Kimmel

APRIL 10

By Faith, Not Sight

Trust in the L*ORD* *with all your heart and lean not on your own understanding; in all your ways submit to him, and he will make your paths straight.*

—PROVERBS 3:5–6 (NIV)

AS A PET sitter, I was blessed to care for all shapes, sizes, and breeds of pets. They all wrapped around my heart in unique ways. And one, a shivering Chihuahua that was going blind, held a special place in my being. When Louie met me, he began biting at my ankles. He couldn't see this new stranger, but he needed to defend his home. I learned early on that UGG boots were great for meeting new dogs, especially Chihuahuas that liked to nibble ankles. Nothing could bite through those.

Each visit, I had a specific and involved procedure for eye drops and meds that needed to be given to Louie. I had to hold him so he wouldn't hide from me between my giving him his different eye drops. This cuddle-and-med session took about thirty minutes, and it became so special. Both Louie and I looked forward to the sessions. In between drops, he would nuzzle my neck and give kisses. Sometimes he would get so comfortable, he would fall asleep.

Though he couldn't see me, he trusted this stranger who came in twice a day to care for him and to keep him away from danger when he was outside. On his own, he might have ended up down the street at another house, but leaning on me, he got everything he wanted and love to boot.

If I trusted God as surely as a blind Chihuahua trusted me, how different would my path be? Not just dependence on God, but radical dependence, as if I were sightless, is where real trust begins.

God, please be my vision. When my trust falters, strengthen it for me. Amen.

—Devon O'Day

APRIL 11

A Refining Glory

Dear friends, do not be surprised at the fiery ordeal that has come on you to test you, as though something strange were happening to you. But rejoice inasmuch as you participate in the sufferings of Christ, so that you may be overjoyed when his glory is revealed.

—1 PETER 4:12–13 (NIV)

I KNEW THAT SOMETHING was not right as soon as I spotted the butterfly. Picking up a small stick, I carefully lifted its struggling body from the wet grass. Its vivid yellow, orange, and blue wings lay limp.

"Will it be able to fly, Mom?" my oldest son asked.

"The rains last night washed it down to the ground, perhaps just after it emerged from its chrysalis," I explained to him. "It was not able to hang and properly dry out its wings, so it won't be able to fly. But we can admire and learn from it."

As the butterfly we named Winston hung inside the butterfly net we fashioned for him underneath our crab apple tree, my children and I sat and watched in wonder as his new wings hardened.

I feel like Winston at times. It can seem as though the circumstances pressing in around me stifle the beauty and strength God wants to bring forth. Yet as we watched Winston, he offered us important lessons about time, hope, process, and transformation. We discovered that even when we get knocked down, God wants to use our lives and our stories to bless others and turn our eyes and hearts to Him. We can trust Him with our brokenness and watch Him transform it into beauty.

Dear Lord, help me to lay every part of me that is broken down at Your feet. I trust that You are able and willing to refine my brokenness into glory. You can make much of my story. Make known Your power in my life, that others will see in me a display of Your grace, glory, and love. Amen.

—Eryn Lynum

APRIL 12

Magic's Gentle Spirit

Rather, it should be that of your inner self, the unfading beauty of a gentle and quiet spirit, which is of great worth in God's sight.

—1 PETER 3:4 (NIV)

"DO YOU THINK your grandchildren would like a visit from Magic?" Debbie, a friendly blonde woman asked, as she held the lead of a beautiful black miniature horse.

Would they!

We were on a family vacation in Florida. While there, I took part in a business meeting with the owners of an organization of miniature therapy horses. Meanwhile, my two young granddaughters were experiencing days packed with swimming, theme parks, and other activities. They were amped up. I only worried that they might not be able to calm down enough to fully appreciate the little horse's visit.

The horse trailer pulled up, and Debbie knocked on the door. The girls were delighted from the moment they saw Magic. They laughed gleefully and pulled at my hand, anxious to meet her. Despite their enthusiasm, little Magic remained still and calm. She nuzzled up to the girls with a gentle, feather-light touch. Before they could even start running around, they somehow instinctively calmed and knew to treat Magic gently.

The apostle Paul reminded Christians to always be gentle. Gentleness is not one of the first qualities we might think of when we think of leading a godly life. But Paul wanted the followers of Christ to be clothed with compassion, kindness, humility, gentleness, and patience. If we treat others in a kind and tender manner, we will likely experience the same in return.

That day, I saw the awesome power of gentleness modeled in a miniature horse.

A horse gallops with his lungs, perseveres with his heart, and wins with his character. —Federico Tesio

—Peggy Frezon

APRIL 13

Raise Your Voice!

They raise their voices, they shout for joy; from the west they acclaim the LORD's majesty.

—ISAIAH 24:14 (NIV)

I HAD NEVER SEEN so many alligators in my life—from hatchlings, with their blank-eyed stares, to the granddaddies, tipping the scales at four hundred pounds and stretching out to fourteen feet. My family learned all sorts of fascinating facts about them at Orlando's Gatorland. Did you know President John Quincy Adams briefly lodged an alligator in the unfinished East Room of the White House?

But the most interesting fact that stood out in my mind was that alligators are one of the few reptiles with a "voice." They bellow. They growl. The babies give a high-pitched *yerp* before they hatch from their leathery eggs.

I realized at the time how I take my own voice for granted. Not only can I growl and yerp, I've even been known to bellow occasionally. But I can also do so much more. I can sing and soothe. I can laugh. I can reveal emotion through the tone and volume of my voice. I can cheer during a football game or tell a joke. I had never really thought about what a blessing a voice box is. If you've ever suffered from laryngitis, you know how frustrating not being able to speak can be. How thankful I am for my voice—yet another blessing from the Lord.

Walk of Faith: *Use your voice today to praise God, to thank Him for your many blessings. Take time to offer encouraging words to someone you meet.*

—Shirley Raye Redmond

APRIL 14

Fear Not the Chickens

David also said to Solomon his son, "Be strong and courageous, and do the work. Do not be afraid or discouraged, for the LORD God, my God, is with you. He will not fail you or forsake you until all the work for the service of the temple of the LORD is finished.

—1 CHRONICLES 28:20 (NIV)

AS WE ENJOYED dinner on a friend's deck, another friend sitting next to me suddenly jumped up from her seat and nearly into my lap. "Sorry," she said. "Birds are one of my biggest fears. I know, it's irrational!" I looked over her shoulder to see half a dozen chickens wandering the yard and making their way toward the deck. I chuckled as our host shooed the birds back toward their pen. They refused to go inside, instead huddling under a nearby tree. My friend sat on the edge of her seat all evening, keeping one eye on the chickens.

Just as my friend's irrational fear of chickens kept her from fully engaging in our evening together, fear keeps me from fully engaging in God's best. Irrational fears have robbed me of sleep and health. Fear of rejection has kept me from reaching out to new friends or connecting in current relationships. Fear of failure has prevented me from trying new things or moving forward in a directive God has given.

King David's reminder to his son Solomon encourages me in the midst of my fears. I can be strong and courageous because God is with me. He has an assignment for me, but He doesn't leave me alone to accomplish it. He will be with me until all the work of my life is finished.

Our host that day understood my friend's fear and kept the chickens away. And God sees our fear and will walk with us through it. He will not fail us or forsake us.

Walk of Faith: *What fear has held you captive? Bring it to the Lord today. He will be with you until all the work of your life is complete. You have nothing to fear with Him by your side.*

—Amelia Rhodes

A Goat by Any Other Name

To him who overcomes I will give some of the hidden manna to eat. And I will give him a white stone, and on the stone a new name written which no one knows except him who receives it.

—REVELATION 2:17 (NKJV)

MY GRANDSONS WERE adamant. They wouldn't accept the new goat's name. The two-week-old kid was named Eustace after a C.S. Lewis character. The name means fruitful, and he was the first successful birth on the farm.

My oldest grandson decided he would call the goat Tom Brady after the (then) New England Patriots' quarterback because "Tom's the G.O.A.T!" (Greatest of All Time). And the youngest said, "I'm calling him Dave because I can pronounce the name."

My daughter laughed at the boys' struggle. "Apparently Eustace is a hard name for children. When my friend brought her little guy over to see the goat, he called out 'Hi, Useless!'"

Eustace was already a joy to me. I had never had goats while growing up or raising my children. I had no idea until now how joyful they are, and my attachment to him was strong.

Names are so important, getting them wrong can cause lasting harm. Growing up, I didn't like my name; it was too common. I was happy when friends nicknamed me Xena for my warrior spirit. It helped overcome some of the damage my grandfather had caused by describing me as useless when I was a girl. Perhaps that's why I came to Eustace's defense.

Even the best name, though, won't compare with the name we receive from our Father when we're home with Him at last. He, alone, knows our true identity, revealed in the name He gave us before time began.

Walk of Faith: *When people struggle to refer to me by my given name, the way my grandsons struggled with Eustace's name, I remember that even that is only part of my earthly identity. God knows my true name, and it awaits me in eternity.*

—Lori Stanley Roeleveld

APRIL 16

Little Shadows

The righteous care for the needs of their animals.

—PROVERBS 12:10 (NIV)

MY MOTHER HAD an affinity for the smallest of dogs. I think she preferred a tiny breed that could sit with her on the sofa or be held in her arms.

Tina, a Chihuahua-mix pup, needed a home, and Mom welcomed her gladly. Tipping the scale at around two pounds as an adult dog, Tina reminded me of a tiny black stallion—elegant and slender, with shiny fur. She was so small, we had to be careful we didn't step on her. But her high-pitched bark made her presence known in our home until she died of old age.

One day, while jumping and playing in our backyard, where my siblings and neighbor kids gathered on summer days, Tina fell from a ledge and broke her skinny leg. My mother, who didn't drive, ran out to the yard and then managed to find a ride to the veterinarian.

I had seen a white plaster cast on a friend at school who had broken her arm; all of us in the classroom signed our names on it. But to see a similar plaster cast on a tiny dog's stick-like leg touched my heart. It represented to me the tender care of a human for a hurting animal.

Tina's three good legs somehow supported her broken leg as she trotted across the floor, with a resilience that made my heart melt. When someone said her name, she persevered to come for a loving pat. Soon her cast came off, and she was good as new.

Toy breeds are said to be their owner's "little shadows." I realize now how Mom must have loved her buddy at her feet, as busy as she was raising a large family.

After Tina died, other dogs joined our family. But for me, the tiniest one holds the most endearing memories in my heart.

Dear God, thank You for the "little shadows" at our feet—those tiny blessings in fur that follow us around to let us know they need and love us too. Amen.

—Kathleen Ruckman

APRIL 17

Known by Our Love

Let me give you a new command: Love one another. In the same way I loved you, you love one another. This is how everyone will recognize that you are my disciples—when they see the love you have for each other.

—John 13:34–35 (MSG)

EACH YEAR WHEN we take our family vacation, we eat at one of our favorite restaurants on the bay. Afterward, we love to walk around the marina to take in the view and admire the boats—from fishing boats to beautiful yachts. There is even a dispenser where you can purchase a handful of fish food to drop in the water. Our kids always enjoy doing that. It's amazing to watch the frenzy of fish surfacing to try to get one of the pellets of food.

But watching the fish reminds me of the frenzy we sometimes see on social media—people attacking one another over differing opinions. People being critical, sometimes even bullying. I've had to bite my virtual tongue on more than one occasion to keep from jumping into the fray. I've also struggled with guilt for not standing up for someone who was attacked because I was afraid to speak up. I imagine it pains God to see His people tearing one another down.

Those swarming fish also remind me of the desperation in our world. Those who lash out could be hurting. We're called to have compassion, to show the way with our love for one another.

Dear God, when we're tempted to attack when we disagree with someone or we're tempted to turn away from the desperation and injustice we see, please give us wisdom to discern the right action. Lord, we want to be reminded of Your love for each and every one of us, even those with whom we disagree. Amen.

—Missy Tippens

APRIL 18

Safety of Hedges

Why have You broken down her hedges, so that all who pass by the way pluck her fruit? The boar out of the woods uproots it, And the wild beast of the field devours it.

—PSALM 80:12–13 (NKJV)

DO YOU EVER have those days when everything goes wrong? The psalmist definitely must have been feeling the same when he complained to God about wild boars uprooting Israel's vineyards.

We never owned a boar, but a large Saint Bernard named Princess kept our lives interesting. A gift from my brother's girlfriend, Princess was the cutest puppy I had ever seen. She loved to wrestle and play with me before retiring to the floor vents for frequent naps. The warm air eased her into deep sleep without delay.

As the months passed, Princess grew by leaps and bounds. While she was a patient woman, my mom began to notice the collateral damage of having such a large dog in the house. Whenever we let Princess out of my brother's room, the dog would race back and forth, barking excitedly. After one such romp, a favorite knickknack souvenir from our Wisconsin Dells trip lay in pieces on the linoleum.

"Buster!" Mom yelled. "Get your dog outside."

He and I took Princess for a walk, but our absence failed to make Mom's heart grow more accepting of letting the dog live indoors. That very day, Buster began building a kennel in the backyard. He dug the holes deep. With Dad's help, he set strong metal posts with concrete. When they added thick-gage metal fencing across the posts, Princess had a sturdy new home, including a fashionable doghouse.

Princess taught me the value of sturdy boundaries around my heart. By choosing God's way, I'm safe and secure from danger. Like my furry friend, I sometimes wish to run wild. But love, as explained in God's Word, constrains me.

I am profitably engaged in reading the Bible. Take all of this Book that you can by reason, and the balance by faith, and you will live and die a better man. —Abraham Lincoln

—David L. Winters

The Persistence of Birds

Ask, and it will be given to you; seek, and you will find; knock and it will be opened to you. For everyone who asks receives, and he who seeks finds, and to him who knocks it will be opened.

—MATTHEW 7:7–8 (NKJV)

OH, THE PERSISTENCE of birds! We have a porch with hanging plants, plants that used to be real but are now artificial because of the persistence of birds. The house finches come back every year to build their nests and have their babies in the same spots—my hanging baskets. Once the babies are born, I can no longer water the pots, so I've changed to fake flowers to accommodate my finch friends.

One unseasonably cold spring, I delayed putting out the baskets because it was too cold for flowers to survive and those baskets would have looked silly. The birds were waiting on the rail. They were hinting, but still the baskets remained inside. They finally built a nest on the wreath of the door. I promptly removed the nest, only to have them build it again. Persistence! So I took down the wreath and put those baskets up. Persistence paid off.

God seems to like persistence. He tells us to knock and He will answer. He tells us to never give up. He tells us to be patient. These things don't come easy for me. I would rather have answers yesterday, thank you. But God's timing and answers are far superior to anything I could imagine and always work out best if I just have the persistence, the patience, the faith to stick to it. The birds reminded me to continue my prayers for ongoing situations. Persistence pays.

Father, let me be like the birds. Let me persist in prayer until Your timing is achieved. Amen.

—Linda Bartlett

APRIL 20

But I Like Chicken

For what I want to do I do not do, but what I hate I do.

—ROMANS 7:15 (NIV)

MAX IS JUST a great big black dog with very few teeth and stinky, itchy ears. He used to have teeth, and he used to be smaller, but he has ALWAYS had stinky, itchy ears. From the time he was old enough to have checkups, veterinarians have prescribed antibiotics and antiyeast medicine, and I tried all sorts of natural and internet cures, but nothing helped my big old dog get relief. Max cried pitifully every time I cleaned out those ears.

Then one day, I was shopping for food and supplies in a smaller, more rural town. I asked if they had any remedies for stinky ears that I had not tried. And the young woman behind the counter said, "It's probably the chicken."

What? Isn't chicken always the preferred protein for all living creatures? Isn't it healthier? All the questions popped into my head. But as it turned out, many dogs have reactions to even high-end chicken kibble. So, I spent a little extra on salmon food, and the itching and stinkiness stopped almost immediately. No medicine. No cleaning. His ears just healed.

But despite the positive result, whenever I had chicken of any kind, Max would stare at me, begging. He would salivate or try to steal any chicken scraps from the garbage. He wouldn't give up because, though it was bad for him, he just loved chicken. How many of us are like that? We insist on something we know will cause repercussions if we do it, yet we are drawn to it.

There is no understanding why the moth is drawn to the flame, but God has a way of showing us the flame and equipping us with the strength to resist it. The more we resist, the easier it gets to walk away.

God, it isn't easy to walk in the ways You have planned for me as I'm drawn to the flames of my past. But will you ease the pull it has on me? In Jesus's name. Amen.

—Devon O'Day

APRIL 21

The Great Kid Chase

Suppose one of you has a hundred sheep and loses one of them. Doesn't he leave the ninety-nine in the open country and go after the lost sheep until he finds it?

—LUKE 15:4 (NIV)

CAMP SCOTTIE DAY CAMP was in for a rare treat—a local family had brought several farm animals to visit. They placed an adorable kid goat inside the slatted-fence interior of the GaGa Ball pit, a perfect pen. Older children began hanging over the rail with food for the tiny darling, which he greatly enjoyed. I loved capturing photographs of the wonder in their faces.

Eventually, groups scattered, and I began to walk back to the main lodge. The goat did not appreciate being left alone. He frantically ran around the pen, bleating loudly and clattering against the fence. In an instant, he was over it. He circled me quickly, then headed straight for the campers sitting nearby.

I followed the goat and chased him away from the campers, then watched him go behind a cabin. Knowing he would get lost in the thick woods surrounding the area, I picked up the pace. Campers cheered while I followed him in hot pursuit. Suddenly, the goat saw his food bin on the picnic table and hopped up on top. I let him eat some food, then slyly moved the bin to guide him off and into his cage.

Like God, shepherds always search for their lost sheep. I have to admit, though, that sometimes I am more like a darting goat. Distractions are around me from the minute I open my eyes. I focus on everything else but God, not realizing that He is right behind me. His pursuit of me is real. God continues to call me. I only need to let Him guide me home.

Lord, help me to put my phone down and turn the TV off when the time is right. Forgive me when I let distractions pull me away from You, the most important One in my life. Amen.

—Twila Bennett

APRIL 22

Bubbles

My sheep listen to my voice; I know them, and they follow me.

—John 10:27 (NIV)

MY FRIEND CHRISTOPHER shared with me that he used to be a dolphin trainer for an amusement park some thirty years ago. Recently, he returned to the park with his family. When the staff realized he used to work there, they gave him a backstage tour.

"I was amazed at how different things are now," said Chris. "So many improvements and state-of-the-art equipment."

Then he walked over to the new dolphin tank, and the guide described several of the mammals, calling them by name.

"Many of these are the offspring of our oldest, most beloved matriarch, Bubbles."

Chris's jaw dropped, "Did you say 'Bubbles'? I trained her!"

At the sound of his voice, Bubbles swam directly to Chris and began interacting with him, having recognized an old friend. For several minutes, Chris and Bubbles enjoyed their unexpected reunion as the dolphin matriarch followed him around the perimeter of the tank.

"That made my day," Chris said as he closed his story.

But I couldn't stop thinking about Bubbles. She knew Chris's voice and his face.

Obviously, the voice matters when it comes to training. As I walk out my journey of faith, it's Christ's voice I want to follow. Over the years, I've trained my ear to recognize the Trainer. But it wasn't always this way. There were times I followed other voices or followed none at all.

Even now, strangers call for my attention, enticing me away from the Master. It's those times I must dive into the Word and spend time meditating on the guiding influence of the Father.

Lord, thank You for calling me Your own and placing my identity in You alone. Teach me to know Your voice better, trust Your direction, and follow You all the days of my life. Amen.

—Tez Brooks

APRIL 23

Mister Feathers Speaks Up

Whether you turn to the right or to the left, your ears will hear a voice behind you, saying, "This is the way; walk in it."

—ISAIAH 30:21 (NIV)

WHEN I WAS a kid, our family had a parakeet named Mister Feathers. He lived in the kitchen, and from his cage, he could see everything that went on in the kitchen and part of the living room as well.

Now this was the 1960s, and in the evening after dinner, our family would retire to the living room to watch television. Mister Feathers sat quietly, letting forth the occasional *chirrup*, but every now and then he would decide he did not like what we were watching. We never could figure out what it was about certain shows that bothered him—whether the frequency of sound or tone of an actor's voice. It wasn't volume, because we tried turning it down. But when Mister Feathers decided he didn't like what was on TV, he would screech and squawk and make such piercing noise that we simply had to change the channel. There was no point in trying to watch. Mister Feathers wouldn't have it. We would grumble, but once we changed the channel, he would quiet down, and peace was restored.

Remembering Mister Feathers's clear and insistent call for a channel change made me think of those times God's voice has been loud and clear in my life and prompted me to change my thoughts or actions. As I learn more about His will for my life through reading Scripture, I'm better able to "hear" Him. He guides my good conscience, providing me with my best protection against disobedience and its consequences. But, where I felt frustrated by Mister Feathers's screeching, when God makes Himself impossible to ignore, I rejoice!

Thank You, Father, for making Your good and perfect will known to me. Help me to be obedient and gladly follow You. Amen.

—Marianne Campbell

APRIL 24

Misty, Then and Now

Finally, brothers and sisters, whatever is true, whatever is noble, whatever is right, whatever is pure, whatever is lovely, whatever is admirable—if anything is excellent or praiseworthy—think about such things.

—PHILIPPIANS 4:8 (NIV)

THE LAST TIME I saw Mom's cat, Misty, things were different. In the past, the little gray feline would stop in her tracks, hiss, and run off to hide.

Misty was a kitten when Mom got her, and those early formative months for socialization weren't happy ones. Mom's second husband had cast a negative shroud over the household. His misguided attempts to manage the kitten resulted in him shooing her away whenever she got underfoot and trying to chase her out of corners. The poor little kitten spent most of her time hiding under the bed.

Now Mom lives alone, and the home at last feels peaceful and harmonious. This is evident in the change in Misty. I recently arrived from out of state for a visit. When I walked into the house, she calmly looked at me and swished her tail. As I approached, she even took a step toward me and leaned into my stroke. "Mom! This is the first time in sixteen years she let me pat her," I said. "It's wonderful to see her so happy."

When our home is stressful, even our pets can feel it. The same is true for me when I surround myself with negativity, such as crowded schedules, an unhealthy diet, or toxic people. God's Word reminds me to surround myself with things that are positive, uplifting, and beautiful. Focusing my mind on such things transforms me from pessimistic and discouraged to positive and hopeful, just as a peaceful setting transformed Misty from an anxious kitten to a trusting adult cat.

A cat's purring on your lap is more healing than any drug in the world, as the vibrations you are receiving are of pure love and contentment. —Anonymous

—Peggy Frezon

APRIL 25

The Bright Side of Life

You will show me the path of life; in Your presence is fullness of joy; at Your right hand are pleasures forevermore.

—PSALM 16:11 (NKJV)

OH, MAN—WHAT WAS that?" I exclaimed, wiping something warm, wet, and gooey off the back of my neck. I was changing the oil when a slobbery tennis ball rolled underneath my car and lodged in my collar. Already hot, cramped, and uncomfortable, I grumpily cranked my head around to find Riley, my son's yellow Lab, down on her front legs, peering at me with a playful look. I couldn't stay grumpy.

Riley is a beautiful, energetic, and loving dog with one intense passion: fetching tennis balls. She will chase as many balls as you want to throw and go as far as you want to throw them. She chases the last ball with the same bounding energy as the first. Every time you stand, she lets you know she is ready to chase the ball.

My wife and I recently moved to Colorado to be closer to our family, including Riley. When the bright sunshine breaks through our bedroom window each morning, my first thought is, *Good morning, Lord,* as I thank Him for the day ahead. I want our fellowship to be my intense passion, something I am ready to do with Him at a moment's notice, any moment of the day—as ready as Riley is to fetch a ball.

Riley is the epitome of life lived in the happy lane. She brightens the room with her excitement to see me. She has taught me how I want to greet my Lord each day with spontaneous joy. Her enthusiasm is magnetic—it draws me to her. It makes me want to stop all the busyness of life and spend time with her. I imagine my heavenly Father feels the same way about me when He sees sincere love coming from His child.

Joy is the infallible sign of the presence of God.
—Pierre Teilhard de Chardin

—Randy Benedetto

APRIL 26

The Creator's Camouflage

If you say, "The LORD is my refuge," and you make the Most High your dwelling, no harm will overtake you, no disaster will come near your tent. For he will command his angels concerning you to guard you in all your ways.

—PSALM 91:9–11 (NIV)

ON A WALK through our daughter's college campus, we emerged from the woods into a hilltop clearing. A young doe nibbling grass on the wide lawn saw us and froze. She had nowhere to go: behind her curved a large brick building, to the side was a busy road, and we blocked her way back into the woods. *What would she do?* I wondered.

She shot past us into the woods, where her spotted coat blended perfectly with the warm brown underbrush and dappled light filtering through the trees. She was much closer to us than she had been before, but she was no longer afraid. Blending perfectly into the landscape, she felt safe. Danger was all around, but trusting her camouflage, she could relax. We passed, and she bounded off.

As I thought about that little deer, I realized that danger also surrounds me on every side, yet I'm called to enter places where I feel exposed, where people may hurt me—intentionally or inadvertently. When I feel scared, I tend to panic and start trying to control the situation. Often, I'll back myself into a corner or make things worse by being confrontational.

How much wiser was this doe? She knew instinctively how God had created her and leaped directly into her refuge. Faced with adversity, I have the choice of which way to leap. I have a refuge as perfectly fitted to me as the fall woods are to a deer. When I turn first to God, the danger doesn't go away, but the angels concerning me will guard me.

Dear Creator, You know our nature and have created perfect camouflage for us. In times of trouble, help us to recognize it and choose refuge in You so that we may feel Your strength and find the best path forward. Amen.

—Lucy H. Chambers

APRIL 27

Persistently Preparing

Therefore, since we are surrounded by such a great cloud of witnesses, let us throw off everything that hinders and the sin that so easily entangles. And let us run with perseverance the race marked out for us, fixing our eyes on Jesus, the pioneer and perfecter of faith.

—HEBREWS 12:1–2 (NIV)

FROM MY SEAT on my front porch, I glimpsed a speedy blur of brown whizz past my driveway. I blinked, then brought my gaze back to my computer and my impending deadline. But a few minutes later, I again saw the blaze speed past, this time toward the stone wall in the front of my house.

It was an adorable chipmunk, its cheeks so full I didn't see how it could breathe. It scurried into a hole between the stones and disappeared . . . but not for long.

Soon the little guy flew by again, repeating the same path and returning once again with burdened cheeks, then emptying them somewhere within the stone wall. This time, I crept alongside the back of the house to follow its path. It scurried to the foot of the birdfeeder, where it hastily filled its mouth. All day, from my spot on my front porch, I watched this chipmunk in its persistent foraging for food. I could only assume, on this warm spring day, that it was preparing for a time when food would not be so plentiful.

I thought of the race this little guy ran with persistence, its eyes on the prize of food. I thought of one of my favorite verses, a prodding to run this race of life well, to keep my eyes on the prize of Christ and His finished work. If God had planted such an innate ability in this sweet chipmunk that worked so hard for something of temporal consequence, I wondered, how much harder should I run toward things of faith?

Lord, You've done the hard work already. You are the Perfect One, and the Author of our faith. Help us to look to You, to race onward toward the eternal prize of Your glory. Amen.

—Heidi Chiavaroli

APRIL 28

The Most Beautiful Day

The flowers appear on the earth; the time of singing has come, and the voice of the turtledove is heard in our land.

—SONG OF SOLOMON 2:12 (NKJV)

MY BIRDS TALKED up a storm on the sunporch. After a winter cooped up in the house with the rest of us, our lovebird and sun conure tweeted happily. From the perches in their cages, they could see me pulling weeds in the backyard gardens.

After a crazy workweek, nothing relaxed me more than hanging out in the garden and working at my own pace. *With the tulips fully in bloom, it won't be long until time for planting annuals,* I thought. The soft spring breeze felt so good as I struggled with a long-rooted invader.

My mind revisited the highs and lows of the week. A difficult conversation with a customer pried its way into my idyllic Saturday, but the birds reminded me to let it go. Suddenly, I thought about Tuesday morning. I was driving along the George Washington Memorial Parkway when an intoxicating wind blew through my thinning hairline. That was a sweet moment worth remembering.

In my life, I dread trouble coming to call, but how often do I just praise God for these peaceful times? This glorious day brought out my inner baritone, usually reserved for the shower. So I sang in full voice, "Praise God from whom all blessings flow." The dog next door howled a little.

After my weeding and prepping ended, I poured a glass of iced tea and opened the cages of the birds. At their own pace, both flew over to me. Peaches perched on my shoulder, while Sunny dove inside the collar of my shirt. He peeked his head out at the newly spruced-up garden, chirping his approval. The birds just wanted my companionship—like God, I imagine. Thankfulness filled my heart.

Lord, thank You for wonderful days when trouble remains far away and joy fills my heart. Praise Your name for lavishing grace and love on Your people. I seek Your presence and rejoice in Your everlasting kindness. Amen.

—David L. Winters

APRIL 29

How Big Is Your God?

He upholds the universe by the word of his power.

—HEBREWS 1:3 (ESV)

MAY I PET your dog?"

The question was a common one when I took our Leonberger, Lancelot, out in public. Eventually growing to more than 130 pounds with the height to match, he was a gorgeous tan, black, and rust-colored dog that stopped people in their tracks with his looks and size.

But Lancelot would also stop in his tracks when he saw strangers. Once a puppy that adored new people, our dog became fearful as he grew, eventually requiring us to work with a professional trainer to reduce his paranoia to a livable level.

Never aggressive, my giant-breed dog would simply try to flee if strangers reached to pet him. My job when taking him out in public was to protect him from such well-meaning advances.

I told the man on this occasion that my dog was too fearful for him to pet.

He looked at my Leonberger and shook his head. "Doesn't he know how big he is?"

It seems accurate to assume such a large dog wouldn't have reason to be afraid. But I realized later that a similar question could be asked of me.

I'm often plagued by worry, and I'm downright terrified of danger. At such times, someone could ask me with the same incredulous tone, "Don't you know how big your God is?"

The truth is our God is bigger than we can imagine. He is bigger than anything we fear. He is big enough to uphold the universe with a word of His power.

He is big enough to keep us safe in His loving care forever.

Lord, help me to remember You are bigger and more powerful than even the worst things I face. Help me to trust in Your promise to always provide refuge in Your everlasting arms. In Jesus's name. Amen.

—Jerusha Agen

APRIL 30

Don't Judge Me by What She Said

A perverse person stirs up conflict, and a gossip separates close friends.

—PROVERBS 16:28 (NIV)

CHEYENNE DOESN'T WARM up to people easily," I was told before the sweet spotted saddle horse was brought to my rescue ranch. "She has been mistreated and abused and doesn't trust easily."

That was what I knew about Cheyenne before ever laying eyes on her. I was worried about how she would work out with my other horses. As the gate opened on the trailer the night she was delivered, she quietly and carefully stepped out and looked around the pasture. I put her in her own paddock, so she could socialize and get to know the other horses with a fence between them. I didn't know if she would pull the lead rope from my hands and run or be aggressive.

But instead of reacting to what I had been told about her, I watched her and acted accordingly. She seemed very quiet and happy to be out of the trailer. Although she caused quite the stir with the other horses, it was curiosity, not anxiety, that bubbled between them. Cheyenne didn't run from me or charge me but gently came to me when called and checked my hands for a treat . . . which I had.

Instead of creating a nervous force field based on fear of what might happen, I chose to welcome a new horse like family. My internal feelings were discernable to both her and the other horses, and since I was calm, all else was calm. Instead of believing what was said about this horse, I took Cheyenne at her own merit. This is how we can avoid heartache with people too.

Making assumptions about people I have never met based on someone else's irritation or angst can discount the chance of a wonderful friendship. May I always remember that allowing a friendship to naturally develop based on actual experience can bless me beyond measure.

Dear God, close my ears to others' judgment and
awaken me to the good in people. Amen.

—Devon O'Day

May

MAY 1

Beneath the Ripples

Now faith is confidence in what we hope for and assurance about what we do not see. This is what the ancients were commended for. By faith we understand that the universe was formed at God's command, so that what is seen was not made out of what was visible.

—HEBREWS 11:1–3 (NIV)

TODAY, MY FAMILY and I went for a hike to a beautiful little pond that's filled with fish. To get there, we followed a trail through woods that are home to many animals and creatures. I've seen photos other people have taken from this same trail and know it's a rich habitat with everything from birds to foxes, raccoons, deer, and dragonflies. The thing is, on this particular afternoon, I couldn't seem to spot any of them! When we got to the lake, the same comical pattern continued. Everyone else in my family saw fish jumping, but not me.

Then as I watched the still waters, I heard a splash and turned to see if I could spot the fish. I was too late to catch it before the fish dived underwater, but I did see something else that was even more interesting—rings of widening ripples bending the flat surface of the water, ripples that extended far beyond the place that fish had jumped.

The fact is, there is a diverse ecosystem that exists beneath, above, and beyond those waters. I don't need to see it to know it exists or to recognize my own part in this intricate design. As I watched those beautiful ripples, I was reminded of God's work in and through me. I, like that fish, create ripples from my own life. Sometimes I can't see what God is up to. Maybe I can hear the sound; sometimes other people notice and tell me what they've seen. But I don't always *need* to see to trust His ways are good. The ripples of redemption are ever spreading toward shores of grace whenever I simply turn to Him.

I alone cannot change the world, but I can cast a stone across waters to create many ripples. —Mother Teresa

—Ashley Clark

MAY 2

God's Convoy of Love

There is no fear in love; but perfect love casts out fear.

—1 JOHN 4:18 (NKJV)

I WOKE UP IN the middle of the night, unable to go back to sleep. Getting up out of bed, I walked through the dimly lit rooms into the kitchen. I grabbed a small glass from the cupboard, then proceeded to the fridge and poured myself some milk. In my agitation, I gulped it down, then headed to the living room to walk off my fears.

I knew my fears were silly, but they built up during the day and often kept me awake or woke me up in the dead of night. No matter how hard I tried, the fears covered me to the extent that I could not get back to sleep. Fighting my midnight fears had become an unplanned routine for me.

As I walked the darkened living room, I suddenly felt something soft and furry against my ankle. *Princess!*

I let out a laugh seeing our youngest cat, Princess, whom we had taken in as the runt of her litter. She had come to us tiny and scared, hiding under the bed for days. But after a month of loving care, where I would ease myself under the bed and pet her, then cover her with a warm shirt of mine, combined with prayer from Terry and me, Princess began to grow strong and confident, no longer afraid. She was covered with love that could only come from God, and she knew it.

Tonight, with Princess walking at my side—proof of God's love covering her—I am inspired to claim God's love covering me now. I feel His convoy of love, with Him, Princess, and me walking together, casting out all fear.

He shall cover you with His feathers, and under His wings you shall take refuge. —Psalm 91:4 (NKJV)

—Sandra Clifton

MAY 3

Branching Out

Therefore go and make disciples of all nations, baptizing them in the name of the Father and of the Son and of the Holy Spirit.

—MATTHEW 28:19 (NIV)

A YEAR AFTER MY mother passed away, Dad moved into an assisted living home. My husband, Stan, and I spent the next several weeks cleaning out his house. One day, I sorted through a desk while Stan worked on a hall closet. He came to the bedroom door holding a trash bag full of sheepskins we had used on Mom's chair.

"What do you want me to do with these?" he asked, peering into the bag. Suddenly, he snapped it closed and ran for the back door. I reached the patio just in time to see a flying squirrel leap from the bag and race up a tree. The tiny creature had somehow found its way into the house and nested in the nice, soft sheepskins.

Like the little squirrel, I want to stay in my comfortable routines and familiar spots. But God doesn't tell me to hunker down and stay put. He says, "Go!" Go spread His Word, not only to those in my immediate sphere but to people I wouldn't meet otherwise. That doesn't mean God is calling me overseas as a missionary. But I have worked locally with eyeglass clinics in poor areas of town, taught vacation Bible school, and spoken to groups about my faith.

The last time we saw the flying squirrel, it was running along a branch high above our heads. While it enjoyed its cozy spot in Dad's house, it was isolating itself from others. I often do that too. It takes a deliberate effort to leap from my comfortable nest and branch out, but when I do, I have the opportunity to impact the world with a life-changing message.

Walk of Faith: *Pray that God will bless and empower your efforts to spread the good news. Is your church planning an outreach program, a short-term mission trip, or backyard Bible study? Find a way you can "go!" and tell others about Jesus.*

—Tracy Crump

MAY 4

The Black Swan

This man is my chosen instrument to proclaim my name to the Gentiles and their kings and to the people of Israel.

—ACTS 9:15 (NIV)

I SPOTTED NORMAN, THE black swan, in the middle of the pond in our hotel's outdoor lobby. When I opened the food I had purchased to feed the swans, Norman glided toward me through the dark water. His long neck arched as he nudged his way through the crowd of white swans headed my way. Norman didn't care if he didn't fit in or if the other swans looked different from him. He moved to the front of the pack and brought smiles to people's faces with his grace and courage.

After I surrendered my life to Jesus, I didn't look like most of the Christians around me. Some people couldn't see beyond the blackened feathers of my past. As I read through the Bible, I realized all God's people are like Norman.

According to Scripture, Saul was still uttering murderous threats against the disciples when he encountered Jesus on the road to Damascus. At first, Ananias didn't believe Saul had been changed or chosen by God. But the Lord transformed Saul and immediately empowered him to preach the gospel with a new name: Paul. People doubted God would use such a man. But Paul grew more and more powerful and proved that Jesus was the Messiah the Jews had long awaited.

God is still changing me. He chose me and is allowing me to share His truth and love wherever and whenever He gives me the opportunity. Like Norman . . . and Saul . . . I don't have to fit in or look like anyone else. My black feathers are my testimony of God's life-transforming power.

Father God, thanks for loving us as we are and making us more like You while we learn more about You and share You with others. Amen.

—Xochitl E. Dixon

MAY 5

The Reluctant Gardener

The earth is full of the goodness of the Lord.

—Psalm 33:5 (NKJV)

I PUSHED OUR NEW lawnmower through the overgrown backyard grass. Hundreds of little flying insects rose in waves as I plowed through their resting place and then descended as I passed. *They're playing jump the grumpy guy's lawnmower*, I thought. When we purchased our home during a Midwest winter, I really hadn't paid much attention to the gray and sparse backyard. It was now spring, and the gray tundra had turned into an overwhelming growth of plants, shrubs, and grass. I emptied the last bag of clippings, moaning, "Lord, how am I supposed to get this yard under control?"

I was a reluctant gardener. Our first thirty years of marriage had been spent in rental units, and our first homeownership had been in the Southwest, where gravel was my landscape of choice. Here, I was faced with rampaging vegetation.

A squirrel perched on the fence, chewing an acorn, and studied me. "Great," I griped, "I've got a supervisor." Moving on to weed the dirt beds, I uncovered a seemingly choreographed army of brown-colored beetles marching in single file. Each little shelled bug purposefully worked its way across the ground. These beetles knew their job and went about it sight unseen. I heard no complaints coming from the beetles. I suddenly felt a bit foolish. These beetles certainly didn't need my mentoring in yard maintenance. They were instinctively performing the job for which God had created them. I had elevated myself to the position of yardmaster. The real Master wanted me, to the best of my God-given abilities, to simply be a good servant of His land and its creatures—He would handle the rest.

Thank You, Lord, for the blessings of the intricate working system of creatures like the beetles that You have placed here to support Your earth. Let me never take them for granted. Help me to be a wise steward of the land around me, especially that which I live on or own. Amen.

—Terry Clifton

MAY 6

A Not-So-Sweet Surprise

He will call on me, and I will answer him; I will be with him in trouble, I will deliver him and honor him.

—PSALM 91:15 (NIV)

WHEN MY GOOD friend Dee was only nine months old, her mama carried her outside, along with a bundle of wet laundry. The family's freshly washed sheets had to be hung on the clothesline to dry. And Dee needed to be near her mama. But the day was hot and too harsh for the baby's comfort.

So Mama plunked Dee upright in a shallow creek, only a few feet away. The baby splashed and giggled as her mama pinned sheets to the line. When the work was finished, Mama picked up her dripping daughter, took her inside the house, and sat her on the wood floor. She pulled a diaper from a pile of clean laundry, folded it on the floor, and prepared to change her child. Then, she noticed something amiss. Horrifying, in fact.

A little snake slithered out of Dee's diaper. A harmless water snake, no doubt. But the image made me shudder when Dee told me about it all these years later. What must her mama have thought? Perhaps after recovering from a first fright and tossing that snake out the door, she was grateful Dee was safe in her care. No harm would touch her baby.

The story reminded me how something bad can sneak into our lives, unseen at first. We may never notice it until it slips out and makes itself known. Maybe in a frightening way. But God is our ever-present help in times of trouble. And we need not worry. Because He loves us, He longs to rescue us.

Go to sleep in peace. God is awake. —Victor Hugo

—Cathy Elliott

MAY 7

Be the Person . . .

The LORD your God is with you, the Mighty Warrior who saves. He will take great delight in you; in his love he will no longer rebuke you, but will rejoice over you with singing.

—ZEPHANIAH 3:17 (NIV)

I RECEIVED A WONDERFUL gift for my birthday this year—a soft blue T-shirt, featuring an image of a retriever and the words *Be the person your dog thinks you are*. I love this message, yet I often feel as though I'm undeserving of the reputation my dogs bestow upon me.

Last week, I had a less-than-stellar interaction with a family member, and I returned home brooding about how I could have handled the situation with more grace. As I sank into the sofa, my dog Ernest snuggled up next to me and looked at me with pure, unreserved love. Ernest already thought I was patient and kind.

Another morning, I was berating myself for having eaten too many sweets the day before. When I looked in the mirror, I saw someone overweight and unattractive. Yet when Petey padded up and looked at me, his smiling eyes and wagging tail demonstrated his love. My dog wasn't concerned about the spare tire around my middle.

What is it about my dogs that enables them to see me as so wonderful? The way God sees me. God knows that underneath the cracks and flaws, the extra pounds and wrinkles, I am still worthy of His love. After all, He created us in His image. To be sure, my dogs love me; yet, this love pales in comparison with God's immense adoration. His unconditional love is a gift I will always treasure.

Dear God, Your love for me is without limits. It isn't based on my successes or limitations. Help me to accept Your grace and to extend that grace to myself when I feel I don't measure up. In Jesus's name. Amen.

—Peggy Frezon

MAY 8

Butterflies Everywhere

I can do all things through Christ who strengthens me.

—PHILIPPIANS 4:13 (NKJV)

THE BUTTERFLY FLUTTERED out of the foliage of the peaceful English garden. I smiled, knowing that God had sent it just for me. Later that day, I saw another one. Before going to sleep that night, I noticed two framed embroidered butterflies on the wall beside my bed.

Butterflies had become my symbol of rebirth and freedom during a long season of rebuilding my life from scratch after abandonment and divorce. Going to England and Scotland with my friend Julie felt like the gutsiest thing I had done since starting over in my childhood hometown. Because low vision keeps me from driving, I work from home and spend most of my time in familiar places where I won't risk getting lost. But I had also dreamed of traveling, which required a ten-hour flight (I'm not a fan of flying) into the unfamiliar. And now here I was, farther away from home than I had ever been in my life. Each step of bravery—navigating crowded London Tube stations, talking to people I didn't know, venturing out to a café alone while Julie slept in—felt scary at first, until I did it and felt like a butterfly spreading her wings. Seeing my special symbol of rebirth three times in one day felt like God's way of telling me, *You are living outside the cocoon now. This trip is only the beginning.*

Even exciting steps can be a stretch, forcing us to remember "I can do all things through Christ who strengthens me." But when we feel the joy of freedom that comes with those challenges and see how God grows us through each one, something in us truly is reborn.

Walk of Faith: *What are you hesitant to do because it requires stepping out of the familiar? Write Philippians 4:13 on a card to keep with you as you pray for the courage to take on the challenge. Ask at least one friend to join you in prayer for this step of bravery.*

—Jeanette Hanscome

MAY 9

A Mama Bear's Love

For I am persuaded that neither death nor life, nor angels nor principalities nor powers, nor things present nor things to come, nor height nor depth, nor any other created thing, shall be able to separate us from the love of God which is in Christ Jesus our Lord.

—ROMANS 8:38–39 (NKJV)

MY HUSBAND AND I enjoy vacationing in the Great Smoky Mountains, with its breathtaking scenery and native wildlife. While driving along a winding highway one afternoon, we happened upon a group of people staring across the road at a wooded hillside. Curious, we pulled over to ask what was going on. An onlooker pointed out a black bear that had wedged herself beside a large tree to nap while two cubs chased each other up and down the steep hill. What a sight! A park ranger standing nearby politely answered our questions about bears. However, he made the purpose of his presence clear when he quipped, "I'm here to keep everyone on the non-people-eating side of the road."

No doubt a mother bear will lash out at any threat to her offspring, but she would only be acting according to her nature. She loves and protects her cubs.

God loves me with the same ferocity. Because I became His child through repentance and faith in Jesus Christ as Lord, nothing will separate me from His love—not death or life, not the present or future, not anything in all creation. Nothing.

I enjoy watching bears from a distance but would never want to get between a mama bear and her cubs. Since becoming a mother and grandmother, I understand the fierce love that drives her. But how much more does God love me as His child? What a comfort to know I am loved with such an overwhelming and unconditional love.

When you are in the throes of adversity, it is easy to feel abandoned. So it is crucial at such times to tell yourself the truth: Nothing can separate you from God's loving presence. —Sarah Young

—Tracy Crump

MAY 10

Freedom Seeker

You say, "I am allowed to do anything"—but not everything is good for you. You say, "I am allowed to do anything"—but not everything is beneficial.

—1 CORINTHIANS 10:23 (NLT)

MIKE WAS ABANDONED with his litter of puppy siblings, some of which did not survive in the woods where they were left. One defied a car on the road and lost his life for his courage. Mike saw all the hunger, felt the cold, and must have been affected by the death he saw.

Yet when he was safe in my pack at the rescue ranch, no fence could keep him in. No matter the material I used, he managed to find his way out in seconds. However, he seemed to have learned the lessons of the past in that he never went near the road or even ventured near a vehicle. He never wandered far from the yard or pastures he knew were his. There was no bringing him inside until he was good and ready. It was maddening for me but exhilarating for him.

You see, the farm was his calling. He loved herding his horses and sleeping in the pasture as they grazed. He loved guiding our blind steer in from the back field when it was time to eat. And most of all, he dearly loved his barn cats. While most pit bull mixes were notorious cat terrorists, Mike adored the feral litter of kittens, and they loved him. He would climb on the hay bales, and soon the cats were lavishing him with purrs, kneading him and using him as a big, warm pillow.

While it's often tempting to stray outside the boundaries of protection my heavenly Father has placed around me, Mike has taught me that it is not the fence that holds me in but the love and security that keep me where I can thrive. The love of Someone who patiently waits for us to return is the true freedom we all seek.

God, help me see and stay within the good, loving boundaries in which I can find my true freedom and safety. Amen.

—Devon O'Day

MAY 11

Social Lessons from a Snake

If it is possible, as far as it depends on you, live at peace with everyone.

—ROMANS 12:18 (NIV)

SNUGGLING UP WITH a snake would not have been my first choice for how to spend a morning, but my grandchildren felt differently. We were visiting the nature center of a local zoo where reptiles and amphibians abounded. The children scurried from tank to tank, marveling at the geckos, turtles, and fish. Then a movement caught their attention. In the corner of the building was a naturalist with a four-foot boa constrictor draped around his neck.

"Would you like to hold the snake?" he asked, noticing the children's fascination. Four-year-old Caroline nodded hesitantly. The naturalist positioned her hands to support its weight. As she lifted the snake from his grasp, it raised its head until it was eye-level with her face.

"It likes to see who's holding it," the naturalist said. "It's very curious."

"So is Caroline," I said as the two checked each other out, eye to eye, gazing into each other's face.

I learned a lesson from Caroline's interaction with the snake that day. Sometimes I bring fears, prejudices, and preferences into my encounters with people. They may look different than I do, come from another country, or speak another language. Their customs, diet, and culture may be as strange to me as Caroline was to the beady-eyed, legless reptile. But when I make an attempt to connect, to look deeply into their eyes and learn about them, I usually come away with a new appreciation. Caroline and the boa constrictor assumed the other was friendly, initiated eye contact, and waited patiently while each worked through any initial hesitation.

I don't know if Caroline will remember her playdate with the snake, but I'll remember the lesson I learned from it for quite some time.

Walk of Faith: *The next time you encounter someone whose looks, speech, or actions are different from yours, assume that person is friendly, make eye contact, and reach out. Prepare to be pleasantly surprised at what you discover.*

—Lori Hatcher

MAY 12

Leaving the Fishbowl

Enlarge the place of your tent, stretch your tent curtains wide, do not hold back; lengthen your cords, strengthen your stakes.

—ISAIAH 54:2 (NIV)

TWO ETHEREAL FANTAIL goldfish circled the murky water of the fishbowl. I grimaced, dreading the chore in front of me, my stomach already revolting against the odor of algae and fish. The smell hadn't bothered me before pregnancy, but morning sickness made maintenance of the fishbowl unbearable.

"What if we release Lilly and Angel into the koi pond at the park?" my husband suggested, surprising me.

"Won't they get eaten?"

He laughed and assured me that goldfish don't eat goldfish.

After checking to be sure it was okay, the next day we carried our fish to the pond and poured them into their new home. It took a second for them to adjust, but soon, two tiny goldfish were swimming happily beside monsters. We visited them every day until we moved to a new home in preparation for our baby. A year later, we returned to the park to see how they fared. In the place of the tiny fish we remembered, two enormous fish with Lilly's and Angel's coloring slipped beneath the surface of the inky waters. My mouth hung open. I had no idea our fish babies were capable of growing that large. They may have resented the change at first, but if they had never expanded their boundaries, they would never have reached their full capability.

A similar thing happened when my husband and I decided to have a baby. I feared what lay beyond our safe, familiar world. Were we ready to be parents? Yet enlarging our tent made room for God to fill our lives with good things. As I learned from two fantail goldfish, sometimes we have to leave the familiarity of our safe, little bowl and slip into the depths of God's faithfulness. Only then will we grow to our full potential.

Help me, God, to trust You in the unknown. Enlarge my life so I might be filled to the measure with Your fullness. In Jesus's name. Amen.

—Tracy Joy Jones

MAY 13

The Cicada Choir

While we live in these earthly bodies, we groan and sigh, but it's not that we want to die and get rid of these bodies that clothe us. Rather, we want to put on our new bodies so that these dying bodies will be swallowed up by life.

—2 CORINTHIANS 5:4 (NLT)

CHILDREN ARE FEARLESS when it comes to bugs (and most everything else except doctors and green vegetables). They don't hesitate to scoop up a roly-poly, chase down a cricket, or capture a spider.

One day, my granddaughter Lauren spotted a cicada clinging to a tree trunk in my backyard. Cicadas are common in the South, but we seldom see them. The three-inch-long, bug-eyed insects spend their days in the tops of pine trees, filling the air with their loud songs. This was a rare opportunity. Plucking the creature from the tree trunk, Lauren took a look. "This one's dead," she announced.

"No, it's not," I said. "Look closely. That bug's not dead, that's just its exoskeleton. The cicada grew too big, so it split its skin and climbed out. It's up in a tree somewhere, happily singing its song."

Although cicadas and humans are entirely different species, we have something in common. One day, my inner being will grow too big for my body, and it will burst out. No longer bound by the limitations of human frailty, I'll rise to meet my Lord in the sky and take my place in the heavenly choir, filling the air with loud songs of praise.

The body I leave behind will look empty and lifeless, because I'm not in it. If I've lived my life well, those who look upon my body will know it's just a shell. The real me will be brand-new and more alive than I've ever been.

There are better things ahead than any we leave behind. —C.S. Lewis

—Lori Hatcher

MAY 14

No Better Friend

Two are better than one, because they have a good return for their labor: If either of them falls down, one can help the other up.

—ECCLESIASTES 4:9–10 (NIV)

MY NIECE KACEY loves to hike. Just out of college, she often kidded her family that she would like to abandon all career paths so that she was freed up to explore as many national parks as possible. Two years ago, she adopted five-month-old Smokey, an adorable black Lab puppy. He has become her constant companion as they explore the wilds of Utah, Nevada, and Arizona.

Kacey always makes sure to bring extra water for herself and her dog when they venture out into the unforgiving heat of the desert. One day, they departed for a planned six-mile round-trip hike. Their destination was the falls, and Smokey made it there just fine. He ran around, splashed, swam, and rested in the shade before it was time to begin the journey back home.

But Kacey could tell he was tired. He was sluggish, didn't want water (though he desperately needed it), and lay down and didn't want to get up. Fighting panic on behalf of her dog, Kacey picked up her sixty-five-pound friend and carried him a mile back to the trailhead. Each time she found a creek, she practically threw him into the water, sitting immersed with him to help him cool down. When they reached her car, Smokey seemed much better and slept in her lap most of the way back to town.

Kacey's loving care of Smokey reminded me of the friends I have who help lift me when I am exhausted or feel unable to carry on. There are people in my life I can count on if I am in need, if I want to go on an adventure, or if we just want to sit quietly in the backyard and enjoy the sunset together. The Lord has placed me in these relationships to teach me how to both give and receive love and encouragement.

Everyone thinks they have the best dog. And none of them are wrong.
—W.R. Purche

—Liz Kimmel

MAY 15

The Wind beneath My Wings

Those who hope in the Lord will renew their strength. They will soar on wings like eagles; they will run and not grow weary, they will walk and not be faint.

—Isaiah 40:31 (NIV)

MY HUSBAND AND I pushed off against the shore of Courtois Creek. We situated ourselves on the two seats of our canoe and settled in for a leisurely ride down Missouri's waters. As the canoe glided over the clear water, a bald eagle began circling overhead. After a few minutes, another eagle joined the first. As we continued our journey, more eagles made their appearance, flying just above the treetops. We counted seven eagles that afternoon. As we pressed our paddles against the water, propelling us on, the eagles seemed to glide effortlessly above our heads. And that's precisely what their flight was: effortless.

Eagles use the wind to fuel their journey. Riding upon the breeze and wind gusts, they have been known to fly up to 125 miles in a day, but it all depends on the wind. We will "soar on wings like eagles," God's Word tells us. I saw it that day, with eagles circling overhead. Wherever I am in my journey, and however far I have yet to go, God is the One who propels me. It is He who will renew my strength and carry me, just like the wind underneath an eagle's wings.

There is something quite magnificent about depending on the wind. More magnificent, even, to depend on our Lord and Savior to be the wind beneath our wings, to carry us onward by His love, mercy, grace, and power.

Dear Lord, wherever You have for me to go in this life, whatever the journey ahead may bring, carry me forward by Your great love. When I try to control the pace or direction of life, remind me that You have an incredible plan and to trust that You will give me everything I need along the way. You will carry me there. Amen.

—Eryn Lynum

MAY 16

Majestic

Lord, our Lord, how majestic is your name in all the earth!

—Psalm 8:1 (NIV)

MOST EVERYONE IN the cabin still slept. Our infant daughter and I began our morning routine. My brother, Bill, had left for a morning walk. I loved the peace of vacations in the mountains.

Bang! Bill burst through the door. "There's a bear across the creek!"

At first, I didn't believe him. Knowing I loved bears more than most, Bill liked teasing me. But he grabbed his camcorder and ran outside, leaving me sitting on the floor with the baby. Not for long, though. I scooped her up and followed him out.

There, across the creek not twenty yards from the cabin, stood an enormous black bear. Awe mixed with the excitement of seeing a bear in broad daylight so close to us.

As Bill and I watched, the bear nosed its way through the dew-wet grass, the sun glinting off its dark fur. It didn't seem to care about the astonished, staring viewers. Now and then, it lifted its shaggy head and looked at us.

While we were watching, the bear stood and rubbed its back on the trunk of a nearby hemlock, then began to amble away. We continued looking at him for several minutes, amazed at the majestic scene we had just witnessed.

The Bible refers to the Lord as "majestic," meaning deserving of dignity, full of greatness. If that black bear seemed majestic to us, how much more majestic should we think our God is? He made the heavens and earth, the people, the mountains, and the black bear. He gave His life that we might live. That alone makes Him worthy of being called "majestic."

In majesty, God reigns above,
watching over us in love. —C.M.

—Cathy Mayfield

MAY 17

The Stone of Remembrance

These stones are to be a memorial to the people of Israel forever.

—JOSHUA 4:7 (NIV)

FOR MY DAD'S fiftieth high school reunion, he invited the whole family to join him and my mom. My family enjoyed a fun-filled, restful time in our log cabin on Ice Lake in the Upper Peninsula area of Michigan. The kids were particularly excited about fishing.

After some successful crawdadding, our youngest, Joshua, age six, felt a pull on his line and, with some coaching, pulled in a dandy perch. After the hurrahs and some picture taking, though, I saw him gently pull out the hook.

Then he said, "Bye, fish," and threw it back in.

I'll always remember that moment, because my mom captured the scene in a watercolor painting, which Joshua now has.

Important life victories deserve to be remembered. More than once in the Bible, God instructed the Israelites to remember victories by making a memorial with stones. This was true after the Israelites escaped from Egypt and after they crossed the Jordan River, as well as after they won a battle. The point was that the stones would always remain as a reminder of God's faithfulness.

I love having visual markers in our home—a piece of artwork or a souvenir or a photograph—because they remind me that God loves me, cares about my needs, and orchestrates the details of my life. Whenever I get in a stew because of a worrisome situation, I can point to that photograph or read my gratitude journal to recall God's fingerprints over my past to orient me in the truth that He is still with me and will guide me through whatever may be ahead.

Lord, I remember with gratitude Your faithfulness throughout my life. Because I can remember those times, I know that You are with me today and will be with me through whatever challenges I may have ahead. Amen.

—Janet Holm McHenry

MAY 18

Queen Bee

I am the vine; you are the branches. If you remain in me and I in you, you will bear much fruit; apart from me you can do nothing.

—JOHN 15:5 (NIV)

WHEN MY HUSBAND and I first became beekeepers, it was on a whim. A friend was relocating a hive that had taken up residence in a local church, and he needed a place to move them. He asked if we would consider taking the hive, and after very little thought, we replied, "Of course." After all, how could we say no to "Gospel bees"?

We frantically began reading and studying as much as we could about beekeeping, and I was amazed to learn how many resemblances the beehive had to the body of Christ. It was an unexpected discovery, and it increased our passion for beekeeping.

A week later, our hive arrived, but it didn't take long for us to realize that the hive wasn't thriving. The bees were working hard, but there seemed to be fewer honeybees every time we checked. We soon discovered the problem . . . our hive had no queen. She had been lost in the move.

The queen is absolutely critical to the hive's survival since she is the only one that can lay eggs to hatch new bees. Worker bees live for only six or seven weeks, so there has to be a constant production of new bees to keep the hive growing. Without a queen to lay eggs, our Gospel bees would all be dead by the end of the summer.

Fortunately, we were able to call a bee farmer, and three days later a very nervous postal worker delivered a package with our new queen. The hive now had a chance to thrive.

The resemblance to the body of Christ once again amazed me. Just like those honeybees need their queen to thrive, I need Jesus. I must remain connected to Him first and above all else, otherwise all my efforts will be in vain.

King Jesus, You are the very heartbeat of Your people. Thank You for Your presence and power in my life enabling me to bear fruit for Your kingdom. Amen.

—Joy Pitner

Cute as a Bug's Ear

But ask the animals, and they will teach you, or the birds in the sky, and they will tell you; or speak to the earth, and it will teach you, or let the fish in the sea inform you. Which of all these does not know that the hand of the LORD has done this? In his hand is the life of every creature and the breath of all mankind.

—JOB 12:7–10 (NIV)

HAVE YOU EVER heard someone described as "cute as a bug's ear"? Do bugs even have ears? I decided to find out when we took our five-year-old grandson, Sev, to the Harrell House Bug Museum in Santa Fe. Intrigued by huge Madagascar cockroaches and scorpions, Sev was in insect heaven. With a shudder, I scurried away, leaving my husband to admire the giant millipedes with him.

I ventured into the room with thousands of mounted insects on display—most of them beetles. Many had jewel-like colors, from iridescent emerald-green to sapphire-blue. I've always appreciated the beauty of God's creation, but I never fully realized how much the Lord loves variety. God could have settled for one or two kinds of beetles—or even a dozen. That day I learned there are twelve thousand different kinds of beetles in the United States and three hundred thousand kinds worldwide.

When I stopped to consider that God's biodiversity extends to all categories, from people to birds and fish to flowers, I was amazed. I found myself praising the Lord's creativity as I stared in awe at the beautiful—yes, I'll admit it—beautiful array of beetles. Only after we had left the museum, did I realize I had forgotten to ask about bug ears.

How many are your works, LORD! In wisdom you made them all; the earth is full of your creatures. —Psalm 104:24 (NIV)

—Shirley Raye Redmond

MAY 20

Gray Doesn't Give Up

Then the Lord said, "If they do not believe you or pay attention to the first sign, they may believe the second."

—Exodus 4:8 (NIV)

GRAY WAS A kitten that showed up one day wearing a flea collar, which let me know he belonged to someone. I was outside sitting under the carport, talking to a friend on the phone, when this kitten began mewing to get my attention. I had some canned cat food for my cats in a cupboard outside, so I opened a can for him. He ate voraciously.

This became a nightly ritual, and soon Gray (the name I gave him because he was . . . gray) could just come to the back door and paw at the screen or howl until he got the food he wanted. He is so insistent when he wants attention or affection; if one way of getting what he wants doesn't work, he tries another. He will not stop until I respond.

I have often wondered if we have dreams and desires that we try to fulfill and give up on if, at first, we don't get the desired result. For example, have you ever reached out to someone who was too busy at the moment to give you the time you needed? Did you continue to reach out for other things, or did you quickly give up, blaming yourself for not being enough to get the person to be the friend you needed?

Sometimes our lives just get so busy, insistence is the only way to break through the noise. When we truly seek interaction and connection, we can continue in kindness, patience, and compassion so that even if we do not get the response *we* want, we give what we desire to others.

God, please give me guidance on how to persist in love and how not to take things so personally when busy lives get in the way. Amen.

—Devon O'Day

MAY 21

Eyes to See

The word of the LORD came to me: "Son of man, you are living among a rebellious people. They have eyes to see but do not see and ears to hear but do not hear, for they are a rebellious people."

—EZEKIEL 12:1–2 (NIV)

MY DAUGHTER RAN in one recent morning proclaiming that I must come outside. "There's a big grasshopper on the back porch!" she insisted. I followed her to the back porch, but to her disappointment, the insect had moved. We hunted for a minute before she spotted it in the grass. I bent down for a closer look. "No, that's just grass," I said.

She knelt and insisted, "It's definitely the grasshopper." I got on hands and knees for a closer look. "Are you sure? I'm not seeing it." Then as if on command, it jumped! What I had thought, from six inches away, was a big blade of grass was indeed a grasshopper.

I often have eyes to see but miss what God is trying to show me. Like the Israelites during Ezekiel's time, I can be rebellious. An opportunity to obey God can be in front of me, but I will choose the easier path. I'll stay in bed and scroll social media instead of opening my Bible to read and listen to the Lord. I'll harbor bitterness rather than doing the work of forgiveness. I lose patience with my children rather than responding in love. When prompted to speak an encouraging word to a stranger, I stay quiet in my comfort zone. Over time, my ears stop hearing God and my eyes stop seeing Him.

Just as my daughter directed me to see the grasshopper right in front of me, God makes His instructions and will clear through His Scripture, the Holy Spirit, and godly believers. I must be willing to open my eyes and ears and then obey as He directs.

Lord, open my eyes and ears to You today.
Give me strength to obey as You lead. Amen.

—Amelia Rhodes

MAY 22

Envying Lady Amherst

A heart at peace gives life to the body, but envy rots the bones.

—PROVERBS 14:30 (NIV)

THERE I STOOD, envying a pheasant. Which is ridiculous, of course, it being contained behind a metal fence and me free to walk about the farm. Well, and the fact that it's a bird. Still, as I gazed at him, my heart flooded with envy.

It was its exotic design that raised my hackles. God blessed this Lady Amherst's pheasant with jewel-like feathers of brilliant hue—indigo, mango, ruby, gold, emerald, ebony, and pure white. It dazzled as it strutted, surrounded by hay and farm feed. Beside it, I felt lacking. Irrationally, I brooded as the caged fowl came to embody all I felt I wasn't.

Following a season of caring for a loved one during his last days and then the ensuing grief, I had fallen into a state of disrepair myself. The ornamental creature left me feeling the extra weight, the graying locks, and every wrinkle. Here was a shining example of God's creative handiwork, and all I could think was, *Why didn't our Father design me with such beauty and grace?*

Thankfully, God nudged my spirit into merciful awareness that I was falling prey to a foolish temptation. Nothing robs a person of beauty faster than envy and self-pity! Immediately, I chose to worship the Creator rather than envy His creation.

Here I was, witness to my Father's splendid work displayed in the feathers of a farm fowl. The owner told me that every summer the Lady Amherst's pheasant plucks out its tail feathers and they grow in anew. That was a reminder that certainly God can also replenish my heart and inner beauty after a season of loss.

Walk of Faith: *When you're tempted to envy what God has given others, remember what God warns in Proverbs—that envy rots the bones—and seize the opportunity to admire His work and find life and peace in that.*

—Lori Stanley Roeleveld

MAY 23

Tiny Helicopters

How many are your works, LORD! In wisdom you made them all; the earth is full of your creatures.

—PSALM 104:24 (NIV)

I SAT WITH MY eighty-five-year-old friend on her front porch, sipping our coffee. While Kristen was old enough to be my mother, she remained young at heart. Soon, she would move out of state to live near her daughter.

I wondered if I would see Kris again this side of heaven. As we shared thoughts and memories, one of God's unique creations came to visit us: a red dragonfly, also known as a red-veined darter. I had never seen one before and was struck by its color. It flew like a tiny helicopter and landed for several seconds where we could observe its beauty. The ruby veins in the dragonfly's transparent wings resembled the artwork of an ultrafine calligraphy pen.

Red-veined darters are much different from other dragonflies, as proven by their behavior and genetic variances. They are found in Europe, the Mediterranean islands, and Asia. They have also been seen in southwestern Washington and along the Oregon coast—thus, this rare beauty found its way to us, sixty miles east of the Oregon shore, on the porch of my dear friend.

Dragonflies move each of their four wings independently, flapping each wing up and down and rotating each wing forward and backward on an axis. They can fly straight up or down, hover, and make hairpin turns. No wonder Kris and I watched in amazement.

"The red dragonfly visits me, Kathy," Kristen told me that day. "I watch for it."

Kris loved the Lord and is home now in heaven. But her words still ring in my heart. If we *watch* for these visiting miracles—like "little helicopters" that land on the airstrip of our experiences—we will be enriched in our souls and blessed by God, who created all things.

Dear God, thank You for the memory of dear friends, especially when combined with miracles in nature that come from Your hand—sometimes on wings of intricate beauty.

—Kathleen Ruckman

MAY 24

Lean into the Wind

He got up, rebuked the wind and said to the waves, "Quiet! Be still!" Then the wind died down and it was completely calm.

—MARK 4:39 (NIV)

I WALKED UP TO my car after work and noticed a lime-green katydid perched on the side rear window. Backing out of my parking spot, I could see from my mirror that it stayed on the car. I assumed it would fly off when I bounced down the dirt road, but it held on—still waving its spindly antennae in the air like a flag.

The true test was on the straightaway to my house. Driving fifty miles per hour, I tooled along, cheering on the little creature as it held fast. We rounded several corners near home, and I lost sight of it. After pulling into the driveway, I jumped out and was overjoyed to see it standing strong.

A miracle in aerodynamics, this insect held tight despite the intense pressure of the wind.

A few days later, I visited my young friend Maddie, who is facing cancer for the third time. Her parents are in the midst of a difficult divorce; her childhood home was sold. Her beloved grandfather recently passed away. Her sophomore year of college was paused to transition into a medical treatment plan.

How do you move forward when the floor is slippery and your feet fall out from under you?

Sitting next to Maddie, I told her about the katydid. Even with the slightest of handholds, an insect that weighs next to nothing pushed against the gale-force winds and prevailed. I urged her to lean into those same winds. Our Father, the same One who created that tiny katydid, had created her. He keeps them both in the palm of His hand.

When everything seems to be going against you, remember that the airplane takes off against the wind, not with it. —Henry Ford

—Twila Bennett

MAY 25

God Doesn't Make Mistakes

There are different kinds of gifts, but the same Spirit distributes them. There are different kinds of service, but the same Lord. There are different kinds of working, but in all of them and in everyone it is the same God at work.

—1 CORINTHIANS 12:4–6 (NIV)

I LOVE VACATIONING AT the beach with our family. Every year, I look forward to it for months and can barely stand waiting for the week to arrive. My favorite part is sitting in my chair under the beach umbrella with my toes in the sand, reading book after book as the waves break and roll toward us. I also love watching the birds and grabbing my phone to snap photos—not of the seagulls, but of other birds that walk along the edge of the water.

Two birds in particular entertained me on our last visit. One was fairly large, long necked, and a bit awkward. It would slowly plod along with its head bobbing. And in my head, I could imagine a rather deep, slow voice that sounded a little like Eeyore from *Winnie-the-Pooh*. The other was tiny and moved so quickly it almost looked like a cartoon character in fast motion. As I watched its tiny feet, I "heard" cartoon sounds in my head mimicking its frantic, itty-bitty steps as it headed toward the water and then ran away as each wave neared closer.

The birds couldn't be more different, but both made us laugh. And both have a place in creation, just as we each have a place. We're each given certain gifts and roles.

I don't have the energy of that tiny seabird. Honestly, I'm probably more like the lumbering long-necked bird. Either way, God can use me just as I am. God loves each of us just as we are—just as He created us to be.

Dear God, thank You for making us exactly how You planned. Help us to accept that You love us and made each of us special. God, we praise You that You don't make mistakes. Amen.

—Missy Tippens

MAY 26

Enough

And God is able to make all grace abound toward you,
that you, always having all sufficiency in all things,
may have an abundance for every good work.

—2 CORINTHIANS 9:8 (NKJV)

LIBBY THOUGHT SHE was a night owl, not a calico cat. It never failed. Once I got myself tucked into bed for the night, she would jump up and pace back and forth along the length of my body, as if she were walking on the boardwalk. When she neared my face, she purred and begged me to pet her. Then she would walk back down the boardwalk toward my feet and curl up next to me as if I were her heater. She knew how to get comfortable. Repeat over and over. Then all of a sudden, just when I thought the petting had fulfilled her needs, she would jump off the bed to run and have a bite to eat. She sought satisfaction and found it in being petted, in being comfortable, and in being fed, but never for long!

I'm a lot like that, if I'm being honest. I seek satisfaction through temporary fixes. I desire comfort. I gain a wanted possession and realize it doesn't really fill the void the way I thought it would. And I seek to be "petted," too, in the form of praise or attention. Even when others give me the recognition I think I need or deserve, I'm not satisfied. And just like Libby, once I realize the comfort-seeking isn't fulfilling me, I go to comfort food to make me feel better.

When I evaluate the "why" behind my dissatisfaction, I realize it's because only God is enough. Only God can fill a God-size void. My heavenly Father has been there all the time, wanting to meet my needs. He sent the Comforter to be my comfort. He whispers words of affirmation to my soul. He provides spiritual bread that leaves me feeling full. What more could I want?

Dear Lord, may I find "soul-fill-ment" *that goes beyond fulfilment as I receive God's comfort, affirmation, and provision. You are enough. Amen.*

—Kathy Carlton Willis

MAY 27

Landing the Big One

Then He said to them, "Follow Me, and I will make you fishers of men."

—MATTHEW 4:19 (NKJV)

MY BROTHER AND I couldn't have been more excited as we boarded the boat. We had none of the fear adults do about sunburn, seasickness, or drowning. Whale watching sounded like an adventure.

Mom slathered each of us with suntan lotion. Dad tried to lower expectations. "Don't count on seeing a whale today, let alone getting a picture. Just enjoy our time on the boat."

Three hours into our adventure, I felt ready to turn for home. My big brother had seen no whales. On the other side of the boat at the time, Mom and I had seen two whales briefly. But by the time she got her phone out, the whales had ducked back under the water.

Buster looked dejected. I prayed that God would help him catch at least a peek at one whale. God answered fast.

"Hey, there's one, out by that buoy!" he exclaimed a few minutes later.

My brother snapped picture after picture as the whale rose out of the water and fell back. He literally jumped for joy. His camera caught great photos of the big one. Dad smiled and patted Buster on the shoulder.

Although a great father in many ways, Dad was not a believer. Mom, my sister, and I prayed for him for years. Unlike my prayer for the whale that day, this prayer waited a long time for an answer.

Just two years before he died, Mom called to tell me Dad had accepted Christ as Lord. Hearing the news, I felt overwhelmed with joy. "He believed and prayed for salvation last night," Mom said. "He was too sick to get out to church, so our minister came over and baptized him in the bathtub."

When Dad came to know the Lord, I felt like God landed the big one, at least the big one in our family.

For by grace you have been saved through faith, and that not of yourselves; it is the gift of God. —Ephesians 2:8 (NKJV)

—David L. Winters

MAY 28

Help Not Wanted

In my distress I called upon the Lord*; to my God I cried for help. From his temple he heard my voice, and my cry to him reached his ears.*

—Psalm 18:6 (ESV)

I KNEW WE WERE in trouble when our Bernese mountain dog puppy, Zander, threw himself to the ground in his first obedience-training class. He wasn't happy with the idea of walking politely on a leash, and he decided he just wouldn't do it.

Our dog's stubborn streak only increased as he grew older. I sometimes thought we had ended up with a mule instead of a dog. His favorite trick was pinning himself against the floor when we wanted him to get up, daring anyone to try to lift his 135-pound body.

When Zander suddenly fell ill and received a cancer diagnosis, I thought his stubbornness might be an asset, providing the will to survive the disease. Instead, I soon saw we were in trouble once again.

The disease weakened his hind legs, and he had difficulty lifting his huge body to stand. I would rush over to help whenever I saw him struggling to rise. But the moment he spotted me coming, he would drop back down, as though pretending he hadn't wanted to stand.

I would linger near, assuring him I was happy and able to help him to his feet, but he wouldn't budge. His stubbornness wouldn't allow him to accept my help.

As I shook my head at the trouble his stubborn streak was causing, I realized I'm the same way. I have a hard time admitting I need God's help. I often try to muddle through on my own, neglecting the Bible, prayer, or help from friends. All the while, God is hovering close, reaching out a strong hand, assuring me He is happy and able to help me to my feet.

Walk of Faith: *What are you struggling to handle on your own? Ask God for help today, and welcome the help when it comes.*

—Jerusha Agen

MAY 29

Be Careful Who You Follow

I will give him and his descendants the land he set his feet on, because he followed the LORD wholeheartedly.

—DEUTERONOMY 1:36 (NIV)

I WAS A JOGGER in my younger years. We lived on the county line just outside a small town called Chisago City in Minnesota. The distance from our house into town was two miles, so it was a perfect location for a four-mile run. Leashes were not needed in the county, but the city of Chisago did have a leash law, and therein was the problem.

I enjoyed running in the early morning, but I was often followed by unwanted company. Four golden retrievers lived in our neighborhood, and they also liked early morning runs. And with no leash law, they were free to join me. I would often have one, two, and sometimes three of them joyfully joining me. It wasn't that I disliked the company; I just didn't want the responsibility. It was dangerous for the dogs on the county road.

Days turned into weeks with the local police ignoring the canine parade. However, one day, one of the dogs decided to cross the road right in front of a car. I screamed, the car slowed, and disaster was avoided. But timing is everything. The police officer, who had ignored these dogs for a while, had just passed me and made a U-turn. "Are these your dogs?" he asked.

"No, but I do know where they live," I admitted.

"Okay, I'll need names and addresses," he stated as he opened the back of his car. I called the dogs over, and to my surprise all three hopped in. To this day, one of the funniest sights I've ever seen is three grinning golden heads in the back of the squad car.

Recalling that sight now reminds me to think about who I follow and where I go. Some leaders look and sound good, but I need to check them out with the collar of God's Word and the leash of prayer to keep me on the right road.

Father, Your words and example are all I need to stay on the right path to life eternal.

—Linda Bartlett

Heron Visits

And God said, "Let the water teem with living creatures, and let birds fly above the earth across the vault of the sky."

—GENESIS 1:20 (NIV)

I LOVE WATCHING BIRDS at the end of the day as they fly to roost before sunset. Flocks of blackbirds, thousands it seems, fly and dance in complex formations, swooping up and down, and not one ever goes opposite the group. Mockingbirds fly to their favorite holly tree in my yard. The robins in the spring return to their nest in the crook of my waterspout.

I was used to all these birds. But one sunset brought the silhouette of a large blue heron against the sky. Not being around the swamps where I had grown up seeing these beautiful birds, I wondered how one had ended up over the flat farmland where I now lived.

But every evening, the lone blue heron flew over my barn as I did chores, sounding its haunting siren call. Where was it going? Then a neighbor told me that another neighbor had a pond he had stocked with freshwater shrimp. So this beautiful bird had navigated by faith and instinct to a pond teeming with living creatures, counting on the promise its Creator had granted from the first chapter of His Word.

We have promises for us and the instinct to claim them within us as well. Our biggest roadblock to trusting in God's provision is our own intellect that tells us that provision is impossible. Who trusts shrimp to be inland on landlocked farmland? A bird . . . that has never been let down when it trusts its instinct rather than logic to guide its journey.

Lord, teach me to trust You with my heart rather than depending on the negativity in my head. Amen.

—Devon O'Day

MAY 31

The Path of the Bats

You make known to me the path of life; you will fill me with joy in your presence, with eternal pleasures at your right hand.

—PSALM 16:11 (NIV)

OVER MEMORIAL DAY weekend, we drove out to West Texas to see a colony of Mexican free-tailed bats. My uncle said up to 10 million bats would swarm out of the cave at sunset.

We scrambled up the rocky hillside and waited. Dusk fell. The cave mouth remained quiet. Fearing we had come in the wrong season, we packed to leave.

A few swallows began twisting over the cave mouth. Like dark smoke, bats trickled out. The sky filled with the beating of wings, and bats streamed out in an ever-widening spiral—millions of bats, furry creatures that can fly up to sixty miles per hour, climb to a thousand feet, and travel a hundred miles in one evening. We were awed, then stunned.

Red-tailed hawks and peregrine falcons hovered just beyond the ridge. When bats left the spiral, the predators swooped in and picked them off. The bats had an ever-widening path and hundreds of square miles in which to fly freely, feasting on insects. When they stayed together in the prescribed pattern—in the center or near the edge—they were safe. But when they strayed off alone, raptors caught them.

God has provided a path for me too. Sometimes I fear this path limits my creativity or independence, but watching the bats that evening, I realized my path is wide and far reaching, leading to my heart's desire. God is not a limit on how high or far I can go, but a refuge that provides the freedom to soar in ways that will sustain me and fill me with joy.

Dear Lord of the heavens and the earth, I can be so stubborn and proud, wanting to fly off and do things my way. Help me to have patience to find lasting joy on Your path and trust that it provides all I need. Amen.

—Lucy H. Chambers

June

JUNE 1

Noise Control

A gentle answer turns away wrath, but a harsh word stirs up anger.

—PROVERBS 15:1 (NIV)

THERE IS A moment when you realize that your parenting techniques might not be working.

My boxer dog, Tyson, had begun to communicate to me by barking. At some point in his growing-up years, I allowed a bit of freedom and, boy, he grabbed it and ran. To be fair, I was raising a human baby at the same time he was a puppy. Babies get priority over puppy training, so Tyson became the crazy one.

That dog thinks bark-yelling at me will get him the attention he deserves. And just as a mother knows the different cries of her baby, I know the different barks of my dog.

Short, persistent barks? "Gotta go; gotta go."

Crazy, obnoxious barks accompanied by bouncing? "Good, you're home. Feed me now!"

Barking with a few low growls? "You told me no to a dog treat, and I don't like it. I will talk back to you, then move to *extremely* loud barking."

My husband's words to me when I arrive home and Tyson starts barking at me? "He didn't do this when you were gone." I give up. The harshness of consistent barking from Tyson makes me annoyed and angry, and if I yell at him, he runs away and hides.

If I respond to Tyson, or to those around me, with harsh words or respond sharply to an innocent question, I push them away. Instead, my responses should be in love. Gentleness is always the best answer. I want my words to draw others close.

Reaching for Tyson, I pull him in for a hug. He snuggles close. Maybe I didn't really know what that barking meant after all.

May these words of my mouth and this meditation of my heart be pleasing in your sight, LORD, my Rock and my Redeemer. —Psalm 19:14 (NIV)

—Twila Bennett

JUNE 2

Something's Fishy

Can a man scoop fire into his lap without his clothes being burned? Can a man walk on hot coals without his feet being scorched?

—PROVERBS 6:27–28 (NIV)

MY SHORT-TERM MISSION trip to the tribal villages along the Amazon was ending. Our host invited us to go fishing for piranhas. Adventurous by nature, I agreed to go.

Piranhas are known for their aggressive character and razor-sharp teeth. In his book *Through the Brazilian Wilderness*, Theodore Roosevelt says they are "vicious creatures." We baited the hooks on our bamboo rods. Before long, we were filling a bucket with piranhas.

Claudio, a native Brazilian familiar with the river, was with us. He knew how to grab the fish without getting bitten. As he unhooked one of the cunning creatures, he forgot to watch where his other hand was going.

CHOMP! Claudio dropped the fish and grabbed a rag to stop the bleeding. A chunk of his finger the size of a penny was torn back.

After that, I lost interest in fishing for these nibblers. I decided to stay as far from those jaws as possible. I wondered why someone would consider catching piranhas when so many other delicious fish were in abundance.

Wisdom tells me to avoid hazards. The book of Proverbs is filled with warnings against playing with danger, risking it all to see how close I can get without succumbing to temptation, until I've plummeted overboard, moving farther away from God instead of toward Him. I want to be steadfast and diligent, so I remain far from temptation and live a life pleasing to God.

We're 100 percent responsible for the pursuit of holiness, but at the same time we're 100 percent dependent upon the Holy Spirit to enable us in that pursuit. —Jerry Bridges

—Tez Brooks

JUNE 3

A New Self

Do not lie to each other, since you have taken off your old self with its practices and have put on the new self, which is being renewed in knowledge in the image of its Creator.

—COLOSSIANS 3:9–10 (NIV)

WHILE VISITING MY in-laws back East, something shiny on the outside wall of our vacation rental caught my eye. A freshly metamorphosed dragonfly glittered in the sunshine! Sticking to the wall just below it was its former larval skin looking dead and useless. I was struck by the beauty of the dragonfly's iridescent wings and the perfection of its delicate yet strong design in contrast to the ugly, desiccated skin it had shed. Once it fully recovered from casting off its old form, it would be ready to begin its life as an adult.

Looking at the dragonfly's cast-off shell, I was reminded of how I've taken off my "old self" and "put on the new" through faith in Jesus Christ. And like the dragonfly transforming into a shining adult, I can grow into a more spiritually mature version of myself. Since I'm transformed, I can rid myself of habits and practices that too often hold me back from living my Christian life to the fullest, and replace them with more beautiful, Christ-like attitudes and behaviors.

Is it easy? Or simple? No, I'm definitely a work in progress, often following the "one step forward, two steps back" pattern of growth. But what a blessing to know my new self, which is being renewed in knowledge every day, will be strengthened and equipped to live the way God would have me live for my good and His glory. My new self and my salvation are secure in Jesus Christ.

Be guided only by the healer of the sick, the raiser of the dead, the friend of all who were afflicted and forlorn, the patient Master who shed tears of compassion for our infirmities. We cannot but be right when we put all the rest away, and do everything in remembrance of Him.

—Charles Dickens, *Little Dorrit*

—Marianne Campbell

JUNE 4

Beauty for Ashes

He has sent me to bind up the brokenhearted, to proclaim freedom for the captives and release from darkness for the prisoners, to proclaim the year of the LORD's favor and the day of vengeance of our God, to comfort all who mourn, and provide for those who grieve in Zion—to bestow on them a crown of beauty instead of ashes.

—ISAIAH 61:1–3 (NIV)

THERE'S A LOT to like about working part time at Walmart. Being inside on a beautiful day is not one of them.

I left my station behind the pharmacy counter one beautiful day this past summer and headed outside where I sat on a bright-blue metal bench beside a display of hanging baskets that boasted petunias and begonias. The small outdoor corner smelled like cigarette smoke, but I chose a spot behind the flowers and soaked in the much-needed sun.

I longed to enjoy the remainder of the day outside, working in the yard or walking on the beach, but I knew that was not to be. Suddenly, a sparrow flew down, landed right at my feet, and pecked at a soggy cracker on the cement. It pecked again, then looked up at me, tilting its head as if to inquire why I was so blue (aside from the color of my smock) on such a beautiful day. I smiled at the bird, watching it hop with little steps to reach for the green of a plant on display. It lifted up, flew to a hanging basket, then flew back down, this time even closer to my feet. After spending almost my entire break with me, it flew away with a chirp.

Before I returned to the pharmacy, I tilted my head to the sky in thanks. I may not have been able to witness what I considered ultimate beauty that day—the wide-open ocean or the feel of grass beneath my knees—but God had nevertheless brought a slice of beauty to me.

Heavenly Father, thank You for Your gifts, filled with beauty, that always abound if only we have eyes to see. Amen.

—Heidi Chiavaroli

Second-Chance Dog

The Lord is not slow in keeping his promise, as some understand slowness. Instead he is patient with you, not wanting anyone to perish, but everyone to come to repentance.

—2 PETER 3:9 (NIV)

I HAD BEEN AFRAID of dogs since I was a small child. But when my daughter begged to adopt an eighty-five-pound mutt from a shelter, I gave in on one condition: Bandit would be my daughter's dog. Two weeks later, she moved away for college, and Bandit decided that *I* was his person. He followed me everywhere—whining outside the bathroom door, trotting behind me as I worked in the kitchen, wedging himself between any visitor and me.

Big and beefy, with a shiny black coat and white blaze, Bandit had been abused at some point. His tail had been hacked off, leaving him with a stub, and his muzzle was peppered with gray. He was a second-chance dog if ever there was one.

One rainy morning, I put the teakettle on the stove, then stepped backward, tripping over Bandit. "Quit following me!" I yelled. Bandit hung his head. I stomped into the bathroom to take a shower. Over the water's spray, I heard frantic barking. He couldn't be without me for five minutes? Maybe I would give him back—I didn't care much for dogs anyway. I wrapped myself in a towel and opened the door, wagging my forefinger. "Hush!" But he kept barking and running to the kitchen, until I followed.

On the stove, the teakettle glowed bright red, and smoke filled the kitchen. I switched off the burner, grabbed a mitt, and flung the kettle out the back door onto the wet grass. Bandit flinched when I reached for him—and my heart melted. I sank to my knees and buried my face in his fur, begging his forgiveness. As Bandit licked away my tears, I became a dog lover. Like our merciful God, he was willing to give me a second chance too.

[When it comes to God] we can't run out of second chances . . . only time.
—Robin Jones Gunn

—Linda S. Clare

JUNE 6

The Gobbling Goat

Above all else, guard your heart, for everything you do flows from it.

—PROVERBS 4:23 (NIV)

MY FAMILY RECENTLY took a day trip to a farm complete with cotton, rows of sunflowers, and farm animals. My favorite part? The goats. Always the goats. There's just something about goats that gets me—baby goats especially. For a minute, I even considered whether my backyard was large enough for my own pet goat . . . but then quickly decided my dogs wouldn't be as thrilled as I was by that prospect.

As I walked over to see the goats, the family ahead of me began feeding them one of the sunflowers from the farm. Quickly, I realized I had come empty-handed and had little chance of getting the goats' attention if I had to compete with a sunflower lunch. So, I turned around and grabbed a handful of tall grass growing outside their fence. Would you believe those goats gobbled it down as if it were ice cream? Or whatever the goat equivalent of ice cream is.

While this willingness to eat anything works well for goats, the same does not hold true for people, whether we are feeding our stomachs or our hearts. All too often, I allow my heart to gobble up things that will make it sick. I feast on gossip, worry, and fear. I, like the goats, indiscriminately eat whatever is held out to me. Too rarely do I pause to consider the nutritional benefits of what I consume—whether it strengthens my heart, mind, and spirit. Whether it aligns with those things God has called me to meditate upon. Instead, I consume headlines and social media, as well as entertainment, based on what is most convenient—the metaphorical grass on the other side of the goats' fence. Why am I surprised, then, whenever my heart grows weak and weary? What I often forget is that God's prescribed diet is for my own benefit. When it comes to feeding my heart and spirit, I know I need to be intentional about the things I let in. That way, my own words, in turn, can be life giving.

For the mouth speaks what the heart is full of. —Matthew 12:34 (NIV)

—Ashley Clark

JUNE 7

The God of Beginnings

Behold, I will do a new thing.

—ISAIAH 43:19 (NKJV)

I WAS ON THE way to my doctor's clinic, nervous as usual about my monthly blood-pressure test. At home, my reading was normal, but at the doctor's office, it would go through the roof. *Lord, if only my blood pressure would be normal at the clinic,* I silently prayed, feeling frustrated and discouraged.

I asked my husband, Terry, to wait in the car for me. When I entered the waiting room, I noticed a new fish tank stretching across an entire wall. The aquarium contained a sunken ship with colorful treasures—and an abundance of fish.

As I sat down in front of the glass, one little fish came forward and studied me. Sturdy and little, with a bold crimson tail, it swam so smoothly and with such confidence.

Surrounding my new friend were other fish—gold ones, creamy ones with black zebra stripes—that moved in a soothing ballet behind my little friend. The more I gazed at this scene, the more it drew me in, relaxing me. It was like watching an underwater Broadway show.

"That's Cedric," whispered the office manager to me. "He's a bloodfin tetra, known for his blood-red tail. Look at how gracefully he moves. I think he likes you."

Later, as my arm was cuffed for the blood-pressure test, my mind was on little Cedric, his red tail and his smooth maneuvers. My reading was normal . . . a first!

As I got into the car, Terry asked, "So, how did you do?"

My answer? "Just swimmingly."

I was reminded anew that God truly is a God of firsts and new beginnings. His mercies are new every morning. Only God could have set me up with a smooth-moving fish to give me this prayed-for first.

Dear Lord, thank You for the firsts and new beginnings You bring into my life. Thank You that every new day is a gift from You. In Jesus's name. Amen.

—Sandra Clifton

JUNE 8

Strength in the Waves

My hand will sustain him; surely my arm with strengthen him.

—PSALM 89:21 (NIV)

FRUSTRATED AFTER A flare-up of muscle spasms and chronic pain forced me to spend the first three days of our Hawaiian vacation in our hotel room, I strolled the short distance from our car to the beach. My husband, Alan, had suggested we give my body time to recover, so we stayed close to our accommodations.

I sat on a nearby bench, pouting as Alan ventured closer to the water. I watched waves crashing against the rocky shoreline. Why did I have to miss out on so much? I wanted to walk with my husband instead of being stuck on the sidelines of life.

Alan pointed toward the waves and yelled over the wind. "Sea turtles."

Staring at the choppy waters, I noticed a turtle-shape shadow in the curve of a large wave. With large flaps spread wide, it remained still in the current. I spotted sea turtles raising their heads above the surface and riding the waves. I even saw a few resting on the rocky shoreline.

As I watched the turtles swimming gracefully in the turbulent waters, I considered the Ruler of the surging sea—the One who made the turtles and me—God. The psalmist sings of the Lord's faithfulness and affirms that God rules over the surging sea, fully in control no matter how rough the storms may seem. And when the waves mount up, He stills them.

While I continue enduring my seemingly endless waves of chronic pain and fatigue caused by multiple injuries to my neck, shoulders, and upper back, God's hand will sustain me and strengthen me.

Maker and Ruler of All, thanks for affirming You are with us, You are working, and You are always in control. Amen.

—Xochitl E. Dixon

JUNE 9

Two Little Piggies Went to Market

Whatever you do, work at it with all your heart, as working for the Lord, not for human masters.

—COLOSSIANS 3:23 (NIV)

MY FRIEND'S BOYS, both in 4-H, asked to raise hogs to sell at the fair. With a few conditions, their parents agreed and purchased two piglets, Tank and Susie.

The boys took on the responsibility of swine ownership and control of the feeding and care of Tank and Susie. But their charges were also pets and provided much amusement for the family. Susie used to sit on her hunches like one of the dogs. And the boys' tiny twin sisters rode her piggyback.

Apart from work, mixed with fun, the experience was a teaching time for the boys. They were required to visit every participant who attended the fair's swine sale, whether or not the participant had bid on the boys' pigs. The boys also thanked each buyer for participating in the fair. This taught them proper business practices and began to establish their good reputations.

When the time came to say goodbye to Tank and Susie, the boys had earned good money for the sale of their pigs. According to the family's plan, 10 percent of the earnings went to a tithe for church and a thousand dollars went into a savings account. The rest? The boys could spend what was left on whatever they wanted. A happy result of all the hard work.

While I might sometimes complain about it, I am thankful for work and the joy it gives me. And I need to remember that it is a gift from God and that my hard, honest labor can lead me to the wonderful things He has in store.

The reason a lot of people do not recognize opportunity is because it usually goes around wearing overalls looking like hard work. —Often attributed to Thomas A. Edison

—Cathy Elliott

JUNE 10

Horses Grieve Too

The Lord is close to the brokenhearted and saves those who are crushed in spirit.

—Psalm 34:18 (NIV)

I GOT MESSAGE FROM a friend saying that she was entering hospice with an aggressive cancer and that she needed a favor. She wanted me to take her horse and promise to love and care for her.

The rock in my heart pulled me under for two reasons: because I grieved for what my friend was going through and because she chose to let her best friend, her beautiful spotted saddle horse, Cheyenne, go to another home. I could not imagine this weight or having to make this choice.

Cheyenne arrived at my farm, and we put her in her own paddock as the rest of my herd got to know her behind the safety of a fence. Rocky, my gelding, was the first to welcome her. But Cheyenne watched the horizon for her mama-person to come see her. She ate well and enjoyed brushing. But there was something in her eyes that wouldn't lift easily.

Extra treats and time began to soften her sadness. Eventually, she began to respond in small ways to the kindness she was receiving. Her restlessness began to settle, and she felt like a part of the family. Rocky stayed close and attentive, and soon they were bonded as if they had been horse friends for years.

When we lose someone, the pining and sadness are a normal part of grief. We all experience it differently, but we all experience it. Surrounding ourselves with those who will patiently keep loving us even when we are not ready to receive that love is the key to healing. God is ever close and knows just who to send our way.

Dear God, please heal my broken heart and keep sending love till I'm ready to open my heart to it. Amen.

—Devon O'Day

JUNE 11

Letters to Ernest

Be completely humble and gentle; be patient, bearing with one another in love.

—EPHESIANS 4:2 (NIV)

IT WAS THE last day of the school year, and the first-grade class gathered around. Although filled with joy as they anticipated the impending summer vacation, the students were also sad to say goodbye to their book buddy, our golden retriever, Ernest. We had brought him in regularly for story time, when the kids practiced their reading skills as he lay at their sides and listened.

On this last day, the students had written letters to Ernest, expressing what he had meant to them. Ernest sat attentively, his golden head on the child's lap, as each child read a heartfelt note. I found myself tearing up at their words: *You are nice to everyone. You look nice every time I see you. You are kind. You are a good listener. You make me smile. You make me happy. I feel good when you come to our class.*

Wasn't it wonderful that the children found all these positive qualities in a dog? He's kind, a good listener, and nice to everyone, and he makes people happy. He sounds like a good friend to me. The kind of friend I would like to have. The kind of friend I would like to be.

God supplies us with many guidelines for how we should treat others. He asks us to love our neighbors and to treat others the way we want to be treated. He uses words such as *forgive* and *encourage* and *honor.* When I listen to God, I know everything I need to know about being a good friend. And when I observe my dog, I also learn, because surely God created the loving heart in Ernest that sets such a fine example.

A dog will teach you unconditional love. If you can have that in your life, things won't be too bad. —Robert Wagner

—Peggy Frezon

JUNE 12

My Therapy Dog

I pray that out of his glorious riches he may strengthen you with power through his Spirit in your inner being.

—EPHESIANS 3:16 (NIV)

I MET FRANK IN the United Kingdom. My friend Julie and I had arrived, frazzled and exhausted, at a cozy house in the English countryside. It was my first trip overseas and Julie's first-in-decades stay in England for something other than visiting her daughter. We had spent the first four days in London, seeing exciting places but often feeling overwhelmed. That morning, the handle of my suitcase had broken in the train station. But we had made it to our Airbnb in East Hampshire, where our hosts greeted us with tea, let us relax in their garden, and introduced us to their dogs: a lap dog named Nettie and Frank, their fox-red Labrador.

Frank immediately ran over with a toy, ready to play.

"Frank," our host said, "leave them alone."

"It's okay," I insisted. Something about playing fetch with Frank in a garden that looked like it belonged in a storybook refreshed me and Julie. Later, he followed us around as we explored. We took turns rubbing his warm ears and feeling him snuggle against us for a hug. We started calling Frank our therapy dog. I didn't even mind when he insisted on playing fetch with a soggy apple instead of a ball. This encounter with Frank became a sweet reminder that God was with us on our adventure, supplying what we needed for each day.

God knows exactly how to strengthen His children, whether we are feeling like weary travelers, having a hard day, or being tossed in the throes of a crisis. Those moments when He sends what our hearts need can become evidence that the One who knows us best is with us on the journey.

Walk of Faith: *Think of someone who needs strengthening right now. Ask God to inspire you with one thing that you can do to not only brighten his or her day but also to send a reminder that He is with them.*

—Jeanette Hanscome

JUNE 13

Reflecting on Reflections

So all of us who have had that veil removed can see and reflect the glory of the Lord. And the Lord—who is the Spirit—makes us more and more like him as we are changed into his glorious image.

—2 Corinthians 3:18 (NLT)

KNOCK, KNOCK, KNOCK. The sound slowly penetrated my consciousness. *Knock, knock, knock.* There it was again. *Who could be knocking at this hour of the morning?* my sleep-thick brain wondered. My husband and I were enjoying a weekend alone in a remote mountain cabin in the foothills of the Blue Ridge Mountains, and no one we knew was nearby.

Knock, knock, knock, knock, knock. The sound grew insistent. Forcing my eyes open, I discovered an angry male cardinal dive-bombing the floor-to-ceiling window that made up the eastern wall of the house. The rising sun had turned the glass into a mirror, allowing him to see his reflection. Assuming that what he saw was an enemy, a rival bird, he had launched an all-out attack. *Bam, bam, bam.* Into the glass he flew, beak aimed for war and feathers flying.

Sometimes, like our cardinal visitor, I see things I would rather not see in my reflection: insecurity, inadequacy, fear, faithlessness. I perceive myself as the enemy and go on the attack. *You'll never be smart enough, accomplished enough, connected enough, skilled enough,* the voices in my head tell me.

But this isn't why my gracious God, through His Holy Spirit and His Word, allows me to see my inadequacies. He doesn't show me so I can attack and defeat myself. He shows me my weaknesses so I'll realize my need to fully rely on Him. He can work in and through me *despite* my inadequacies. In my weakness, He is strong. In my frailty, He is mighty. In my ignorance, He is wise.

Walk of Faith: *Today, instead of attacking yourself because of your perceived inadequacies, try to acknowledge them and surrender them to God. Ask Him to grow you and change you to become more like His Son. Invite Him to make up for what is lacking and glorify Himself through you.*

—Lori Hatcher

JUNE 14

Beyond the Wave

For the LORD does not see as man sees; for man looks at the outward appearance, but the LORD looks at the heart.

—1 SAMUEL 16:7 (NKJV)

THE FIRST TIME my son's bearded dragon waved at us, we were in a pet store deciding which cold-blooded creature would be part of our lives for the next fifteen years.

"Mom, we have to get that one! It's a friendly dragon. Look, it's waving!" One little wave, and we knew we had the right dragon. We waved back and brought it home.

As we later learned, bearded dragons don't wave in friendliness. They wave as a sign of submission when they feel threatened. One clawed "hand" rises slowly and circles to a deliberate conclusion back in the sand. The result is a wave so cute, it's almost impossible not to return the gesture.

The other day, Drax the Dragon waved as I entered the room carrying a load of laundry. On instinct, I lifted my hand and then stopped. What was I communicating to him in a language I didn't understand? I meant friendship, but he might see hostility or an act of submission. Maybe I had just declared him my ruler. I laughed to myself, wondering how often I have misinterpreted people's actions and body language through a lack of understanding. Maybe they spoke out of wounding, and I interpreted it as hostility. Or perhaps they acted in arrogance when their hearts were bound with insecurity.

The Bible cautions against judging others based on externals. As with Drax, if I don't take time to understand others, I can easily assign motives that aren't there. Thankfully, God is never confused by my outward posturing. He sees my heart and longs for me to know His heart in return. And when I learn to understand someone else's heart, I stop misunderstanding the actions, and I finally see beyond the wave.

Lord, help me to know Your heart today. Help me to see beyond the externals in the people around me and love others as You love me. Amen.

—Tracy Joy Jones

JUNE 15

My Meow-Meow

I will give you hidden treasures, riches stored in secret places, so that you may know that I am the Lord, the God of Israel, who summons you by name.

—Isaiah 45:3 (NIV)

MY HUSBAND AND I recently adopted a pair of teenage American shorthair tuxedo kittens, which my grandson named Dab and Hype after his two favorite contemporary dance moves. This is our first experience with cats in many, many years, and it's been a learning experience every step of the way.

One of the most challenging issues at the beginning was that these brothers look remarkably similar. When I look closely, I can see minor differences. The bottom of Hype's jaw is completely white. Dab has a black spot on his belly. But when they're running around creating mischief, it's harder to tell which is which.

My grandson has come up with a clever solution. He merely picks up the cat. If it meows, it's Granny's cat, Dab. If it remains silent, it's Grampy's cat, Hype. Dab's vocalizing is, in fact, probably the easiest way to differentiate between them.

So, without realizing it, I started calling Dab my Meow-Meow. Now he comes to me when I call him by that name. I'm not entirely certain at this point he even knows his given name is Dab. But he affectionately responds to Meow-Meow.

God likewise has a name by which He calls us. Just as my Meow-Meow responds to me, I should thankfully run into the arms of Jesus.

Therefore God exalted him to the highest place and gave him the name that is above every name, that at the name of Jesus every knee should bow, in heaven and on earth and under the earth, and every tongue acknowledge that Jesus Christ is Lord, to the glory of God the Father. —Philippians 2:9–11 (NIV)

—Deb Kastner

JUNE 16

A Place Called Home

But our citizenship is in heaven. And we eagerly await a Savior from there, the Lord Jesus Christ.

—PHILIPPIANS 3:20 (NIV)

I THOUGHT THAT PERHAPS, in my exhaustion after driving twelve hundred miles over three days with our three-going-on-four children, my eyes were playing tricks on me. Yet there they were, these sixty-thousand-pound creatures, raising their fins high above the surface of the Pacific Ocean. It was as if the gray whales were waving—greeting my family to their waters.

As we made our way up the Pacific coast that week, we discovered the whales in several inlets. These pods of resident whales are set apart from their migratory relatives. They remain at these inlets and feed. When they do travel to California, they can always be depended on to return here, to the Oregon coast—to their home.

These stunning animals were the first to greet us at the outset of our two-month-long road trip. The week before, we had sold our home and set off in an RV across the Pacific Northwest. And yet, just like those whales, we would find our way back home. After eight weeks, we were eager to return to our church family, our community, and the soil we call home in Colorado.

Watching those whales, knowing the journey they make across deep waters, leaves a deep and lasting understanding of the word *home*. Amid long journeys and arduous travels, they know where they belong.

Wherever life takes me, and whatever path the Lord may lead my family on, I can be certain of where I belong. I can hold to His Word and promise that we are only passing by and that my eternal home is fixed in heaven by His side.

Dear Lord, when I feel out of place or uncertain of where You would have me go, assure me of Your presence. Remind me where I belong—by Your side. You died and rose to reserve for me a place of belonging in heaven. My home is with You. Amen.

—Eryn Lynum

JUNE 17

Freeze Tag

We also have the prophetic message as something completely reliable, and you will do well to pay attention to it, as to a light shining in a dark place, until the day dawns and the morning star rises in your hearts.

—2 PETER 1:19 (NIV)

SUMMER HAS A variety of sounds unique to that season of the year—among them is the croak of the bullfrog. And one thing my grandchildren love to do is bullfrog catching. With flashlights, they go with their friends looking for them after dark along the creek area behind their house.

Their first experience at bullfrog catching was during a birthday party. The adventure started when they quietly followed what others call the *jug-o-rum* sound in the dark and then turned their flashlights toward the noise.

Oddly enough, bullfrogs will freeze in the light, stunned motionless.

Those moments of pause, though, were just long enough for my grandkids and their friends to grab the olive-green creatures with brown side splotches. They didn't hold the luncheon plate–size things very long—just long enough to say they had.

Just as light dazzles some animals, including bullfrogs, it dazzles—even stuns—me too. I squint when I step from a dark room right into sunlight. And for a moment, it's hard to find my way.

But just imagine what measure of brightness heavenly light will flash into my face when I step into God's kingdom! I will not need lamps or even the sun. There will be no confusion or frustration or humiliation. Just light and truth and the peace that the presence of the Lord will provide. What a stunning day of rejoicing that will be! Even more exciting than catching a bullfrog.

And the city has no need of sun or moon, for the glory of God illuminates the city, and the Lamb is its light. —Revelation 21:23 (NLT)

—Janet Holm McHenry

JUNE 18

In His Steps

Trust in the LORD with all your heart and lean not on your own understanding.

—PROVERBS 3:5 (NIV)

PRINTZ WAS AN adorable ball of fluffy, brilliant white fur. As a pup, he resembled a polar bear cub with lively black eyes. A Japanese spitz, Printz proved typical of the breed: personable and easy to train. He was also trusting. I remember the first time we took Printz to Ishikawa Beach in Okinawa. When his little paws sank into the deep sand, he locked his legs and looked up at us uncertainly. We moved ahead of him, coaxing him to follow. Reassured, Printz took small prancing steps until he felt safe enough to break into a clumsy run.

As we moved closer to the waves, he hesitated again. The sand felt firmer, but wet—another new sensation. Again, Printz looked up, as if asking for permission to move forward. We reassured him again, but paid close attention, not wanting him to get swept away in the undertow.

Looking back on that family outing, I can clearly see how I should be more like Printz. As I face new situations in life, it is in my best interest to turn to my heavenly Father for guidance and reassurance. Just as we watched over Printz's puppy steps, the Lord watches over me, urging me forward when it's safe to take the next step. It's when I don't look to Scripture for guidance, when I don't pray for wisdom and insight, that I'm more likely to get swept away into difficulties. God loves me. He loves you too. He wants the best for us. We can trust Him completely.

Never be afraid to trust an unknown future to a known God.
—Corrie Ten Boom

—Shirley Raye Redmond

JUNE 19

Harsh Condition Survival

Blessed is the one who perseveres under trial because, having stood the test, that person will receive the crown of life that the Lord has promised to those who love him.

—JAMES 1:12 (NIV)

VISITS TO MY in-laws' home always include fun sightings of the animals on neighboring farms. On the last trip, as we turned the corner to their home, we saw shaggy, long-haired cows grazing across the hill. Long horns protruded from underneath hair that nearly covered their eyes. We had never seen cows like them before. We later discovered they are Highland cattle, originally from the Scottish Highlands. This hardy breed is known for its high survival rate in harsh, wet, cold climates. It makes sense that Michigan farmers would choose such a tough breed!

I've often been tempted to believe that as I follow the Lord, life should be easy. Resentment can creep in when I scroll social media and see all the blessed posts when my life feels anything but blessed. Yet, as He has done for the Highland cattle, the Lord has provided everything I need to endure harsh trials. Not long ago, I suffered the betrayal and false accusations of a close friend. Some mornings, the pain was so deep I wasn't sure how I could breathe. Yet each day, the Lord provided His strength so I could persevere. He fought lies with truth from Scripture. He sent friends to remind me I was His beloved daughter. He provided peace as I prayed. Jesus promised that we would have hard times in this life. But He also promised that we can take heart because He has overcome the world.

Whatever harsh environment today brings, we can endure—just like the Highland cattle. Through Jesus Christ and His Holy Spirit, God has given us all we need to not just survive but even thrive.

For our present troubles are small and won't last very long. Yet they produce for us a glory that vastly outweighs them and will last forever!
—2 Corinthians 4:17 (NLT)

—Amelia Rhodes

JUNE 20

Peeking through the Window

My Father's house has many rooms; if that were not so, would I have told you that I am going there to prepare a place for you?

—JOHN 14:2 (NIV)

I ENTERED THE EMPTY house located beside a small pond. We would move in the next day, so I was doing a final walk-through. My wife and I were especially excited about the views of the pond through all the windows on one side of the house.

As I entered the living room, I noticed movement outside the window. A raccoon was standing on its hind legs peeking through the pane of glass—no doubt curious as to who was in this house that had stood vacant so long.

I inched closer. It saw me and scurried into the bushes. I noticed dozens of paw prints and nose smudges streaking the glass. Apparently, this wasn't the first time it had tried to inspect the interior of the house. I wondered how many visits the little fellow had made to make the window so dirty.

Grinning, I couldn't help but compare its curiosity to my own. How many homes had I, too, peered through the glass at as we shopped for the right place to live?

I wish I could do the same when curious about my heavenly home. God's Word tells us some of what to expect, but not everything. Much of what Christians will experience is still a mystery. Jesus said He was going to prepare a place for us. Is He finished yet? Still working on it? What will our final home look like?

If it were possible, I'm sure our prints would cover the window. One day, we will finally see home and see our Father face to face. Until then, let us live expectant, awaiting His return.

Father, as we toil on this earth, work our jobs, buy homes, and live our lives—remind us that we're only passing through. One day, Your children will see You face to face, and it's going to be glorious! Amen.

—Tez Brooks

JUNE 21

Letting Go Is Tough

I have told you these things, so that in me you may have peace. In this world you will have trouble. But take heart! I have overcome the world.

—JOHN 16:33 (NIV)

ONE DAY, WE were chasing butterflies in the meadow, and the next we were at the veterinarian hearing that Henry's organs were shutting down. He just stood and stared blankly at a spot on the floor. When a dog is very old, many people struggle with making a decision to ease the dog across the bridge without pain. We hold on tightly to the last days. We spend fortunes on anything that might buy us more last days.

I have counseled many people that a dog will tell you when it is ready to leave. My fuzzy little black dog, Henry, was waiting for me to tell him that it was okay for him to cross the rainbow bridge. I believe dogs often outlive their bodies because they are afraid to leave us alone. Some wait for us to get another dog to take over the job. And some wait until we let them know we will be all right if they leave. Neither is easy on the heart when we love a pet.

But when we know we are giving a gentle passing to our loyal friend, even in sadness, we find peace. In life we have many situations that are just plain painful. Loss. Regret. Change. And in every troubling instance, God reminds us that in even the darkest, most painful experiences, there is no pain He has not overcome. He shares that hope with us and never leaves us in our darkness. He is greater than any troubles we face.

God, please help me see light in this dark time, and remind me that there is nothing You cannot overcome as I go through this. Amen.

—Devon O'Day

JUNE 22

A Squirrel in the Bread Keeper

There is no fear in love. But perfect love drives out fear, because fear has to do with punishment. The one who fears is not made perfect in love.

—1 JOHN 4:18 (NIV)

I'VE ALWAYS THOUGHT squirrels are cute. I even admit to talking to them on occasion in the trees around my back deck. But I have had one run-in with a squirrel that was too close for comfort.

When I was a senior in college living in an apartment, I began to hear noises in the kitchen. One day, I finally went searching for the source. When I opened the cabinet door high up over the stove, I froze in horror as I came face-to-face with a furry creature inside our Tupperware bread keeper. When it suddenly moved, I slammed the doors shut and ran from the room screaming. I didn't stop until I had torn out the front door. I stood there squealing, fearing the animal had been about to attack.

My terrified elderly neighbor came hurrying out to check on me. Relieved that I wasn't harmed, she calmly told me it was probably a squirrel. But no way was I going to go back inside to look. I did what I had done every other time something scared me. I called my dad.

He came to investigate and had a good laugh at my overreaction. The squirrel had eaten its way inside our apartment through the top of the cabinet, had carved out a huge hole in our bread keeper, and had been happily chowing on the loaf of bread inside.

The event was funny after I realized the attack animal was a harmless squirrel caught snacking, but it was tough when I was in a moment of true fear. Just as I was grateful to my dad for helping me with my furry visitor, I'm also thankful I have a heavenly Father I can go to with even my smallest fears.

Walk of Faith: *Think of a fear that has stopped you from moving forward recently. Take that fear to God now, and let Him calm your fear.*

—Missy Tippens

JUNE 23

A Close Encounter

"Woe to me!" I cried. "I am ruined! For I am a man of unclean lips, and I live among a people of unclean lips, and my eyes have seen the King, the LORD Almighty."

—ISAIAH 6:5 (NIV)

I THOUGHT I LOVED cows.

My husband and I drove through farm country enjoying the view. Every pasture held a different variety of cattle. The day was warm and bright. The fields were green. And the distant cows brought me peace. Couldn't we get a little closer for a better view?

We found a pasture where the fence was near the road and the cows were grazing close enough for great photos. I drank in the pastoral scene. The black-and-white bovines stood close enough that I could distinguish one cow's pattern from the next. It was bliss, right up until the moment a cow I hadn't noticed grazing directly next to the car raised her head and, suddenly, we were nose to nose.

Old Bessie was as shocked as I was and bellowed a complaint right into my face! Her breath was hot, and if she had cared to, she might have licked my face. Instead of being thrilled, the close encounter rattled me. I felt terribly small beside the cow. Rather than imagining her a peaceful, docile creature, I now saw wild, enormous eyes, a speckled nose the size of my face, and shoulders that testified to weight that could crush me at will.

This is akin to how I feel when I come into the presence of the living God. If I keep God at a distance, I can imagine Him as peaceful and domesticated. A close encounter in His presence, however, reminds me that He is holy, majestic, and greater than I. I was safe with Bessie, and I'm safe with Him, but the nearer He is, the more I respect His power.

Walk of Faith: *When Isaiah saw God, he rightly realized God's magnificence and power. Likewise, when we come closer to Him, we may feel small, but remember this today: while God is never tame, He loves us, and we have nothing to fear in Christ.*

—Lori Stanley Roeleveld

JUNE 24

Fox Alert

Catch for us the foxes, the little foxes that ruin the vineyards, our vineyards that are in bloom.

—SONG OF SOLOMON 2:15 (NIV)

A RED FOX WALTZED across the backyard as my daughter Julie and I watched from the window, sipping our morning coffee. We had never seen a fox in person until our visit with my aunt in Connecticut. Smaller than we had imagined, the fox had upright triangular ears and an upturned snout. A long, bushy tail distinguished it from a neighbor's dog.

I was reminded of what Jesus said about foxes, how they have dens to sleep in, yet He had nowhere to lay His head. As we think of a den of pups, foxes can be endearing—but they are also a metaphor for caution. King Solomon had a vineyard in Israel requiring many keepers. As with other images in the Song of Solomon, foxes are symbolic. If blossoming vines represent the growing romance between Solomon and his bride-to-be, the foxes would be potential problems that could damage their relationship.

Foxes eat the grapes, not the flowers, and they must be driven out before the grapes are ripe. They gnaw branches, dig holes, and spoil vines and roots. The key is to protect the fruit.

My own little "foxes" are things like gossip that flies as chaff in the wind and hurts others and "small sins" of commission or omission. The enemy of my soul is cunning and may come as an angel of light, cute and charming, waltzing across the backyard of my life. I must watch out for his tactics and remember that, like Solomon's little foxes, he is a spoiler.

Julie and I watched the fox traipse out of my aunt's backyard, as slyly as it had come. We wondered if it knew we were eyeing it when it intruded into her manicured yard.

A little thorn may cause much suffering. A little cloud may hide the sun. Little foxes spoil the vines; and little sins do mischief to the tender heart.

—C.H. Spurgeon

—Kathleen Ruckman

JUNE 25

Lost Right Where I Left Her

Be still before the Lord *and wait patiently for him.*

—Psalm 37:7 (ESV)

I LOVE TO HIKE and always wanted a dog that would stay close in the woods around our home while having freedom to run and explore on its own. Bay, my small chocolate Lab, would do just that.

I trained Bay to heel, stay, lie down, stop, and come with both voice and hand signal commands. If anyone approached or I heard another animal, I wanted her to stop and stay even if she couldn't hear my voice. The training proved very important and probably saved her life on several occasions. We were as close as human and dog can be.

We had been hiking together for a few miles when it dawned on me that Bay wasn't nearby, and I hadn't seen her for several minutes. Even though we were in a wide-open national forest, it was unusual for us to break sight of each other. I immediately turned in my tracks and started searching.

I came upon a small rise, and there she was—sitting at attention and patiently waiting for me. Bay watched carefully for my command to come. Only then did I remember saying to her, "Sit, stay," while I listened to a birdcall. She was simply being trustingly, patiently, and lovingly obedient. How proud I was of her, and how embarrassed I was of me. I had forgotten my friend!

O Father, I prayed silently, *forgive me for not having the trust in You at times that Bay has in me.* He reminds me over and over in Scripture to trust in Him and wait patiently for Him. God has often revealed His love for me through this loyal, loving Labrador.

"Stand still"—keep the posture of an upright man, ready for action, expecting further orders, cheerfully and patiently awaiting the directing voice; and it will not be long ere God shall say to you, as distinctly as Moses said it to the people of Israel, "Go forward." —Charles Haddon Spurgeon

—Randy Benedetto

JUNE 26

Loving Devotion

Be strong and courageous. Do not be afraid or terrified because of them, for the Lord *your God goes with you; he will never leave you nor forsake you.*

—Deuteronomy 31:6 (NIV)

OUR FORMER NEIGHBORHOOD was mostly surrounded by woods, so we got to experience a lot of wildlife. Deer families were some of our favorite sightings. If we remained very still and quiet, we could watch them as they wandered through our yard, across the street, and into the neighbors' yards as they headed back into the heavily wooded areas.

One year in particular, I was touched by the devotion of one of the herds we got to watch. One of the fawns had either been born with a disability or been injured. It walked with a limp and was always slower than the rest. My heart hurt as I watched the fawn struggle to keep up. I feared that "nature" would take over, and the doe and other fawns would eventually leave it to its own devices. I feared it wouldn't survive.

But that never happened. The others would hurriedly cross the street, but then they would wait for the slower deer to catch up. Months went by, and the family always waited.

Oh, that I would be so loving and devoted! I fear that I might not be so patient, especially if I felt in danger, exposed, or at risk the way those deer must have felt.

Lord, please give us the courage to stand up for others. Give us the patience and desire to help others who are struggling or who aren't as fortunate. And Lord, thank You for those who have loved us enough to wait for us in times of difficulty. Please bless them for their devotion. Amen.

—Missy Tippens

JUNE 27

Taking Care of God's Creatures

In the same way, I tell you, there is rejoicing in the presence of the angels of God over one sinner who repents.

—LUKE 15:10 (NIV)

TERRY SCAMPERED INTO the room, wagging her tail. She had just returned from an outing with the dog walker and quickly realized I had come home from work. Jumping onto my lap, she repeatedly licked my face. I couldn't stop laughing.

A terrier mix, our dog loved to wrestle me for her toys. When she got down from my lap, she retrieved her plastic squeaky bear and offered me the other half. She pulled and refused to let go. I tugged and tried to get it from her, but she held fast. A few pretend growls didn't deter me. When I finally released my grip, she dropped the toy in front of me. Her expression seemed to say, "Why did you give up so easily?"

Imagine my dismay the very next afternoon as the dog walker texted me. "Terry slipped her collar and ran off. Searching now."

Worry built inside me, and I prayed for her safe return. Instead of going straight home, I searched the streets near our house. Up and down, Terry seemed to be nowhere to be found. Finally, I dejectedly headed home.

There on the front stoop, Terry sat, wagging her tail. She came back to where she knew she would find love. Soon, her dog walker joined us in front of the house. We hugged the dog and welcomed her home.

Our joy at seeing the pooch come home safely provided only a glimpse of the joy in heaven when a prodigal comes home to God. Angels rejoice when a previously lost person finds his or her way to the Savior. How beautiful to know our Father keeps watching, calling us home to Himself.

Are not two sparrows sold for a copper coin? And not one of them falls to the ground apart from your Father's will. —Matthew 10:29 (NKJV)

—David L. Winters

Fear and the Friendly Snake

For you did not receive the spirit of slavery to fall back into fear, but you have received the Spirit of adoption as sons, by whom we cry, "Abba! Father!"

—Romans 8:15 (ESV)

I HELD REX IN my hands and smiled at the boy in front of me. "Would you like to touch him?" The fear that tightened the child's features as he shook his head was familiar. I had seen the same expression on the faces of many zoo visitors when I showed them the Florida king snake.

The day I first volunteered at the zoo in the hands-on children's area, I had the same reaction when the zookeeper prompted me to touch the snake.

Remembering the fear that had held me back then, I told the boy what I had needed to hear. "He's not slimy or gross at all. Rex actually feels really smooth and cool. You'll be glad you touched him."

As this same scenario played out with a variety of visitors, I learned something about fear. It affects all kinds of people, all ages, male and female. Sometimes a big burly guy would back away from Rex. Other times, the little girls would be the first in their group to feel the snake's sleek, slightly bumpy scales.

The visitors who chose to walk away without petting Rex left with fear in control of their choices, limiting what they could do and experience in life. I said yes to petting Rex, and I'm glad I did. But how many other times do I say no to frightening things and walk away with fear still in control of my life?

Rex, the friendly snake, taught me that fear itself is more dangerous than the object of my fear. If I choose to follow Christ instead of fear, a life of freedom awaits.

He who has overcome his fears will truly be free. —Aristotle

—Jerusha Agen

JUNE 29

Cry of the Loon

When I consider your heavens, the work of your fingers, the moon and the stars, which you have set in place, what is mankind that you are mindful of them, human beings that you care for them?

—PSALM 8:3–4 (NIV)

THERE IS NOTHING like the cry of a loon to remind someone that he or she is a Minnesotan. I am blessed to live with a park in my backyard, and that park includes a lake. My dogs and I walk around this lake most mornings at a time when the loons call one another. Along with the call of the loons, we hear the screech of red-winged blackbirds, the chatter of chickadees, the knock of woodpeckers enjoying breakfast, and the hoot of the occasional owl. It is the most glorious symphony of sounds.

Some people walk in the park with their earbuds in or while constantly checking their phones, but not me. I don't want to miss out on the free concert. When I was younger, I took for granted all the beautiful sounds of nature. But no longer. Now it is a marvel to me how God created not only one bird species but hundreds, probably thousands, each with its own special characteristics. Birdsong sounds to me like a great praise fest to God's majesty.

I may not sing like a bird, but as I listen to the chirps around me, I silently praise the One who created it all and gave me the awesome ability to hear and respond. And I realize that my response should be—like nature—a reflection of God's goodness.

Heavenly Father, Creator of All, the birds have their songs, the stars mirror Your brilliance, the ocean waves pound out Your perfect rhythm. May I reflect even a smidgen of Your love to others in my orbit as praise to You. Amen.

—Linda Bartlett

JUNE 30

Saying Goodbye to Jessi

But you, God, see the trouble of the afflicted; you consider their grief and take it in hand. The victims commit themselves to you; you are the helper of the fatherless.

—PSALM 10:14 (NIV)

JESSI WAS A street dog that found her way to me. Out of all the people she could have chosen, she chose me, and it seemed she could look right into my soul. Some nights were hard as I walked through valleys of pain that I could tell no one about, but Jessi was right there. Putting her head under my hand to divert my attention from my own troubles to her beautiful brown eyes was sometimes the only thing that tethered me to this world.

When I found the courage to leave an awful living situation, I had nowhere to take Jessi, so I asked a dear friend if he could keep her temporarily. Having a safe place for pets is often the catalyst for leaving an abusive home. Steve loved Jessi and treated her like the queen she was. As I started over in my new life, so did Jessi. Though it was meant to be temporary, I soon realized that she was in the perfect home for her. Steve cooked for her every night, and I was always able to visit.

Age was taking its toll, so Steve and I met at his house and held on to the old dog that shared our hearts. Her breathing was labored as she began to transition. We told her how we appreciated her and gave her permission to fly. As the hospice meds from the vet took her into an easier place of passage, we encircled her with love. There is grief in all powerful passages, but gratitude for the gift is the best way to start healing. Jessi was sent as many fur angels are, and in her passing, I know she was telling me I was now safe to move on.

Lord, thank You for sending the perfect angel to help me move from the hard place where I had imprisoned myself. Heal the empty place where she has been. Amen.

—Devon O'Day

July

JULY 1

Mercy in the Morning

The steadfast love of the Lord never ceases; his mercies never come to an end; they are new every morning; great is your faithfulness.

—Lamentations 3:22–23 (ESV)

I BELIEVE THAT MY dogs destroy my favorite possessions out of revenge. I know, I know. Dogs cannot possibly understand what they do. Or do they?

Case in point: my first boxer, McKenzie, decapitated a vintage Raggedy Ann doll that once belonged to my grandmother. My fifteen-minute trip to get milk gave him enough time to remove the doll's red-haired head and toss stuffing everywhere.

Our current boxer, Rocky, gleefully rips book covers, chewing them to pulp. He destroyed my favorite journaling devotional. He knocked my *Pioneer Woman Cooks* cookbook from the counter and gnawed on it. I bought a new one, and he did it again. Does he still smell the roast beef left on the pages? Today, I walked into the living room to discover him chewing on an envelope he stole from my backpack.

These dogs want attention. McKenzie wanted to go for a ride. Rocky wants more water in his bowl and hates getting dinner late, even when it is three hours before the appropriate time. Those big eyes look innocent, but is this how my own face looked when, as a child, I misbehaved for attention?

Even when I have been defiant, my Father keeps loving me. Scripture promises that the mercy of the Lord never comes to an end. God's forgiveness and grace never cease to amaze me. The same is true with my dogs. Mercy arrives when I clean away the evidence, sit down on the couch, and feel my dog get up to snuggle next to me. How can I resist? I will forgive over and over again for the one I love.

Lord, Your mercy is vast and incomprehensible. My human heart wants to compare my sins to the sins of others, but You look at them all the same. As the sun rises every day, You forgive me and welcome me back to Your side. Amen.

—Twila Bennett

JULY 2

Cheesecake

If it is possible, as far as it depends on you, live at peace with everyone.

—Romans 12:18 (NIV)

THE CAPYBARA, A four-foot-long rodent from South America, is known for being friendly and easy to tame. After visiting Brazil recently on a mission trip, I learned of an animal rehab and recovery farm that cares for a capybara named Cheesecake.

Cheesecake is known for being unusually kind and gentle to any human or animal she encounters. Her friends include a crane, a zebra, a wallaby, a buffalo, a tortoise, and a hare—she mingles with them harmoniously, regardless of the species. She accommodates any new animal that comes to the farm.

When I meet people who are different from me, I'm not always eager to become instant chums. My caution doesn't come from prejudice or ignorance but from insecurity and fear of rejection. It takes time for me to trust them, appreciate their uniqueness, and see if they desire a reciprocal relationship.

When I first met my neighbor from Russia, I was skeptical of getting past mere pleasantries. What if we couldn't relate?

I took a chance and made a point of engaging beyond discussing the weather. Soon, we were sharing dinners and dog sitting for each other. We are now trusted friends, and I've learned about his culture and beliefs. He's even attended church with me.

I don't know yet where our relationship may lead. But what might I have missed out on had I followed my instincts and never introduced myself?

Much like little Cheesecake, I was willing to embrace the uncomfortable, which led to blessing. Welcoming those different from us enriches our lives and provides opportunity to learn, grow, and show the love of God to others.

Walk of Faith: *Who is God challenging you to interact with today? Start small, and invite that person to join you for dessert this week. Maybe cheesecake . . . ?*

—Tez Brooks

JULY 3

Hidden Things

Nothing in all creation is hidden from God's sight. Everything is uncovered and laid bare before the eyes of him to whom we must give account.

—HEBREWS 4:13 (NIV)

EVERY YEAR, MY family and I go to our local county fair, and one of our favorite attractions to visit is the Great American Petting Zoo. This educational cage-free zoo has a variety of common farm animals wandering about but also includes some more exotic animals such as Bennett's wallabies. These small members of the kangaroo family have dark expressive eyes and plush fur that invites petting. And without fail, when we visit the zoo, we pet the wallabies, ask the keepers how they're doing, take photos, and promise to return.

One year was different, though. A wallaby was in a small enclosure rather than hopping around with the other animals. We asked why and were told she had a joey hidden in her pouch. Imagine our surprise and delight when the baby wallaby popped its head out of Mama's pouch! What had been hidden was hidden no more.

This made me think about how nothing in my life is hidden from God. Everything I've done will be uncovered and laid bare. I can't conceal anything from Him. This is both mortifying and comforting. Mortifying because I'm imperfect and sinful and God sees it all. Comforting because though God sees it all, He loves me anyway. In fact, He took my sin and nailed it to the cross with His Son, Jesus. The joey's appearance surprised me, but I don't need to be afraid that any hidden thing will pop out to separate me from my salvation. When it comes time to "give account," Jesus has already taken care of that for me. Praise be to God!

Leave the broken, irreversible past in God's hands, and step out into the invincible future with Him. —Oswald Chambers

—Marianne Campbell

JULY 4

The Seal of Freedom

It is for freedom that Christ has set us free. Stand firm, then, and do not let yourselves be burdened again by a yoke of slavery.

—GALATIANS 5:1 (NIV)

FOR MY THIRTY-EIGHTH birthday celebration, my husband took me and my sons to Cape Cod. Our first stop was the expansive beach of Cape Cod National Seashore. We walked along the sand, collecting rocks.

"Look! A seal!" My husband pointed into the crystalline water.

My heart sang as I spotted the dark creature bobbing at the surface, even as I wondered if the form wasn't really someone's dog out for a swim. But as we walked closer, we saw the enormous sleek body, the very seal-like head. We followed it along for a good while. It came closer and even stuck its head up from the surface, staring at me.

Now, I've been to SeaWorld in Orlando, Florida. I've been to Mystic Aquarium in Connecticut. I've *seen* seals. But never like this, out in the open ocean, dipping beneath the water, then coming up to observe the humans intent on watching their every move. To me, the experience was almost magical. This seal was free. It didn't have to stay and let us observe. It wasn't lured by food or stuck behind a glass tank. And yet it chose to come.

I sometimes wonder why God doesn't make people turn to Him. Why the Lord of the universe doesn't demand glory. And here, with this seal, I understood. He gives us our freedom—not only in freeing us from the shackle of sin, but also in giving us free will. How much more precious when we choose to abide in Him? I am confident that the same beauty I witnessed in sharing a moment with this gray seal will be a hundredfold on the day I see His face.

Lord, thank You for freeing us from the burden of our sin. May we come to You with open hearts and empty hands. May we abide in You alone. In Jesus's name. Amen.

—Heidi Chiavaroli

JULY 5

The Hard Goodbye

"For I know the plans I have for you," declares the LORD, "plans to prosper you and not to harm you, plans to give you hope and a future."

—JEREMIAH 29:11 (NIV)

A FEW SUMMERS AGO, our kids asked if we could raise baby chicks. Truth be told, I had wanted chickens for a while. The problem was, we lived in a neighborhood that had a no-chicken policy. We knew it would be difficult to convince our neighborhood homeowners' association to change the policy, but we decided to give it a try.

We explained our plan to the kids. We would go ahead and get chicks, but we had to convince the homeowners' association to let us keep them before they were big enough to move outside. If we weren't successful, at eight weeks old they would go to live in the country with a friend.

The kids were on board, and a couple of days later we picked up four adorable one-day-old chicks. Of course, it didn't take eight weeks to fall in love with chickens. By day one, we were all in. We held them constantly, letting them sleep on us while we read books or watched movies at night. We learned their individual personalities, each of us bonding with one of them. We watched them explore the outdoors for the first time, get their first bug, and then come to snuggle up and rest on our laps. Every night, the kids prayed we would be able to keep our chicks.

Sadly, however, after eight weeks of petitioning and pleading, our HOA was unmoved. We had to say goodbye. There were so many tears.

What we didn't know was that by closing this door, God would open our eyes to an opportunity He had for us that we otherwise would have missed. He said no to our prayers because He had something better in mind. A few months later, we moved out to a homestead where our family thrived . . . alongside a whole flock of chickens.

Thank You, Lord, that Your ways are higher than ours. Thank You that we can trust Your plans for us and that we can have peace, knowing You are in control. Amen.

—Joy Pitner

JULY 6

Pecked by Problems

That is why, for Christ's sake, I delight in weaknesses, in insults, in hardships, in persecutions, in difficulties. For when I am weak, then I am strong.

—2 CORINTHIANS 12:10 (NIV)

I HAD A POWERFUL cat named Tarzan. Snow white and sleek, he was fearless. He dozed in the dappled sunlight under a big oak, and the blue jays and other birds gave our yard a wide berth. Then Tarzan had an accident. A car hit him and broke his leg. When it healed, nerve damage left him lame. He couldn't run or hunt as he had before. Now, more than ever, he wanted to relax in the sunshine.

The blue jays saw he was wounded. They came back and began pecking at him. For a few days, I kept rushing out to shoo them away. But Tarzan didn't panic. He walked around the yard, dragging his lame leg until the blue jays came closer. Then he leaned back on his good leg, leaped up, and caught one. Blue feathers flew, and soon, Tarzan napped contentedly under the tree.

How often do I blame setbacks for keeping me from living the life that I desire? When I see Tarzan keeping the blue jays at bay, I remember that everything that happens can be used for good. Yes, others may torment me, and old ways of coping may not work anymore. My strength will fail. But my weaknesses offer opportunities to draw closer to God, who will provide new understanding and new ways to deal with the incessant pecking of life's challenges.

Dear Creator, life knocks me down in so many ways. Problems arise just when I feel the least able to cope. But when I am weak, You are strong. When I feel damaged, help me trust that You will reveal a path forward that brings me closer to You. Grant me strength to face each day just as I am and grace to bask in the warmth of Your love. Amen.

—Lucy H. Chambers

JULY 7

Gliding toward Our Father

The eternal God is your refuge, and underneath are the everlasting arms.

—DEUTERONOMY 33:27 (NIV)

THE TINY CREATURE was like nothing I had ever seen before. Part flying squirrel, part cuddly koala, part bat, it scurried into the pocket of its owner, who had presented it to my family and me at a local fair.

A moment later, the little animal poked its head from the man's pocket, climbed on the fingers of its owner, and peered at us in an incredibly personable fashion.

"Do you want to hold it?" the man asked.

I held out my hands, unwilling to turn down the opportunity to hold the sugar glider. The soft possum burrowed beneath my fingers, its tail hanging down as I held it against my body, fearful I would drop it.

I shouldn't have worried, for the next moment, it peered over my fingers, searching for its owner. Before I could stop it, the sugar glider jumped from my palms, spread its arms and legs open, and glided effortlessly to the waiting arms of its "father," who was more than three feet away.

I marveled at the fearlessness of this small creature. Yes, the gliding possum knew its capabilities in jumping, but it also knew something else: its caretaker was there to catch it.

For a tiny moment, I envied the wide-eyed marsupial. It was so obviously confident of its position with its owner that it knew where it belonged and where it wanted to be.

How often do I hesitate when coming to my heavenly Father? How often do I look for something or someone else to satisfy my deepest longings? How often do I stand, trembling at the edge, instead of jumping into His waiting arms?

This is faith. This is trust. As simple—and as complicated—as the jump of a sugar glider, lunging into the waiting arms of a loving father.

Lord, You are waiting with open, loving arms. May I not hesitate to jump into Your lavish love and grace. Amen.

—Heidi Chiavaroli

Millions of Blessings

Give, and it will be given to you. A good measure, pressed down, shaken together and running over, will be poured into your lap. For with the measure you use, it will be measured to you.

—LUKE 6:38 (NIV)

WHEN MY KIDS were little, one of their favorite books was *Millions of Cats*. Being a cat lover, I never minded reading it again. But recently, when I saw a local news report, my heart broke. Four hundred cats had been discovered on a woman's property. She had tried to care for the kitties by herself until she was hospitalized. I watched in sadness as disease-ridden and starving cats roamed the rural yard.

Some blamed the woman for hoarding felines and allowing them to breed. But one of the woman's relatives cradled a calico kitty and begged for donations of cat food and medicine. Still, I fretted. I sent in a small sum, but it felt like a drop in a very big bucket. Surely, God wouldn't abandon these innocent creatures?

A few weeks later, I was watching my young grandchildren when a follow-up report announced that several organizations had come to the kitties' rescue. The same relative held a bright-eyed ginger tabby, thanked those who had offered help, and vowed to find homes for all four hundred cats. My three-year-old granddaughter pointed to the TV. "I like that one and that one and that one!" Her older brother added, "Can we get some?"

I hugged them and smiled, knowing my own weakness for strays. "Maybe," I answered. I couldn't help thinking that whenever I feel my life's problems spiraling out of control, God always helps me find a way out. Instead of leaving me with four hundred problems to solve, God can turn a bunch of troubles into hundreds of little blessings—including the two blessings sitting next to me. I switched off the TV and pulled out our dog-eared copy of *Millions of Cats*.

He who feeds a hungry animal feeds his own soul. —Charlie Chaplin

—Linda S. Clare

When a Rascal Dies

In his hand is the life of every creature and the breath of all mankind.

—JOB 12:10 (NIV)

RASCAL'S SEND-OFF WAS more poignant than her final years might have warranted. The last, lingering pet of our children's childhood, the Siamese hadn't endeared herself to me in old age. Suffering from feline dementia, she exhibited a persistent disdain for her litter box.

Rascal was my daughter's beloved companion for years. She was a scamp who stole socks from the laundry and delivered them to Hannah's bedside, a vocal feline taken to late-night caterwauling, and an attention-deficit mouser—often cornering a mouse and then abandoning it in a flash of boredom.

But while my daughter had grown and moved, Rascal seemed intent on setting an endurance record for living. I might have been relieved to see her go, but instead, my husband, Rob, and I stood weeping in the exam room as the vet prepared the needle.

We had only just come from the hospital where Rob received an unexpected, life-altering diagnosis. In those moments, cradling our last living attachment to our children's childhood, the enormity of life and death made the room a holy sanctuary.

"You've been a good, old, faithful friend, Rascal. We forgive you for the last couple of years, old girl."

"You brought us joy, you silly cat."

Rob looked at me through tears, "With what's ahead of us, I can't help thinking about the day you all say goodbye to me."

"It's not here yet. Today is not your time."

We held her as she breathed her last. How powerful, that moment bridging life and death. Only a gasp and yet so significant, even the passing of a house cat can have lasting impact. Rascal's final gift was a reminder that every life has holy value.

Dear God, You blessed all the life You created and called it good. It's easy for me to take it for granted, but when I remember Rascal, I think about her final moments when life left her and thank You for the hope of eternity. Amen.

—Lori Stanley Roeleveld

Libby Came Around

Turn, LORD, and deliver me; save me because of your unfailing love.

—PSALM 6:4 (NIV)

THE RESCUE DELIVERED Libby to me in a carrier and warned me to be careful when I let her go. She was a Snip and Tip (a trap, neuter, and release program) feral cat, and I was giving her a farm to live on rather than the danger of inner-city streets.

Libby had issues. She had fended for herself in a cruel, cold world. There was no way to imagine the hard things she had experienced. But it was evident that trust was something she was not going to give easily. I fed her and talked to her every day. Though she ate with ferocity, she ran from me anytime I got within several feet from her.

Then one night as I was feeding the horses over the fence, I felt a kitty rubbing against my shoulder. I could hear the purr. I turned, expecting it to be one of the more docile cats that resided at the farm. But it was Libby. She kept talking to me as she purred and continued to rub against me. I raised my hand, and she put her head against it. And this time, she didn't run. It had been a year of constant trying to tame her and get her to trust—and a year of disappointment.

But without trying, love had suddenly won. That's how love works. We can't make someone respond to kindness or care, but it matters that we do it. It matters that we don't give up. And one day, all that consistent love might just move a mountain in someone's heart.

Dear God, give me a heart big enough to keep loving when the loving isn't easy. Amen.

—Devon O'Day

JULY 11

Attuned to Him

My sheep listen to my voice; I know them, and they follow me.

—JOHN 10:27 (NIV)

MY COCKER SPANIEL, Schroeder, has unbelievable intuition. If I stub my toe, he comes from the other side of the house to be by my side in seconds. On one particular night a few years ago, I fell in the garage and broke my foot. Schroeder was there beside me, his little paws on my shoulders, even before I realized how badly I had hurt myself. He's a little shadow, always responding to where I'm going and what I'm doing. He stays in my presence because he desires to be with me.

Every night when the rest of the house is quiet with sleep, Schroeder follows me to the refrigerator where I get a glass of water before bed. Even if he has been sleeping, he doesn't hesitate to rise and come with me. He doesn't deliberate, as I would in his position, whether the occasion is worth the effort or if he'll get a treat out of it. When I move, he responds. He simply comes and sits beside me. He's actually sitting beside me even as I write this devotion.

Rise and come. I believe God desires this refrain, this response, from all of us. When I trust that He loves me, responding to His voice becomes a natural thing. I stay when He lingers and come when He tells me to follow. I don't have to work hard to figure out His plans as if they were a riddle. I can allow my own plans to be flexible and attuned to the moments He rises and tells me to come along—whether that means encouraging a stranger or taking steps that mean sacrifice toward even bigger dreams.

Walk of Faith: *In what areas of my life have I tried to force my own plans rather than listening intentionally to the ways God is already speaking? How can I train my heart to respond throughout the day as He leads, even if it may be inconvenient for my own schedule?*

—Ashley Clark

JULY 12

No Mistakes

For You formed my inward parts.

—PSALM 139:13 (NKJV)

IT HAD BEEN a rough season for my husband, Terry, recovering from serious surgery, and for me as his caregiver. My prayers had been for my dear husband to fully recover. I needed assurance from God that He heard my prayers.

Knowing I needed a treat, Terry had reserved an hour for me on Beau, my favorite horse at the local riding stable. This was to be followed by a mani-pedi at my favorite salon.

After my ride, I reported to the nail salon. Joan, a dear friend, was standing at the front desk paying for her manicure. She turned and greeted me, "So how was he this morning?" With my mind still on Beau, the horse I had just ridden, I responded with, "Well, he was ornery this morning. When I greeted him, he bared his big pearly whites at me, snorted loudly, and stomped his foot!"

Joan gripped her throat and whispered, "Oh, dear." The pitiful look on her face told me she was picturing my husband being guilty of that behavior and not Beau the horse. After we each recovered from tear-filled laughter and I reassured her that hubby Terry was fine, I pondered, *Am I making my prayers clear to God?*

Suddenly, a rush of words came, like a whisper: *All clear here. I know your needs even before you ask. I answer your prayers in My perfect time.*

I had my answer.

My favorite horse, Beau, ornery as he had been, had not only given me the joy of a morning ride but provided a vehicle for laughter and, ultimately, reassurance from God.

Walk of Faith: *You can be at peace that God, being holy and perfect, knows your prayers as yours alone. He will answer them, from His heart directly to yours, in His complete, beautiful, and sometimes unusual ways.*

—Sandra Clifton

JULY 13

Bee Strong

The grass withers and the flowers fall, but the word of our God endures forever.

—ISAIAH 40:8 (NIV)

MY SON BRIAN volunteered at a nature center's wildlife rehab facility and often came home with fascinating stories. One day, he accompanied a beekeeper who came to inspect and medicate the center's hives. Honeybees are susceptible to an array of parasites and diseases that can wipe out entire colonies, but how do you medicate insects? In my wild imagination, I pictured rows of the tiny creatures lined up, each waiting openmouthed for a dose of medicine.

In reality, Brian and the keeper spread medicated powder along the openings to the hives. As the bees entered, the powder stuck to their legs and wings. Being tidy insects, they cleaned themselves, ingesting the medication that would protect them.

As I walk closely with God, Satan tries to lure me away. Like the bees, I need protection. How can I bolster my spiritual immunity? By ingesting the Word of God, I find strength for the battle. Too often, I skim through a passage without internalizing what I read. When I slow down and meditate on the words, I absorb God's wisdom, which fortifies me and safeguards my heart to keep me close to Him. Renewed, I can face another day's challenges.

As a child, I watched honeybees flit from flower to flower in my front yard. Not anymore. They have all but disappeared from the wild. But beekeepers work tirelessly to protect and perpetuate the species. Bees may not open their mouths for medication, but I can open my heart to the Bible. I, too, find powerful protection from the world's dangers by taking my daily dose of God's potent Word.

Thank You, Lord, for Your enduring Word, a defense against discouragement, a comfort during sadness, and wisdom in times of indecision. I can be strong because You have shown me the path to follow and bestowed promises of life eternal. Amen.

—Tracy Crump

JULY 14

Brother to the Rescue

No one has ever seen God; but if we love one another, God lives in us and his love is made complete in us.

—1 JOHN 4:12 (NIV)

WHEN MY SISTER'S husband was terminally ill several years ago, she needed help transitioning into town from their country home of almost forty years. Bob's passing came relatively quickly, and Mari found herself overwhelmed with the tasks of preparing the country home for sale. Enter our brother David, an Arizona transplant, cowboy hat, boots, and all. He planned to come for a month to help clear out years of collected clutter but fell in love with the property and became its new owner!

David escapes the Southwest heat every summer, driving the seventeen hundred miles to Minnesota, where he continues to make numerous improvements to his home. One day, he noticed a hungry stray cat that appeared to be pregnant. She watched him warily and kept her distance.

He soon earned her trust and affection, as each day he set out food and water for her. She followed him around the property as he worked, hiding as soon as visitors came. When the kittens arrived, they were tucked safely under brush and broken window frames angled against the home's foundation. We tried our best to behold their cuteness without disturbing their nest.

When the babies were old enough, David called a pet rescue organization, and two women took the family into town. After making sure the cats were healthy, they found homes for them all, even the mama cat.

I am inspired by my brother's tender heart. I may not be able to move across the country as he did when he saw a need arise. But if my eyes are fixed on Jesus, He will show me who I can help and how I can be a blessing to the people I meet in my own neighborhood.

Father, I want to reflect Your heart that cherishes and nourishes others. Make me aware of opportunities before me where I can reflect Your nature and become more like You. Amen.

—Liz Kimmel

JULY 15

Praying for a Llama

Is anyone among you sick? Let them call the elders of the church to pray over them and anoint them with oil in the name of the Lord.

—JAMES 5:14 (NIV)

FOR MORE THAN twelve years, Rojo the llama served God by spreading joy whenever he went to schools, assisted-living communities, children's hospitals, and facilities for children and adults with disabilities. After enjoying over a decade of ministry throughout the Portland, Oregon, and Vancouver, Washington, area, the certified therapy llama retired. A few weeks later, my friend Becky, a volunteer at the Mtn Peaks Therapy Llamas and Alpacas, informed me that Rojo needed medical treatment and prayer. A prayer chain for a llama? Absolutely!

God's people quickly responded. I read through a few of the comments, then added my prayers on behalf of the adorable llama. Though I expected the prayer response would bless Rojo and his family, I never dreamed God would use the process to deepen my faith as I suffered another setback in my healing journey.

I had recently stopped asking for prayer, afraid of becoming a burden. I trusted God to continue working in and through my healing journey. But I had forgotten how He used intercessory prayer to refresh my spirit and breathe hope into the moments I feel most alone.

James the apostle invites believers to pray by faith and to welcome others to come alongside us with bold prayers. As believers care for one another, God strengthens our resolve and emboldens our testimony.

Like Rojo, I know people who are willing to pray for me when I'm weak and weary. Seeing the outpouring of loving prayers for this sweet llama affirmed that a prayer request blesses the one who prays and the one who asks for prayer. Rojo reminded me that prayer support is a priceless gift.

Lord, please give us courage to ask for prayer and confidence to pray for others with unshakable faith. In Jesus's name. Amen.

—Xochitl E. Dixon

JULY 16

Here Kitty, Kitty

As the Father has loved me, so have I loved you. Now remain in my love.

—JOHN 15:9 (NIV)

I'VE BEEN A dog person my whole life. In fact, almost the very first thing my husband and I did years ago when we were newlyweds was to adopt a terrier mix we named Lady.

Since then, at least one dog and usually two live in our family. At times, the number of dogs climbs up to five when we babysit our "grand-puppies" for our three adult daughters. But we never considered owning a cat. I have allergies, and I didn't believe I had the right personality to enjoy a cat.

So I think it surprised everyone when, a couple of months ago, we adopted a pair of American shorthair teenage male kitties that were nearly identical black-and-white "tuxedo" brothers.

There's definitely been a learning curve. While our dogs sit patiently hoping for a table scrap, the cats fly by at Mach 3, grabbing chicken off my salad on the run and hoping I *don't* notice. The dogs always want to snuggle. Cats? Not so much. But when they do decide to grace me with their presence, there's something heartwarming about having one of them curl up on my chest, rubbing my chin with his engine purring.

Dogs and cats show love in different ways, and people do too. For some, love may be physical, with lots of hugs and touch. For others, a genuine smile will do. And for others, love is best shown through words. It's up to us to recognize and respect that each individual's love language may be different.

God's love, too, is often shown in different ways, from the beauty of His creation to the unique way He's made dogs and cats and to the ultimate sacrifice of love when Jesus gave His life for us.

Lord, help me to recognize the different love languages in which Your people speak. And let me also acknowledge the many ways You show Your love to me and others and be grateful. Amen.

—Deb Kastner

JULY 17

Maggie's Cagey Makeover

The Lord is my helper; I will not be afraid. What can mere mortals do to me?

—HEBREWS 13:6 (NIV)

WHEN HER HAMSTER, Maggie, gets a little stinky, my "grandgem" Sidney knows it's time—past time—to clean out her cage. Sidney dreads the deed. But Maggie cannot do it herself, so Sidney must.

She sets to work and cleans the hamster house: sponging down the exercise wheel and tube, laying out new bedding, and filling Maggie's bowls with fresh food and water. Soon the place sparkles and smells sweet. Sidney's heart lifts as she watches her happy hamster root through the fragrant bedding, sniff and sip her fresh water, and roll around in her food. In fact, Maggie practically dances with delight.

After one such cage cleaning, I asked Sidney if she enjoyed the task.

"Not much," she said. "But when I see how happy Maggie is after all my work, I'm happy too. Because I love her."

I'm reminded of how often I find myself in a mess, even one of my own making. I have no idea how to solve the problem. But then my good Father comes to the rescue, cleaning up what I cannot. And in the doing, He gives me a fresh, new start.

God uses rescued people to rescue people. —Christine Caine

—Cathy Elliott

Stuck

Evildoers are snared by their own sin, but the righteous shout for joy and are glad.

—PROVERBS 29:6 (NIV)

THE SMELL OF a skunk is unmistakable. When I was a child, we would often smell the striped fellows as they prowled the marshes around our house hunting for food. Our garden was usually the target of their late-night raids.

One hot July night, we not only smelled a stinky fellow but heard it—ripping down the cornstalks in our garden. "We'll just have to wait 'til morning to see what's left," my dad said with a shake of his head.

The next morning, we discovered our corn-eating bandit stuck like a cork in a bottle under the fence between our yard and the neighbor's. In Winnie-the-Pooh fashion, its gluttonous feast had expanded its belly so much it couldn't escape.

I don't know how many times I've been trapped, like that engorged skunk, by the effects of my cravings. A desire for affirmation, power, prestige, money, love, respect, or possessions isn't wrong, just like food to fill a hungry skunk's belly isn't wrong. But while these things fill me up temporarily, they can never truly satisfy me. Only my relationship with God can.

When I attempt to satisfy my cravings with the things of this world, I become trapped. When I feast on the things the Lord has for me, I experience freedom. I can sing and be glad.

Thank You, Father, for the freedom and deep satisfaction I can find in Jesus. Amen.

—Lori Hatcher

JULY 19

Well Done!

His master replied, "Well done, good and faithful servant! You have been faithful with a few things; I will put you in charge of many things. Come and share your master's happiness!"

—MATTHEW 25:21 (NIV)

I LEANED OVER AND patted my two-year-old golden retriever, Petey. "Goood booooy," I said, drawing out the *o*'s. I say this often. It makes us both happy. My preschool granddaughters even copy my intonation when they say, "Goood boooy."

Recently, people posted photos on Facebook of their dogs, just before and just after being called "Good boy." Big dogs, little dogs, fluffy dogs, all manner of dogs, each posing for the camera. In the before photos, the dogs' ears are flat, their heads down, and they often looked disengaged. But after the words of praise, their ears are perked, their chins are lifted, and their eyes are wide. And best of all, they actually appear to be smiling. Clearly, the praise has a positive effect.

I wondered, what would it look like if there were photographs of us just before and after being told we had done a good job? I imagine that our expressions would change from those of boredom, apathy, or discouragement to those of joy. Our eyes would widen, furrowed brows would soften, and we would smile. Thinking about this makes me want to encourage others. Everyone loves to receive approval and praise.

Of course, there is no greater praise than what we will hear on the judgment day. Ultimately, how our faces will shine when one day we're told, "Well done, good and faithful servant."

Oh! the sweet rest prepared for the faithful,
will be His blest and final "Well done." —Lucie Eddie Campbell

—Peggy Frezon

JULY 20

The Runaway

But they will never follow a stranger; in fact, they will run away from him because they do not recognize a stranger's voice.

—JOHN 10:5

HAVE YOU EVER had a dog that was not food driven? What that means is that the word *treat*, which would make any other dog sit, roll over, or fetch, does nothing. I have one dog that couldn't care less about a bowl of food in front of him if he wants to play. His chasing games are his kryptonite, his hardest quality to live with. No trainer has been able to teach him differently because he has absolutely no interest in treats.

My runaway is a brown mutt that just showed up one day. He was hungry and needed care, but he would not come to any food I offered. He would move toward me yet run away any time I lifted my hand with food. The interesting thing about dogs is you must search for their motivator. If not food, then what?

I sat down and softly began speaking to this puppy, and he got closer and closer till soon he was cuddled in my arms. His motivator . . . was my voice.

How many times have we been in a dark moment and that soft voice of God wooed and beckoned until we felt peace? It's unexplainable. While others around us are motivated by money or position, we find no peace in those motivators. Our true peace comes from time spent in the comfort of God's company.

Instead of trying to fit into the world's template, I have decided to relish my time in the quiet as God sings over me. I do not have to justify my motivators to the world, but as I walk in God's peace, I have found that the world is drawn to it, wanting to know more.

Dear God, I hear Your sweet voice. Guide me gently into the life You have prepared for me. Amen.

—Devon O'Day

JULY 21

The Pelicans Still Remind Me

But God demonstrates his own love for us in this:
While we were still sinners, Christ died for us.

—ROMANS 5:8 (NIV)

W*RITE ABOUT THE pelicans,* I noted in my travel journal. While in Edinburgh, my friend Julie and I had told our Airbnb host about the pelicans we had seen in London's St. James's Park the week before. Our host shared an interesting "fact"—that during famines, mother pelicans would pierce their breast and feed their chicks with the blood. What a perfect illustration for Jesus's sacrifice for us. I couldn't wait to write about it.

But when I researched the details, I discovered that the story about mother pelicans was a myth. The belief that they pierced themselves for the sake of their young had become such a common symbol of Christ's sacrifice that pelicans appeared in Christian art and even an early edition of the Bible, but in reality, they were no more sacrificial than any other bird.

Though I wasn't shocked, I felt a wave of disappointment. Until I recalled one of the pelicans I had seen and realized they can still remind me of Jesus. Pelicans may not be selfless enough to sacrifice blood for their children, but He was. Their image in Christian art may be based on a made-up story that started who knows where, but the story of Jesus is true.

As a parent, I am willing to give up a lot for my sons, but I will never be able to provide what Jesus can give them. The more comparisons I came up with, the more thankful I was that God allowed me to hear about that pelican myth; it prompted me to think about my Savior and all He endured so we could be His children.

This is love: not that we loved God, but that he loved us and sent his Son as an atoning sacrifice for our sins. —1 John 4:10 (NIV)

—Jeanette Hanscome

JULY 22

The Masterpiece

Every good gift and every perfect gift is from above, and comes down from the Father of lights, with whom there is no variation or shadow of turning.

—JAMES 1:17 (NKJV)

I HAD BEEN SITTING at my computer for more than two hours, just staring at the screen. I was hoping for some inspiration for a book-cover design that was due the next day. I had been praying for an idea to drop into my mind's view. I had even looked up current covers on the market to jump-start an idea. Nothing. Was my greatest fear—that I was creatively bankrupt—becoming real? What would I do for income if this had finally happened? I was not getting any younger. Panic had reared its ugly head and immobilized me.

I knew I needed to break this mental monologue of fear and went out to our small backyard garden. I prayed the Lord would help lift me out of this fog. As I approached the storage shed, I nearly ran head-on into an enormous hairy gray-and-white spider. My first instinct was to make a hasty retreat. But I was halted by the sight of the massive web on which the spider perched. The orb-like, intricate latticework was covered with iridescent droplets that glistened in the sun. The web's symmetry and design were magnificent. *How many hours or days had this little creature spent weaving this beautiful tapestry?* I thought. I suddenly felt convicted. It was as if the Lord was whispering in my ear, "Surely, more time than you have given Me to give you a creative idea."

I left the spider to its work of art and went back to my desk, encouraged that the same God who gave the spider its creative gifts would undoubtedly help me with mine.

Walk of Faith: *If you are doubting your abilities to overcome a personal challenge, I encourage you to lean into the Lord, who created you with your own unique gifts. He will be there to overcome any stumbling block or obstacle you are facing.*

—Terry Clifton

JULY 23

Everlasting Light

The sun will no more be your light by day, nor will the brightness of the moon shine on you, for the LORD will be your everlasting light, and your God will be your glory.

—ISAIAH 60:19 (NIV)

AFTER DAYS OF nonstop summer thunderstorms and high humidity, I took advantage of a break in the rain and went for an evening stroll with my service dog, Callie. The dark skies paled to my mood as my pain level increased during our walk. I had expected to feel better, hoping my last procedure would have yielded longer-lasting results. Instead, my doctor informed me that I would be wise to embrace the possibility of a lifetime of chronic pain management and limited mobility. My healing journey had become a seemingly endless trek through the wilderness.

I stopped next to the creek that runs beside our home and loosened Callie's leash so she could sniff the grass. Listening to the water trickling in the darkness, I gave in to my grief. How could I feel hopeful when my future looked so bleak?

Wiping tears from my cheeks, I stared at the wildflowers covering the creek's bank and noticed tiny blinking lights. As more fireflies joined us, cutting through the darkness and illuminating the night, I smiled. My focus shifted toward Jesus, the Light of the World. Though I had grown weary during my battle with chronic pain, my hope remained anchored in His unchanging goodness, not my ever-changing circumstances.

When the Israelites wandered in the wilderness, the Lord affirmed He would be their "everlasting light." God assured them that He would bring them to the land He had promised them. He secured their future as they trusted His plan and pace, even when relief didn't come when or how they expected.

Watching the fireflies, I thanked God for being my everlasting light as He led me forward in Spirit-empowered faith.

You, LORD, keep my lamp burning; my God turns my darkness into light.
—Psalm 18:28 (NIV)

—Xochitl E. Dixon

JULY 24

Looking for Lions

The Lord *is my portion; therefore I will wait for him. The* Lord *is good to those whose hope is in him, to the one who seeks him.*

—Lamentations 3:24–25 (NIV)

IT TOOK MY parents, my husband, and myself a single day of hard travel to drive from East London, South Africa, to our lodgings on the border of Kruger National Park. In spite of being carsick and tail sore, I couldn't wait for our journey through the park the next day. I dreamed of watching elephants lumbering across the African bushveld, giraffes craning their necks to the tops of the acacia trees, and most of all, lions lounging in the thatch grass or chilling my blood with their golden-eyed stares. At least, that was the plan.

Unfortunately, no one told the plan to my dad. To him, the park speed limit was just a suggestion, not to be taken seriously by those set on breaking the cross-park record. Trees and grass flew by our windows in a blur of green, yellow, and brown. I asked him to slow, and he dropped his speed a little. I asked again, this time with no result. Eventually, my husband and I started to laugh. There may have been lions hiding in the yellow grass or elephants between the trees. We would never know.

I didn't see any lions that day, but I immediately saw the lesson. How many times have I been blind to God's presence when I am driven by my own agenda through the frantic pace of life? "Where are you, God?" I ask as I speed on my way. Yet only when I slow down, open my eyes, and seek Him am I finally able to see—He's been there all along.

I remain confident of this: I will see the goodness of the Lord *in the land of the living. Wait for the* Lord*; be strong and take heart and wait for the* Lord*.*
—Psalm 27:13–14 (NIV)

—Tracy Joy Jones

JULY 25

Recognizing my Father

Then the two told what had happened on the way, and how Jesus was recognized by them when he broke the bread.

—LUKE 24:35 (NIV)

MY HUSBAND AND I have a yearly pass for the Denver Zoo because it's never the same visit twice. It caters to hubby's double-stroke disabilities by providing a scooter.

We always enjoy visiting all the animals, big and small, especially when we bring our grandson Boo. As a bonus, our niece now works as an official zookeeper there, so we often get to see some behind-the-scenes views that others may miss.

During our last tour of the zoo, we spent extra time watching the zebras frolick around their enclosure. I'm a huge fan of horses, and I truly enjoy every second watching zebras, with their similarities and differences. We had our usual teaching time with Boo, talking about how the stripes work as camouflage in the wild. My niece added something new—every zebra has a distinct, unique stripe pattern, as individual as fingerprints, and foals recognize their mamas that way! What I see as a blur of uniformity is actually the combined signatures of unique individuals.

Observing the herd of zebras, I realized that distinctive stripe patterns are certainly something I would have missed without an expert there to point them out to me. And that got me thinking about the ways, like the zebra foal, I recognize my eternal parent—God—in my everyday life. Do I recognize His distinctive, unique patterns and acknowledge the many ways He works in my life—or do I walk on by, too caught up in my own worries to notice?

Some people can be so disoriented to God that when he begins to work around them, they actually become annoyed at the interruption! —Henry Blackaby

—Deb Kastner

JULY 26

Lucky

As a shepherd looks after his scattered flock when he is with them, so will I look after my sheep. I will rescue them from all the places where they were scattered on a day of clouds and darkness.

—EZEKIEL 34:12 (NIV)

MY BROTHER DAVE was an electrical lineman working a job in Nogales, Arizona, a busy hub for produce coming into the States from Mexico. One day, his job brought him in contact with lots of big trucks arriving with their deliveries. As he walked across a lot, he spotted a tiny tiger-striped kitten cowering and immobilized by fear as the monster vehicles lumbered around it.

Dave stooped to pick up the little bundle, wondering why it wasn't scurrying for cover on its own. When he looked at it more closely, he saw that the kitten had something wrong with its eyes and could not have navigated its way to safety if it had tried.

A trip to the vet confirmed a bad case of conjunctivitis. This is very dangerous for cats and, if left untreated, can lead to eye damage, blindness, and even death. The vet's first suggestion was that this cat should be put down because it would be too much work to nurse it back to health. He wasn't serious, of course, for he knew Dave and was familiar with the tender heart that lived inside the tall, dusty lineman. After dispensing the needed medication, he encouraged Dave to find a home for the kitten (knowing full well this one would likely end up joining the other cats, dogs, and horses that were cherished by Dave's family). Lucky had found a new home.

There have been times in my life when I have been immobilized—by blindness, illness, or fear. And each of those times, God has sent just the right person, Jesus with skin on, to set me on the right path again.

Father, thank You that You never leave me stranded and alone. I may feel lost, but You know where I am; You see and direct me to a place of safety. Amen.

—Liz Kimmel

JULY 27

All Creatures, Great and Small

The King will reply, "Truly I tell you, whatever you did for one of the least of these brothers and sisters of mine, you did for me."

—MATTHEW 25:40 (NIV)

JUST BEFORE DAWN, I let our dog, Max, out. Beautiful pink clouds filled the sky. When I looked down at their reflection in the pool, I saw a baby possum clinging to the edge. I put Max inside so he wouldn't try to eat it, then I scooped the little creature out and placed it under the big leaves of an oak-leaf hydrangea.

I looked more carefully to see if it had drowned or was just playing dead, and I noticed its thin tail and long snout. *You're not a possum, you're a rat!* I thought. Then it woke up and stumped away under the hydrangea. It was clearly a possum.

All morning, I found myself pondering, *If I thought it was a rat, would I have tried to save it? Is a possum better than a rat?* If rats invade my space, I want them gone. But I don't want a rat to drown in my pool. Yes, rats can cause problems, and they scare me, but they're an important part of the ecosystem, a purposeful part of creation. All creatures deserve a chance at life.

I thought about the people I see around me every day: successful people and people who are down on their luck; people who obviously contribute to society and others whose contributions are not as obvious; people like me and people very different from me. Do I extend them all the same grace? That little possum reminded me it's not my job to decide who is worthy of my care. If a creature is drowning, it's my job to help. Possum or rat, prince or beggar, when one is in need, I want to help.

Dear Lord of all, help me to see the sacred wholeness of Your creation and to care for all Your creatures, even if I don't fully understand their role. Amen.

—Lucy H. Chambers

JULY 28

With Me!

*This is love, that we walk according to His commandments.
This is the commandment, that as you have heard
from the beginning, you should walk in it.*

—2 JOHN 6 (NKJV)

WHILE WALKING OUR dog, Kenai, on our road, I continue his training, though he's no longer a puppy. When my husband walks him, he doesn't keep him in a heel by his side. Because of this, Kenai pulls to be in front.

As we walk, I repeat the new command for *heel* I learned during puppy classes: "With me." I also pause periodically, reinforcing the rule for him to stop and sit beside me whenever I stop. Kenai loves the treats he gets along with my praise.

While stopped, we work on the "wait" command. I walk ahead of him, stop, pause, and even tug on the leash. He isn't to come after he's told "wait" until I call him. The command "stay" means to stay sitting until I come back to him. Kenai does well with these two commands and receives much praise for his obedience.

However, during our return to the house, he pulls harder, anxious to get home, and I say over and over, "With me! With me!" Some commands come easier than others.

I wonder how often Jesus says that to me. How often do I pull ahead and want to be in front like Kenai, to be in charge instead of following? *With me,* His spirit whispers. How often does He make me wait or stay in order to get my attention, sometimes having to force me to stop in the first place?

Oh, that I would learn the lessons and not even care about the "treats" or praise, until my footsteps take me into heaven and I hear that final one: "Well done, my good and faithful servant!"

*Along life's road, I charge ahead day after day.
Jesus whispers, "With me, child. I alone know the way."* —C.M.

—Cathy Mayfield

JULY 29

Pass the Bucks

Hold them in the highest regard in love because of their work. Live in peace with each other.

—1 THESSALONIANS 5:13 (NIV)

ENTIRE HERDS OF mule deer call my husband's ranch "home." All summer long this year, eleven bucks with growing antler racks sought out the cool of his pine windbreak during the heat of the day. Then as the sun began to sink, they would head into his wheat field, get their fill of grain, and bed down there for the night.

He thinks they sought refuge in the field because last year a doe herd fed and gave birth there. In fact, as he was cutting hay that year with his swather, he had to pay special attention, as the babies would rest in the wheat. The males among those fawns must have grown into full adult bucks, while the doe herd wandered through our mountain town from one cozy yard to another.

Craig welcomes their company—even though they eat his crop. He can drive his pickup truck or any of his equipment right by them, and they won't budge unless he stops and stares at them.

I told him, "That sounds like deer-topia."

I can learn from ranchers and farmers who coexist peacefully with the wildlife around them. I can offer simple respect and dignity to my neighbors. I can chat with others in the grocery line. And I can take a meal to a friend in need or donate clothes to a local charity. Living in peace with others around me simply means treating them as I would like to be treated—and that's not hard to do.

People must learn to hate, and if they can learn to hate, they can be taught to love, for love comes more naturally to the human heart than its opposite.

—Nelson Mandela

—Janet Holm McHenry

JULY 30

Pepper Holds a Grudge

Do not seek revenge or bear a grudge against anyone among your people, but love your neighbor as yourself. I am the Lord.

—Leviticus 19:18 (NIV)

SCHNAUZERS AREN'T USUALLY the most gregarious, choosing instead to cling loyally to their person . . . the one they pick, not necessarily the one that picks them. And if they feel wronged in any way, they never forget it.

Pepper, my miniature schnauzer, was often the instigator in my pack. I was usually around to be the alpha and stop any fights that might happen, but one day, I went to the feed store for a few minutes, and a fight happened while I was gone. Pepper escaped graphic injury, but she had some swelling and pain. She would yelp dramatically anytime I got near her. Months after her complete healing, she still ignored me and kept her distance. She held me responsible for a fight she probably started, even after the pain was over. She was angry I hadn't protected her and held on to her resentment instead of receiving the affection she craved.

We also hold on to grudges, as if by hanging on to them, we will get some sort of satisfaction. That never happens. Revenge doesn't make us feel better. And the only way to feel peace is to let go of blame even if it's justified. Those burdens make the journey heavier than it was ever meant to be. Love only returns when we decide not to hate, not to blame, and to move on in peace.

Lord, take the burden of resentment off my heart and replace it with forgiveness. Amen.

—Devon O'Day

JULY 31

Breaking In

God disciplines us for our good, in order that we may share in his holiness.

—HEBREWS 12:10 (NIV)

WHEN WE FIRST moved out to the country, we were delighted to find that many of our neighbors had horses. Our favorite was Adele, the beautiful, not-quite-two-year-old mare next door. Our neighbor was a skilled equestrian, and she had purchased Adele because of her potential to be a successful show horse. However, before our neighbor could compete with Adele, she had to train her . . . and Adele had never even been ridden before.

I'll never forget the first time I saw Adele "throw" our neighbor. We were watching over the fence as our neighbor mounted Adele, then sat confidently in the saddle. Then, without warning, Adele began rearing and bucking like a bronco at a rodeo. Our neighbor was flung around like a rag doll until she finally lost her grip and went crashing to the ground. We all breathed a deep sigh of relief when she stood up, but then to our amazement she grabbed the reins and began working Adele on the lead line. This happened three more times: Adele bucked our neighbor off and then our neighbor wore her out on the lead line.

Afterward, I talked to my neighbor, who was bruised and sore, and she explained why she persisted. If she had stopped, Adele would have "won." The mare had to learn who was in charge, because only by submitting would she be able to really come into her full potential. Our neighbor knew what Adele was capable of; she had a vision for the amazing life that Adele was made for. Out of love for that horse, my neighbor was willing to persist.

In that moment, I saw such a beautiful picture of God's sanctifying work in my own life. Not only does He love me relentlessly, but He knows exactly what I am capable of. So, if I want all God has in store for me, it begins by learning to submit to His lead in all things.

No discipline seems pleasant at the time, but painful. Later on, however, it produces a harvest of righteousness and peace for those who have been trained by it. —Hebrews 12:11 (NIV)

—Joy Pitner

August

AUGUST 1

Be a Sea Star!

Blessed be the peacemakers, for they will be called children of God.

—MATTHEW 5:9 (NIV)

I DASHED INTO THE pet store to buy a chew stick for my dog, Duncan. Two little girls—obviously sisters in their matching pink sundresses—huddled near a large fish tank, pointing and whispering. Curious, I slowly made my way toward them, hoping to catch a glimpse of whatever it was they found so fascinating. It appeared to be a chubby orange starfish with brown bumps sprinkled all over it.

"That's a chocolate-chip sea star," the clerk commented, making her way over to them. The girls giggled. Upon closer examination, I could see that the bumps did resemble miniature Hershey kisses or chocolate chips. When their mother joined them, the clerk explained the dos and don'ts of adding such a creature to their fish tank at home.

"All in all, it's a good choice," the clerk said, smiling. "The chocolate-chip sea star tends to be peaceful, and it plays well with others."

"I'm a chocolate-chip sea star too!" one of the little girls quipped.

"Me too!" the other piped up.

Their mother and the clerk laughed, and the girls were promised a new addition to their fish tank.

Instead of laughing, I marveled. Even as young as they were, the girls understood the merit of being peace-loving individuals who get along with others. Jesus called such peacemakers "blessed." I want to be a chocolate-chip sea star too.

Walk of Faith: *Consider what you might say or do today to be a peacemaker in your family or community.*

—Shirley Raye Redmond

AUGUST 2

Rest on the Rock Together

If one part suffers, every part suffers with it; if one part is honored, every part rejoices with it. Now you are the body of Christ, and each one of you is a part of it.

—1 CORINTHIANS 12:26–27 (NIV)

I SAT NEXT TO the natural spring, watching my husband and kids splash in the clear water below. As the sun danced on the water, I noticed a bright yellow movement to my right. I turned my head and saw two yellow-and-black swallowtail butterflies resting on the rock next to me. Their wings slowly moved as they basked in the sun. A few minutes later, a third butterfly joined the pair. The three butterflies stayed together on the rock for nearly the entire hour we swam.

Through creation we see that God designed us for community. Even insects congregate! Paul reminds us that through Jesus Christ we are one body. When one of us suffers, we all suffer. When one of us receives honor, we celebrate together. We honor Christ when we share life—all parts of it.

One of my dear friends recently suffered the tragic death of a family member. In the midst of her grief, she asked if a group of us could hang out one morning so she wouldn't be alone. We surrounded her in the sunny corner of a coffee shop, telling her all the beautiful things we saw the Lord doing in her life. We laughed, we cried, but mostly it was just good to be together.

Our time that day reminded me of the butterflies gathered on the rock at the spring. God has designed us to do life together. Some days, it is good to just sit in the company of others and take refuge on the rock of Jesus Christ.

Walk of Faith: *Who can you sit next to today and offer encouragement? Ask God to show you how to be this kind of friend or to bring one into your life.*

—Amelia Rhodes

AUGUST 3

A Chorus Line

Sing to the Lord *a new song; sing to the* Lord, *all the earth.*

—Psalm 96:1 (NIV)

ONE MUGGY AUGUST evening in Oregon, I felt lazy and definitely not motivated to work in my garden. I had settled back into my patio chair, when suddenly the raspberry bushes erupted in sound. *Ribbit!* I pictured the plump, warty toads of my Arizona girlhood, but to my amazement, the singer turned out to be a tiny male Pacific tree frog, small enough to fit in the palm of my hand. His intense green coloring blended perfectly with the raspberry leaves, and I might not have seen him if not for his song. I marveled at how he made himself sound like a chorus of frogs, all to make females come running.

I stood stock still, fascinated by this impromptu concert. Mr. Frog's throat ballooned out, becoming nearly transparent with each call, then shrank back under his cream-colored chin. When a bug came into range, he twitched one of his little padded toes. The insect came closer, and the tree frog's tongue shot out so fast that he nearly bounced off his leaf. He munched his dinner and started singing again. The last rays of the summer sun lit up his skin, a translucent emerald nestled among plump red raspberries.

I don't know if the little frog found a mate that night, but my ho-hum mood evaporated as he sang his song over and over. His tune was more like high-pitched *cre-ee-eeks* than the low croaks of amphibians in the desert. I stood there in the bushes until my legs cramped and the mosquitoes came out.

Mr. Frog wanted to attract a mate, of course, but his loud chorus also reminded me that all creation—from the most important to the least—sings praises to our Creator. The frog's song left me in awe, and as I went in for the night, I hummed a song of praise of my own.

Walk of Faith: *As weather permits, go outside and listen for all God's creatures singing praises.*

—Linda S. Clare

Elephants Help Me Remember

For great is the Lord *and most worthy of praise… Splendor and majesty are before him; strength and joy are in his dwelling place.*

—1 Chronicles 16:25, 27 (NIV)

I'LL NEVER FORGET the first time I saw an elephant. From my first glimpse, I was awed by its sheer size, its balance of power and gentleness. With the strength of its mighty trunk, an elephant can lift a tree. That same trunk tenderly intertwines with another elephant's in an expression of affection. While videos of the antics of baby elephants abound on the internet, researchers have noticed that even older adults are playful. For example, in their "floppy run," the elephants swing their big ears and trumpet as they trot along.

Elephants can detect water from miles away and will determinedly use feet, tusks, and trunk to make watering holes. They are fierce in the protection of their young and weaker members of their herd. The popular saying that an elephant never forgets probably stems from a matriarch elephant's ability to learn and remember where she found water, when a lion's roar means immediate danger, and other things important to the herd's survival.

I was immediately smitten by these magnificent creatures, and I began buying keepsakes of my visits to their enclosure at the zoo. And from there my collection grew. People who visit our home notice my affinity for elephants. They grace our living room and some of our artwork, they appear as finials on some of our lamps, and they adorn our bookshelves.

What is the attraction? Elephants embody tenderness and fierceness. They are playful, hardworking, and wise. They are huge and majestic. I can imagine that the Ultimate Designer assembled elephants to mimic aspects of His own persona.

When I see an elephant—whether a real one or one of my small keepsakes—may it always remind me of God's amazing characteristics: His strength, majesty, wisdom, and fierce protection. And above all, His tenderness, protection, and affection for me, His child.

Lord, You are amazing. Thank You for the beauty and majesty You have blessed us with. Help me to see the many facets of Your nature through all Your beautiful creation. Amen.

—Liz Kimmel

AUGUST 5

The Shepherd's Voice

My sheep listen to my voice; I know them, and they follow me.

—JOHN 10:27 (NIV)

I LIVE IN A rural community, where the high school graduates about twenty-five students a year. Despite its size, the school has a terrific agriculture program that has won state and national awards. Along with animal barns, a greenhouse, and gardens, the program has its own sheep herd.

Because my English classroom overlooked most of the ag operation, I could see when sheep got out. But after a quick call to the ag teacher, the sheep would soon be rounded up. Seemingly, they knew the shepherd's voice, and sometimes it took just a word or two to scoot them back home.

One weekend day, I was out walking and decided to pass by the high school, only to notice that the whole flock had escaped to the football field.

"Go back home," I said, waving my arms. But they only scattered even farther.

I tried again, but they would not listen to me. I was not their shepherd. I was just the silly English teacher. So I called the ag teacher, who calmly walked over from his nearby house. All it took was one look for them to head back to the barn.

There are many confusing voices that would try to send me this way or that: Folks on social media promote and sell. Hollywood figures try to influence my ballot choices. Newscasters offer a continual stream of commentary. Sometimes it's hard to know what to believe.

However, I know I can always find my way to the Shepherd's voice by reading the Bible, which speaks truth and life into me when I am confused or weary. He never leads me astray.

Lord, sometimes I get completely lost. I lose my sense of purpose and direction. In those times, I know I can look to You and Your Word and that You will bring me home to Yourself. Amen.

—Janet Holm McHenry

AUGUST 6

Making a Personal Connection

Philip found Nathanael and said to him, "We have found Him of whom Moses in the law, and also the prophets, wrote—Jesus of Nazareth, the son of Joseph."

—JOHN 1:45 (NKJV)

FORTY-FIVE MINUTES I sat trying to make a personal connection with a chicken.

I was surrounded by chickens and two roosters, as well as a muster of peahens. They wandered around oblivious to my observation, wholly engaged in chicken activities. Occasionally, the lot of them would shift from one side of the path to another as if on some signal to which I was not privy.

After a time, I could distinguish between the two roosters, but I was largely unmoved by any individual fowl and feeling lacking. How is it that other individuals establish bonds with these farm critters?

A nearby groundskeeper cleared his throat. "May I help you?"

I shrugged. "It's a writing assignment. I'm trying to establish a personal connection with a chicken, but I'm failing miserably."

He stopped his work to help me out without even a snicker. He explained the chickens' behaviors, pointed out personality quirks, and introduced the ones he had named. After a while, I developed an affinity for the anxious rooster that managed his hens with ruffled feathers and stomping. The other rooster was a calm nudger, but this guy was frazzled in his work, and I could relate.

I glanced up to thank the groundskeeper, but he had left me to my new feathered friends. I wondered if that's how people who don't know Jesus feel when they attempt to connect with God but wind up just feeling mystified and somehow lacking. When a believer comes along to facilitate that personal connection, it can make all the difference.

Walk of Faith: *Am I available, willing to set aside my own work, to take a moment and explain the things of God to someone trying to make a personal connection? How can I do that today?*

—Lori Stanley Roeleveld

AUGUST 7

Royal Dwelling

A lizard can be caught with the hand, yet it is found in kings' palaces.

—PROVERBS 30:28 (NIV)

NOW TWENTY YEARS old, Gary the day gecko became a member of our family when he was a baby. Our son Mark received Gary as a gift, purchased by a friend at an exotic pet store.

Quick as lightning, the gecko scampered across the ceiling the day Mark received him, and Mark had to catch him, upside down, in a cardboard box. This unique creature needed the safety of a terrarium, equipped with a heater and light, and crickets or mangos for a menu.

A type of lizard, day geckos are vibrant in color and said to be "forms of living art." People who own them usually display them as a decorative focal point in a room or garden. Kelly green with brilliant orange and red markings, Gary displays the work of our Creator's paintbrush, but if scared or traumatized, he might turn gray.

In the book of Proverbs, King Solomon wrote about lizards in the king's palace. Some Bible versions use the word *spider*, which is properly translated as "gecko" in Hebrew. The *shmamit batim* is the Mediterranean gecko found in Israel and likely what Solomon spoke about.

Designed with sticky webbed feet, these exquisite beauties would have been able to run up the marble walls of Solomon's palace and across the ceiling. Could it be the king saw such a gecko when he penned the proverb about them? Theologian J. Vernon McGee suggests the gecko is a metaphor for "holding fast," without falling, to our faith and the promises of God.

Gary is healthy in his old age, although a bit slower, and his vision has dimmed with cataracts. Symbolic of how small and insignificant we may feel at times, the gecko reminds us that we are welcomed into the "palace" of God's presence, holding fast to His Word and eternal love—as He holds fast to us.

Dear Lord, thank You for the lizard that reminds us that we can live in the glory of Your royal fellowship forever.

—Kathleen Ruckman

AUGUST 8

How the Hippopotamus Became My Favorite

She gave this name to the Lord who spoke to her: "You are the God who sees me," for she said, "I have now seen the One who sees me."

—Genesis 16:13 (NIV)

A FAVORITE MEMORY FROM my childhood is the piglet that followed me around my grandfather's farm. When I was four, Mom made the four-hour drive from Denver to Lamar to visit Granddaddy's horse-and-pig farm on the edge of town. One of the piglets trailed behind me as I explored the dusty property. I loved it.

Later that summer, Mom took me to the Cheyenne Mountain Zoo in Colorado Springs, and the baby hippo followed me too. It pursued as I walked from one end of the cement enclosure to the other. I don't know how long Mom sat on the bench while I walked back and forth, but that day the hippopotamus became my favorite animal. For years, hippos beat out even cuddly bears for the top spot in my heart.

Those memories stand out because, for a few brief moments, I was the focus of their attention. That piglet and hippo made me feel special. As an only child of a single parent, at times I felt like I was in the way. Mom faced all the responsibility of raising me and didn't always have the space or capacity to play with me.

With their eyes on me, that piglet and hippo reminded me I was seen. I was someone worth noticing. But I don't need to be followed around by animals to know this. I can look to God's Word to know how He sees me. He loves me, and He promises to always be with me.

Lord, thank You that You are always with me. Help me to know You're here even when I can't feel You. Amen.

—Crystal Storms

AUGUST 9

Taking That First Step

Wait for the Lord*; be strong and take heart and wait for the* Lord*.*

—Psalm 27:14 (NIV)

SOMETIMES I RUN kicking and screaming when I'm told to do something. Other times, I jump in but feel resentful. Or I start out compliant but then rebel.

That is what our elderly dog Duke did after he was diagnosed with several eye problems by his veterinary ophthalmologist. At our first visit, we learned he was having eye pain—enough that his third eyelid had closed. (I didn't even know dogs had such a thing!) The vet prescribed multiple eye drops to be given every few hours for several weeks.

Duke did great at first. I think the drops eased his pain, so he stood there and let me hold open his eyelids. But after the first week or so, he got tired of me messing with him. He quit complying and would stubbornly slam his eyes shut. Or he would jerk his head away. Eventually, he began running from me anytime I got near. Smart fellow.

His reaction reminds me of a child who doesn't want his teeth brushed. Or a teen who doesn't want to do her homework. Or an adult who dreads going to work . . . or who dreads putting eye drops in an uncooperative pup's eyes.

It also reminds me of myself, when I know God wants me to do something I don't have the time, the courage, or the desire to do.

But just as Duke's eye drops were what he needed for healing, sometimes the jobs God has for me end up being exactly what I need at the time. Often, I only see this in hindsight. But I won't know until I step up and try.

Walk of Faith: *With courage and a willing heart, let's make that first step to do what God is calling us to do.*

—Missy Tippens

AUGUST 10

Chihuahua in a Tutu

A happy heart makes the face cheerful, but heartache crushes the spirit.

—PROVERBS 15:13 (NIV)

IT'S INCREDIBLE HOW God puts little stress reducers in our path on days we really need them. They might not fit a mold one would expect. I was in the middle of helping a friend close her antique store after eighteen years. We were working on a deadline, and it was overwhelming to both of us. It's always easier to move in than to move out because suddenly everything that has to be done is on someone else's timeline.

New tenants were waiting for keys, and there was still so much to do. Just about the time we were about to sit on the floor and cry, in walked someone to help, and with her was her Chihuahua in a pink tutu. This pup pranced around like she was our entertainment: in the door and out the door in that little pink dress, begging for bites of pizza, jumping in and out of boxes. Basically, she would not let anyone ignore her, and with that she didn't let us focus on what wasn't getting done. We laughed, and she lifted everyone's spirits.

When life becomes unmanageable with more stress than I can handle, God often sends moments and God-winks that let me know I am not alone. It might be a dog that irritates me with a paw to the knee until I put down my phone. It might be a cat that insists on lying on my computer until I pay attention. Or it might be as fanciful as a Chihuahua in a tutu that appears in my stressful day and makes me laugh. I want to pay attention and not miss the precious moments that God sends to lift burdens.

God, please send me moments to save me from the stress of my days, and when I stop paying attention, make it as obvious as a dog in a tutu. Amen.

—Devon O'Day

AUGUST 11

Dog's Day of Summer

But let patience have its perfect work, that you may be perfect and complete, lacking nothing.

—JAMES 1:4 (NKJV)

I TURNED DOWN THE thermostat, but it felt like a losing battle against the outside 105°F temperature. Even Barnie and Rudy, our cats, lay dormant on their backs. The heat made it hard for me to concentrate on my overdue freelance assignment. My wife, Sandra, took mercy on me and said, "Why don't we go get some ice cream." I am not a big ice cream fan, but at that point, I was drawn to anything cold.

When we drove into the ice cream store parking lot, we discovered that we were not the only ones seeking something cold. Customers were standing three-lines deep at the counter. I usually avoid drive-through lanes but figured it had to be better than getting out of the car.

After twenty minutes of stop-and-go in the line, I mumbled, "Great, we are trapped in this line and can't get out." I noticed the driver's window of the car in front of us open, and the head of a dachshund wearing a service-dog vest popped out and excitedly sniffed the air. "He's probably getting a treat for a job well done," my Sandra surmised. "Well, I hope he doesn't mind waiting," I groused. That wiener dog didn't mind at all. He got more excited as he approached the pick-up window. His head stuck out so far that his snout seemed to actually grow. His enthusiasm was rewarded with a "pup cup," a scoop of ice cream topped with a biscuit bone.

I felt convicted. That dachshund was singularly focused on the prize. My impatience had kept me focused on the process, and I had lost sight of the reward.

Lord, help me to be excited and expectant of the good things You have for me as I approach any finish line. I have faith in Your perfect timing, even when the waiting seems to take longer than I would like. Amen.

—Terry Clifton

AUGUST 12

Press On

Brethren, I do not count myself to have apprehended; but one thing I do, forgetting those things which are behind and reaching forward to those things which are ahead, I press toward the goal for the prize of the upward call of God in Christ Jesus.

—PHILIPPIANS 3:13–14 (NKJV)

EVERY WEEK, SPUNKY Hettie conquers another exploit. She is the most adorable two-pound Boston terrier we have ever seen. She seems convinced she is a stunt puppy, jumping and running and taking risks like a fearless daredevil.

You can see determination in her eyes. They also tattle on her when she's about to do something audacious! A teeny little creature, she faced off with two recliners, jumping from one opened recliner to another—with a good amount of space between. She negotiated the odd angle she needed to navigate her jump.

The first jump ended in a fail. She plopped to the ground rather than hitting her mark. She shook it off, from shaking head to wiggly tail. Then she started all over again. The second jump missed the goal but came closer. I lost track of how many jumps she attempted. Each time, Hettie's stubborn determination motivated her to try again.

You can imagine our elation when she made it.

Watching her has inspired me. I pray that I will have Hettie's ability to not be distracted by my past failures and press on toward the goal until I fulfill the challenge. I remind myself not to let the times I miss the mark rob me of my vision to succeed. I want the outcome of following Jesus to motivate me more than the worry of getting it wrong. With dogged determination, despite multiple attempts, with God's help I will achieve daunting tasks.

Genius is divine perseverance. Genius I cannot claim nor even extra brightness but perseverance all can have. —Woodrow Wilson

—Kathy Carlton Willis

Renaissance Javelina

Do not be afraid, you wild animals, for the pastures in the wilderness are becoming green. The trees are bearing their fruit; the fig tree and the vine yield their riches.

—JOEL 2:22 (NIV)

WHEN RAIN FINALLY arrived that summer afternoon, I was hiking a trail outside Tucson, Arizona. The dry landscape came to life as I took cover from both the deluge and thoughts of my friend's recent death. As I ducked raindrops, a family of thirsty peccaries, aka javelinas, charged into view, darting in and out of the rare showers. Young ones jumped and frolicked, and adults opened their mouths to the downpour, while others shook themselves. I couldn't stop watching them play in the rain.

My friend Rhett had died holding a fishing rod in Oregon, but he had also loved to play in the Arizona desert. Artistic and creative, he was truly a Renaissance man. His many careers included a stint as a US Marine and another as a bookmobile-driving librarian in New Mexico. He had also been an Oregon sign maker and orchardist. His sketches and drawings were as whimsical as his writing, and he could be irreverently funny.

Maybe that's why Rhett loved javelinas—a pig that's not really a pig. Adult peccaries look a lot like wild boars, with pointy tusks that can be dangerous. But they're also super family-oriented, living in large social groups. Most would rather eat prickly pears than bully one another. Rhett had loved to eat too. A pair of young peccaries chased each other in circles, mud flying from their little three-toed hooves. I chuckled softly. Their short, wiry coats reminded me of Rhett's scraggly beard; their antics were much like the jokes Rhett slyly hid in his prose and pictures. Tears poked at my lashes.

Sun peeked through the clouds as the herd melted back into the desert. Playful, funny, family-oriented—just like Rhett. I smiled as a rainbow arched across the sky.

Blessed are those who mourn, for they will be comforted.
—Matthew 5:4 (NIV)

—Linda S. Clare

AUGUST 14

Black Dog Blues

Do not judge according to appearance, but judge with righteous judgment.

—John 7:24 (NKJV)

BLACK IS THE most overlooked color in shelters. Black dogs like Maggie, Lilady, and Bear were adorable, lovable, and adoptable, but people didn't adopt them. If only we could paint them like rainbows, they would be out the door lickety-split. That's why when we had a chance to take dogs out to advertise them, we often took black dogs. But some had stayed at the shelter so long that the real world scared them.

When a new volunteer wandered into the shelter, our kennel tech paired her with Maggie. Maggie had grown up in the shelter and was now afraid to leave the shelter grounds. We hoped Kathy, the new volunteer, could ease her back into normal life. Kathy began to work with Maggie daily. Trust was renewed.

We were looking forward to taking Maggie to our next adoption event, but we didn't have to. Kathy fell so in love with Maggie that she took her home. Once Kathy spent time with Maggie to find her lovable nature, she saw beyond her color and knew Maggie was special. Maggie was loving and loyal, and she worshipped Kathy.

I'm so glad that God is able to look beyond the darkness of our souls and see the soul that longs to do good. We have so many human flaws, but because of Jesus who covers our sins, God is able to accept us, and someday He will bring us home.

Father of all creatures, thank You for accepting us as we are; thank You for sending Jesus to cover our sinful nature; thank You for providing a forever home for us. Please, dear Father, help us to be loving and loyal to You. Amen.

—Linda Bartlett

AUGUST 15

The Miracle of Flight

"How then were your eyes opened?" they asked. He replied, "The man they call Jesus made some mud and put it on my eyes. He told me to go to Siloam and wash. So I went and washed, and then I could see."

—JOHN 9:10–11 (NIV)

JOHN BALL ZOO in Grand Rapids, Michigan, was hosting Monarch Day, and I was going to celebrate with them by releasing a monarch into the wild.

At my scheduled time, I peeked inside the cellophane envelope and saw a gorgeous monarch. The zoo had raised caterpillars to chrysalises, which had recently hatched for release. These monarchs would migrate from Michigan all the way to Mexico, part of their amazing cycle of life. On the count of ten, I carefully slipped the butterfly out of the package, and my vibrant friend lifted away.

Looking around, I teared up as I noticed how many people were participating. Hundreds had gathered to watch the butterflies fly high. Flashes of orange contrasted with the brilliant blue sky. Little kids held monarchs tenderly. Cameras were everywhere. It was a beautiful moment.

Nearby, I saw a monarch with a crumpled wing fluttering on the ground. A volunteer rescued it and explained that zookeepers would remove the injured section and repair the wing, using one from a deceased monarch. This delicate surgery would give it the ability to fly again.

Months later, my pastor was teaching about the blind man who was healed by Jesus. Once healed, he probably ran around town telling friends, ready for a new life. As I reflected, I couldn't help but wonder how that healed monarch was doing on its cross-country trip, happy to be living the life God created it to live. Fly on, little one; fly on.

Dear Lord, I am in awe of how the touch of a hand can heal. Your hands on that blind man's eyes. The skill of surgeons on humans and butterflies. The hand I hold when times are hard. May we use our hands well and for Your glory.

—Twila Bennett

AUGUST 16

Sticking to It

Let us not become weary in doing good, for at the proper time we will reap a harvest if we do not give up.

—GALATIANS 6:9 (NIV)

WINTER, THE FAMOUS dolphin featured in two Hollywood movies, lives in Saint Petersburg, Florida. Thousands of visitors come to see her and hear about her miraculous recovery after losing her tail from a fishing-net accident.

My family and I were blessed to meet Winter and interact with her at the aquarium. We listened to her story and learned the seemingly impossible odds she overcame in learning how to swim with a prosthetic tail. My young daughters had the privilege of petting Winter, touching her man-made appendage, and taking home a wonderful photo of the moment.

How easy it would have been for this injured sea mammal to reject the mechanical device and give up. But Winter was tenacious. She had a strong will to survive and thrive, becoming an inspiration to hundreds of disabled people around the world.

Whenever I revisit that memorable photograph, I'm inspired to keep going when things get tough. We are never promised an easy journey when swimming through the ocean of life. The nets of discouragement can wrap around us, cutting off the blood flow to hope. We can be tempted to give up.

With prayer, we can ask God to restore our determination and endurance. He provides the steadfast grit and tireless diligence we need to hold fast and swim against adversity toward resolution and victory. Are you losing your drive to continue in the journey? Cry out to the Lord and rediscover your tenacity today. He will meet you where you are and lift you up.

Walk of Faith: *Consider watching the film* A Dolphin Tale *with your family or friends this week, and then discuss the importance of persistence and perseverance. Write down three scriptures or famous quotes that encourage you to persevere through trials.*

—Tez Brooks

AUGUST 17

Take a Deep Breath

He makes me lie down in green pastures, he leads me beside quiet waters, he refreshes my soul.

—PSALM 23:2–3 (NIV)

BRUISER LIVED NEXT door. A retired military guard dog, Bruiser was a Belgian shepherd—intelligent, loyal, and extremely protective. The poor dog didn't seem to realize he was now off duty. He constantly paced the perimeter of our neighbors' yard. He never seemed to relax but remained ever vigilant.

President Herbert Hoover had the same kind of dog. Like Bruiser, King Tut patrolled the perimeter of the White House. He stressed out over the constant stream of official visitors who came to see the president. Agitated and uneasy, Tut stopped eating. He wore himself to a frazzle, as did my mother's friend Diane, who for many years cared for her ailing husband. He suffered with Alzheimer's disease. A diligent caregiver, Diane appeared reluctant to let anyone share her responsibilities.

Bruiser, Tut, and Diane had something in common: they didn't understand the importance of rest. After my heart attack, I learned just how important it is to rest, both physically and spiritually. I do not need to do everything that needs to be done. Others are willing to help. I learned to let them. Sadly, Diane didn't learn that lesson. After her husband's death, she collapsed from exhaustion—literally. President Hoover had to send King Tut to a relative's home in the country because the exhausted dog grew weak and unresponsive. Fortunately, Bruiser learned to relax. He enjoyed being simply a dog, rolling in the grass and chasing a ball. I am not being lazy when I sit on my porch swing listening to Christian music or reading a devotional book. Rather, I am letting the Lord restore my soul.

The Lord replied, "My Presence will go with you, and I will give you rest."
—Exodus 33:14 (NIV)

—Shirley Raye Redmond

AUGUST 18

Clinging for Life

Because you are my help, I sing in the shadow of your wings. I cling to you; your right hand upholds me.

—PSALM 63:7–8 (NIV)

THINNER THAN PAPER, the luminescent wings were the first thing I noticed. Sunlight shone off them, drawing my attention to the spot where a dragonfly clung to my shoelace, its long body and legs anchored around the lace as if life depended on it.

I crouched down to get a better look. It still didn't move. I studied its spindly insect legs, tight around the fabric of my shoelace. Cautiously, I poked its backside.

Nothing.

A wind came, sweeping over the road and fluttering the wings of my tiny friend, and still the dragonfly clung tenaciously to my shoe. I marveled at the will of the small creature. For how often am I led astray by the poke of well-meaning but unwise advice? How often am I swept up in the winds of my own circumstances? How often am I rushed into the urgency of the world instead of the urgency of God?

As I watch this winged insect, I think of how I often fail to cling to the only One who can sustain me. And yet, in a mystery of faith, a familiar stir of hope fills my chest almost immediately, and I know it is God, reminding me it is never too late.

Again and again, He pulls me back—gently, sometimes with near scandalous love. His Right Hand—the One I trust as my Savior—is always there, directing me toward His grace. I cling to Him, and in the clinging, Jesus upholds me. As the dragonfly finally flutters away, my own heart lightens. God's grace is sufficient. For in the clinging, I am set free.

Jesus, You tell us what's best for us in Your Word—to draw close to You. Help us to cling with reckless abandon, when it doesn't make sense, when it's hard. Help us to trust You more, for everything, always. Amen.

—Heidi Chiavaroli

AUGUST 19

Caught

Immediately Jesus reached out his hand and caught him.

—MATTHEW 14:31 (NIV)

MY CHILDREN HAD some doozies among steers they raised to show at the county fair. The most challenging one had a misnomer for a name: Rosebud. He was no sweet thing. Perhaps his name should have been Thorny.

When twelve hundred pounds of Angus determination wants something, there's not much that can stand in its way. The second day on the fairgrounds, our daughter Rebekah led Rosebud to the scales chute for weigh-in, and all went fairly well until he left the chute, broke away from Rebekah's grip on his halter, and took off. She yelled, "Help!" as he headed down a grassy stretch toward a red barn that housed small animals like rabbits and poultry.

But just in time, a nearby angel disguised as a cowboy grabbed Rosebud's halter and yelled, "Whoa!"

I knew horses responded to "Whoa!" but I'd never seen that work with cattle.

Much to my surprise, though, Rosebud stopped and stood there as calm as could be. Minutes later, he was back in his stall munching hay.

When I'm overwhelmed or need help or am sinking into fear, I need someone to grab me and tell me "Whoa!" Jesus did that. When Peter stepped out of the boat to walk on the water toward Jesus, the wind caused him to worry, and he started to sink. He cried out, and Jesus caught him.

Life can often make me feel as though I am sinking out of control. Whether I am overcome with worry about my health or about finances, all I need to do is pray, *Help!* God will catch me, reassure me of His presence, and lead me in the right direction each and every time.

Don't be afraid to ask for help when you need it. I do that every day.
—Barack Obama

—Janet Holm McHenry

AUGUST 20

River of Refreshment

As the deer pants for streams of water, so my soul pants for you, my God.

—PSALM 42:1 (NIV)

LATE SUMMER MORNING sun warmed the river, causing a magical mist to rise in front of our kayaks. My daughter and I paddled in silence, taking in the awe and quiet of the early morning. As we rounded a bend in the river, my daughter sighed, "Oh, Mom, look!" I followed her pointing finger to see two does standing in the center of the river. We slowed our kayaks in the hope of observing them a while longer. They stared at us for a few seconds before splashing back to the bank and bounding into the woods.

The psalmist described his desire for the Lord as the need that draws a deer to the stream. Just as water provides life-sustaining refreshment for deer, I've found the Lord to be my source of life, hope, and strength. During a recent season of intense pressure in my work life, I found myself longing for the Lord and His help like never before. I fell asleep each night and woke each morning reading Scripture-filled note cards I had taped next to my bed. His life-giving promises to provide my daily bread and fill me with His Spirit sustained me in the midst of deep anxiety and heart-racing panic attacks. When I felt as dry as kindling, I stood in the river of His promises, drinking deeply from each word.

As I floated toward the deer that morning, I remembered the beauty of quietly coming to the Lord each day and believing His promises. In every challenging season, I've learned His promises are true. When we come to Him, as a deer drawn to the river, we will find His refreshment.

We can't anticipate and provide for life's trials, but the Lord can and does. The Lord wants us to thirst not after a quick fix to our problems but after the life-altering refreshment of His provision. —Priscilla Shirer

—Amelia Rhodes

AUGUST 21

Jailbirds

You were bought at a price. Therefore honor God with your bodies.

—1 CORINTHIANS 6:20 (NIV)

WHEN MY TWO escape-artist dogs got out of the fence and took off while I was at work, they were picked up by the county animal control. They both had tags and collars and were microchipped, but they would be spending the night in dog jail until I could pick them up the next morning.

At first, all I could be was grateful they were safe and had not gotten picked up by a stranger or hit by a car. Then I worried they would have to spend the night in a cell. After all the money spent on fencing, premium beds, and food I cooked for them every night, they still took off into a world of danger, leaving safety and love in their rear view.

The next day, I paid their bail. And even though it was apparent I had done everything I could to contain them, I was penalized for letting my dogs run free. They came out as the animal control officer commented how obedient and well cared for they were. Tails wagging and joyful, they hopped in the back seat as if they'd had a glorious adventure. They never realized the danger they had escaped or that someone had paid the price for their safety. They didn't realize they had caused any problem at all.

We do this too. We break from the safety of home, family, church, good health choices, or any choice that serves our best and highest interests. Then, when someone has our back and God covers us in protection, we return as if nothing happened, happily blind to all the ways we have been covered and blessed. Even when we do not realize how precious we are to God, He loves us through our adventures and constantly wants to give us a way back to His arms.

God, thank You for always loving me back to You. Amen.

—Devon O'Day

Loving Ernest-ly

"Which of these three do you think was a neighbor to the man who fell into the hands of robbers?" The expert in the law replied, "The one who had mercy on him." Jesus told him, "Go and do likewise."

—LUKE 10:36–37 (NIV)

THE WOMAN SAT at a picnic table outside a McDonald's, wearing layers of heavy sweaters despite the August heat. Two tattered trash bags and a backpack, with a coat and blanket tied to the top, lay at her feet. I imagined these were all her worldly possessions.

We were returning from a trip. "We had better walk the dogs away from there," I said.

My husband went inside to get food, while I took the dogs and headed away from the picnic-table lady. However, my golden retriever, Ernest, strained at the leash and pulled with all of his eighty-five pounds. This wasn't like him, a mellow fellow. But he tugged me right toward the woman I was trying to avoid.

I struggled with myself. Why was I turning away from her? Didn't God teach us to love one another? Shouldn't I show her kindness and compassion? With Ernest leading the way, I finally approached the woman.

"Hi!" I said.

"He's not going to bite?" she asked.

"Oh no," I said. "Are you having a nice day?"

She looked at us curiously. "You know?" she said. "I guess I am."

I wasn't sure what to do or what she needed. "Well," I said, smiling. "I just wanted to say hi. Ernest here suggested I come over."

"He did?" Her eyes grew wide. I could tell she wasn't exactly a dog person, but her gaze softened. "No one ever says hi to me. Thank you, Ernest."

As we walked away, I knew I had done the right thing. But I couldn't take all the credit. It was Ernest's idea.

Dear Father, teach me how to be compassionate to those I meet. If they need help, show me what I can do. If they need attention, give me the words. Thank You.

—Peggy Frezon

AUGUST 23

Where Have the Bats Gone?

Indeed, he who watches over Israel will neither slumber nor sleep. The Lord watches over you—the Lord is your shade at your right hand.

—Psalm 121:4–5 (NIV)

SUMMER IS FINALLY waning, so I have been spending more time outside at dusk. Any Floridian such as I will tell you that during the summer, you don't want to be anywhere near the outdoors just before nightfall because you'll get eaten up by mosquitoes. But the fall and winter months are a different story entirely.

The other day, I was outside at twilight with my dogs when I saw a bat flutter over my house. I know bats evoke fear in some people, but I welcome them. As far as I'm concerned, they can eat their fill of mosquitoes from my yard. I love to watch their erratic flapping and graceful swooshing as they chase pesky bugs.

Funny thing is, before that sighting, I hadn't seen that bat or any others in the longest time. At first, I thought it was a new bat . . . or that it had returned after being away awhile. But then I realized it wasn't the bat that had been absent. I was the one who had been hiding inside all summer, away from the mosquitoes and their predators—bats.

The same is true on a spiritual landscape. It's easy for me to feel as though God has appeared out of thin air and come to protect me—or conversely, to wonder where He has gone. But perhaps the better question in those times is, Where have I gone? Have I hidden on the other side of walls as He fights my battles on the horizon? Or have I simply stepped outside to discover He was there all along?

Father, help me to remember in my hours of doubt that You are ever with me. You are ever steady, ever alert, and ever capable in watching over me. You are my keeper, and I do not have to hide in isolation or retreat. I know You go before me and will never leave me, even when my own eyes can't see. Amen.

—Ashley Clark

AUGUST 24

Puddles in the Parking Lot

Behold, I will do a new thing, now it shall spring forth; shall you not know it? I will even make . . . rivers in the desert.

—ISAIAH 43:19 (NKJV)

I SAT IN THE grocery-store parking lot feeling the weight of a recent loss. My father's passing had ushered in an extended estrangement from family with whom I had been very close. Grief changes things. It impacts so many areas of life—some in ways we can anticipate and others in ways we don't see coming.

Everything I had tried to bring about reconciliation had failed. Others had intervened. Mature Christians had become involved but all were rebuffed. Now, it seemed clear, there would just be this sad, indefinite separation, and I had no recourse but to wait on the Lord. But, how? How would I fend off hopelessness and believe He would make a way through this seemingly impassable divide?

Just then, a sparrow flew past my windshield and landed in a puddle in the next parking space. It danced, flapped its wings, and hopped from one end of the transitory pool to the other, clearly enjoying an impromptu cooling dip. It had been such a dry stretch; I imagined the bird must be thrilled for this unexpected reprieve.

And then I knew. God was reminding me that just as surely as He makes puddles in the parking lot, so He makes streams in the desert and finds a way when there is no way. This puddle wasn't there yesterday, but here it appeared, as far as the sparrow knew, out of nowhere. I smiled at the tiny, joyful creature that reminded me where I would find my hope—in the One who makes a way where there is no way, in the One who *is* the way.

Are not five sparrows sold for two pennies? And not one of them is forgotten before God. —Luke 12:6 (ESV)

—Lori Stanley Roeleveld

AUGUST 25

The Truth Is Like a Lion

It gave me great joy when some believers came and testified about your faithfulness to the truth, telling how you continue to walk in it.

—3 JOHN 3 (NIV)

I'VE ALWAYS WONDERED why lionesses do all the work, or so it seemed to me, while the male lions get to laze around and sleep. After all, the lionesses have to carry the pregnancies, birth the cubs, and take care of the family. They're also the primary hunters in their prides, going out most evenings to bring home the family's meals.

However, things aren't always as they appear at first glance. The male lions do, in fact, have a very important job to do, and that's protecting their pride. Every evening, especially if there are other prides nearby, the male lions prowl around the perimeter of their pride's space, marking it as theirs and roaring again and again to let everyone in earshot know to whom this land belongs. They are, in a sense, walking their truth—and they make sure everyone knows it.

Scripture tell us to faithfully walk in God's truth. Do the people around us know we are Christians? Like the lions, we should be vocal in sharing His love with others.

The truth is like a lion. You don't have to defend it.
Let it loose and it will defend itself. —Anonymous

—Deb Kastner

AUGUST 26

Free Indeed

It is for freedom that Christ has set us free. Stand firm, then, and do not let yourselves be burdened again by a yoke of slavery.

—GALATIANS 5:1 (NIV)

WITH THE SUN fading around us, we could hear the eerie bugles of bull elk. In an hour, this meadow would be closed to hikers like us, a window of time given to let the elk migrate across Rocky Mountain National Park.

As we turned a bend in the trail, a ten-point bull lifted his head from the field of grass a few hundred feet away.

"What do you notice about him?" my husband asked our four young children.

"I see how big his horns are!" our eight-year-old exclaimed.

Our one-year-old's vocabulary was limited, but upon spotting the magnificent animal, she found the only word she needed: "Whoa!"

We live next to the Rocky Mountains, so this is not the only close encounter we have had with elk. In Estes Park, a town right next to the national park, they can be found roaming the streets downtown during certain seasons. And although it's quite the sight to watch them relaxing on the golf course or napping in the yards of vacation rental homes, it's never lost on me how truly wild they are. I'm always reminded, when we come upon them in the wilderness, that God fashioned this animal for freedom, and He has placed the same spirit of freedom within me. Just as He never created the elk for the confines of town life, He has not created me for the chains of insecurity, shame, guilt, comparison, depression, sin, or anxiety. When I see these incredible animals make their way out of town and back to the wilderness, I'm reminded that Christ has invited me into the realm of freedom, and I'm compelled to leave behind the chains of this world and live free indeed.

Dear Lord, I find myself time and time again returning to the confines of this broken world. When I feel trapped in a chained place—somewhere You never intended me to be—show me again the freedom that You bought for me on the cross. Help me to discover, more than ever before, what living in that freedom looks like. Amen.

—Eryn Lynum

AUGUST 27

Surprised by Joy

These things I have spoken to you, that my joy may be in you, and that your joy may be full.

—JOHN 15:11 (ESV)

DURING A SUMMER road trip through northern New Mexico, my husband pulled the car over to read a historic marker near Clayton. A quick perusal of the plaque revealed that this stretch of highway paralleled an old cattle trail once used to herd thousands of head of cattle from Texas to Dodge City, Kansas.

While Bill hiked down the path to take a closer look at the natural spring where cowboys watered their thirsty herds, I strolled over to the kiosk to study the colorful map mounted there. My attention was caught by birdsong. I could hear it all around me, but there were no trees for birds to perch in—only brown grass, scorched by the summer sun.

As I ventured into the tall grass, dozens of western meadowlarks fluttered up around me, their bright yellow breasts gleaming in the sunlight against a turquoise blue sky. Their exuberant trilling filled the air. It was truly an exaltation of larks—the poetic distinction for such a flock.

In that moment, the unexpected beauty of God's creation took my breath away. I felt a joy so intense I thought I might cry. That unforgettable experience helped me understand the difference between happiness and joy. Happiness is a carefree road trip with my hubby. Joy is a gift, the fruit of the Holy Spirit—along with love, peace, faith, patience, kindness, goodness, faithfulness, gentleness, and self-control. I'll never forget that special summer day when I was surprised by joy.

Joy, which was the small publicity of the pagan, is the gigantic secret of the Christian. —G.K. Chesterton

—Shirley Raye Redmond

The Skittish Skink

Be very careful, then, how you live—not as unwise but as wise, making the most of every opportunity, because the days are evil.

—EPHESIANS 5:15–16 (NIV)

MY FEET DANGLED in the cool water of the Floridian natural spring as I watched my husband and teenagers play. Our swim concluded a quick but relaxing vacation. When we returned home, our oldest would start high school. A bit of fear constricted my heart as I felt the years slipping away and recognized how soon my kids would be out in the world on their own.

As I watched my family swim, I noticed a quick movement next to my hand. Something scurried under my son's shirt lying on the shore. I lifted the clothing, and a small lizard, a skink, greeted me. It slithered deeper into the pile of clothes as I called my teens over to look. We huddled around the clothes for a few minutes, catching glimpses of its shiny scales as it kept burrowing deeper to find safety. We watched until it eventually scampered under a large rock.

I often feel like that skink; I just want to run and hide from the world. Newsfeeds confirm that the days are evil. I recognize I'm often powerless to protect my teens from heartache and hurt.

But I'm learning that rather than running and hiding under a rock like the skink, I am called by God to face this challenging culture head on. With His courage and wisdom, He helps me make the most of every opportunity—even the hardest hurts—to point my children toward His character and heart for them. I've learned to say with confidence that the Lord is my helper.

Father, grant me Your confidence and courage today. Help me not shrink back in fear but rather to make the most of every opportunity You provide today. I desire to point others to You. Amen.

—Amelia Rhodes

AUGUST 29

Quiet Joy

He leads me beside the still waters. He restores my soul.

—Psalm 23:2–3 (NKJV)

I HAD STEPPED INTO a crowded coffee shop for breakfast after an early morning doctor appointment. I had been experiencing painful nighttime cramps in my legs that worried me, and I wondered where all this was leading me. The cacophony of voices competing with the high-decibel music filled the restaurant. *I guess I am showing my age,* I thought, *but there is too much jangling music and crass talk these days. Where is there any calm and quiet?*

An elderly smiling woman caught my attention. She was holding the lead of a large golden retriever wearing a service vest. They stood patiently at the host's station, waiting to be seated. Despite their surroundings, they seemed to carry a sense of peace about them.

Her companion dog, sensitive and aware of the commotion around them, was, at the same time, solely focused on its owner. As the duo was guided to a booth, other diners stopped and halted their own conversations. It was apparent that the two of them carried a powerful bond of mutual, quiet serenity. They emitted an inner heavenly joy that was stronger than any loud surface noise in the room.

It had to be God who placed those two together, I thought.

Since I had been facing health concerns about my own future mobility, I was reassured and comforted that the Lord would provide the perfect companion dog for me when I needed one.

I know you love me and invite me, even when I am antsy and anxious.
—Henri J.M. Nouwen

—Sandra Clifton

AUGUST 30

Pamela the Possum

When a Samaritan woman came to draw water, Jesus said to her, "Will you give me a drink?"

—JOHN 4:7 (NIV)

THE FERAL CATS eat a LOT of food and drink a LOT of water in the area I set aside for them in the barn. I know they do their job taking care of rodents and snakes because I do see the little presents they leave me on the back doorstep. While feral cats sometimes eat their prey, most hunt for the joy of the hunt, not for food. So there was always a crowd at feeding time.

One evening as I was feeding the cats, I saw a young possum at a bowl. It saw me and ran away so quickly I thought it was a cat at first. Pamela Possum became a regular dinner guest, and soon she didn't run when I came to fill the bowls. The cats didn't seem to mind that she joined them at dinnertime.

It occurred to me that God welcomes me to provision even in unlikely scenarios. Have you ever been at a gathering when someone showed up who didn't fit in? Maybe you were that person, invited by a friend but realizing after you walked in that you were totally out of your element. We are all welcome at the well God has provided for us, and we are all required to share the water with others. Love and kindness break through the barriers of appearance and fear, and we get better the more we use them.

Lord, keep me open to sharing love and kindness to all You bring to the well with me and dispel my fear when I feel I do not fit in. In Jesus's name. Amen.

—Devon O'Day

AUGUST 31

Compassionate Chatter

The words of the reckless pierce like swords, but the tongue of the wise brings healing.

—Proverbs 12:18 (NIV)

MY FRIEND TEDDY serves as a caregiver for wounded wildlife through the Tri County Wildlife Care. She invited me to be a member of an online group committed to praying for her and the animals God entrusted to her. One day, she introduced the group to Norma, an injured infant squirrel. We prayed as Teddy nursed Norma back to health and prepared to release the squirrel back into the wild.

In one video update, a stronger Norma perched on a branch in her cage and nibbled on a nut while Teddy hid behind some brush to record her improvement. The tiny squirrel noticed the intruder—her well-meaning caregiver. Norma chattered fiercely and leaped toward Teddy.

To my surprise, Teddy responded with joy. She wanted Norma to maintain her natural instincts and remain territorial, which would help her thrive in the wild. Teddy explained that squirrels weren't meant to live in cages and injured animals don't always know how to respond to caregivers.

Injured people don't always do well in that department either. During my ongoing battle with chronic pain and fatigue, caused by a back injury, my physical limitations have often made me feel caged and helpless. When frustration, discouragement, weariness, or fear have snuck up on me, I've lashed out at my well-meaning caregivers. I've had to seek forgiveness from God and from those I've hurt with careless words.

Unlike Norma, I don't need to thrive in the wild. No matter how I feel, I can choose to love God by responding to others with compassionate chatter.

Lord, please help me acknowledge the destructive power of careless words and respond to others with love, compassion, gentleness, and respect. Amen.

—Xochitl E. Dixon

September

SEPTEMBER 1

The Best Day

He will wipe every tear from their eyes. There will be no more death or mourning or crying or pain, for the old order of things has passed away.

—REVELATION 21:4 (NIV)

KATE AND I share a heartbreaking experience: the loss of a child. Though it happened many years ago for both of us, we tear up right away when we talk about our boys, gone to heaven too soon. So many sad things to remember. But happy things too.

When Kate's oldest son, Travis, was about seven, he did his best to adjust to the death of his little brother, Jesse. But Travis missed him terribly. What helped fill his heart most was his scruffy rescue dog, Rusty. The dog adored Travis, and in turn, Travis was crazy about Rusty. They were inseparable.

One day, Rusty disappeared. The family helped Travis search but couldn't find the dog anywhere. They went door to door in the neighborhood, asking if anyone had seen Rusty. But no one had. They checked at the pound with no luck. Travis had lost his brother not long before. Now his dog was gone too. The family's prayers seemed to vanish in the clouds.

Many months passed without a trace of Rusty. Then one day, the dog came loping down the sidewalk, dragging a rope tied to his collar. When Travis saw him, he thought his heart would burst. And he rushed to scoop up his beloved Rusty. At last, they were together again.

As Kate watched her boy hug his dog, she thought, *This must be what it's like to be reunited in heaven—the absolute joy of recognizing your loved ones!*

That will be the best day of all.

Earth has no sorrow that heaven cannot heal. —Thomas Moore

—Cathy Elliott

SEPTEMBER 2

Bee Mighty

Truly I tell you, if you have faith as small as a mustard seed, you can say to this mountain, "Move from here to there," and it will move. Nothing will be impossible for you.

—MATTHEW 17:20 (NIV)

MY FAMILY SAT at the picnic table on a lovely late-summer evening. I tried to simply enjoy our weekly dinner. But truth be told, as I looked from daughter to son to grandchild, I couldn't help thinking about the events of their weeks, the struggles in their lives—and worry.

All the while, a swarm of bees was having a family gathering of its own around the foundation of my house. I watched them squeeze into a crack in the mortar. A buzzing queue lined up as bees awaited their turn to enter. I understand the benefit of bees and their place in the ecosystem; however, having them invading my foundation and swarming around my back steps was not ideal.

"You don't want to get stung," I told my grandchildren, whisking them away. I didn't have to encourage my adult children—they had already abandoned their hot dogs and burgers and taken refuge inside. "Bees!" they cried as they ran. They might as well have been shouting "Bear!" or "Stampeding elephants!"

What a tiny creature, I marveled, studying a single bee lighting atop a stone. Yet, I had to admit, such is my faith—sometimes so small I'm ashamed. Why do I look at my family members and worry when it won't change a thing? If only I would call upon my faith—even the puny amount I can muster—and trust that God has everything under control. After all, Scripture tells us that even a tiny seed of faith is powerful enough to move mountains. Just like the bee—tiny in size but powerful enough to send grown men and women fleeing.

Dear Lord, I'm reminded that my family is in Your loving hands, where worry cannot enter, and faith and love can take flight. In Jesus's name, amen.

—Peggy Frezon

SEPTEMBER 3

Our Creative Creator

May the glory of the LORD endure forever; may the LORD rejoice in his works.

—PSALM 104:31 (NIV)

EVEN THOUGH I'VE battled a lifelong fear of the water, I consider sea life one of the clearest reflections of God's creativity and sense of humor. I was reminded of this when my family went to the Academy of Science for my nephew's birthday and I found myself mesmerized by a small tank of sea dragons. They looked like seahorses dressed as plants for Halloween.

I watched one float in front of me, gracefully dipping downward then up again. It stayed still just long enough for me to get a photo.

I laughed and told my sister, "God was having fun the day He created those." Instead of picturing Him saying, "It is good," I imagined God joyfully exclaiming, "This is so much fun!"

The next day, I looked at the picture of the sea dragon and smiled again. I read that they are some of the best-camouflaged creatures on the planet, able to blend in with the seaweed and kelp around them. Those facts reminded me that God's artistry always has a purpose, but being a creative at heart, I could still revel in the idea of Him enjoying the process. Did He take just as much pleasure in creating me and my two sons, even when it came down to the details of what we would look like and what we would need to survive in the world?

When I read the Creation account, I sense that God, who looked at everything He made and called it good, experienced a special kind of joy when He made us. After all, unlike sea dragons, each of us is created in His image and with a unique plan in mind.

How many are your works, LORD! In wisdom you made them all; the earth is full of your creatures. There is the sea, vast and spacious, teeming with creatures beyond number—living things both large and small.

—Psalm 104:24–25 (NIV)

—Jeanette Hanscome

Silently at Work

One of those listening was a woman from the city of Thyatira named Lydia, a dealer in purple cloth. She was a worshiper of God. The Lord opened her heart to respond to Paul's message.

—ACTS 16:14 (NIV)

OUR NEIGHBORHOOD'S FACEBOOK page was all abuzz. "Is anyone else having trouble with moles in your yard?" one resident asked. "Yes!" another replied. "They're everywhere." The neighbor on the corner who spends every Saturday fertilizing, mowing, or trimming was especially frustrated. "I spend hours and hours on my lawn, and these critters ruin it in a day."

I admit it's disconcerting to step off my porch expecting *terra firma* and instead finding *terra squishy*. The expanse of underground tunnels a mole can accomplish in a single night is impressive. Although I've never seen one, I see evidence of the moles' work everywhere.

I never thought I would compare God to a mole, but as I've pondered the subterranean rodents' handiwork, I've discovered some striking similarities. Not because God tears stuff up, but because He's always at work—silently, imperceptibly, in ways I can't even imagine. If I look closely, I see signs of His presence everywhere. He does His greatest work, however, unseen, deep in the hearts of people.

Like the moles soften the hard ground of my lawn, so God softens the hard hearts of the people around us. And knowing God is at work even when I can't see Him gives me confidence and hope for my lost loved ones. It reminds me to pray for those whose hearts appear hopelessly hard toward spiritual things and encourages me never to give up.

Walk of Faith: *Is there a person in your life who appears hardened toward spiritual things? Have you been tempted to give up on them? Renew your commitment to pray for them, asking God to soften their hearts to believe.*

—Lori Hatcher

SEPTEMBER 5

It's Not How It Appears

I will give you hidden treasures, riches stored in secret places, so that you may know that I am the Lord, the God of Israel, who summons you by name.

—Isaiah 45:3 (NIV)

MY HUSBAND AND I are huge fans of animal documentaries, and the story of Orangutan Jungle School in Borneo caught our eyes and heart. Orangutans are indigenous only to Borneo and Sumatra and are on the critically endangered list. Baby orangutans are often orphaned when their mothers are run over by cars on the busy highways. This is where compassionate conservationists have come in, creating a school for orangutans where they quite literally take classes to learn, from the ground up, how to be an orangutan, with the final goal of release back into the wild.

The littles have a class of their own where they learn basic moves and are cared for until they can forage for fruit (with help from their keepers).

Then comes elementary school where the orangutans learn the most basic of ape skills, everything from plucking fruit off moving branches to using leaves to create hammocks. Every ape has its own name and personality, from shy to crazy outgoing, a laugh a minute.

On one episode, two of our favorite orangutans were held back, kept in their overnight cages while they watched their class being called out to the jungle for the day. Their reactions were priceless. They thought they had been left behind! But they hadn't been left behind. They had actually graduated and would be moving up to the next class.

This made me wonder how many times in my life I have misunderstood God's will for me, thinking I've been left behind when, really, He has somewhere new and exciting for me to be. As with the baby orangutans, maybe I'm not going where I'm expecting to go, but I can always trust God for it to be in the right direction.

Dear Lord, when things don't go quite as planned,
help me look to You to point the way. Amen.

—Deb Kastner

SEPTEMBER 6

The Hummingbird's Flight

Finally, brothers and sisters, whatever is true, whatever is noble, whatever is right, whatever is pure, whatever is lovely, whatever is admirable—if anything is excellent or praiseworthy—think about such things.

—PHILIPPIANS 4:8 (NIV)

ONE OF MY favorite things about the summer season is the end of it. Not because here in the South I melt in the heat—though that's true—but because the end of the summer is when a group of hummingbirds returns yearly to my yard.

This summer was particularly special because I was in the middle of writing about hummingbirds in a novel when one flew up to the window and hovered there, staring right at me. Needless to say, I was fixated! I knew God had just sent me a message—that He sees me and my dream . . . in my case, that particular story went on to be contracted for publication a few weeks later.

The special thing about hummingbirds is they are always searching out beauty in the world around them. The nectar of colorful flowers sustains them from flight to flight. Rather than studying the weeds or rotten, dried-up things, they actively seek out the next bloom for nectar to drink. I believe God's command to "think on these things" is much the same—I am better off when I, like those hummingbirds, look toward the grace of Christ that is abundant all around me. Even my small garden is full of promise. How much more so is the rest of the world? By taking time to meditate on what is true, noble, right, pure, lovely, and admirable, I allow my soul to be fed by God's abundance. When I discipline myself to see the world in this way, there is no end to the beauty I see.

Walk of Faith: *Ask yourself: Are the thoughts I'm nurturing noble and lovely, or are they weeds? I know that what I grow determines what I will attract. How can I be more attuned to see the things of beauty God is growing within me?*

—Ashley Clark

SEPTEMBER 7

A Bulldog's Comfort

My comfort in my suffering is this: Your promise preserves my life.

—Psalm 119:50 (NIV)

THAT SEPTEMBER AFTERNOON, I crouched on a school playground, plucking dandelions. The grass had been mown, along with most of the weeds our pet bunny loves to munch. I felt mown down too. What had begun as pain relief was now my grown son's full-blown addiction—and I was hurting. I needed a shoulder to lean on for comfort.

Looking up, I spotted a twentysomething woman I had seen there before, sitting beside her brindle-colored English bulldog. I said, "Just gathering dandelions for my pet bunny," and held up my bag of weeds. The dog ran over, still rhythmically chewing a squeaky rubber ball. The woman confessed that Dex the dog probably wouldn't drop it for me to throw—he would rather chew and suck on it. She added, "Don't worry, he's friendly." To prove it, Dex sat on my foot, still chomping on his slobbery ball.

The young lady and I chatted while I picked weeds and Dex kept us entertained with his ball chewing. There's just something fun about bulldogs, we agreed, with their oversized heads and droopy eyes. Dex, she said, was really sucking on the ball as if it were a pacifier. "It comforts him." Comfort. I mentioned that I write about the addiction that runs rampant in my family, and she hugged Dex. "I've been in recovery for several years now," she said softly. "I would never have made it this far without Dex here." The bulldog sat there with a smile plastered across his doggy face.

Soon my dandelion bag was full. We said goodbye, but I admired how my new friend's bulldog had helped her recover. All the way home, I marveled at the way animals can bring us together to show us God's love. I felt a little lighter too, smiling every time I pictured Dex and his squeaky ball.

Lord, whenever my hopes dwindle, remind me that the animal friends in my life love me no matter what. Amen.

—Linda S. Clare

SEPTEMBER 8

Wild Turkeys in the City

Look at the birds of the air; they do not sow or reap or store away in barns, and yet your heavenly Father feeds them. Are you not much more valuable than they?

—MATTHEW 6:26 (NIV)

LIVING IN AN urban setting somewhat limits one's opportunities to interact with nondomesticated animals. It is very common to see robins, sparrows, and even crows in the trees and lawns around homes. But it is surprising to see a flock of gigantic wild turkeys strutting down the city street. That is a regular sight in my sister's neighborhood, and my grandsons were especially delighted to be witnesses to these occurrences.

Cathy cared for the boys while the rest of us were at work. She lived in a little valley at the bottom of a steep wooded hill and would take the boys out for a walk every day when the weather allowed. Most days, they would find foot-long feathers to add to their collections. Sometimes, if they happened to be looking up at just the right time, they would catch a glimpse of one of the adult birds taking off or landing nearby. Their four-foot wingspan was impressive against the bright-blue sky.

One time, four-year-old Cody got close enough to actually touch one. He ran into the house to tell Cathy that he had almost caught a turkey. She teased him that he had let their Thanksgiving dinner go free.

I never got as close to the turkeys as Cody did, but I've often waited patiently while the entire flock crossed the road in front of my car. I am so amazed at how they have adapted to an environment that is clearly not natural to them. When God puts me in an unfamiliar setting, I pray that I will be able to adjust as well as the turkeys have.

Lord, You are the master of the unexpected, but You are never surprised. Thank You for providing for my every need, as You do for all Your creation.

—Liz Kimmel

SEPTEMBER 9

A New Confidence

For we do not have a high priest who is unable to empathize with our weaknesses, but we have one who has been tempted in every way, just as we are—yet he did not sin. Let us then approach God's throne of grace with confidence, so that we may receive mercy and find grace to help us in our time of need.

—HEBREWS 4:15–16 (NIV)

SURELY, I THOUGHT, the wild antelope would deviate from their course in order to escape the rumble of our SUV on the dirt road. We kept a careful distance as the herd ran down the road before us.

"Aren't they pretty?" my husband asked our children as they watched the sixteen antelope running forty miles an hour ahead of us.

"Watch them jump," I added when the animals neared the fence.

"I don't think they will," my husband said as he kept our vehicle's speed steady, allowing the antelope as much room as they needed. "They're not even trying."

We stayed with the herd until they found a safe place to escape to a surrounding prairie, and my husband was right: they did not jump the fence. Instead, they found a place where they could duck beneath it.

Although one of the fastest land animals on earth, antelope have a weakness that has threatened their migration: they will not jump fences. Ranchers have adapted their fences by choosing a smooth wire over a barbed one for the lowest rung or using a clip to raise the fence into an arched opening, making it easier for the animals to pass through.

The antelope, with help from those who have adapted their fence lines, have a newfound confidence in their annual migration voyage. I, too, find new assurance as I witness how patient God is with my own weaknesses, and how He always makes a way.

Dear Lord, when I feel the ache of my own weaknesses, turn my eyes to You and Your patience and power. Remind me that You are merciful and gracious toward my weaknesses, and that You are going before me, preparing me in Your strength to clear every obstacle along the way. Amen.

—Eryn Lynum

SEPTEMBER 10

The Runaways

After spending some time there, they were sent off by the believers with the blessing of peace to return to those who had sent them.

—ACTS 15:33 (NIV)

I NEVER SOUGHT A life of animal rescue; it found me. A cat would follow me home, a dog would jump into my car, and suddenly rescue was my life.

I became adept at saving the unsavable. I also learned the hard way when to say no. When you are full, you are full, and the most humane thing for those in your care is to protect your own pack by saying no to more intakes. And then there are those animals that just show up. You have to care for them at least for the night, right?

One evening, my dogs were going crazy as I let them out in my fenced backyard where they found two cute puppies. My dogs were unusually welcoming to the two pups, so I fed them and got them water. I tucked them into an outdoor kennel, and soon they were curled up together on the dog bed. I began the process of calling my network of rescuers, sharing pictures through texts, wondering if they belonged to someone or were strays.

The next morning, I went out to check on the pups, and they were gone, just as mysteriously as they had arrived. Later, I found they were from down the street and had just gone home. I will admit that though I didn't need the worry of rehoming puppies, I was sad when they weren't in the kennel that morning. But the blessing for me was knowing that they had been safe, warm, and well fed before they found their way back to their family. Sometimes people pass our way, and they are never meant to stay forever in our lives. We are just a blessing God planned for them along the journey.

God, please let me hold all who pass my way with open hands, blessing as I can and letting go when they are ready. Amen.

—Devon O'Day

SEPTEMBER 11

Here Be Dragons!

And I saw, coming out of the mouth of the dragon and out of the mouth of the beast and out of the mouth of the false prophet, three unclean spirits like frogs.

—REVELATION 16:13 (ESV)

I COULD HARDLY WAIT to see the Komodo dragons at the San Diego Zoo. As a teen, I had read about William Douglas Burden and his adventure-loving wife, Catherine, and how they journeyed to Indonesia in the 1920s to capture one of the enormous beasts to bring to the United States. I had been fascinated by those creatures ever since.

With eager anticipation, I led my husband and children to the dragon exhibit. My heart pounded. My pulse raced. And then . . . there they were, a pair of them. I had seen photographs, but I expected the dragons to appear more impressive in real life. They were not. They didn't seem nearly as frightening as the gigantic crocodiles and alligators I had seen elsewhere. I knew if this huge lizard came hurtling through the jungle at me, I would be scared to death. But here in its clean, sunny enclosure, the dozing dragons did not live up to their reputation. I felt so disappointed.

In comparison, Jesus has never disappointed me. In the hymn, " 'Tis So Sweet to Trust in Jesus," there's a line, "How I've proved Him o'er and o'er." That's so true! Yes, other people have disappointed me, and yes, I've occasionally found myself in difficult, heart-wrenching circumstances where I felt alone in my suffering. However, the Lord used those occasions to prove that He is good, true, and merciful. His loving kindness endures forever!

A life totally committed to Christ has nothing to fear, nothing to lose, and nothing to regret. —Pandita Ramabai

—Shirley Raye Redmond

Among the Pronghorns

And let us run with perseverance the race marked out for us, fixing our eyes on Jesus, the pioneer and perfecter of faith.

—HEBREWS 12:1–2 (NIV)

ON A LONG-AWAITED adventure, my husband, Tom, and I drove through southeastern Oregon with its ponderosa pines, sage, and aspen-dotted hills. This corner of the state includes the beginning of the Great Basin and is the gateway to the majestic Steens Mountain Wilderness.

In the distance, a herd of antelope-like creatures called pronghorns outran our vehicle. We drove on, drinking chilled water from our cooler on this hot Indian summer day. Then just ahead, we spotted a van that had broken down.

We stopped and shared our cold drinks with the family and waited with them for help to arrive. As time went by, we had the blessing of lingering among the pronghorns, which are small but relentless and amazing to behold.

We watched these animals stop to graze, but they seemed focused on their run—the reason they are named "marathoners of the American West." Pronghorns are the fastest land animal in North America, able to run up to sixty-five miles per hour, and are second only to the cheetah as the fastest on earth.

Named for their unique antlers, pronghorns are often called American antelopes. But scientists have determined they belong to the *Giraffoidea* group, their closest relative being the giraffe. These reddish-brown creatures with their striking white embellishments resemble baby giraffes, if you allow your imagination to take you there, especially on a hot, open range.

Divine interruptions become blessings when we trust the One who orchestrates it all. We were sent to minister to the stranded family until help arrived, allowing more time among these beautiful, athletic creatures. And as we continued our journey to explore more of God's glorious creation, the pronghorns ran alongside us—graceful and free.

Dear Jesus, keep our eyes focused on You as we run the race of life, strong, relentless, and enabled by Your grace. Amen.

—Kathleen Ruckman

SEPTEMBER 13

More Than Hanging On

I came that they may have life, and have it abundantly.

—JOHN 10:10 (NRSV)

RECENTLY, I HURRIED out of the house on my way to an appointment. As I turned onto the main road and began to accelerate, I noticed a grasshopper on my windshield! I couldn't stop and do anything at that moment, so I told the poor thing to hold on for dear life. And it did.

I got up to a pretty good speed, but the little grasshopper clung to the glass, its wings flapping in the wind, and somehow managed to make the journey safely.

Aren't we like that sometimes? Simply holding on for dear life, the winds of grief, strained relationships, and disappointments buffeting us as we try to keep plugging away with our lives. We try to make ends meet, try to save for retirement, try to support our kids and grandkids, try to meet all our obligations, and on and on.

But as I read God's Word, I realize He wants more for me. He doesn't want me to just barely get by, with my hair blown back and my fingers clawing to hang on. He doesn't want me to feel like that poor grasshopper clinging to the windshield at forty-five miles an hour. God wants me to live life abundantly.

Lord, I give my life to You—every detail. It's all too much for me to handle alone. Please guide me to the abundant life You have planned. Amen.

—Missy Tippens

SEPTEMBER 14

Carrying a Butterfly

Be kind and compassionate to one another, forgiving each other, just as in Christ God forgave you.

—EPHESIANS 4:32 (NIV)

A NEAT THING ABOUT living along the Gulf Coast is that every September, I get to see swarms of Gulf fritillaries. We have their host plant, the passion vine, growing along our fence line. As the whimsical purple flowers open toward the sun, the butterflies seem to come from north, south, east, and west. Then they lay eggs, and a new generation of butterflies is born. I love watching the orange caterpillars, with their menacing black spikes, and the beautiful butterflies they become.

Last week, a cold front came through and brought with it some heavy winds. My son and I were playing outside during a break in the rain, and as we were running, I noticed an old butterfly with worn wings climbing up a tall blade of grass amid the storm. I reached out with care, and it climbed onto my finger. Naturally, I thought about keeping it forever, but instead, I used my other hand to block the wind from its wings while I searched for a better spot in the yard for the butterfly. I settled on a thick bush full of flowers, where it could get nectar and burrow between the leaves as needed between gusts of wind.

The butterfly immediately unrolled its wings and began to drink from the flower, as I stood in awe that for the second time in two weeks, a butterfly had crawled onto my hand. I thought about how a similar principle holds true with the people around me. Sometimes, when the winds of life pick up, others who are struggling may be more apt to accept encouragement or help. I hope and pray that I'm able to see them and take the opportunity to block the wind for a little while. May I always remember the difference I can make in others' lives.

Walk of Faith: *Did someone who is hurting come to mind as you read these paragraphs? How can you encourage that person amid struggle, depression, or loss?*

—Ashley Clark

SEPTEMBER 15

Needing an Advocate

My little children, these things I write to you, so that you may not sin. And if anyone sins, we have an Advocate with the Father, Jesus Christ the righteous.

—1 JOHN 2:1 (NKJV)

MISTY PADDED INTO the family room and gave us her muted bark. I knew this meant she needed to go outside, but I waited for our household's newest teenager to respond. Jackie's first reaction suggested she planned to ignore the dog. Misty would have none of it. She let out her full-on yappy bark.

Grabbing the leash, Jackie exited for a hasty parade around the block. My daughter rode her skateboard, and Misty ran alongside at a clip appropriate for Pomeranian legs. I smiled from the driveway.

When they returned, it seemed like a good time to reinforce my daughter's responsibility for cleaning up after the dog. "Jackie, before you head inside, grab the hose and take care of Misty's droppings in the backyard."

"Oh, Dad, can I do it later?"

"If you won't take care of the dog, there could be consequences," I said.

"You won't get rid of Misty. You love her as much as I do. Look at that cute face."

Jackie had a point. I loved the dog. "Who said anything about getting rid of the dog? I'm talking no cell phone for a week."

With that, my daughter hurried around the house to get the hose.

Looking back, I realize that Jackie was acting as an advocate for Misty. It touched my heart that she argued on behalf of a little being that couldn't defend herself. This made me think about Jesus. He served as our ultimate advocate by dying on the cross, but He didn't stop there.

When we sin, Jesus pleads our case to the Father. He argues for mercy. I couldn't survive without God's grace. I am so thankful.

Lord, thank You for being our advocate in heaven. I need Your grace every day. Show me those opportunities when I can extend grace to others. All praise to You. Amen.

—David L. Winters

Prone to Wander

My sheep hear my voice, and I know them, and they follow me.

—JOHN 10:27 (ESV)

WHEN WE GOT a young pygmy goat to be a companion for our pony, Jack, I was surprised to learn we wouldn't need to use a fence or training to prevent him from wandering. Instead, all we needed to do was keep Moni the goat in the barn for a few days with Jack.

Sure enough, when we led our pony out to the pasture a few days later, little Moni followed without being directed. He had attached to Jack and would never stray far from the pony's side from then on.

Called imprinting, this phenomenon of animals bonding to others is still not completely understood, but observing our goat and old pony made one thing obvious. Moni chose to remain near because he felt safe by Jack's side.

Sometimes, Moni would get so busy grazing, following the allure of fresh grass, that he would lose track of how far he had strayed. When he looked up and couldn't see his pony, he would bleat and trot back to the pasture, clearly happy to reunite with Jack. After that, Moni would become more cautious for a while, staying closer and looking back at Jack to make sure he was near.

Little Moni reminds me of myself. I get so caught up in busyness and the allure of worldly pleasures that I wander away from God, my shepherd. When something goes awry, I finally look up and realize I can't see Him close anymore. He didn't wander; I did. As Jesus's sheep, I need to keep my eyes fixed on Him, always staying close to the One who loves me and will keep me safe.

Walk of Faith: *Have you checked lately to see how close you are to Jesus? Take five minutes to return to the Good Shepherd and thank Him for His protective, guiding love.*

—Jerusha Agen

SEPTEMBER 17

Casper the Unfriendly Dog

In Him we have redemption through His blood, the forgiveness of sins, according to the riches of His grace.

—EPHESIANS 1:7 (NKJV)

I'VE ALWAYS BEEN drawn to "bad boys," and I certainly met one at the no-kill dog shelter where I volunteered. His name was Casper, but he was definitely not friendly. He was more like thirty pounds of mean. Casper looked angelic with his white tuxedo chest and white-tipped paws, but he had a cranky attitude. If any potential adopters stopped at his kennel to check him out, he greeted them with a snarl and a growl—not the way to find a forever home. Casper was going nowhere fast.

Casper loved to walk and knew that was my business as a volunteer, so he made an exception for me and was kind. I assumed that would be his life.

But I felt sorry for him when his kennel mate found a home. Casper was so bonded to his friend that he went into a depression. Not even his walks helped much. Of all the two hundred-plus dogs at the shelter, Casper tugged at my heart. With his grumpiness, he would never charm someone into taking him home.

There was only one thing to do. He had to be mine. And that's how Casper became Cesar, ruler of our household.

Life often throws us curveballs to deal with, and sometimes, like Casper, we have a tough time. It's in those times that God can lift us and promise us a better tomorrow.

Love that reaches up is adoration. Love that reaches out is compassion. Love that stoops down is grace. Father, thank You for Your grace. When life is hard, let me not despair. Let me look to You for comfort and peace. Amen.

—Linda Bartlett

SEPTEMBER 18

The Secret Life of a Woodland Mouse

For there is nothing hidden that will not be disclosed, and nothing concealed that will not be known or brought out into the open.

—LUKE 8:17 (NIV)

MY HUSBAND, DAN, and I were sleeping in our Jeep's rooftop tent when I awoke with a start to an odd sound. It frightened me for a minute, then it stopped.

The next morning, I was ready for coffee. Opening the tailgate for my cookstove, I noticed a rip in the trash bag stored inside. We had broken a glass bottle, and shards had shredded the plastic. Annoyed, I picked up the mess, then began preparing breakfast.

Soon, I was enjoying a hot beverage and food, soaking in the peaceful morning. Dan was facing the open tailgate and calmly remarked, "I just saw a mouse run inside the Jeep."

My freshly caffeinated brain connected the noise and the ripped bag. Uh-oh. I was not so calm.

Back and forth, the mouse teased us, running behind the cooler, then out again. The show-off even jumped onto the tailgate hinge, swinging up like a circus performer.

Later that evening, we finally believed the mouse was gone. We hadn't seen it in hours, but I arranged my stove so I could keep an eagle eye out anyway. After a few minutes of cooking, I glanced up. Peeking over the bumper was a tiny head with its nose sniffing the air.

Scripture reminds me that I can hide nothing from God and that everything will be exposed. Yet like the mouse, I sometimes still try to hide. At times, I have truly believed that God cannot know what I have done. The greatest gift that He can give me, though, is exposure. The freedom from guilt and shame sets me on the path toward healing.

Dear Lord, cleanse my heart of my sin. I don't want to hide anything from You. I've been holding something close for too long, and I need Your forgiveness.

—Twila Bennett

SEPTEMBER 19

Kind-Hearted Mysteries

Bless those who persecute you; bless and do not curse.

—ROMANS 12:14 (NIV)

THE TINY EGYPTIAN plover, aka crocodile bird, lives in Africa. Locals think the creature is either extremely brave or stupid. It walks around inside a crocodile's mouth, cleaning the reptile's teeth. The plover is looking for a free meal—bits of leftover food stuck between the croc's fangs. The relationship is symbiotic—the bird, using its sharp beak like a toothpick, gets an easy meal, while the large lizard receives dental care.

It makes sense. Working to help someone else is an easy decision when both parties get something out of it. It's not so fun when there's no favor returned—especially when dealing with our enemies.

How do you explain why a prairie dog would warn a rattlesnake (its mortal foe) that a hungry roadrunner is nearby? It's a mystery. Or what about the inspiring stories we hear of dolphins protecting humans from sharks? There is nothing these animals get in return, so why do it?

Perhaps God enjoys using nature to model how we should live as His followers. Jesus tells us to love our enemies, do good, and bless those who mistreat us.

This can be hard for me if the other person is indifferent or has hurt (in word or deed) me or a loved one. However, laying down my rights to serve those who don't deserve my kindness both kills my pride and helps me grow in charity toward the unlovable.

Performing acts of goodwill for strangers or enemies isn't always reciprocated. We may get nothing in return from others. But what a blessing from God for those willing to try.

Walk of Faith: *Without expecting anything in return, who will you be kind to this week?*

—Tez Brooks

SEPTEMBER 20

Skunk Perfume

Therefore, my friends, I want you to know that through Jesus the forgiveness of sins is proclaimed to you.

—ACTS 13:38 (NIV)

EVEN AN INDIRECT hit from a defensive skunk can "perfume" the head of a dog you love, and it's a fragrance that lives with you for a long time. I have tried tomato-juice baths, charcoal shampoo, and a million other things when one of my dogs goes after a skunk.

Mike is my most curious and energetic dog and loves to play more than he loves to do anything. He acts as if every living creature were made to be his playmate. He irritates some with his enthusiasm. He terrifies others. And one night, he chose a passing skunk as the focus of his attention, and that skunk sent a gift cloud his way. This didn't even faze Mike, who also didn't understand why bed snuggles weren't welcomed after that encounter. To him, it was just something that happened and then it was over.

To me, it was something that happened and I couldn't get past it. I did everything to get him clean. But every time his coat hit moisture, I received a nice strong whiff of Pepe LePew. This olfactory reminder was like all the times someone in my life reached out to me and all I could do was remember something bad they had done in the past. Life would move on, but I couldn't. I would hold on to things long after the event, and forgiveness just wouldn't come. I could not forget any more than I could wash away the scent of a skunk. Time and letting God cleanse my heart was the only way to bring the sweet aroma of forgiveness.

God, wash my heart memories and bring forgiveness where I cannot. Amen.

—Devon O'Day

SEPTEMBER 21

Dolly Llama

I call to remembrance my song in the night; I meditate within my heart, and my spirit makes diligent search.

—PSALM 77:6 (NKJV)

AT JUST THE right time in my life, I was privileged to meet Dolly Llama. Now, Dolly isn't a llama, and she's not famous like the religious leader for whom she was named, but this alpaca still had a profound influence on my spiritual life.

One Saturday, I visited my neighbor's farm for a dozen fresh eggs and a pint of grape tomatoes. It was the last day of summer. Fall was just kissing the air, so rather than rush my errands, I wandered the property.

After enduring a season of grief, I had begun to learn the value of slowing down, learning to breathe deeper, to walk more, and to notice my own heart and the world around me. I had also been relearning the habit of meditating on God's Word.

On this Saturday, I reached Dolly's pen, and the beige alpaca trotted to the fence to greet me, hoping I had brought a treat. Seeing I had none, she wasn't dismayed. Instead, a lump rose up her long throat and landed in her mouth. Calmly, she began to chew.

After a time, she swallowed, but the lump returned, and she chewed again. There she stood, she and I, contemplating each other quietly as she chewed her cud and I exhaled.

Now, when I run to life's fence hoping for a treat but find none, I will remember Dolly and her ruminating. God has filled me with truth that I can call to mind at any moment, to nourish my soul and steady my heart, so I can live as peacefully as Dolly Llama.

Walk of Faith: *When you are dealing with anxious thoughts that try to fill your mind, instead recall a Bible verse or passage. Sit or walk quietly and let it run over and over in your thoughts, relishing each phrase and meditating on its truth.*

—Lori Stanley Roeleveld

SEPTEMBER 22

Stay or Stray?

How can a young person stay on the path of purity? By living according to your word. I seek you with all my heart; do not let me stray from your commands.

—PSALM 119:9–10 (NIV)

WHILE DRIVING ON a narrow country road, I found my route blocked by a doe and her fawn walking in the middle of the road. The doe immediately moved to the right shoulder and jumped down into the brush to get out of the way of my approaching car, but the fawn chose to stop and stare at me for a moment. I slowed to a crawl and pulled to the left, hoping to "herd" the young deer toward its mother, but it stubbornly refused to move out of the way and, instead, trotted a few feet ahead of me. Coming to a stop, I watched as the mother deer patiently climbed back up onto the road and joined her fawn. She appeared to have a little deer discussion with her offspring before they both sauntered off into the surrounding forest.

I had to chuckle. Ah, youth! No matter the species, inexperienced youth thinks its way is best. I know I thought so when I was young. Had the fawn followed its mother, it would have been safe. Instead, it ignored her wise example and kept to its own risky path until she intervened.

Sadly, choosing risky paths isn't reserved for youth. Like the fawn, I often choose my own way, through ignorance, arrogance, or laziness, rather than act according to God's Word. In many cases, a quick prayer or look inside my Bible to seek guidance would have kept me safely on His path. Thankfully, each day is a fresh opportunity for me to seek Him "with all my heart." And I want to! After all, He gave me His Word for my good.

Jesus, keep me near Thee, never let me stray,
Keep me, precious Savior, faithful every day.
—William Harrison Horner

—Marianne Campbell

SEPTEMBER 23

At the Crossroads

Have I not commanded you? Be strong and courageous. Do not be afraid; do not be discouraged, for the Lord your God will be with you wherever you go.

—Joshua 1:9 (NIV)

DRIVING HOME FROM dinner during a thunderstorm, I came to a four-way stop. At the crossroads, a great white heron bent intently over a manhole cover. The headlights cutting through the rain made the bird glow in the darkness. I watched for a minute, and when the storm let up, I got out of the car to get a closer look. Not frightened by the weather, the car lights, or me, the big bird dined contently on a frog. I got close enough to see the ridges of its strong beak and the wispy variations of its feathers. When it finished eating, it focused its yellow eyes on me, shrugged its wide wings, and lifted up into the sky.

The months preceding this evening had been particularly exhausting. A major project at work had gone steadily downhill, with no end in sight. Friends were too busy to get together, and I couldn't say anything right to my family. When I tried to pray, all I could think of was the project failing. I felt all alone.

Herons live all over our town. But seeing this one calmly eating in the middle of the stormy road knocked me out of the ruts that anxiety had carved in my thinking. As the big bird lifted up like a prayer, it helped me turn the corner. I felt the cool mist. I heard the chirping of lucky frogs. And I understood that whatever happened with the project the next day, I would not be alone as I dealt with it.

Dear God of herons and frogs, sun and rain, help me to trust that You are always with me, even when I am too worried to notice. When I am overwhelmed, help me to get out of my head and focus on the signs of Your presence. Amen.

—Lucy H. Chambers

SEPTEMBER 24

Fixing Our Gazes

Finally, brothers and sisters, whatever is true, whatever is noble, whatever is right, whatever is pure, whatever is lovely, whatever is admirable—if anything is excellent or praiseworthy—think about such things.

—PHILIPPIANS 4:8 (NIV)

AS I CAME around the bend in the woods, a blur of brown crossed my line of vision. I inhaled a sharp breath—not so much at the doe eyeing me through the brush, but because everything seemed to take me by surprise of late. Everything seemed to make me want to jump out of my skin.

Health issues, impending deadlines, a child I was having trouble connecting with. It had all seemed to pile up within me until I had sought the woods for solace and prayer, looking for a way to ground myself in something bigger.

Now I stood, still as could be, studying the female deer. Her gaze met mine, and I cautiously walked around a tree to get a better look. She ducked her head around a tree of her own to get a better look at me.

While I had seen deer from a distance before, I had never had one so boldly inquire of me. We stood for minutes on end, staring at each other. Beneath her gaze, I breathed deeply, accepting this gift that the Lord had bestowed upon me in this moment, knowing it was for me.

As we finally parted our ways, I felt peace. The reminder of God's greatness had quieted the thoughts of fear and doubt circling my heart of late. In their place were thoughts of a gentle gaze, of the wonders God performs if I have eyes to see, of the reminders He gives of His everlasting grace.

Lord, we may not always get a special creature in our path to remind us of Your goodness, but I pray that You help us keep our thoughts fixed on not only the lovely but also the truth of Your Word. In Jesus's name. Amen.

—Heidi Chiavaroli

SEPTEMBER 25

Annie's Favorite

Lord my God, I called to you for help, and you healed me.
—Psalm 30:2 (NIV)

AFTER MAJOR SHOULDER surgery, I contacted a physical therapist. I wasn't exactly looking forward to the weekly appointments—a friend had warned that painful exercises with colorful stretchy bands awaited me. I grumbled going into my first PT session but was greeted by the therapist's assistant: a beautiful golden retriever named Annie.

Despite my lingering shoulder pain and stiffness, Annie the Greeter Dog instantly put me at ease. I stroked her soft, reddish-gold fur, gazed into her deep brown eyes, and could almost feel my blood pressure lowering. Then my therapist led me down a hallway, and Annie followed, plopping down in the treatment room's corner as I lay back on a padded table.

Annie slept when the therapist demonstrated helpful shoulder exercises I should do. But whenever I stretched my shoulder farther or tried a painful maneuver, Annie jumped up and poked her wet nose into my palm, as if trying to comfort me. Week by week, Annie and I got to know each other. I learned her favorite spot to scratch for a belly rub, and she learned which exercises gave me the most trouble. After a couple of months, I had made significant progress and worked those stretchy bands harder, just for her. I was sure I was Annie's favorite patient.

When I told the therapist, she smiled. "All my patients think Annie loves them best." I was crestfallen, until I thought back to that first appointment, when I was in near-constant pain and my arm was as stiff as a toy soldier's. Because of Annie's encouragement, my shoulder movement was getting better all the time and I was much stronger. Modern medicine cures many things and physical therapy is vital to the recovery process. Still, I wouldn't trade Annie's gentle nature and wet-nosed support for all the stretchy bands in the world.

Annie's encouragement (even if I really wasn't her favorite) reminded me that I can do the same thing: bring healing and help to others I encounter, through uplifting words and kind actions, every day.

Dear Lord, may I follow Annie's shining example of encouragement to everyone You bring to me today. Amen.

—Linda S. Clare

SEPTEMBER 26

My Friend

No longer do I call you servants, for a servant does not know what his master is doing; but I have called you friends.

—JOHN 15:15 (NKJV)

I HAVE A FAVORITE walking path that I love to take each day. It is on the edge of town, bordering a dairy farm with a postcard-perfect red barn that houses the cows. I stop there frequently to take in the beauty of the white-and-black cows grazing on green pastures.

Lately, a self-appointed greeter makes her way to the fence where I am standing. This calf waits for me to finish my accolades, appearing not to mind at all if I take the next eight hours to complete them. Her bright disposition made me name her Sunny.

As the weeks go on, I notice that Sunny appears less often at the fence, then not there at all. "What has happened?" I ask the Lord.

In the distance, I see a little boy leading my Sunny into the big red barn. Why, of course, she is being trained as a dairy cow. This little boy is treating his calf with love and respect—a pet that will soon be a much-appreciated dairy cow in service for years to come.

Seeing that Sunny is so happy with this little boy, I am delighted. I will still get to see my friend Sunny. My best friend, Lord Jesus, all but told me so.

For the things which are seen are temporary,
but the things which are not seen are eternal.
—2 Corinthians 4:18 (NKJV)

—Sandra Clifton

SEPTEMBER 27

Sweet Substitute

And I will pray the Father, and he shall give you another Comforter, that he may abide with you for ever.

—John 14:16 (KJV)

MY MOTHER HAD a soft spot for animals, whether domestic or wild. She owned several pets throughout the years—six cats roamed her house at one point—but her heart belonged to her dogs, the most recent, a rat terrier named Jack.

When Mom had to be hospitalized one summer, Jack stayed behind with my dad. We anticipated only a few days' separation, but days turned into weeks and weeks into a month. I stayed with Mom day and night and had frequent meltdowns from exhaustion. Every time we thought she could go home, a new complication cropped up, and Mom became weaker and increasingly despondent. It looked as though she would have to go into a long-term facility.

Then one day, a nurse peeked in the door. "Does your mother like dogs?" Did she! In walked a brown-and-white sheltie mix named Misty. She poked her nose into Mom's hand, and it was love at first nuzzle. Mom cooed over the therapy dog and caressed her ears until Misty and her handler had to move on. Mom perked up after that. Misty wasn't Jack, but she was a sweet substitute. Surprisingly, I, too, felt calmer and more at peace after the little dog's visit. Boosted by her encounter with Misty, Mom soon left the hospital and returned directly home to her beloved Jack.

I'm so glad that when Jesus had to leave this earth, He sent the Holy Spirit to lift my heart the way Misty lifted Mom's. But this Comforter will never leave. He resides within me, giving me strength and power, until I am reunited with my Savior in heaven. What a sweet substitute.

Walk of Faith: *When you feel discouraged or life drags you places you don't want to go, turn to the Holy Spirit. He is your advocate, your prayer warrior, and your counselor. But most of all, He is "another" comforter, like Jesus, who will never leave you.*

—Tracy Crump

SEPTEMBER 28

Human Alpacas

Above all, love each other deeply, because love covers over a multitude of sins.

—1 PETER 4:8 (NIV)

MY GRANDCHILDREN ENJOYED feeding the animals at the zoo. They giggled when a camel snuffled grain from their palms and squealed when squirrel monkeys snatched Cheerios from their eager fingers. They fed a deer a fistful of straw and scattered grain for chickens. As they raced from one exhibit to the next, their enthusiasm rose, buoyed by each positive animal encounter . . . until we reached the alpaca enclosure.

"Oh, gross!" the woman in front of us exclaimed as we walked up. "It spit at me. That's absolutely disgusting!" As she pulled tissues from her purse to wipe the slime from her neck, I steered the children in a wide arc around the exhibit.

"Why did the alpaca spit, Gigi?" my granddaughter asked. "All she was trying to do was feed it."

I had no good answer for Lauren's question, but the spitting animal reminded me of humans I've encountered. Have you ever met a human alpaca?

Human alpacas may be in a challenging season of life, struggling with grief or hurting. They need kind and caring people around them, but they're not always receptive. When we reach out, they snap, bite, or spit.

Their negative response hurts and discourages us. Sometimes it makes us steer a wide path around them instead of risking another unpleasant encounter.

Yet God calls us to feed, care for, and love everyone—even human alpacas. Sometimes they need the services of a professional. Usually, they just need someone to love them, even if it means occasionally getting spit on.

When I'm tempted to avoid those who are needy but difficult, I remember Jesus. He was scorned, spat upon, and crucified by those who needed Him most. Yet He endured it to bring about our salvation.

In light of Christ's example, what's a little spit between friends?

Walk of Faith: *Is there a "spitting alpaca" in your life? How can you reach out to him or her today—in Jesus's name?*

—Lori Hatcher

SEPTEMBER 29

The Courage to Care

Finally, all of you be of one mind, having compassion for one another; love as brothers, be tenderhearted, be courteous; not returning evil for evil or reviling for reviling, but on the contrary blessing, knowing that you were called to this, that you may inherit a blessing.

—1 PETER 3:8–9 (NKJV)

I LOVE TO WATCH the fearless antics of frisky squirrels frolicking through our yard. Squirrels chase one another in high-speed pursuits, climb electric poles, and risk the tightrope walk across cables lacing the sky above our lawn. Oh, to have the energy of these furry friends.

One day, I noticed a squirrel with something in its mouth. Curious, I crept closer, trying to identify the object. Was it food? Something to add to its home? But then I recognized its cargo. It should not have come as a surprise, though somehow it did. A wee baby squirrel! Mama squirrel resourcefully relocated her infant from one baby bed to another—even though it meant more danger during the transfer.

Quicker than a blink of my eyes—one second mama and baby were there and the next they were gone. Somewhere high above us dwelled this caring mother and her baby, clueless to the risks its mother just made to keep it safe.

I was reminded of caregivers of all sorts: parents caring for children, grandparents caring for grandchildren, adult children caring for elderly parents, and those who care for the sick. Like the brave mama squirrel, caregivers put their own needs aside to help their loved ones have not just longevity of life but quality of living as well.

Seeing mama squirrel gave me new gratitude for the way God cares for me and inspired me to keep up the good work as I care for Mom in my home. It is my joy to see her smile. For me, strengthened by my caregiving heavenly Father, helping her is not just about helping her sustain life but also helping her *live* life.

Father, bless and strengthen the caregivers. They bless the ones You've placed in their care. Amen.

—Kathy Carlton Willis

SEPTEMBER 30

Boundaries, Baby

Trouble and distress have come upon me, but your commands give me delight.

—PSALM 119:143 (NIV)

WHEN JOSIE IS afraid, she strikes out at the other dogs or cats or any creature that might be around her. She is not afraid of them, but a crash of thunder or a loud siren could trigger her to attack them.

If any dog or cat gets near her food, she loses her composure and lunges. If another pet gets too close while she is getting human attention, she growls and snaps at it. Any moment her boundaries are encroached upon, she strikes back. But the interesting thing about her boundaries is that they are only with other animals. Any admonishment from me, and she hits the ground in submission. She actually borders on terror. Because she's a rescue, a foundling, we will never know her story. But you can actually see when fears are triggered from the past and she is filled with angst and distress. In those moments, her aggression leaves, and she needs comfort desperately from me. I am her alpha, her provider, and her boundary maker. Love brings her back.

When fears from my past are triggered within life, they can affect my relationships, my work, and my day-to-day well-being. Have you ever had a moment when a trauma or event from the past flashes back and derails you? These flashbacks can feel as real as when they happened. We can fall into their trap, or we can reach for the lifeline of love from our Provider and our Boundary Maker. God offers a way to be free within His endless boundary of love, which heals anything our past can throw at us.

God, hold me in Your love boundary until I hurt from my past no more. Amen.

—Devon O'Day

October

OCTOBER 1

A Good Grip

For I am the Lord *your God who takes hold of your right hand and says to you, Do not fear; I will help you.*

—Isaiah 41:13 (NIV)

WHEN I TAKE my service dog, Callie, for a walk, I give her time to explore the creek beside our house. We've seen ducks, muskrats, raccoons, and even a snapping turtle. But my favorite visitors are the tiny yellow finches that flitter from twig to twig.

One day, the wind rustled the brush on the creek bank and bent the tall weeds and wildflowers. I inhaled the sweet air and exhaled a prayer. Our cross-country move had been physically, emotionally, mentally, and financially challenging. Being away from my sons had proved much harder than I had expected. I had been struggling with increasing pain management and fatigue. Discouragement pulled me into a whirlwind of despair.

Just as my emotions overwhelmed me, I spotted a tiny yellow finch resting on a long, single twig by the creek. As I watched the little bird, the wind picked up. It kept its tight grip as it leaned into the swaying branch. How had I forgotten to lean into the One who promised to never let me go?

In Isaiah, the Lord reminds His people of His constant presence. Though their journey would be difficult, God would keep them in His hands and help them. He promised to send them a Servant—the Messiah—who would bring forth justice. If the Israelites could trust God, then so could I.

I watched the tiny finch flitter to a nearby tree. I smiled. I may not always feel strong enough to hold on to my faith, but God always has a good grip on me.

The Lord *is trustworthy in all he promises and faithful in all he does.*
—Psalm 145:13 (NIV)

—Xochitl E. Dixon

OCTOBER 2

Tardy Hummingbird

To everything there is a season, a time for every purpose under heaven.

—ECCLESIASTES 3:1 (NKJV)

IT WAS EARLY morning, and I stood at the living room window studying the merlot redbud tree I had recently planted in our small backyard. I worried that I had put it in the ground too late and it would not survive the coming Oklahoma winter. I surveyed the tree's thin limbs and its slender trunk. The rope ties that I had secured to the ground were the the redbud's only defense against toppling over from even a small wind.

An abrupt movement in front of the little tree distracted me from my anxieties. A gray red-throated male hummingbird, held in immobile suspension by his rapid-firing translucent blue wings, stared at me. "Well, it's about time you showed up," I said to the tiny bird. My wife, Sandra, and I had hung a hummingbird feeder from the patio awning in early summer. We had faithfully changed the liquid nectar with little success in attracting our favorite birds. We had pretty much lost hope of seeing any of these beautiful tiny creatures before they migrated south.

"I think I'll name you Tardy, since you're pretty late," I said. "Everything is set up for you." As if in response, Tardy glided, turned, and hovered at the feeder. His long slender beak took in the nectar. He then darted away from the feeder and settled on a sliver-like branch of the redbud sapling. The limb, gently swaying in the breeze, was the perfect size for my new little friend, who seemed pleased with its new digs. *Tardy*, I thought, *it looks like the Lord's perfect timing had me plant that tree there just for you.*

Lord, I am in awe of the unfathomable and minute intricacies of Your workmanship in designing creatures like Tardy. Help us, Your creation, not to worry but to trust and dwell in Your perfect timing and plans for us.

—Terry Clifton

OCTOBER 3

Eyes on the Prize

We want each of you to show this same diligence to the very end, so that what you hope for may be fully realized.

—HEBREWS 6:11 (NIV)

IN MY FRIEND'S Wisconsin city, ponds dot the landscape. They help balance the ecosystem, and their central fountains provide restful beauty for folks and fowl. Ducks, geese, swans, and the like are attracted to the area, their number increasing each year as feathered families expand.

One day, my friend was driving on a three-lane section of the highway. On her right was a pond populated with an assortment of ducks, and a similar group had gathered near the pond to her left. Then, without even a honk, a beautiful goose on the right-hand side stepped onto the road and began to walk across the street as cars cruised by. Apparently, there was someone it longed to visit on the other side.

To my friend, it seemed a wonder. The goose didn't look to the left or right. It never slowed its pace but continued on as if oblivious to the surrounding vehicles. Yet it never was hit by a car or caused a kerfuffle. No driver swerved to miss the waterfowl. No brakes screeched. The traffic flowed normally. The goose walked on until it got to the grassy median between the lanes, which was occupied by a few fellow creatures. Once there, it gave a goosey greeting and stopped as if to celebrate.

My friend's amazing story reminds me that I am called to pursue my goals in such a way that I win the prize. Face front and focus. Keep moving. Trust in God. And—with God's help—like that persevering goose, I'll make it.

By perseverance the snail reached the ark. —Charles Spurgeon

—Cathy Elliott

OCTOBER 4

We Can All Get Along

The wolf will live with the lamb, the leopard will lie down with the goat, the calf and the lion and the yearling together; and a little child will lead them.

—ISAIAH 11:6 (NIV)

A FRIEND WASN'T BEHAVING in a very friendly way lately, and a coworker had been difficult. I found myself going out of my way to avoid these people. *Thank goodness for the weekend,* I thought. I was looking forward to Saturday and story time at the library, where I would share my book about how animals help kids.

That day I read a few chapters while the kids visited with the animals—I had brought my golden retriever, Ernest, and several of the animals featured in the book: a Jack Russell terrier, a potbelly pig, and a couple of therapy rats.

Then Barb, the "mom" of the rats, said, "How about if we put Honey on top of Ernest?" Ernest is a docile and patient golden retriever, but I wasn't sure how he felt about rats. Barb, however, was confident. She carefully set the rat on Ernest, while I held his leash. Ernest looked back, unfazed. Then, Barb put Honey on top of the pig! The pig and the rat walked around the library, with Ernest following. The kids all laughed and cheered.

"Look how they all get along!" a boy said.

His words hit me hard. Had I been getting along well with others—*all* others? Even those who might be a little prickly? Some people love to stir up trouble; others have hidden needs. It's up to us, as God's people, to try to understand one another and live peaceably with everyone. It couldn't have been clearer than at that moment.

Only God could orchestrate such a lesson. And I have the sweetest picture of a rat riding on a pig to remind me.

If it is possible, as far as it depends on you, live at peace with everyone.
—Romans 12:18 (NIV)

—Peggy Frezon

OCTOBER 5

The Squirrel Situation

Whatever you do, work at it with all your heart, as working for the Lord, not for human masters.

—COLOSSIANS 3:23 (NIV)

I SAT OUT ON the screened-in porch one evening, as the fading light bathed squirrels dancing up and down the oak trees. Thankful for cooler temperatures, I munched popcorn and let my mind wander.

Thinking back on the past week, I couldn't come up with one accomplishment. So many distractions had me darting in every direction, much like the squirrels out back. The water heater broke on Monday, which meant a lot of mopping and setting up fans. No work on Tuesday; I waited forever for the water-heater repairman. On Wednesday, training a new employee at work took up most of my day. The last two days seemed awash in pop-up customer demands and information gathering for my boss.

Just outside the porch, a chubby squirrel ran along the deck railing with a huge acorn in its mouth. Gracefully letting itself down to a large, round planter, it tucked the acorn underneath an inch or two of soil. After looking around furtively, the squirrel scurried away.

God used that moment to teach me about the usefulness of working. Although I don't know who or how much others benefit, my diligence will bring results in due time. Like a nut hidden now feeds the squirrel on a cold day this winter, a client served today will bring in income for the company next month. Repairs to the water heater will pay off in hot showers.

When progress seems slow, I remember the squirrel situation. Working hard today will pay off tomorrow. With God's blessings, my best efforts day after day will mean success in years to come. Whether my current employer notices, I will keep doing my best. In due season, God will provide a harvest of rewards.

Lord, teach me to trust You as I work. You are the rewarder of those who diligently seek You. Let patience teach me to wait on Your outcomes. I will always thank You. Amen.

—David L. Winters

OCTOBER 6

Zoey the Cat Herder

I am the good shepherd; I know my sheep and my sheep know me—
—JOHN 10:14 (NIV)

MY SISTER SHERRY'S house is a menagerie of cats and dogs. Recently, Sherry added a shorthair Australian shepherd named Zoey. She hasn't had any formal dog training yet, but her natural herding instincts have come through in her interactions with the other pets—specifically, her routine of herding the cats, Luna and Cosmo, from the yard when Sherry wants them to come in for the night.

All Sherry has to do is open the door to the area where the cats hang out and say, "Zoey, go get Luna and Cosmo," and Zoey runs out, nudges one cat and then the other, then coaxes them across the yard and into the house. The image of Zoey herding cats is fascinating enough on its own, but what strikes me even more is that Luna and Cosmo let her do it. Recently, when I was at Sherry's house, Zoey tried to herd me up the stairs, and I gently shooed her away. But Luna and Cosmo, though they hesitate occasionally, know that Zoey is the one who ushers them inside before the coyotes and owls come out. They've grown to trust her as a friend who looks out for them.

Today, after a moment with Zoey, I considered my journey of learning to trust God's divine herding techniques in my life and with those I love. It has included many moments of resistance. But the more I get to know Him and watch His plans unfold, the more quickly I recognize nudges that urge me from my favorite resting places at His loving direction, either out of harm's way or to an exciting new purpose.

Heavenly Father, thank You for looking out for me and those I love. Fill my memory with reminders of times You moved me for a good reason, so when I am tempted to resist a change, I will trust You enough to go where You want me. Thank You for being such a kind shepherd. Amen.

—Jeanette Hanscome

OCTOBER 7

Under His Wings

He will cover you with his feathers, and under his wings you will find refuge; his faithfulness will be your shield and rampart.

—PSALM 91:4 (NIV)

THE SKY WAS gray and heavy as my husband and I drove home from an appointment. The atmosphere in the car wasn't much better. I had recently had some negative feedback about a project that was dear to me. In the confessional of our car, I poured out my heart to both the Lord and my husband. Feeling forgotten and discouraged, I didn't know whether to keep going or let go.

As we crossed the Arkansas River Bridge, I noticed a flicker of movement outside my window. A second later, I lost every negative, whiny thought as a bald eagle pulled level with our car. The tip of its massive wing stretched no more than five feet from me.

"Matt," I whispered.

"I see it," my husband whispered back.

I could see every detail, from the crown of its white head to the tip of its feathery tail. A tear slipped down my cheek as peace and comfort flowed through me.

"God is with you, honey," my husband said. "He has you in this."

"I know." The moment I saw the eagle, I knew.

The majestic bird stayed with us to the end of the bridge, riding an invisible current. At the same time, half a dozen scriptures lifted my heart as if I, too, had found my current. We all need a reminder that God is our refuge, that He hides us in the shadow of His wings. And when we are tempted to give up, that's when we need to remember the eagles.

But those who hope in the Lord will renew their strength. They will soar on wings like eagles; they will run and not grow weary, they will walk and not be faint. —Isaiah 40:31 (NIV)

—Tracy Joy Jones

OCTOBER 8

Stinky the Marsh Crab

As for you, you were dead in your transgressions and sins, in which you used to live when you followed the ways of this world and of the ruler of the kingdom of the air, the spirit who is now at work in those who are disobedient.

—EPHESIANS 2:1–2 (NIV)

MY GRANDKIDS AND I were enjoying an early October getaway at Edisto Island, South Carolina. Combing the beach for shells and other treasures, we filled our buckets with gifts from the sea. We searched for moon shells, coral, and the ever-elusive shark's teeth. Four-year-old Caroline discovered a rare find—a tiny marsh crab.

"It's dead, Gigi," she told me, "but I love him." She demonstrated her love, too, by carrying the little creature everywhere. Down the beach, across the dunes, even into the ocean. She ate her lunch with one hand while cradling her crab with the other. When we headed back to the cottage, her crab went with her. "He's a little bit stinky," she observed, "but I don't mind. I love him."

Caroline's crab reminds me a lot of myself. The Bible tells me I was "dead in my transgressions and sins." Compared to God's holiness, I stank to the high heavens. Yet God saw me as valuable. He picked me up, cradled me to His heart, and loved me. Then He did what Caroline couldn't do for her crab—He gave me new life. "Because of his great love for us, God, who is rich in mercy, made us alive with Christ even when we were dead in transgressions—it is by grace you have been saved" (Ephesians 2:4–5 NIV).

Somewhere between Edisto Island and Lexington, South Carolina, Stinky the marsh crab "disappeared." His lesson, however, lingers like a sweet fragrance, reminding me of God's great love for me.

Walk of Faith: *Ponder for a moment how lost you were before God found you. Thank Him for choosing you as His treasure, carrying you all your days, and loving you—even when you're a little stinky.*

—Lori Hatcher

OCTOBER 9

Mile High!

Many peoples will come and say, "Come, let us go up to the mountain of the Lord, to the temple of the God of Jacob. He will teach us his ways, so that we may walk in his paths."

—Isaiah 2:3 (NIV)

I ABSOLUTELY LOVE TO go horseback riding in the mountains with my sister, who runs a sanctuary for horses and other animals. So, when she suggested we go for a fall ride, I was all for it. There's nothing more beautiful than the Colorado Rocky Mountains in all its fall splendor.

I was so excited that I wasn't paying that much attention when she asked if I would like to try riding Ginger, even though I knew she was a draft horse. But when it came time to mount the enormous mare, I knew I was in trouble.

Being more than a little stubborn, I first tried it on my own, even knowing my bad knee would in no way cooperate. Only after I hopped around a bit, coming nowhere near being able to swing my other leg over, did I humble myself and ask for help. Even then, it took the assistance of a willing nearby boulder and my sister and husband pushing and pulling to get me up in the saddle. Color me blushing.

What was first a long way up was also a long way down, but I soon got into Ginger's gentle rhythm and thoroughly enjoyed our ride. It gave me a whole new appreciation of seeing the world from a mile high, and it was truly a mountaintop experience in all the best ways.

If I had talked myself out of riding Ginger, I would have missed a spectacular opportunity to view the mountains at her height. It's a good reminder to me to stretch myself in all of life's great adventures, whether physical, emotional, or spiritual, and look for the path God has set before me.

Over every mountain there is a path, although it may not be seen from the valley. —Theodore Roethke

—Deb Kastner

OCTOBER 10

Bark-tober Fest

A gentle answer turns away wrath, but a harsh word stirs up anger.

—PROVERBS 15:1 (NIV)

NOT A SINGLE soul was stirring, and the only sound in the living room was the gentle snore of my rescue pack. All shapes, sizes, and breeds gathered at night and had their tuck-ins. The peace was palpable as each dog curled or stretched out on its dog bed of choice.

Then, just as my eyes would close in hypnotic sleep, with those sweet and peaceful dog dreams all around me, my largest dog, a Saint Bernard mix, would bounce from slumber into full-on "get away from my house" barks. His brother would join in, and soon all the dogs in the pack would be awake and in a territorial defense choir. This only happened when I tried to close my eyes. They were either protecting me or angry with me for falling asleep on the job of protecting them.

And then as barks escalated, soon they weren't barking at a passing cat or car outside or telling the wind not to blow. They were aggressively barking at one another. Fights would begin between two, then another would join, and if I didn't jump in and become the alpha peacemaker, a horrible fight and maybe a veterinarian visit would result.

This also happens with all of us, especially with family. One person raises a voice in irritation, then one answers the same way, and in defense and offense, voices lift and feelings are hurt and love walks out the door. All it takes is one to softly change the volume on a heated moment and pull things toward peace. A gentle heart is always the best diffuser to an anger explosion.

God, please keep my answers soft and my heart loving in each situation. Amen.

—Devon O'Day

OCTOBER 11

A Grander Narrative

Your eyes saw my unformed body; all the days ordained for me were written in your book before one of them came to be.

—PSALM 139:16 (NIV)

OUR THREE BOYS stood with their noses pressed against the glass windows. Watching them completely absorbed in the moment was nearly as relaxing as watching the salmon swimming by in front of them. The windows allowed us a glimpse into the migratory life of these fish. Here, at the Columbia River Gorge, the salmon begin their journey to the ocean, where they will spend two to five years before returning upstream, to these very waters, to lay their eggs before their own story comes to a close.

One week after our visit to the hatchery, the forest surrounding it would be enveloped in a wildfire. The very campground we stayed at would be consumed. The world around these waters would be in chaos, yet the fish would remain steadfast in their journey.

It's easy for me to feel as though the unpredictable circumstances in my life are up against God's plans. Yet His Word assures me that He has marked out the days of my life. I can trust that He has written a great story for me and that my story fits right into His grander narrative. Just like the lives and migration of the salmon play a part in a much bigger design, so God has a bigger plan and purpose for my life than I can see. Nothing happening in the world around me is able to deter the plans of God. Neither fire nor sickness nor tragedy nor any other unexpected circumstance can make His pen slip. No letter, word, punctuation mark, or twist in the plot is lost to Him. He is steadfast, and His plans for me are good.

Walk of Faith: *Take an hour to sit quietly and make a list of ways God has been faithful in your story. If making this list feels overwhelming, begin with the past year. Spend time on the details, searching for ways He has shown up in unexpected circumstances.*

—Eryn Lynum

OCTOBER 12

What I Cannot See

Love is patient, love is kind. It does not envy, it does not boast, it is not proud.

—1 CORINTHIANS 13:4 (NIV)

WHILE ON A break during a recent national writers' conference, my husband and I were enjoying cool bottles of water out on a deck with a lovely view. In addition to a white gazebo, a lazy stream meandered around the hotel. From our perspective, we could see a couple of elegant swans and the cutest family of ducks ever. Mama and Daddy Ducks were followed by six fuzzy ducklings just learning to swim.

I watched the ducks for a long time, marveling at how they moved across the water, barely causing a ripple. And yet I knew if I were to see underneath the water, the ducks' webbed feet would be paddling along at a rapid speed to keep them going.

Since my husband's double stroke three years ago, I often feel as if I'm paddling like crazy just to stay above water, and I'm definitely *not* doing it as gracefully as the ducks. I look at others who seem to have it easier, and sometimes I admit to being envious.

Why can't it be that way for us? Why do we have to struggle over every little thing? Yet the truth is, I can't see what's happening underwater with other people any more than they can see with me. Just because they appear as graceful as the ducks on the water doesn't necessarily mean they don't have their own sets of problems.

I think that's why God warns us against being envious. Because, as with the ducks, we really don't know how hard people are paddling to keep their lives afloat. And anyway, we should be counting our own blessings, not other people's.

Heavenly Father, thank You for the ducks and for Your reminder not to be envious of others. Thank You, Jesus, for the many blessings You give me every day. Amen.

—Deb Kastner

OCTOBER 13

Vulture Ballet

So God created great sea creatures and every living thing that moves, with which the waters abounded, according to their kind, and every winged bird according to its kind. And God saw that it was good.

—GENESIS 1:21 (NKJV)

TAKE ME HOME, country roads." I've spent most of my life in country settings. Back roads the snowplows never heard of, a creek rippling outside the back door, graceful deer crossing our yard, and vultures.

In real life, vultures do not look or act like the cute creatures in cartoons. To me, they looked scary and just plain ugly. And being dive-bombed by one attempting to divert me from walking near the recent roadkill showed their mean streak. For more than fifty years, I considered them repulsive, only useful for ridding the roads of carnage.

One morning, I watched the day come alive from the deck of our daughter's home. I noticed some large black birds opening and closing their huge wings in a tree at the far end of the field. Grabbing binoculars, I had a close-up view of more than twenty-five vultures, sunning themselves in the morning rays. This kettle of vultures, their wings extended to the sun's warmth, exuded grace and beauty.

Another morning at a different daughter's house, I sat outside, again viewing the dawn's awakening. A trio of vultures floated on the air currents, the sun glinting off their black wings as they dipped and twirled through the sky. They seemed to dance, as though entranced by the new day. Once more, I had a glimpse of the splendor with which God filled even these repulsive, ugly creatures.

Beauty, in this case, had not been in the eye of this beholder. It took God's gentle reminders that He made all things beautiful . . . even vultures. May I view all creation—animals and people—as He does: beautiful, beloved, and blessed.

O Lord, Your creatures, small and grand,
Fill life with beauty from Your hand. —C.M.

—Cathy Mayfield

OCTOBER 14

The Bee Dance

But ask the animals, and they will teach you, or the birds in the sky, and they will tell you; or speak to the earth, and it will teach you, or let the fish in the sea inform you.

—JOB 12:7–8 (NIV)

BEEKEEPING IS HANDS down the most fascinating aspect of homesteading I have engaged in yet, more than gardening or raising chickens and pigs. The bees constantly amaze me.

When my first hive arrived, I set it up in a cleared area of the woods on the property. What I didn't know is that it would also create a perfect environment for pests.

So, a few weeks later, upon the advice of an experienced beekeeper, I relocated the hive into a bright and sunny spot beside the orchard. I didn't want the bees to go back to their original location looking for the hive, so I sealed up the hive for three days.

After the third day, I created a small opening, and the drone bees quickly set out to find a food source. They buzzed around in all directions, then when one found food, it returned to the hive. The rest soon followed, and the relocation was successful!

Later, we learned that the bees communicate direction to one another by dancing. The worker bee can tell the rest of the colony the exact location of food in respect to the hive by moving its abdomen in such a way that communicates the distance and direction based on the angle of the sun to the earth.

Watching the bees reorient themselves to the new location and find food together was fascinating. No one trains them to do this. They are simply born knowing this is their job and what to do. God's divine order and attention to the smallest detail are all around me, declaring His glory, even in the smallest of creatures like the bee.

For since the creation of the world God's invisible qualities—his eternal power and divine nature—have been clearly seen . . . so that people are without excuse. —Romans 1:20 (NIV)

—Joy Pitner

OCTOBER 15

The Price of Wrath

Human anger does not produce the righteousness God desires.

—JAMES 1:20 (NLT)

OUR FRIEND LEE presented us with a Siamese fighting fish as an apartment-warming present. We weren't allowed to have furry pets, so Lee felt Attila would be just the creature to keep us company. The fish was amazingly beautiful with its burgundy-and-magenta tail and fins. However, like most male betta, he was feisty. He didn't like people peering at him too closely. Whenever Attila felt threatened or disturbed, he would flare his fins. He often attacked his reflection, butting his face against the glass and flaring. We didn't dare put another fish in the tank with him. Attila was too hotheaded. One day, he injured himself, developed a skin ulcer, and died.

"Anger kills," my husband reminded me.

I nodded. We knew an angry couple that suffered from high blood pressure, stomach ulcers, and strokes. These folks bristled with hostility and were too easily offended. Everyone provoked their wrath. The apostle Paul warned the Ephesians not to let the sun set on their anger. That's good advice. I've tried to remember it over the years. It's dangerously easy to let anger smolder until one day it bursts into flames. I don't want to lash out at others or repay an insult with a stinging retort of my own. I don't want to nurse grudges or plot payback. I don't want my temper to flare like poor Attila's. Thankfully, God can and will bless us with peace and patience—if we ask Him to do so.

Anger is an acid that can do more harm to the vessel in which it is stored than to anything on which it is poured. —Mark Twain

—Shirley Raye Redmond

OCTOBER 16

Follow the Heron

I make known the end from the beginning, from ancient times, what is still to come. I say, "My purpose will stand, and I will do all that I please."

—ISAIAH 46:10 (NIV)

THE MORNING SUN glistened off the water as my husband and I paddled downriver. My husband spotted a great blue heron sitting on a fallen branch in the center of the river ahead. Its gray feathers blended into the scenery, and I had to look closely to see it. As we approached, it leaned forward and took flight, landing in a tree a little farther ahead. The routine continued as it led us downriver, moving just a little ahead each time we approached.

As we followed the bird, I remembered the quiet leading of the Lord. I want God to show me His entire plan for my life at once. Yet the Lord often reveals just the next step. Not long ago, the Lord directed us to sell our house and move into a smaller place in the heart of our town. When no houses were available for purchase, we moved into a tiny rental home for six months. As the lease ended and still no houses were for sale, my faith waivered. I knew God had led us there, but He didn't seem to be showing us the next step.

Even though I doubted Him, God revealed our next move just in time. The perfect house happened to be next door to where we rented! Each morning, I see our old rental house, and I remember that God knows the beginning and the end. I don't need to see the whole picture, only the next move.

Just as the heron led us down the river, one short distance at a time, God is certain to lead us step by step.

Lord, help me trust You more today. It's hard to not see the whole plan. I may not understand what You are doing in my life, but I believe You are working on my behalf and will reveal what's next just in time. Amen.

—Amelia Rhodes

OCTOBER 17

Clinging to the Windshield

Can any one of you by worrying add a single hour to your life?

—MATTHEW 6:27 (NIV)

IT'S SO HARD not to worry. I'm not sure why I thought that once my children were grown, I would be less tempted to worry about them. Seriously, as they grow, they fall in love, have children, bosses, in-laws, and friends, so my circle of concern just expands. It's unhealthy to live in a constant state of worry . . . and it's unbiblical. Yet I'm tempted, as each loved one begins a new venture, takes a trip, or simply goes about everyday life, to think their lives depend on my anxiety.

Then, one day, I encountered a butterfly and a walking stick insect that God used to alter my perspective. I had left my house to run errands when I spied a perfectly formed monarch butterfly lying dead on my lawn. Its wings spanned five inches across and bore no signs of trauma. It was as if, midflight, the creature simply breathed its last and dropped there for me to find.

Just down the road, I spied, clinging to my windshield, a four-inch-long walking stick. *How*, I wondered, *is this skinny creature surviving the g-force of my travels?* Against all probability, it not only survived my six-mile drive but then sauntered casually down the hood of my car once I parked.

How does a monarch drop midflight while a walking stick survives a harrowing ride? Matters of life and death are in God's hands and not in mine. It's that simple, that profound. I had no worry for the butterfly that passed and great concern for the insect that survived. God's wisdom prevailed over both lives and reminded me to leave such things in His capable and sovereign hands.

Those who leave everything in God's hand will eventually see God's hand in everything. —Unknown

—Lori Stanley Roeleveld

OCTOBER 18

Lovable Puffins

If I rise on the wings of the dawn, if I settle on the far side of the sea, even there your hand will guide me, your right hand will hold me fast.

—PSALM 139:9–10 (NIV)

WHEN MY FAMILY and I visited the Oregon Coast Aquarium, our lives were touched by the unique marine life we witnessed. An octopus, jellyfish, seahorses, and even a shark and a killer whale amazed us. But an unusual seabird captured my heart.

I stopped in my tracks, mesmerized by a puffin's snow-white mask and tangerine bill. Almost comical, the bird seemed to look my way and waddled across its rocky habitat, resembling a penguin and a parrot.

Tufted puffins make their home along the Pacific Ocean. They live on coastal cliffs or offshore islands and nest among rocks and burrows. I felt blessed to be among them at the reserve outside the aquarium and later loved learning more about them.

A puffin's scientific name, *Fratercula,* means "little brother" in Latin, referring to its black plumage that resembles a friar's robe. A puffin tends to hold its feet together before it launches, suggestive of the hands of a monk clasped in prayer.

Puffins can dive 164 feet into the ocean and appear to be "flying" underwater for up to a minute. They use their feet as rudders and are great navigators. Not only do they "fly" *down* into the deep, but they fly *up* to the sky at fifty-five miles per hour. They can flap their wings four hundred times a minute and travel thousands of miles per year. Here we see a spiritual parallel in these unique seabirds. If we reach the highest heavens or deepest sea, God is there—and we are lovable to Him and capture His heart.

We'll be visiting the Oregon coast again soon, and I will watch for the "little friars" and thank God for this sweet seabird that always makes me smile.

Dear Lord, draw me close and carry me to the depths and heights of Your everlasting love. Amen.

—Kathleen Ruckman

OCTOBER 19

In the Waiting

I will instruct you and teach you in the way you should go; I will counsel you with my loving eye on you.

—PSALM 32:8 (NIV)

MY LUNCH ALARM reminds me to take a break. I suspect it's my dog Minnie's favorite time of day because that's when we hang out on the deck.

She'll race me down the stairs and then pace in front of the sliding glass door while I make my lunch. Then when I slide the door open, Minnie will charge and announce her arrival with a loud bark. She'll chase lizards while I eat and then sun herself while I check my email.

But none of that happens until I leave my office chair. And I don't immediately jump up when the alarm goes off if I'm finishing a project.

Minnie knows the sound of the alarm means it's time to get up. So when it goes off, she'll run to the door and back to me, eager for me to move. She'll hop onto the ottoman and bark. But depending on how long I take, she'll eventually give up and wait at my feet. Ready to jump up when I do.

My Yorkie reminds me how I should wait. I've been wrestling with some decisions and am undecided about which direction to take. I need clarity before I go forward.

As I seek the Lord and His wisdom for my next step, I'll wait on His direction. And if I grow restless in the waiting, you can find me at His feet, just like Minnie, waiting for Him to move so I can follow His lead.

Lord, thank You for leading me. Help me to wait on You before going forward. To trust that You'll give me what I need when I need it. Amen.

—Crystal Storms

OCTOBER 20

Horsey Conversations

As a fair exchange—I speak as to my children—open wide your hearts also.

—2 CORINTHIANS 6:13 (NIV)

HAVE YOU EVER heard a mama horse talk to her newly delivered foal? She begins the communication breathing her breath into the nostrils of that new baby before it even manages to stand. Sweet low nickers follow, and soon her baby answers. Even when her foal is one of a herd of colts and fillies, she can pick out the high-pitched call from her own, especially when the young one is looking for her.

And there is a call that screams for help, and the mama will answer urgently and do whatever she can to get to her baby's side. There are communications of correction, training, and love that are palpable when you really observe the mama horse and her baby. A mare always has her foal's best interest at heart.

Communication is at the heart of relationship. There are no good relationships that evolve from one-way conversation. In our God conversations, just as in the communication between humans or horses, we feel an innate seeking to be open and complete the circle of understanding, taking everything into a deeper, more real space. Small talk that remains on the surface and without meaning is not enough to sustain us. All God's creatures seek a safe place where there is trust enough to share an open heart.

God needs an openhearted exchange with us; He craves it. It's not the public displays of devotion but the private, real, and true connection that He misses when we get too busy to spend time in His presence. Enjoy taking in the very breath of God today, and let it nourish you deeply in your heart where only He can go.

Dear God, I open my whole heart to Your communication today, a listening and sharing that heals me. Amen.

—Devon O'Day

OCTOBER 21

Leaving the Nest

Even youths will faint and be weary, and the young will fall exhausted; but those who wait for the LORD shall renew their strength, they shall mount up with wings like eagles, they shall run and not be weary, they shall walk and not faint.

—ISAIAH 40:30–31 (NRSV)

SEVERAL MONTHS AGO, my mother-in-law's cat caught a baby blue jay. Lyn quickly rescued the poor bird and nursed it back to health. Eventually, the bird was getting out of the cage and fluttering around the house like a pet. At that point, she knew it was time to gradually release it. She took its cage to the woods near my sister-in-law's house and hung it in a tree with the door open. It eventually braved leaving the cage and spent more and more time outside. However, she continued to bring it food to make sure it was able to take care of itself. When she would arrive and call it, the jay would return and "chat" with her the way it always had. While we were visiting this past summer, we got to witness this amazing bond.

After a few more weeks, the jay began to explore farther from the cage, and eventually it wouldn't come near her. The baby had grown up, was totally rehabbed, and had left the "nest." It was a joy to witness how the two had bonded and touched each other's lives. It had to have been difficult for her to let her bird friend go, but she knew what was best for the jay.

I wonder if God feels that way watching us go out into the world, living the life He's called us to. It must be difficult watching us struggle and fall. Yet God is there, picking us up and pointing us in the right direction.

Lord, thank You for always being there, for molding us, for teaching us, and for loving us . . . even when we fail. Amen.

—Missy Tippens

OCTOBER 22

Rescuing Big Tex

Stretch out Your hand from above; rescue me and deliver me out of great waters.

—PSALM 144:7 (NKJV)

HAVE YOU EVER heard of Big Tex? He is the claim to fame of Beaumont, Texas, where I live. This fourteen-foot, thousand-pound reptilian monster is the largest alligator ever caught in the United States. Only one problem. After Tropical Storm Imelda hit our area, Big Tex went missing. They couldn't find him in his den, despite the four-foot fences designed to keep him there. When you get more than forty inches of rain, with even higher floods, it's nothing for gators to swim right over the top of their enclosures! A number of smaller alligators also disappeared. You can imagine how sleepless nearby residents were when they found out one of these creatures had already shown up in their neighbor's living room!

Thankfully, just days later, searchers found Big Tex in a nearby pond. On pins and needles, I watched his rescue. It took over a dozen workers to capture and return him to his home. Big Tex dug into the pond's muddy border. He didn't know he was in peril if he stayed put. It was alligator-hunting season. And his temporary home was right next to Interstate 10. He resisted the rescue—didn't even realize he *needed* to be rescued.

I wonder how many times I flee in the wrong direction when I sense I'm in danger. How often do I dig in when God tries to rescue me? How often am I on danger's edge and don't even realize I need to be rescued? I tend to go through the motions of my daily tasks and feel like I'm doing just fine on my own.

Sometimes Big Tex and I aren't all that different, but I'm learning. Not only do I want God to place me in His refuge, but I want His protective fence guarding me from harm.

Father, when I run, may I run in Your direction. When I go the opposite way, snatch me up and lead me to Your protective presence.

—Kathy Carlton Willis

OCTOBER 23

Confidence like a Tiger

Then Paul dwelt two whole years in his own rented house, and received all who came to him, preaching the kingdom of God and teaching the things which concern the Lord Jesus Christ with all confidence, no one forbidding him.

—Acts 28:30–31 (NKJV)

THE FAMILY TRIP to the Columbus, Ohio, zoo was always a favorite day of the year. We piled into the several cars necessary to accommodate multiple generations.

Walking around the sprawling zoo complex, we enjoyed the menagerie of animals that otherwise we might never see. Each family member had a favorite. Mom raved about the lions, remarking that someday they will lie down with lambs. My niece with the great sense of humor stared endlessly at the monkeys. She laughed out loud at their antics.

My favorite were the Bengal tigers. Not only because they are the mascot of a favorite football team, but because they sit with such poise. Many times, I've envied their ability to rest majestically, taking it all in. When the time is just right, they rise, run with great speed, and pounce.

According to Scripture, Paul possessed such poise when preaching the gospel. Although adversaries of the gospel beat him, ran him out of various towns, and chased him away from their synagogues, circumstances didn't deter Paul from preaching about Jesus.

I need and want to share my faith with confidence like a mighty Bengal tiger. Truthfully, sharing my faith sometimes has proved daunting. How can I capture tiger confidence to live out my faith?

Then, I remember the Cross. My confidence doesn't come from my ability. It comes from the power of the God I serve. He is up to any challenge. With His Spirit inside me, I can rise to any occasion.

Lord, fill me with Your Holy Spirit. Lead me in all truth as I read and understand Your Word. Raise my confidence, not in my ability, but in Yours. Praise Your name. Amen.

—David L. Winters

OCTOBER 24

The Nature of Squirrels

What good will it be for someone to gain the whole world, yet forfeit their soul? Or what can anyone give in exchange for their soul?

—MATTHEW 16:26 (NIV)

SQUIRRELS—THEY ARE SO, well, squirrely at this time of year. It is fall, and they are busy finding treasure to store for winter. Their frantic pace makes them appear to be extra-hard workers. They scatter to and fro like the falling leaves. They instinctively know time is short and there is work to be done.

That fast pace tends to make them careless, though. They have a bad habit of running helter-skelter in front of my car like World War II kamikaze pilots. On the positive side, their bad habits tend to slow me down, and I am more careful about my driving.

Jesus often compared us to sheep, but I can easily make the case to compare myself to a squirrel. I run helter-skelter trying to store up treasure too. But why? God has promised us all the treasure we could possibly ever want in heaven someday, and what we store here is not coming with us. Temporary treasure? Is it worth my time?

Often gleaning treasure from this world means shortchanging treasure for heaven. I take on more projects, work more hours, and wander stores for that perfect piece of "treasure" only to find that time has been frittered away. Time I could have spent visiting someone lonely, helping with a church project, or just basking in God's grace. We may all have different amounts of money, but we all have the same amount of hours in a day.

Only one life, 'twill soon be past,
only what's done for Christ will last. —C.T. Studd

—Linda Bartlett

OCTOBER 25

God's Ambassador

Now then, we are ambassadors for Christ.

—2 CORINTHIANS 5:20 (NKJV)

HERE I WAS, the picture of diligence, sitting upright at my computer, intent on nothing but work, work, work. Suddenly, I felt a sharp scratch on my kneecap. "OUCH!" I snapped, then added an abrupt, "Not now." The red welt forming on my kneecap could only be from one of my cats. "These guys need to respect my work," I declared, laying down the law by speaking it into the air.

I bent toward the floor to see who the perpetrator was. I came face to face with Barnie, our eldest cat. His dignified demeanor had earned him the title of Elder Statesman. I mechanically reached down to pet Barnie, and as I did, he began to purr.

When I returned to a sitting position at my computer screen, I stared at the reflection that scowled back at me—my own. I was caught not only being myself with an ugly face but also wearing a look that was not at all the one I wanted to wear for my cats. As I shuddered at the frightful face glowering back, I vowed never again to put on that face. It was scary even to me, so I didn't want to think about what effect it was having on my precious fur babies.

A new, kinder face, smiling with love, formed in my head—my own face, as God's ambassador of love. I looked down at my Barnie with my new face. *Isn't this the face God wants me to wear?* Barnie's contented purring confirmed this.

Walk of Faith: *Have you shown love to your pet today? Ask God to show you how to do it in a way that will please God—and your precious pet.*

—Sandra Clifton

OCTOBER 26

Sad Goodbyes and Happy Reunions

My soul waits for the Lord more than watchmen for the morning, more than watchmen for the morning.

—PSALM 130:6 (ESV)

I JUST HATE IT, but I had to do it five days a week—leave my best friend, Bay, and go to work.

Every morning, we went through the same routine. As she sensed I was getting ready to go, she would get antsy for the dog biscuit she knew I would give her just before I walked out the door. She would gently take her favorite treat and prance away, returning immediately without the biscuit to see me off.

Each evening, I would come through the door and drop to my knees, and the party would begin! Jumping, romping, rolling, yelping—well, enough about me, Bay went crazy too!

Suddenly, as if a lightbulb clicked on in her head, she would stop, dash into another part of the house, and trot proudly back with the bone I had given her that morning. She saved her treat all day for my return and our happy reunion.

Now the fun part! Bay would lie down on the carpet with the bone between her paws, a twinkle in her eye and her head cocked sideways, and give a little growl. I would pretend that I wanted to eat her bone, but she would grab it in her teeth and jump a few feet away. Always on the third charade, she would gobble down her biscuit with great delight, and I would bury her in hugs and loving.

People could use as much patience as this dog. When I wonder where God is and feel that He's far away during my lonely times or trials, I remember He promised that He will never leave me or forsake me. He always comes to me, and then we share sweet fellowship together.

Biblically, waiting is not just something we have to do until we get what we want. Waiting is part of the process of becoming what God wants us to be.
—John Ortberg

—Randy Benedetto

OCTOBER 27

Watch Your Step

For you, LORD, have delivered me from death, my eyes from tears, my feet from stumbling, that I may walk before the LORD in the land of the living.

—PSALM 116:8–9 (NIV)

IN SEARCH OF colorful leaves on a beautiful fall day, my husband and I drove north in our Jeep. We took the scenic route, ending at a state park along Lake Michigan. While hiking the wooded trails in silence, I soaked in the beauty.

The terrain eventually changed to sand as it led us to a cliff. We stood hundreds of feet above the beach, sand slipping down a dangerous embankment below us. Looking across the big lake, multiple shades of blue water spanned the horizon while cloudy skies gave way to magical circles of light on the surface below.

I turned back to the trail and noticed a dog playing catch. Greeting the owner, I knelt to introduce myself to Henry, his long-hair dachshund. Henry happily ran straight toward me from the dune, eyes locked with mine. *Wham!* He ran chest first straight into the low-slung cable fence between us, then bounced backward. Everyone laughed.

Later, my husband wisely remarked, "Henry had the end in sight and not the road in front of him." Oh, how I can relate to that dog! Without watching my steps carefully, I stumble down steep hills or run into walls. I move fast toward my goals but don't take the time needed to assess everything first. I fail. I get smacked in the face with something unexpected because I wasn't watching.

I want to walk before the Lord in the land of the living as the psalmist wrote. Without God, I won't be able to do it. He is my deliverer, lifting me away from the obstacles on the path before me. Rescue is near.

God, help me to keep my eyes on You. I am distracted and forget that I need only to run safely into Your arms. Set me on the path that I should go. Guide my tired feet on the journey ahead. Amen.

—Twila Bennett

OCTOBER 28

Reflecting

In the same way, let your light shine before others, that they may see your good deeds and glorify your Father in heaven.

—MATTHEW 5:16 (NIV)

MONKEYS SCREAMED IN the distance as we floated down the Amazon River, a large spotlight cutting through the darkness. This mission trip to Brazil had served as a blessing to many villages. Now, relaxing under the brilliant stars, we searched the shoreline for caiman, a crocodilian species in South America.

As we scanned the riverfront with the help of our light, we caught glimpses of yellow pinpoints of light shining back at us. This was the evidence for which we had hoped—proof we were being watched from the blackness of the jungle. The yellow eyes of caiman reflected our spotlight. Amazed at the sheer number of these animals, we gazed from the safety of our large riverboat.

Here and there, we would notice a pair of yellow eyes momentarily disappear, then show up again—a blink from one of the reptiles.

Later, as I lay in my hammock surrounded by mosquito netting, the gentle rocking of the boat beckoned me to embrace sleep. But I kept thinking about those points of light bouncing back at me from the jungle. As Christians, we, too, are to reflect from our hearts the light of Christ in this darkness.

The world has a threatening absence of light. Often, we're the only source of illumination others see when traveling the ominous waters of this life. God has shone the brilliance of Christ on us, His children, so that we might reflect His Holy Spirit to the world.

All around me are souls, drifting, maybe even sinking, going down for the last time. May I never blink in indifference, lest I cause those searching to lose sight of the hope of Jesus.

The Bible is not the light of the world, it is the light of the Church. But the world does not read the Bible, the world reads Christians! "You are the light of the world." —Charles Spurgeon

—Tez Brooks

OCTOBER 29

Piggles's Share

The greedy stir up conflict, but those who trust in the LORD will prosper.

—PROVERBS 28:25 (NIV)

THE KITTENS HAD just discovered food away from their mama, and they converged on the food bowl as if the food was the most exciting, amazing thing ever discovered. And at that time in their lives, it probably was.

They all made little slurping, gobbling, and growling sounds as they ate voraciously. But one, the fattest male, jumped in the middle of the bowl and reached his little legs across to the edges, blocking the others from eating. They tried to eat around him, but he managed to keep them away just enough so that he could eat his fill.

The growls increased, and there was some boxing and hissing, all over food that was plentiful. There was no reason to worry about lack. But when one decides to let greed rule his actions, the ripples of consequence are not good.

The male kitten's actions led me to give him the name Piggles. And his actions shone light on how many times I worry about losing out on something there is plenty of. I grab tightly, letting fear make me distrust anyone who gets near anything I want. I worry that somehow, someone will swoop in and steal something I have dreamed about, when all the while, God has filled the coffers for all the dreams He has for me.

No one can take God's dream for me, because He is always there to refill my bowl. When I spend my days fulfilling God's call on my life, I put so much more positive out in the world. And that good only begets more good.

O Lord, please clean the corners of my heart and sweep away any greed that might be hiding there. Remind me again that there is always enough.

—Devon O'Day

OCTOBER 30

Miracle Calf

In the same way your Father in heaven is not willing that any of these little ones should perish.

—Matthew 18:14 (NIV)

MY HUSBAND, CRAIG, thought it was a successful fall roundup of his cattle, which had been grazing on nearby pasture. While cattle are a herding animal and typically stick together, sometimes they wander, looking for protected areas in our mountain valley where mountain lions might not see them.

This year, the pairs loaded up pretty easily in Craig's cattle trailer for the two-mile ride back to the ranch. The baby calves paired up with their moms, and Craig checked and double-checked his numbers.

"It was a success," he told me that night over dinner.

Five days later, though, he found that wasn't the case. On a leisurely trail ride, a friend found a black-and-white calf lying by the creek. Kate almost missed the little guy, hidden in the brush. When Craig arrived, he put him right in the truck for the ride home.

"Miracle," we called him, first because he survived so long without his mother, and second, because he not only took a bottle but also sought out any cow that would take him. Miracle then bonded with his mother again—and his twin agreed to share.

Wandering off isn't something only animals do; I do too. Sometimes I get out of the practice of praying and seeking God daily. I forget to give thanks for all I have been given. And I even make choices that aren't the best for me.

But thankfully, I serve a heavenly Father who will seek me out, swoop me up into His arms, remind me how much He loves me, and bring me back into His fold.

Lord, when I wander from You, seek me out and guide me back into Your safe pastures. Thank You for always watching out for me. In Jesus's name. Amen.

—Janet Holm McHenry

OCTOBER 31

Pumpkin Personality

May the God of hope fill you with all joy and peace as you trust in him, so that you may overflow with hope by the power of the Holy Spirit.

—ROMANS 15:13 (NIV)

TEN YEARS AGO, my husband and I rescued a cocker spaniel named Maddie. Little did we know at the time that she would become the most sociable member of our family. Maddie never met a person, dog, cat, or butterfly she didn't like. In fact, she will persistently pursue friendship with any person or living thing that seems ambivalent about her existence, as if it's obvious that knowing her would make their lives better. She isn't wrong about that part.

Maddie's favorite day of the year is an annual fundraiser for the Humane Society, where she gets to wear her pumpkin costume and meet other dogs and new people. As soon as she sees me pull out her costume, her tail begins wagging dramatically. She knows exactly where she's going. Every single year, Maddie makes a fan club full of people who think she's absolutely adorable. I can't help but agree with them.

The thing about Maddie is that she lives her life expecting good things, so she, in turn, *sees* good things. She expects other dogs to be friendly. She expects new people will want to play with her. And she nearly always wins them over.

I want to live my own life more like this. All too often, I meditate on my fears of what could go wrong in life, as if it's up to me, in my own strength, to keep these things from happening. But doing so limits my perspective so that my fears become *what* I see. On the contrary, if I, like Maddie, expect kindness, I will find kindness. If I seek beauty, I will find that too. The same holds true for restoration, redemption, hope, and generosity. I become, in this way, what I see. Maddie's joy spills over to everyone she meets—and she challenges me to see the joy already abounding in the world around me.

Life becomes easier and more beautiful when we can see the good in other people. —Roy T. Bennett

—Ashley Clark

November

NOVEMBER 1

Remembering Love

Remember that at that time you were separate from Christ, excluded from citizenship in Israel and foreigners to the covenants of the promise, without hope and without God in the world. But now in Christ Jesus you who once were far away have been brought near by the blood of Christ.

—EPHESIANS 2:12–13 (NIV)

THE CHESS PIECE was mutilated and nearly ruined. Little teeth had punctured the plastic rook, and yet it still stood. As my son and I set up the game, I ran my thumb over the rough edges of the piece, fondly remembering little Howie's puppy days and his love for chess.

My son looked at the piece in my hand. "Awww, Howie . . ."

We hugged each other, for it had been nearly a year since we lost our special pup, and yet the pain of his absence was still often upon us.

"It's nice to have this," I said, placing the rook on the corner of the board. "To remember the joy and love Howie gave us in his life."

Memories are powerful. So often in my own walk of faith, I tend to be forgetful. Forgetful of what Jesus has done on my behalf, forgetful of that which He has promised to continue to do and will do. The remedy for this?

Remembering.

Just as memories of Howie place him at the forefront of my mind, memories of all that God has done for me so often shift my priorities into focus. Howie left an indelible mark on our hearts because of love—his love for us and our love for him. How much more so has the Lord of Creation left a mark on the hearts of His children?

Jesus, quite simply, You rock. Your grace is sufficient for every circumstance, every day of our lives. Forgive me for my forgetfulness. May I constantly be reminded of Your truth. May I constantly be reminded of Your love. Amen.

—Heidi Chiavaroli

Night Birds

Trust in the Lord with all your heart and lean not on your own understanding.

—Proverbs 3:5 (NIV)

MY HUSBAND URGED me outside the cabin late one night. "It's beautiful out," he said. "Come and sit." We were spending the weekend at a little camp beside a lake. Sometimes we sat outside at night around a crackling fire. Or watched the stars twinkle in the sky. I enjoyed being outside at those times, as long as the fire blazed and the stars shone. It was another story all together, however, when the sky was inky dark.

I tried to ignore the chill down my spine as we sat together in the still, dark night. Then, a flutter of wings flashed past my head.

"Ah, night birds," Mike said.

"You mean bats," I answered, cowering. As much as I didn't like the dark, I didn't like bats even more. I remember the night one got into our house. I watched it move stealthily across a wall using its wings in a strange and creepy manner. Terrifying. Another bat soon followed, swooping low. I ducked. It was a mystery to me why God made such creatures. Why did the night have to be so dark and scary? How was I supposed to enjoy my evening like this?

Then a cloud shifted to reveal a bright glow, and the bats flew off, silhouetted against the moon. Looking at them illuminated in the moonlight, they appeared graceful, even beautiful, and their flight, mesmerizing. I leaned against Mike and let the tension release. Maybe, when we fear something, the best thing to do is to look at it in a different light.

Dear God, the world is full of things I don't understand,
but I need not fear. Help me to see them in Your light. Amen.

—Peggy Frezon

NOVEMBER 3

Courage!

Have I not commanded you? Be strong and courageous. Do not be afraid; do not be discouraged, for the LORD your God will be with you wherever you go.

—JOSHUA 1:9 (NIV)

YEARS AGO, A young opossum began regularly visiting my chickens' feeder. It was only the size of a guinea pig, snowy white, fuzzy, and cute. My daughter named the possum Prince Henry. But despite his cuteness, I didn't want him eating my chickens' food, so when he arrived to dine, I would go outside with a broom and sweep him away . . . literally. He was so small I could easily roll him out the garden gate with my broom. Though he would hiss and growl, he simply wasn't big enough to resist. Out he went!

Today, Prince Henry is the size of a cocker spaniel. One Sunday morning after getting dressed for church, I spotted him outside, munching away. In my dress and high heels, I grabbed the broom and confronted him. He snarled, curling pink lips back from needle-like teeth. I poked him with the broom. "C'mon now! Out!" Prince Henry growled and made a feint toward me. This was new, and I must admit, I felt rather intimidated and vulnerable with bare legs and high heels. Clutching my broom defensively, I slowly backed up and retreated into the house.

Then I laughed. Why so scared? I might not be able to sweep him out the gate anymore, but opossums aren't exactly known for attacking people. How silly of me. I went back outside, but Prince Henry had skedaddled. Standing there in my Sunday dress, I smiled and thought of God's instruction to Joshua: "Do not be afraid." No matter what comes my way—scary possums, scary people, or scary problems—God will be with me wherever I go, and I don't need to be afraid.

Courage is not simply one of the virtues but the form of every virtue at the testing point. —C.S. Lewis

—Marianne Campbell

NOVEMBER 4

Courage and Compassion

When he saw the crowds, he had compassion on them because they were confused and helpless, like sheep without a shepherd.

—MATTHEW 9:36 (NLT)

HE WAS A stray cat, a long-haired tuxedo with a Charlie Chaplin mustache. I had been feeding him for weeks, setting out kibble on my front porch, and I made a box to keep him dry during the drenching Oregon rains. I hoped to lure him into my home for a better life, but he always ran if I tried to touch him. Then I didn't see him for a week, until one morning, there he was when I opened my front door.

Unseasonably wet weather had dumped more than an inch of rain, leaving everything soggy. I gasped. Outside my door, poor Charlie lay in a puddle of water. I scooped him up and drove like a madwoman to the vet, who diagnosed a urinary blockage. He asked if I was willing to save a throwaway cat that might never be tamed. I agreed, not caring about the cost. All I could see were the kitty's pleading eyes.

I was reminded of the time, not long before, when I'd had to rush for help when my child overdosed on drugs. The doctor told me, "Insurance won't cover a suicide attempt." Was I prepared to face financial ruin to save my child? Yes—I would do whatever I could, no matter the cost.

In both cases, the question went far beyond money. I faced my own helplessness. I might not be able to rescue my child or a stray kitty. Should I try anyway? Of course. Love and compassion meant doing whatever I could to help.

Charlie Chaplin never became tame, but he always showed up for kibble. My child still battles addiction. Yet God gave me both the compassion and the longing to try to help. The cat struggled with urinary troubles and my precious child with addiction, but all of us—including those who might be seen as "throwaway" by some—are precious in His sight.

Lord, may compassion and love rule my heart, and may I always be open to help all Your creatures in their time of need. Amen.

—Linda S. Clare

NOVEMBER 5

Cling to Jesus

Because you are my help, I sing in the shadow of your wings. I cling to you; your right hand upholds me.

—PSALM 63:7–8 (NIV)

LIGHTNING FLASHED, THUNDER boomed, and the electricity went out. After the storm moved through, my husband, Stan, and I went to check on my elderly parents. Wind had blown down a huge limb, and Stan stopped to drag it to the curb for pickup. When he turned around, two orange eyes stared into his. They belonged to a bedraggled but beautiful gray bird, its hooked beak open in silent protest and claws clamped onto the branch.

When the bird made no attempt to fly, we texted a picture of it to the director of a wildlife rehabilitation center. She identified it as a juvenile Mississippi kite, a small bird of prey. "It's a brancher," she said. "Old enough to leave the nest but not yet ready to fend for itself. Put it back in a nearby tree, and its parents will return to care for it." Once Stan managed to pry the bird's claws from the branch, he did as instructed. The next morning, two adult kites swooped in to feed their hungry offspring.

The young bird endured a frightening fall and a bumpy ride across the yard, clinging to the only thing it knew for security. What do I cling to when life throws me to the ground? Too often, I look to other people for comfort and refuge. Others may turn to recreation, work, or more destructive diversions, such as drugs or alcohol, to dull the pain. But I've found that only Jesus provides lasting security, offering the assurance that He will stand beside me no matter what trials and hardships I face. Anything else is temporary.

Life often takes me on a bumpy ride. When I turn to Jesus, I find the peace and strength to let go of the "branch" I'm depending on and move forward.

My salvation and my honor depend on God; he is my mighty rock, my refuge. —Psalm 62:7 (NIV)

—Tracy Crump

NOVEMBER 6

Canine Confession

I confess my iniquity; I am troubled by my sin.

—PSALM 38:18 (NIV)

I STEPPED INTO THE foyer, surprised and a bit concerned by the silence. Jazzy, my beagle-mix pup, usually greeted me at the front door. I walked toward the dining room and set my purse on the table. "Jazzy?" Nothing.

Worry pricked the back of my neck as I searched for Jazzy in the living room and then headed to the upstairs master bedroom. Gulping down a knot of fear, I made my way down the stairs. "Jazzy. Come. Now."

My dog slunk out of my husband's office, head lowered, ears twisted forward, and eyes filled with guilt.

I expected to find trash strewn across the office floor but found nothing. I searched the perimeter, then sat on the floor in front of her. "What did you do?"

Jazzy walked toward me, her steps slow. She tucked her tail, lowered her head even more, and twisted her floppy ears so far that I could see the insides. She sat in front of me, scooting closer until she pressed into my leg while avoiding eye contact.

"Were you in the kitchen?"

Tapping the tip of her tail on the floor, Jazzy nudged my hand.

"Oh, Jazzy," I said with a smile. "I forgive you."

Before I could fully open my arms, Jazzy wiggled into my embrace, hopped onto my lap, and slathered my face with puppy kisses.

Jazzy's canine confession reminded me of the psalmist David, who wrote about the burden of unconfessed sin. But her response to my forgiveness filled me with hope.

When I confess my sins to my Master—Jesus—I can count on Him to remain faithful, merciful, and unconditionally loving as He forgives me.

If we confess our sins, he is faithful and just and will forgive us our sins and purify us from all unrighteousness. —1 John 1:9 (NIV)

—Xochitl E. Dixon

NOVEMBER 7

Neighborhood Nessie

Though you have not seen him, you love him; and even though you do not see him now, you believe in him and are filled with an inexpressible and glorious joy.

—1 PETER 1:8 (NIV)

I NEVER SAW HIM, but I believed the stories about the river otter that lived in the man-made lake in our housing development. I affectionately called it the Loch Ness Monster.

It was first spotted by men on the maintenance crew, then by some of our neighbors. Nobody could figure out how a river otter found its way through a suburban neighborhood and into our lake. Where did it come from? We don't have any rivers in our area. What did it eat, other than descendants of the small fish that landscapers planted in the lake years ago? Should someone call animal control? No one did. It wasn't hurting anything, and some of us liked the idea of a river otter choosing our lake.

Occasionally, while taking a walk, I saw a dark spot on the water and wondered if it was my Loch Ness Monster. When I heard news that the otter was gone, I felt sad that I had never seen it. What I missed more was the mystery of knowing it was there whether I saw it or not.

My journey of faith has provided me with a lot of practice in believing in what I can't see. Stubbornly holding on to God through challenges, including some that could've shattered my faith, has deepened my belief not only that He is there but also that He is at work even when I can't see evidence of it. Those are the moments that send me looking for Him and have taken me from believing in Him to loving Him, which is exactly what He wants.

Faith is to believe what you do not see; the reward of this faith is to see what you believe. —Saint Augustine of Hippo

—Jeanette Hanscome

NOVEMBER 8

My Canine Caregiver

"Martha, Martha," the Lord answered, "you are worried and upset about many things, but few things are needed—or indeed only one. Mary has chosen what is better, and it will not be taken away from her."

—LUKE 10:41–42 (NIV)

IT'S NOT EASY being a long-distance caregiver for my senior mother with mobility and vision issues. She lives alone, although she does have services in place to help: a visiting nurse, Meals on Wheels, and a life-alert button. But I have one more secret tool that makes a great difference in her care.

I visit Mom as often as possible. On a recent visit, I sat at the kitchen table making a list, wondering if I had addressed every issue that needed attention. *God, help me to help Mom in the best way I can*. I looked over her bottles of pills. Was she taking her medication? I opened her refrigerator. Had she been eating properly? Was there a doctor appointment that needed scheduling? But while I was taking care of all these details, my golden retriever, Ernest, was thinking about only one thing. He was up on the sofa, draped over my mom's lap, gazing up at her adoringly. He hadn't moved from her side since we had arrived.

It reminded me of the story of Martha and Mary. While Martha hurried to make all the preparations for Jesus, her sister Mary simply sat at his feet, listening attentively. Maybe I needed to take a lesson from Mary—and from Ernest.

I set down the pen and paper, walked over, and sat beside them on the couch. I'm not saying that certain details don't need to be attended to. But Ernest knows what's often needed most. Yes, Ernest is my secret tool. He provides the best TLC—and the finest example—anyone could ever give.

Walk of Faith: *Do you know someone who could use a little extra attention? Part of being a good caregiver is simply spending time with someone lonely or in need.*

—Peggy Frezon

Called to Action

When the Spirit of truth comes, he will guide you into all truth. . . .
He will bring me glory by telling you whatever he receives from me.

—JOHN 16:13–14 (NLT)

I HAVE SOME ESSENTIALS I assemble when I start my day. I gather my Bible, reading glasses (yes, even with the large-print edition), juice, and coffee. Rudy, our seventeen-pound Manx, has his own essential item for me—his favorite toy, a stick-and-string toy dragon. With my right hand, I drink and read. With my left hand, I play "catch the dragon."

When I move to the office to start working on projects at the computer, my recreation-director duties continue as I carry in Rudy's toy. And sometimes, when I'm on a deadline, the combined effort of my computer work and satisfying Rudy's need for activity can become frustrating.

One day when Rudy let me know it was time for fun and games, I sighed and gave in. As I stood to play with him, with my back aching after hours at my desk, I thought, *How long have I been sitting here without getting up?* I looked down at the face of our little four-legged, tail-less ball of energy. "Why, thank you, Rudy," I said as I dragged his toy across the room. "I needed that!"

The experience made me think about how often God uses small, unexpected voices in our lives as prompts to act. Just as I listened to Rudy's much-needed calls to get up and play, I want to always be attuned to the Holy Spirit's reminders and calls to action.

Lord, thank You for the many voices You use to speak to me and nudge me into action. Help me always be listening for Your prompts. Amen.

—Terry Clifton

Flying Cats

Abram believed the Lord, and he credited it to him as righteousness.

—Genesis 15:6 (NIV)

FARM CATS AND farm kittens are incredibly gifted at survival. They are born with the intrinsic belief that they can catch and feed themselves because the ability is within them. The thought that they may not be able to sustain themselves doesn't occur to them. There is no social media to compare lives with other more successful cats. They just patiently do what is within them to live.

Tigre was a feral kitten, part of a litter from a cat that just showed up at my farm. Fed well, she still hunted like a professional from a very early age. She was a climber almost instantly. I watched her sleep in a tree right outside my window, realizing she was preparing her hunting ground. She slept there and became part of the environment, so birds would eventually become used to her and not even see her.

I thought it was cute that she thought she could actually catch a bird in a tree. I mean, cats can't fly. Can they? I would watch her watching birds. She didn't make a move as she studied them. She won't ever catch one, will she?

Then one day, I found the evidence of a bird she had caught. She had brought the bird to her littermates, and her survival skills had won their dinner. I could not believe that she was successful in such a difficult task. But she did not doubt her ability. She believed in what her inner self knew.

We all have inner survival skills and a Creator who has equipped us for unbelievable things. When I patiently wait for God to move me to use the skills with which He has equipped me, then move boldly and believe in my skills, I will be successful in His plan for me.

God, move me past any doubt of Your belief in me, past the unbelief of those around me, into the success You have waiting for me. In Jesus's name. Amen.

—Devon O'Day

NOVEMBER 11

Looking to the Sky

Look at the ravens. They don't plant or harvest or store food in barns, for God feeds them. And you are far more valuable to him than any birds!

—LUKE 12:24 (NLT)

DURING MY SERVICE in the US Navy, I often had to stand at attention. In boot camp, especially, when we were learning "how" to stand at attention, we were sometimes required to stand absolutely still for up to forty-five minutes. Whether during an inspection or a military ceremony, standing at attention is draining both physically and emotionally.

Aside from "don't lock your knees," we weren't given much instruction to help us endure standing at attention, but I developed a few tricks of my own to get me through. One of these tricks was to look up and out. Just using my eyes, not lifting my head, I would scan the sky or trees for signs of life. Almost always, I would spot a bird. Then I would remember what the Bible says about how God feeds them even though they're just birds, and how much more valuable I am to Him than they are. Focusing on the bird and that comforting thought took my mind off my aching back, sore feet, and depending on the weather, feeling too hot or cold or wet.

And my little trick has worked for me in other uncomfortable times in my life. When I begin to feel that everything is out of my control, when people are unkind or unfair, when life just doesn't go my way, when I'm worn out, I look up and out and spot a bird, flying free, cared for by God, and know that God cares for me too.

I will lift up mine eyes unto the hills, from whence cometh my help.
—Psalm 121:1 (KJV)

—Marianne Campbell

NOVEMBER 12

Bunny Therapy

Praise be to the God and Father of our Lord Jesus Christ, the Father of compassion and the God of all comfort, who comforts us in all our troubles, so that we can comfort those in any trouble with the comfort we ourselves receive from God.

—2 CORINTHIANS 1:3–4 (NIV)

MIDDLE SCHOOL IS a stressful time for many kids—hormones, immature friends, peer pressure, growth spurts, and so much more. When my daughter came to me in the middle of her eighth-grade year and asked for a bunny, my immediate reaction was to say no. Instead, I prayed about it. For some unfathomable reason, my heart felt at peace about getting a rabbit. More than that, I felt like it was right. Four weeks later, a sweet little Holland Lop bunny came to live in our house. My daughter named him Beebo, and we all fell in love with him.

But here is the thing that still amazes me. Every time my daughter picks up Beebo, the stress falls from her face and her entire body relaxes. I feel it too. I hold him and stroke his downy softness, listen to the adorable sound he makes eating apples, or watch him hop around our living room, and my stress levels drop. My shoulders relax, and I can't help but smile.

I have no idea why God made bunnies so soft, made their tails so cute, and gave them such big floppy ears. It feels like one of those mysteries of comfort and beauty, strangeness and wonder that He laced all through creation. However, God knew before I did what that sweet little bunny would mean to our family and how much we needed him. After all, He is the God of all comfort, and His comfort comes in all kinds of packaging. Sometimes it comes through His sweet presence, holding us together when we are falling apart. Sometimes, through the compassion of a friend. And sometimes, He sends bunnies.

When anxiety was great within me, your consolation brought me joy.
—Psalm 94:19 (NIV)

—Tracy Joy Jones

We, Though Many

For just as each of us has one body with many members, and these members do not all have the same function, so in Christ we, though many, form one body, and each member belongs to all the others.

—ROMANS 12:4–5 (NIV)

GEMSBOK ANTELOPE AND ostriches often appear within the same enclosures in zoos and wild animal sanctuaries and reserves. Likewise, they'll often be found hanging out together out in the wild. They may appear to be odd bedfellows, but actually, the ostriches do the antelope a great service.

Why? Ostriches have those nice long necks, which make them up to nine feet tall and consequently able to see well above the tall African grass. Predators are much less likely to sneak up on the antelopes' tall friends without being seen, and the ostriches are quick to let everyone know it's time to scatter.

As I watched the ostriches comfortably interacting with the gemsbok herd, I thought about how God has made His people different from one another for much the same reasons.

My husband's double stroke meant my life as I knew it had changed. For most of my life, I was the figurative antelope grazing in the field and my husband was the ostrich that watched out for me. Now that I am his full-time caregiver, our roles have changed, and I'm the one watching out over him. I admit there have been moments when I've questioned God as to why this had to happen, but deep in my heart, I know He has everything all under His control, and I'm deeply grateful I still have my husband around. I've just had to learn to stretch my neck a little and stay on guard.

Walk of Faith: *As each of us walks by faith, may we appreciate the way God has made us and the different roles we play in our own lives and the lives of others.*

—Deb Kastner

NOVEMBER 14

A Break in Pattern

Every good and perfect gift is from above, coming down from the Father of the heavenly lights, who does not change like shifting shadows.

—JAMES 1:17 (NIV)

IT'S ABOUT PATTERN," my husband explained. He stepped carefully down the trail, our toddler daughter sound asleep in his arms. I was surprised a few minutes earlier when he spotted the grasshopper on a boulder ten feet from the trail. After he pointed it out to me, my eyes caught the creature within a few moments, but not for the same reason it caught my husband's attention.

While I was drawn to its unusual bright-neon-orange color, my husband, who is color blind, had noticed the painted grasshopper for its striking pattern. Black and white lines zigzagged across its thorax and long legs, eclipsed by faux wings intricately painted onto its back—an artist's detail from its grand Creator.

"How did you see it?" I asked my husband as we continued down the trail after our three young boys.

"A break in pattern catches our attention. It's a deviation from what we expect. Our subconscious catches it first," he explained.

I wonder how many of these exceptional sights I walk by every day. And yet God's Holy Spirit is within me to help me notice these breaks in pattern. He nudges my attention toward unexpected blessings punctuating ordinary days. As my heart and mind align with His, I become more aware of His presence and His gifts scattered across each and every day. His blessings become a break in pattern, a deviation from the noise and distractions of this world, centering my heart on His beauty.

Walk of Faith: *Turn your attention to seeing God's blessings today. Write down five gifts you see from Him that you would have missed were you not looking for them. Keep your list of five blessings on your fridge, or somewhere you will see it often, as a reminder to search for His blessings throughout your days.*

—Eryn Lynum

NOVEMBER 15

Doe Fight

Let no one seek his own, but each one the other's well-being.

—1 CORINTHIANS 10:24 (NKJV)

HURRYING HOME, I rounded a curve and saw two white-tailed does in the middle of the road, which was not abnormal in our rural area. I slowed to a crawl, thinking they would bolt to the adjacent field. When they didn't, I stopped, my front bumper a few feet from them.

Strange how they seemed oblivious to the danger my car represented. They stared at each other, never glancing my way.

Mesmerized, I watched them each circle to the left, resembling two boxers in the ring. In a sudden move, they reared up on their hind legs and lashed out with their front hooves. I laughed, thinking of a cartoon with boxing kangaroos.

After whacking each other, the does dropped to the ground, circling to the left again. They still ignored me, but I needed to get home. I lowered my window and yelled at them, figuring I might scare them out of the road. It didn't work.

Astounded, I tried the horn. Both turned toward me, then right back toward each other. I beeped again and inched the car forward. After I blew the horn a third time, they turned and fled across the field.

At home, I looked up their strange behavior. I had seen bucks do this, but never does. It seems that both will fight to establish and keep a pecking order. It surprised me to think of shy, gentle does battling it out to be first in line.

Later, thinking about my encounter with the deer, I wondered what my Christian friends would think if they saw how often I whip my cart into the line a clerk just opened in the busy department store or step harder on the gas pedal to beat someone else to the front parking space.

Those who are happiest are those who do the most for others.
—Booker T. Washington

—Cathy Mayfield

NOVEMBER 16

Free to Choose

"I have the right to do anything," you say—but not everything is beneficial.

—1 CORINTHIANS 10:23 (NIV)

EVERY YEAR WHEN the weather got colder, a wren would find her way into my outdoor laundry room and make a nest in an area of the ceiling where some insulation had torn away. I was always careful to watch and make sure she had a way out. It was not an ideal situation because it meant I couldn't close my laundry room until her babies had left the nest.

One day, a repairman needed to turn the electricity off and then on again, which meant he had to get to the control box in the laundry room. When he was finished, he closed the door. I didn't think about checking the door or the little wren for several days till I did laundry. And when I did, I found her body on the floor. Her nest was empty, so her babies had gone, but she had chosen to go back inside to her nest. That was her trap.

It was very sad, because I had tried to be so meticulous in making sure she could come and go. But in that moment, I flashed to all the times I had made choices that had not ended well for me. Some of my choices seemed at the time to be more fun, more exciting, or easier than what I knew to be the right choice. I knew I could make any choice, but I did not always weigh a choice against the feeling in my heart about God's choice for me. That deep knowing and strong pull to do something of sacrifice or against the grain of peer pressure was often ignored to my own detriment. Even in the loss of this little wren's life, God spoke to me of the importance of choosing wisely.

Lord, please speak Your plans into my heart loud enough that I have the freedom and strength to make better choices. Amen.

—Devon O'Day

Good Boy!

His master replied, "Well done, good and faithful servant! You have been faithful with a few things; I will put you in charge of many things. Come and share your master's happiness."

—MATTHEW 25:21 (NIV)

DUNCAN IS A people pleaser. Our Scottish terrier is always eager to hear us say, "Good boy, Duncan," and to receive a pat on the head or an affectionate ear rub. He fetches a ball or his tug toy with tail wagging and brown eyes twinkling. He's leery of strangers, particularly men, but when my husband calls, Duncan comes running as fast as those little legs can carry him. He doesn't have to be coaxed. He knows his master's voice and is eager to please.

Watching him, I have often thought my human family members can learn a lesson from Duncan—and that includes me. Jesus doesn't want me to fetch and carry for Him, but there are things He expects me to do—that He expects all of us to do when we set our feet on the pilgrim path of life and truth. Many of these are clearly stated in Scripture: Be a cheerful giver, take care of widows and orphans, love thy neighbor. There are many others.

I need to remind myself to be as willing to serve God as Duncan is eager to please us. Faithful discipleship doesn't happen instantly, I know. It takes time and effort. It takes perseverance. The apostle Paul compares it to running a good race. One day, I want to hear the Lord call me His "good and faithful servant." I want that with all my heart.

Dear Lord, help me to manage my time and talents in a way that is pleasing to You. Help me chose priorities that line up with Yours. I want to be a good and faithful servant. In Jesus's name. Amen.

—Shirley Raye Redmond

NOVEMBER 18

Safe Dwelling

My people will abide in a peaceful habitation, in secure dwellings, and in quiet resting places.

—ISAIAH 32:18 (ESV)

MY SON AND I worked together to move his portable basketball hoop so he could mow the backyard. It took the two of us a solid fifteen minutes to move the heavy base just a foot off the grass and onto the concrete patio. My son pointed to the dirt where the base had sat and asked, "How did they get there?" I bent down to inspect and saw two large toads staring at us, startled that their secure hiding place had vanished.

"They must have found a small opening to get under the base," I replied. My son stood amazed that they had found a way to stay safely tucked under the hoop without getting squished. I'm sure the toads thought they had found an immovable, secure home. Imagine their surprise when sunlight and fresh air exposed them!

We have a secure, immovable dwelling place in the Lord, no matter what is taken from us in this life. I'm watching my grandmother live out this truth. Her memories are slipping away. She's lost physical mobility. She battles pain. She's lost her independence. Yet in the midst of these losses, a peace enfolds her. "I know where I'm going, and I'm ready," she told me on a recent visit. Her peace testifies to me of the security we have in Christ.

Unlike the movable hiding place in which the toads found themselves, the home the Lord has promised us is peaceful, secure, and immovable. While we may not experience that kind of physical rest in this life, we find comfort knowing that our spiritual home and life are hidden and secure with Christ.

Lord, thank You for being my secure dwelling. I confess that sometimes I fear exposure and what might be taken away from me. Help me trust You and believe my future is secure with You. Amen.

—Amelia Rhodes

NOVEMBER 19

Hot Ears

Therefore consider carefully how you listen.

—LUKE 8:18 (NIV)

MY DAUGHTER WAS holding one of my first "grandbunnies" in her arms. She and Andrew had made several attempts to successfully breed their two Flemish giant rabbits, Galadriel and Radagast, with two tragic failures. At last, Galadriel had given birth to a healthy brood of nine, and they were finally old enough to cuddle and hold.

I didn't have pet rabbits growing up, and neither did my children, so I wasn't accustomed to being so close. The softness of Galadriel's fur was exquisite. The cuteness of her twitching nose was endearing. But what surprised me was the heat pouring off her long ears!

"Wow!" I said. "Is Galadriel not feeling well? Why are her ears so warm?"

My daughter smiled. "She's fine. A rabbit's ears are designed to help regulate its body temperature. Her ears are simply doing their job."

I thought about that later as I watched the evening news. As different broadcasters gave their wildly divergent opinions of the day's headlines, I caught myself thinking they had each heard the news through ears tuned to hear what they wanted or expected to hear. Then I thought about the bunny's regulating ears.

Jesus often warned us that our ears also have the ability to help regulate our soul's temperature. As a communicator, I focus my attention on how I communicate. Jesus, however, warned the crowds to beware how they listen. If we listen ready to react in anger or judgment, that's what we'll find ourselves feeling. If we listen prepared to apply wisdom, patience, and love to our response, we're more likely to respond with souls regulated by God's Word.

Walk of Faith: *Now, when you listen to someone speak or take in the day's headlines, think about your ears as regulating the temperature of your soul. Process what you hear with God before reacting. Though your ears may heat up, your spirit remains steady and calm.*

—Lori Stanley Roeleveld

NOVEMBER 20

Toenail Trauma

You answered me, "What you propose to do is good."

—DEUTERONOMY 1:14 (NIV)

EVERY TIME I try to clip Muffin's nails she screams. She is so old she's barely able to get around, and her toenails grow like fertilized tomato vines. This sedate dog who sleeps twenty hours a day can turn into a snapping, biting Tasmanian devil if I even come near her with toenail clippers.

I have given up on the job. It is now part of a quarterly veterinarian visit, and it's worth every penny. The toenail clipping is too traumatic for me and for my fifteen-pound dog. I can't seem to convince her that I'm not trying to kill her and that all my intentions are for her good.

I'm often that way with God and things I don't want to do or do not want to give up. Have you ever watched people cling to things that are detrimental to their health and well-being by using excuses? I have complained about foot pain when I didn't feel like walking. I have rationalized avoiding healthier eating by telling myself I deserved a treat. I get downright angry when the doctor curtails the overuse of salt or sugar.

How many times am I guilty of the same illogical reaction to good as my little Muffin has to toenail care? God's rules are really not rules at all but a guide to our best quality of life. He wants good for all of us, His children. We are precious to Him, and He wants us to be as healthy and happy as we can be.

Dear God, I know Your intentions are always good for me. Please diffuse my ill temper and impatience as I make any changes You have asked me to make. Amen.

—Devon O'Day

The Wallaby in the Mirror

But the LORD said to Samuel, "Do not consider his appearance or his height, for I have rejected him. The LORD does not look at the things people look at. People look at the outward appearance, but the LORD looks at the heart."

—1 SAMUEL 16:7 (NIV)

WHAT DO YOU see when you look in the mirror? I catch my reflection and am drawn straight to my imperfections. Whether it be the gray hairs that aim for the sky or the fine lines forming around my eyes, I notice what's wrong with me.

When I observed the wallaby at ZooTampa at Lowry Park staring into the mirror, I wondered what it saw. Did it perceive the beauty I saw?

Did it see the advantages of its large feet and long tail as it jumps, or did it just focus on the fact that they were big? Did it appreciate its fluffy white belly that looked perfect for rubbing, or did it wish that belly was flat and toned? Did it enjoy the sweetness of its dark eyes or wish they were another color?

It's easy to focus on all the ways I don't measure up. I fall well below the standards of the magazine covers. I prefer comfortable, flat shoes versus high heels. And the Florida humidity replaces my smooth locks with frizzy hair that grows and grows.

I hoped that wallaby with its nose pressed up against the mirror appreciated its God-given gifts. But I know God saw the beauty He created. I captured the moment with my phone to remind myself I have a choice of where to place my focus.

I can choose to notice all the ways I'm lacking or plant myself in the truth of how God sees me. He looks at me as His masterpiece, uniquely gifted to reflect His glory to the world.

Lord, thank You for seeing beauty in me even when I fail to notice the gifts You've given me. Amen.

—Crystal Storms

NOVEMBER 22

Deceitful Vinny

Do not lie to each other, since you have taken off your old self with its practices and have put on the new self, which is being renewed in knowledge in the image of its Creator.

—COLOSSIANS 3:9–10 (NIV)

WHILE LIVING IN Australia, I enjoyed watching the wild kookaburras, parakeets, lorikeets, and cockatoos flying overhead. My favorite were the pink galahs that hung upside down on the power lines, playing and squawking with one another.

Recently, I observed Vinny, a pet galah that is notorious for deceiving visitors. He kisses his master sweetly, then pretends he wants a kiss from the visitor. However, when the unsuspecting person leans in to give Vinny affection, the galah promptly bites the person on the lip.

Vinny then flaps his wings and laughs. While it might be funny for Vinny and his owner, this rose-breasted cockatoo with his ill-intent is not winning any friends. Most of the victims have learned to ignore or avoid Vinny altogether.

I'm reminded of an old school acquaintance I'll call Carmen who had a way of wooing other students and making us feel valued. She complimented our clothes and bragged about us publicly. But behind our backs, Carmen would roll her eyes and mock us. She amused herself at our expense. Eventually, her betrayal got back to each of us, and one by one, we distanced ourselves.

Sadly, Carmen ended up losing many friends, all in the name of entertainment.

The Bible instructs us to be men and women of our word and warns about deceit—not meaning what we say. Being predictable and transparent is vital in pleasing God. Scripture reminds me that if we are deceitful, we are serving not the Lord but our own desire for acceptance. May I never be like Vinny or Carmen and use others for my own gain.

Father, give me a clean heart to treat others the way I want to be treated. Make me transparent and trustworthy. Help me rid myself of all malice, deceit, hypocrisy, envy, and slander of any kind. Amen.

—Tez Brooks

Out of Our Protective Shell

I will give you a new heart and put a new spirit in you; I will remove from you your heart of stone and give you a heart of flesh.

—EZEKIEL 36:26 (NIV)

AS A CHILD, I loved roly-poly bugs (sometimes called pill bugs or sow bugs). I can remember collecting them from the soil in our yard, watching them curl up into a ball in my hand, then carrying them to the shady front porch. I would lay them down and patiently wait until they unfurled and began to cautiously crawl around, then I would gently touch them to watch them curl up again. After a while, I would return them to their dirt homes.

I guess it was the budding scientist in me that was fascinated. More than a decade later, I would go to college and major in biology. But still, today, I think about those creatures that would roll up in a protective ball. Don't we all do that sometimes? We put on a hard shell to protect ourselves from the barbs that can come our way. We shut ourselves off from those who would hurt us . . . and maybe even from those who would love us. We shut ourselves off from a hurting world and those who need us . . . and maybe even from those whom we need.

Loving and receiving love can be difficult. I am sometimes afraid to risk pain or rejection or disappointment. I'm afraid of failure or that I'll let people down. I put on my armor or roll up to protect myself, shutting out a needy world. Oh, how I love my safety within my shell. But then God reminds me that He's called me to step out of my comfort zone, to risk putting myself out there with my writing and in everyday life. He has a purpose for me, if only I'll listen to His direction and follow.

Lord, even when it's scary, help us to open ourselves to Your plan for our lives. Please be with us as we step forward with a new heart, to reach out with Your power and Your grace. Amen.

—Missy Tippens

NOVEMBER 24

Turkey Crossing

The LORD will fight for you; you need only to be still.

—EXODUS 14:14 (NIV)

I WAS RUNNING LATE to an important meeting—a recurring theme. With a child, husband, full-time job in publishing, and parents with severe illnesses, I was overwhelmed. There weren't enough hours in the day. Pressure weighed heavy on me as I drove across town and past beautiful fall fields and forests.

Out of the corner of my eye, I caught movement. Immediately sensing a deer, I slammed on the brakes. I was shocked to see a wild turkey flying at eye level inches in front of my vehicle. If I had been driving a few seconds faster, Thanksgiving dinner would have landed in my lap.

The turkey crossing had started from the hill on my left side. Brown-and-black wings pumped with all the power it could muster as it struggled over two lanes. Gnarly legs dangled, and a red neck stretched out ahead. I marveled that this huge bird could accomplish such a feat. After it safely landed on the other side of my Explorer, I cheered.

Tears flooded my eyes as I drove on. I connected to that bird's weak flight. Barely having the strength to fly through the hard times, I mostly landed in the middle. I never asked for help. I kept flapping my wings but going nowhere.

God promised that He will fight for me if I am still. Stopping in the middle of my crazy life seemed the wrong thing to do. Peace in the quiet rebuilds me, though. God cannot get my attention when I am straining to fly away. He wants me quiet in order to strengthen my heart and bring reliance on Him.

Lord, help me to stop moving to avoid pain. Bring me healing in the stillness of the morning and in the quiet of the evening. Surround me with love, and remind me that You will help me. Amen.

—Twila Bennett

NOVEMBER 25

The Feel of Thanksgiving

Every good gift and every perfect gift is from above, and comes down from the Father of lights.

—JAMES 1:17 (NKJV)

IT DIDN'T FEEL like Thanksgiving Day to me. My husband, Terry, had just gotten home from the hospital after surgery. His dietary restrictions meant no turkey and none of the usual trimmings. I stood in the kitchen sipping a cup of black coffee, wondering what to do to make it feel like the holiday.

Terry entered the kitchen and suddenly gripped his nose. "EWW!" he uttered in a shrill, nasal tone. He pointed to my ankle. I gasped. It didn't take a rocket scientist to discover that the pungent smell came from our cat, Mr. Rudy. In licking my ankle, he had lovingly left a deposit of stinky mackerel.

"Maybe that was Rudy's way of wishing his mom-cat a Happy Thanksgiving," Terry said as he took his medications.

"Right," I mumbled as I wiped away the smelly residue from my ankle. In that instant, I knew I had better check my disposition. *God is watching*. He couldn't be pleased with my attitude of nongratitude, especially on Thanksgiving Day. Surely, I could stretch my frowning mouth into a smile—for both Terry and Mr. Rudy.

Mr. Rudy's ankle deposit had made me aware of the importance of showing thanks. On this particular Thursday, I knew it was only right that I thank the Lord out loud for all He had done for us. I grabbed Terry's hand, and we bowed our heads, praying and expressing our gratitude. And then it felt like Thanksgiving Day.

Walk of Faith: *Thanksgiving Day is a time to give thanks for all that the Lord has done for us and our families. Make sure to leave room for hope for the Lord's blessings to come.*

—Sandra Clifton

NOVEMBER 26

Last Words

Never let loyalty and kindness leave you! Tie them around your neck as a reminder. Write them deep within your heart. Then you will find favor with both God and people, and you will earn a good reputation.

—PROVERBS 3:3–4 (NLT)

GOODBYES ARE NEVER easy, but good words to good people (and precious pets) are never hard. Our thirteen-year-old Boston terrier, Jazzy, fought a difficult fight with degenerative myelopathy. She had been a loyal dog—making life better despite having to adapt to new surroundings after eight moves with us. Even in her physical struggle, she provided faithful companionship. She entertained with silly antics and snuggled like the best warm, fuzzy blankie. Though her muscles atrophied and her mind betrayed her, her heart remained focused on showing love and brightening our days.

Then *that day* happened—the day we had to let her go. We surrounded her on the table and shared sweet words as her life faded away. "You were a good girl. Thank you for loving us. It's okay to rest now. You lived a good life. Thank you for making our lives better." The last words Jazzy heard were words of love and favor. She earned our praise.

I wonder what last words I'll hear as I move from this life to the next? What will I hear first when I enter heaven? I long for that "well done" my Jazzy received. It all starts by showing love with loyalty and kindness while I live.

Walking away from the vet with tears in my eyes, my heart offered tribute to the gift of Jazzy's life. I determined to take on her attributes and live them out in my own life as I interact with others. May my presence and words be like a warm, fuzzy blanket.

His lord said to him, "Well done, good and faithful servant; you were faithful over a few things, I will make you ruler over many things. Enter into the joy of your lord." —Matthew 25:21 (NKJV)

—Kathy Carlton Willis

NOVEMBER 27

Three-Dog Night

Now, therefore, you are no longer strangers and foreigners, but fellow citizens with the saints and members of the household of God.

—EPHESIANS 2:19 (NKJV)

WHEN I PICTURED a weekend alone at a friend's mountainside home, it all seemed too good to be true. With snow gently falling outside, I would write amazing prose all day and binge-watch old TV shows at night. The one complication might be babysitting Fred, my friend's two-hundred-pound mastiff.

The gilt came off my lily pretty quickly. When I used a hidden key to unlock the oversized front door, Fred appeared reticent about allowing a stranger into the sprawling manse. It took a lot of coaxing and the rest of my roast beef sandwich to get past the canine sentry.

Fred eventually lay down on his dog bed, though he continued to eye me suspiciously while I toured the house. The A-frame looked amazing, like one that would be featured in a design magazine. After grabbing a coffee, I settled down to work at my laptop.

Two hours later, the wind picked up, and off went the power. My laptop fizzled thirty minutes later. No power meant no television. Fred and I sat uneasily together in the dark. At bedtime, we went for a short walk. He growled at me all the way.

Later, I could have used three dogs as I tried to stay warm in the rapidly cooling house. The well-trained Fred balked at joining me on the bed. But the next morning, Fred woke me at seven for his morning constitutional. As we strolled through the woods, God reminded me how badly my relationship with Fred began. Now, he nuzzled my hand like an old friend.

The gentle nudge of the Spirit reminded me of a new family at church. The Hendersons would probably appreciate an invitation for lunch. Had I been as standoffish as Fred? The intimidating pooch reminded me that everyone prefers a warm welcome.

Lord, thank You for gentle reminders. Help me pass Your love along to others, but particularly those of the household of faith. Amen.

—David L. Winters

NOVEMBER 28

Flight Training

Are not two sparrows sold for a penny? And not one of them will fall to the ground apart from your Father. . . . Fear not, therefore; you are of more value than many sparrows.

—MATTHEW 10:29, 31 (ESV)

A DARK OBJECT CAUGHT my eye as I looked out the window. Something brown was nearly buried in the green grass of our backyard. An animal. My heart lurched with the thought, afraid it was injured or dead.

I grabbed my binoculars. Sure enough, the dark blob was a robin. I didn't need to be an ornithologist to know a robin's normal behavior didn't include lying on the lawn, right where my dogs often trekked outside. I searched for signs of injury, but the bird was too obscured to see more than its head.

I would have to risk disturbing the bird to get a closer look. Instead of an injured robin, I saw a fledgling, a baby bird that had been shooed from the nest but couldn't yet fly. After speaking with a nature expert on the phone, I was comforted to know this fledgling was simply on a necessary journey to adulthood.

I kept an eye on the bird and eventually saw that its parents stayed nearby. They would watch over their baby in this difficult phase of life until the day the fledgling began to fly.

I've felt like that baby bird. My circumstances are sometimes hard, the future grim. I've been left alone, unable to do anything but wait for something good to come my way. But seeing this fledgling reminded me that even the darkest moments in my life are necessary steps in the journey God has for me. Like the baby robin, I am never alone—God is always near, keeping watch over me. And in God's timing, I am destined to fly.

Walk of Faith: *Take a step back and look at your circumstances with the objective eye of a bird-watcher. Ask God, "How are You using this to prepare me for flight?" Then trust that He is.*

—Jerusha Agen

NOVEMBER 29

Playful Penguins

For the LORD does not see as man sees; for man looks at the outward appearance, but the LORD looks at the heart.

—1 SAMUEL 16:7 (NKJV)

WHILE ON A trip of a lifetime to Antarctica, I discovered that penguins are a lot like people. They are curious and friendly—so friendly that they will walk right up to you and tap on your boots as if to welcome you. Penguins also take good care of their offspring, with the mom and dad sharing duties. And they are most entertaining. Penguins love to have fun slip-sliding down snow mountains into the ocean. When you combine their antics and their walk, penguins are regular comedians.

But penguins, like people, can be deceptive and naughty too. They steal rocks from one another, precious rocks that are necessary for nest building. A male penguin will never take a rock while being watched. He will wait for an opportunity when rocks are unguarded to steal them. Then he will appear innocent as a newborn babe.

I often try to get away with something, too, something I would never do when someone is watching. Nothing big, just a minor thing like taking a pen from a restaurant or paper from the office. *Technically, it's not stealing,* I say to myself. People expect pens to "walk away." Or I have many times written things at home that were really work-related using my personal supplies, so I am just evening the playing field. My natural nature might be to "steal a rock" from my neighbor, but my better spiritual self asks forgiveness for such thoughts.

If we stop and think, we realize Someone is always watching; we are really fooling only ourselves if we think we get away with our small infractions. God has promised to fix the injustices of this world someday, and until that time, I will daily ask forgiveness for my tiny wanderings in the wilderness of deceit.

Father, keep me from dishonesty. Help me act with integrity as I am reminded that You see my actions and know my thoughts. Amen.

—Linda Bartlett

NOVEMBER 30

Brothers Who Fight

My dear brothers and sisters, take note of this: Everyone should be quick to listen, slow to speak and slow to become angry.

—JAMES 1:19 (NIV)

I WAS GIVEN A litter of feral kittens to socialize and rehome. When they were released into my care, they were so cute and playful. They chose a basket as their favorite sleeping place and couldn't get close enough to one another as they wrapped themselves in sleep. As they chased tails and toys, there was never as much as a snarl between them. These littermate brothers were thick as thieves. Until one day.

As it turned out, they would stay at my farm, and they fit in perfectly. They were here to stay, but as they got older, they weren't sleeping or playing together. The basket they shared was empty as the brothers chose different quadrants of the farm to explore. But upon returning to their food bowls, they would bristle and howl aggressively. Although they were raised as brothers, something as trivial as jealousy could spark unrest. There was no real competition for attention or food, but somehow in their familial circle, the competition they felt was real. It inflated, and there was no way past the wedge between them.

How many times have I let issues with my family members grow into a thorn of destruction? In the grandness of forever, these are petty things . . . possessions, territory, or jealousies that can tear down communication and relationships. Courtrooms are full of these sad bickerings that are hard to heal. If I could only stop for a moment and remember the sweet pictures of our childhoods, when love, joy, and togetherness brought such peace, maybe a forgiveness seed could be planted that would choke out the anger.

God, please heal my family rifts, and let us return to the love we were born into. Amen.

—Devon O'Day

December

DECEMBER 1

Safe in My Father's Arms

Casting all your care upon him; for he careth for you.

—1 PETER 5:7 (KJV)

THE SCHOOLS WERE closed, and the highway patrol warned drivers to stay off the snow-buried roads or risk getting a ticket. It was the perfect day to call off work, and I couldn't wait to take my four-month-old chocolate Lab named Bay out in her first snow.

Oh, what fun to pull her on a sled and watch her jump deep snowdrifts that were way over her head! She burrowed her brown snout into the snow and emerged as cute as a calendar picture. She wriggled on her back, her tiny puppy legs squirming in every direction, and made snow angels. Bay was enjoying herself immensely, but it didn't take long before she became cold and tired. She put her paws on my leg and gazed up at me with a quizzical look. She couldn't explain that she was weary and her winter coat wasn't very thick, but she turned to me for help.

My heart melted. I unbuttoned my jacket, bent down, and scooped her into my arms. She jumped under the cover and safety of my coat, tucked her head under my warm arm, and didn't move all the way home. This was a time when we bonded with each other. She depended on me, and I protected her.

I often find myself feeling worn out and defenseless, concerned about finances, my work, our health, and many other things. At times like these, I open my Bible and turn to the Psalms. It's like climbing onto my Father's lap and letting Him comfort me and warm my worried soul. I feel my Father's love wrapped around me, just as Bay, curled up in a ball beneath my coat, trusted in her master. Safe in His arms, we take the next step in our journey toward home.

A safer place cannot be found, comfort beyond all measure.
Close to the father's heart is everlasting pleasure. —R.B.

—Randy Benedetto

DECEMBER 2

Do Not Fear

You are my hiding place; you will protect me from trouble and surround me with songs of deliverance.

—PSALM 32:7 (NIV)

YEARS AGO, MY quiet time with the Lord meant my Bible in my lap and my parrot, Lorito, on my shoulder. At the end, I would reward him with a neck rub before putting him in his cage and feeding him breakfast.

Living in a condo meant maintenance workers sometimes walked in front of my office window. When Lorito spotted them, his breathing became labored. He would fluff himself up to appear bigger than he was. Parrot or not, he can really be quite chicken.

One day, Lorito observed someone outside and flew to the hallway door. Then he stopped, looked back at me, and ran my way.

I picked him up and reassured him of my protection. Then I pulled him close, lightly covered him with a blanket so he couldn't see outside, and gently rubbed his neck. Soon, he was bending his neck to allow me to better reach his tight muscles.

The next time Lorito spotted someone walking by, he climbed down to burrow in the blanket and snuggled next to me. He allowed his fear to cause him to draw near to me.

In the Bible, the words *do not fear* are often accompanied by the promise of God's presence. Lorito reminded me I don't have to face my fears alone. I can allow my fear to cause me to draw near to my Savior. In His arms, I'm safe and secure. I can find peace in His presence with me. I can walk in the assurance that God is with me.

Lord, when I'm afraid, take hold of my hand and draw me near to You. Amen.

—Crystal Storms

DECEMBER 3

You Are My Rescue

From six calamities he will rescue you; in seven no harm will touch you.

—JOB 5:19 (NIV)

THE SOFTEST BUNNY I've ever held arrived at Camp Roger this past summer. Her name is Olive. She is no ordinary rabbit from your backyard. Olive is a Mini Rex, with gorgeous brown fur that is as plush as a stuffed toy.

My friend Taylor brought Olive to camp after she was discovered in a church parking lot. Olive was outside her cage next to a bag of food and bedding. The day had been scorching hot, and having their own bunnies at home, Taylor's church friends brought her in, out of the heat. Taylor knew that our nature center hosts many critters during summer camp, and the rest is history.

Campers are particularly fond of this cuddle bug. They cradle her in their arms, talking to her and snuggling her tightly. If Olive had not been rescued in that particular moment, the results would have been devastating for her. Now, Olive lives the best life—Taylor's family takes her during the off season, and she goes to camp in the summer.

Over and over again in Scripture, I am reminded that God rescues me. Some days, I cry out to Him for help, and I am aware that He saves me. And some days, I don't even know my Father has rescued me from harm. How can He keep something from touching me? Does He cover me with an invisible shield? However it happens, He promises that in those moments, no harm will come to me.

Afterward, my Rescuer always takes me in His arms. As Olive can calm the jumpiest of kids, God can calm my beating heart and shaking hands like no other, pulling me close.

Guard my life and rescue me; do not let me be put to shame, for I take refuge in you. —Psalm 25:20 (NIV)

—Twila Bennett

DECEMBER 4

Hush

I say to myself, "The LORD is my portion; therefore I will wait for him." The LORD is good to those whose hope is in him, to the one who seeks him.

—LAMENTATIONS 3:24–25 (NIV)

WHILE LIVING IN Australia, we had an unexpected visitor. An Australian possum crawled along our back deck each night.

At first, we were alarmed at its boldness, but we soon realized it was waiting for us. Its overly large eyes would widen when I would come out and whisper to it. I named it Hush because the possum was so quiet.

One night, using his long tail to hold on to the fence, he reached out to me with both his claws.

"I believe Hush wants a handout," I said.

I rushed into the house and grabbed a banana. I presented it to Hush, and he gingerly took it from my hands. I confess it brought me great joy to watch him peel it, then relish every nibble.

My wife was not amused when it became a nightly ceremony to offer our good food to a wild animal, but I couldn't stop. As the weeks progressed, I trained Hush to eat from my hand, and he allowed me to pet him. Eventually, he brought his family to the nightly smorgasbord. I looked forward to these visits, and Hush came to trust me, his bulging eyes expecting only the choicest delicacies from my hands.

Our heavenly Father wants no less for us. He delights in providing for our needs—in seeing our eyes bulge with excitement and anticipation for what He lays in our hands each day.

When I begin to fret over finances, worrying about how I'm going to provide for my family, His Word reassures that it's not up to me. He is our Provider, and I have never seen Him forget about us.

Therefore I tell you, do not worry about your life, what you will eat or drink; or about your body, what you will wear. Is not life more than food, and the body more than clothes? —Matthew 6:25 (NIV)

—Tez Brooks

DECEMBER 5

Joy in the Midst

The LORD is my strength and my shield; my heart trusts in him, and he helps me. My heart leaps for joy, and with my song I praise him.

—PSALM 28:7 (NIV)

WHEN MY PARENTS asked me to watch their fourteen-year-old Labradoodle, Olive, I agreed enthusiastically. Though her body is riddled with mysterious lumps, she has trouble going down the stairs, and she can't see all that well, I looked forward to having a dog in the house again. Our own Howie had passed away a year earlier, and we hadn't yet sought out a new companion for our family.

After my mother dropped off her pet, Olive explored the house, long tail wagging in broad sweeps. She bumped into a table there, a chair here, but a few bumps didn't stop her enthusiasm. Over the next three days, I watched her struggle continuously with her old age—her poor eyesight, her struggle to stand, her apparent fear going down the back steps—all the while retaining a mysterious youthful enthusiasm I couldn't ignore. By all appearances, Olive was filled with joy.

As I prepared her food, leash, and bed for her journey home at the end of my parents' vacation, I pondered this characteristic with a little jealousy. How often do I let my circumstances sour my attitude? How often do I fail to realize true joy, especially in the midst of the difficult? And how much would I be blessed through trials if I could, like Olive, grasp this truth?

Where does Olive find her joy? In life, in living, in her relationships with people. This can be the same for me. God has not only given me the gift of this life and the people within it, but He has given me His everlasting love and strength. There is every reason for joy, and I am grateful Olive reminded me of it.

Heavenly Father, may we find our true source of joy in You. May we not only trust You, but soak ourselves in the strength, grace, and love You have shown us. Amen.

—Heidi Chiavaroli

DECEMBER 6

Tongue Tamer

All kinds of animals, birds, reptiles and sea creatures are being tamed and have been tamed by mankind, but no human being can tame the tongue.

—JAMES 3:7–8 (NIV)

MY SON AND I sat on bleachers with other curious onlookers. The crowd quieted when a young stallion entered the arena. He ran snorting around the ring, bucking and kicking up dust, as the horse whisperer we had come to see explained his plan. Though the stallion had been well cared for, he had grown up wild and distrustful of humans and without any training. The horse whisperer intended to tame the horse as we watched. Using soothing sounds and slow, gentle movements, he talked constantly while getting closer and closer to the horse. Each move showed intent and purpose.

In time, he was able to touch the stallion's flank, his neck, his head. When the horse bucked or shied away, the trainer started over. Eventually, he fit a bit into the horse's mouth, laid a blanket across his back, and saddled him, all the while talking in that same quiet voice. When it came time to mount, the horse whisperer said, "I may end up on the ground, but I'm going to give it a try." Before we knew it, he was seated on the young stallion who only two hours before would let no one touch him.

Mankind has tamed many species of animals, but James says we've yet to tame the most dangerous of all—the human tongue. How I can relate! Too many times words flow from my mouth like a runaway horse. Once they're released, I can't take them back, and we all know words can hurt as well as help. But I have hope. Just as the trainer used patience and consistency to tame his charge, I can strive to bring my tongue under control in obedience to Christ. Will it be easy? No. But just like the horse whisperer, I won't give up.

Set a guard over my mouth, LORD; keep watch over the door of my lips.
—Psalm 141:3 (NIV)

—Tracy Crump

DECEMBER 7

Me and the Mongoose

But our citizenship is in heaven. And we eagerly await a Savior from there, the Lord Jesus Christ.

—PHILIPPIANS 3:20 (NIV)

WHILE STATIONED AT the Naval Submarine Base, Pearl Harbor, I would jog on the Pearl Harbor Bike Path for exercise. One day, I caught a glimpse of an animal I had never seen before. It looked like a cat . . . a cat with red eyes! I asked a local friend what it could be. She said it was a mongoose and gave me a brief history of how mongooses arrived on Oahu, Hawaii.

During the sugar-plantation boom of the nineteenth century, rats from merchant ships invaded the islands. Someone thought it would be a great idea to introduce mongooses to combat the rats. But rats are nocturnal, mongooses are not, and "never the twain shall meet." With no natural predators for either creature, the islands had two invasive species with which to contend. The rats and mongooses didn't belong there.

When I would see a mongoose on the trail, we would stare at each other for a moment before it scurried off, and I would think about its history and how it didn't belong there. But then, neither did I. I was stationed there temporarily, and my hometown was more than two thousand miles away on the mainland. Taking that thought a bit further reminded me that I'm temporarily stationed on earth too. Heaven is my home.

The mongoose and I have God-given work to do on earth for the brief time we're here. Mine is to share the good news of Jesus Christ and love others as He loves me. But my forever home is with Him in heaven. Whenever I'm feeling out of place or uncomfortable in my current earthly situation, it's comforting to know Jesus has a place for me at His side for eternity.

If I find in myself a desire which no experience in this world can satisfy, the most probable explanation is that I was made for another world.
—C.S. Lewis

—Marianne Campbell

DECEMBER 8

Always Working

Let us hold unswervingly to the hope we profess,
for he who promised is faithful.

—HEBREWS 10:23 (NIV)

I SMILED WHEN THE couple looked at my border collie mix, Callie, as we followed my husband into the restaurant. "That doesn't look like a service dog," said the woman with a scowl.

My joy faded, but Callie remained oblivious to the criticism. She walked confidently by my side as we followed the hostess. Once she seated us, I gave Callie the command to rest at my feet under the table. We enjoyed a wonderful dinner and a visit from the restaurant's manager. She handed us our bill and thanked us for choosing her restaurant before moving to the next table to visit with the patrons.

When I rose from my chair, Callie came from under the table and sat by my side. The manager turned toward us. "I had no idea you had a service dog with you."

"That's the point," I said with a grin. "She's always working, even when you don't see her."

God has taught me so much through my relationship with Callie. I see how she responds to my commands out of love, and I want to obey my Master—Jesus—with the same willingness and joy. I notice how Callie draws near to me when she's unsure about a situation, and I want to stay close to my Master, who promises He will care for me in all circumstances. But that night, when I explained how Callie was always working, God reminded me to be confident in His promises to work through what often seems like endless waiting seasons.

God has proven that He is always with me, always in control, and always working . . . even when I don't see Him.

You need to persevere so that when you have done the will of God,
you will receive what he has promised. —Hebrews 10:36 (NIV)

—Xochitl E. Dixon

DECEMBER 9

Traveling on the O Line

I will lead the blind by ways they have not known, along unfamiliar paths I will guide them; I will turn the darkness into light before them and make the rough places smooth. These are the things I will do; I will not forsake them.

—Isaiah 42:16 (NIV)

I PAUSED ON THE path and looked up. Two long, sturdy, vine-like cables traversed the distance from a zoo enclosure to a fifty-foot-tall tower. An orangutan, in a frenzy of flowing orange hair, made its way across the cables. Its long arms reached above its head and moved hand over hand, as its nimble feet walked across the bottom cable. It passed right above my head!

I marveled at the agile ape, as well as the innovation that allowed the orangutan to spend time up high, just as it would in the wild. The zoo-keepers at the Smithsonian National Zoo in Washington, DC, installed the O lines, as they call them, to connect the ape house to a play area. The orangutans travel across them by walking and swinging, just as they would in the jungle.

Watching the orangutan move confidently and swiftly, I wondered what it would be like up so high above the ground, hanging on to mere ropes as I traveled.

Good thing God is my guideline. Even if I find myself precariously swinging from life's challenging rope course, I know that there's nothing to fear. I have the best safety net.

The wild-haired orangutan paused in the middle of its travels to take a break. Before I left the area, I paused once again and looked up . . . this time with gratitude to the One who is with me on my life's journey.

Dear Father, Your wisdom is perfect; Your guidance is precise; Your ways are right; Your love is ample. You enrich my world with wonders, and I am confident that whatever lies ahead is glorious. Amen.

—Peggy Frezon

DECEMBER 10

The Angry One

If only we knew the power of your anger! Your wrath is as great as the fear that is your due.

—Psalm 90:11 (NIV)

THERE IS AN old adage to the effect that if you do not deal with your anger and issues with the one who caused them, you will bleed on the ones who didn't cut you. I have learned that where anger is found, it usually has deeper roots and, through another lens, could more accurately be labeled fear.

Never have I seen this better illustrated than when my heeler hound, Josie, reacts to a thunderstorm. We have tried everything from thunder shirts to drugs and behavior modification. Nothing calms her completely. And with every crack of thunder, instead of hiding, she attacks the nearest dog or cat in her path, as if explosive anger and violence could chase the fear from her spirit. She is old now, and her attacks are not as fierce as in her younger days, but they are terrifying and unjustified for those who receive them.

I have learned that there is something in Josie that is so unspeakably fearful we cannot cure it. I anticipate the storms by staying close by her and wrapping myself around her, and now, as well as throughout the years, love is the only thing that brings her through the rain, thunder, and lightning.

How often do I react in anger to cover the indescribable fear that I feel? The past hides until the lightning of life brings it to the forefront. I chase it away in any way I can—more often than not with the distraction of angry outbursts, which are unfair to everyone. Recognizing that anger is usually fear wearing a scary mask is the first step to healing. God doesn't judge me for my fears, but I must love myself enough to let Him heal me.

Lord, I surrender my anger-covered fear to You for healing right now. Amen.

—Devon O'Day

DECEMBER 11

A Pint-Size Protector

The angel of the Lord *encamps around those who fear him, and he delivers them.*

—Psalm 34:7 (NIV)

MY FRIEND JULIE'S Chihuahua-papillon mix, Finn, has earned the nickname "Ten Pounds of Crazy," even though he might weigh even less than that. Though sweet and playful, he came to her without training, so she had to work with him a lot, especially on not growling at random people and dogs that are five times his size.

One afternoon, Julie and I had Finn with us when we went out for coffee, so we chose a table outside, and Julie kept him on her lap. Finn was surprisingly calm, until a man said hello to us in passing. Then Finn started growling. Thinking he was up to his usual antics, Julie corrected Finn and apologized to the man. When the man stopped to talk to us on the way back to his car, Finn growled even more. Again, Julie shushed him and apologized.

As soon as the man was gone, Julie whispered, "Wow, Finn really didn't like that guy." Both being writers, we exchanged wild ideas about what Finn sensed in that suspicious person. After a while, though, we stopped making up stories and considered the possibility that Finn really had been protecting us.

At the time, I was working through painful memories of being lured in by a predator. Though it hurt to recall how many red flags I had missed, I could also see how God protected me from a much worse scenario. The signs I had ignored could now be lessons on what to pay attention to in the future. Finn's growl became a reminder of God's protective warnings as I learn to trust Him to keep me safe.

Walk of Faith: *Reflect on a time God protected you from harm or a worse scenario. After taking a moment to thank Him, consider how that experience has equipped you with wisdom for the future.*

—Jeanette Hanscome

DECEMBER 12

A Keen Engagement

Whatever you do, work at it with all your heart, as working for the Lord, not for human masters, since you know that you will receive an inheritance from the Lord as a reward. It is the Lord Christ you are serving.

—COLOSSIANS 3:23–24 (NIV)

I NARROWLY CAUGHT THE movement in the peripheral of my vision, a slight jerk of energy in the tall grass outside the car window. "Stop. What is that?"

My husband slowed the car to a stop. "Is it a fox?" There was an eagerness to my question. Here in the foothills of Colorado, wildlife abounds, but a fox can be a rare sight. However, we had happened upon an even more uncommon viewing.

Slowly, the animal stood up from the grass.

"A bobcat!" my husband exclaimed. We cautioned our boys to stay in the car, pointing out the incredible animal. Wanting a better view, I unbuckled my seat belt and eased my upper body out the window until my head was above the roof of the car. "It's catching dinner!" I whispered back into the car.

Despite our cautioning the boys to stay quiet, I knew the cat was acutely aware of our presence. Yet its focus remained fixed on the job of the hunt. Its engagement caught me—fully aware of its surroundings yet absorbed in its work. Its hips moved up and down, one after the other, as it readied, lowered its chest to the ground, then pounced on its find.

Although dinner would come easily for my family that evening, I thought about the other work right in front of me: the work of being a follower of Christ, a wife, a mother, and a writer. Just like the beautiful bobcat we happened upon, I want to be fully aware of my surroundings, while silencing distractions so that I can fully engage in whatever work God has placed before me.

The soul of the sluggard craves and gets nothing, while the soul of the diligent is richly supplied. —Proverbs 13:4 (ESV)

—Eryn Lynum

DECEMBER 13

Eyes on the Bear

Let your eyes look straight ahead; fix your gaze directly before you.

—PROVERBS 4:25 (NIV)

A FEW YEARS AGO, our family took a trip into the mountains of Tennessee. As soon as we got to the Smokies, we hiked out to Spruce Flats Falls. Wanting to see more of the mountains, we found a local stable to take us on a trail ride the next day.

In the morning, we showed up early to the stables, where we were introduced to the guide and the horses. The stable was anything but fancy—an old, rugged building that had probably been there for generations—but the horses were clearly well cared for, and our guide was an old pro.

About halfway through our ride, we crossed a creek bed and then headed up a narrow section of the path that hugged the side of the mountain. As we rounded a corner, we looked above our shoulders to the left, and about twenty feet from the path was a rather large black bear.

Avoiding eye contact, I tried my best to keep my eyes on the bear as we passed by. I don't think I breathed, watching my children pass her, watching their horses to see if they would spook. But to my amazement, those horses didn't even flinch.

Those horses weren't worried about the black bear one bit . . . because their leader wasn't worried. They had followed him through enough trails to know that he would lead them safely back to the stable where there would be a reward waiting for them. They just had to keep their eyes focused on his footsteps and trust him to worry about the dangers around them.

As we headed back to the stables, I couldn't help but think about my own life. There will always be things trying to distract me, to make me fear or worry. But just as the horses kept their eyes focused on their leader, I must focus on my Leader as well—Jesus.

And let us run with perseverance the race marked out for us, fixing our eyes on Jesus, the pioneer and perfecter of faith. —Hebrews 12:1–2 (NIV)

—Joy Pitner

Chickadee in Distress

I lift up my eyes to the mountains—where does my help come from? My help comes from the Lord, *the Maker of heaven and earth.*

—Psalm 121:1–2 (NIV)

AT MY DESK one afternoon, I glanced out the window and noticed a chickadee fluttering at the suet cage. Soon the fluttering became more frantic, and the cage began to sway. Looking again, I realized the poor little bird was stuck.

I hurried outside to help. Sure enough, the bird's tiny foot was entangled in the wires of the suet cage. As I approached, the chickadee fluttered wildly. I knew the little bird was afraid, so I talked soothingly as I slipped on a pair of soft cotton gardening gloves. The more it fluttered, the more the cage swung to and fro.

"Oh, for heaven's sake," I exclaimed quietly. "I'm trying to help you." I was concerned that if it didn't hold still, the bird would seriously injure itself. As I gently grasped its body with one hand, the bird stopped flapping. It regarded me through bright black eyes, perhaps understanding that I was trying to free its foot.

Please, Lord, let me help this poor creature, I prayed. When I finally dislodged its tiny foot, the chickadee flew off. While removing my gloves, I realized that I'm often like that chickadee when I face a crisis. Instead of calmly seeking God's help, I flap and flutter with worry, trying to solve the problem on my own. I need to learn to be still and allow God to help. He wants to, I know. He even answered my prayer to help the distressed chickadee.

Cast all your anxiety on him because he cares for you. —1 Peter 5:7 (NIV)

—Shirley Raye Redmond

DECEMBER 15

Welcome Home

Lift up your eyes and look around; all your children gather and come to you.

—ISAIAH 49:18 (NIV)

VISITING MY GRANDPARENTS on Sunday afternoons holds a lasting memory in my heart. My father and mother would gather us kids, and we would join cousins, aunts, and uncles at the old homestead.

The last house on a steep dead-end street became my grandparents' home shortly after their arrival from Slovakia. The large two-story house, where prayer and Bible study were always a part, and where my father grew up, became a place for grandchildren to run and play.

Grandma would welcome us at the door, but Grandpa usually sat in his chair and greeted us by extending the crook of his cane to draw us near him.

But a memory of a different kind were the two white Samoyed dogs that greeted us. Barking can be annoying to many people, but somehow, when Snowball and Timber came running, their bark became their "welcome-home song." Sometimes, they scampered from the woods behind the house or from the backyard where chickens roamed. These pure-white dogs blended with the frosty snow in wintertime and almost appeared like angels in other seasons.

Samoyeds belong to the spitz breed of herding dogs. Their instincts are to gather and herd livestock out to pasture and back to the security of the barn at the end of the day. Perhaps Timber and Snowball sensed we gathered as a family where it was safe, fun, and full of love.

When Grandpa died, these loyal dogs, known for their understanding of humankind, often waited where Grandpa did carpentry in the shed, as if they were watching for his return.

The big front porch, baked Slovakian treats, parents and grandparents who loved us, and cousins, aunts, and uncles were all a part of our Sunday reunion after church.

And in my mind, I still see Timber and Snowball running to welcome us too.

Thank You, dear Lord, that You love to gather Your children home—and someday, there will be a Grand Reunion Day that will last forever. Amen.

—Kathleen Ruckman

DECEMBER 16

Authenticity

Stop judging by mere appearances, but instead judge correctly.

—JOHN 7:24 (NIV)

I'VE ALWAYS BEEN fascinated by insects, especially the praying mantis after I spent time watching one that was outside our back door at eye level.

When that mantis turned its head to look at me, it was almost human-like. Such an odd creature, with its prayerful hands and big eyes that follow you. When I did some research, though, I learned it is actually a predator. Those "praying" hands have spikes that snare their prey, and they can lash out quicker than the blink of an eye.

It reminded me that things are not always as they seem.

Sometimes we grow envious and think a person has it all. We see wealth or beauty or the perfect family or job or home. But that's not always the complete picture. I have a friend who appeared to have it all on the outside, but in private, her life was falling apart. In today's culture, we often feel pressured to portray a certain image, so we take the best selfies and share our funny stories without sharing the heartache or struggles. We tend to look at all those wonderful photos on social media and assume that everyone else has a perfect life.

I don't want to do that; I want to assume that other people may have struggles just like I do. And I want to try to support them. I want to look beyond the surface, just like I looked beyond the surface of that praying mantis with the cool praying hands and cute bug eyes and learned the full story.

Lord, open our eyes to the pain of others. And help us to show our authentic selves to help others know they're not alone. Amen.

—Missy Tippens

DECEMBER 17

Kangaroo Down

For what if some did not believe? Will their unbelief make the faithfulness of God without effect?

—ROMANS 3:3 (NKJV)

KANGAROOS FASCINATE ME. The bounce in their step could keep me entertained all day. The way their long tails help them balance is like the eighth wonder of the world.

Imagine my excitement at seeing real kangaroos in person. On a trip to Australia, I learned that watching the bouncy beasts on television bears little comparison to the real-life experience. They often move fast. Getting a clear photo proved difficult.

One morning, I felt lucky to see a kangaroo lounging on the grass outside our hotel. My friends chuckled as I crept closer and closer. Supposing the animal might jump up and start kicking me, they pictured me in a hospital instead of the conference for the week.

Kerry the kangaroo barely moved. She lay in the grass as I approached. Wanting a picture, I lay down not six feet away. My friends captured the whole affair on their cameras. After she felt I had gotten close enough, Kerry jumped over me and bounded off down the lane. We all laughed at her reaction, but I treasure the once-in-a-lifetime experience.

My attempts to woo Kerry reminded me of God's love. He came near by sending His Son into our world. Jesus died to open the door of relationship with an ordinary man like me. My failure to recognize Him at first did not make Him less faithful. He kept reaching out.

As I try to share my faith with others, this principle keeps coming to mind. Not everyone will say yes to God right away, but He doesn't give up easily. If I keep sharing Jesus with others, I just might get to be part of a once-in-a-lifetime experience like my encounter with Kerry.

Dear Lord, grant me patience to continue sharing the gospel. When others don't respond right away, remind me of Your unending faithfulness. Fill me with the love that doesn't give up too soon. Amen.

—David L. Winters

DECEMBER 18

Abiding Rest

Remain in me, as I also remain in you.

—John 15:4 (NIV)

I GLANCED OUT THE window on my way to the kitchen but stopped short at the sight of a black-and-white ball of fur lying on top of a stack of wood outside our shed. I stared at the cat, lounging lazily in the shade. It stared back and flicked its tail but didn't seem apprehensive about my presence.

Now, we don't own any cats. In truth, my husband doesn't care for them all that much, and I'm allergic to them. So I found it funny that this little creature would not only be in our yard but also so brazenly rest there, seemingly confident that it belonged.

I kept an eye on the cat for the rest of the afternoon. It never moved, content to be lying in the shade of the shed.

I thought how confident the cat was that it belonged in this place. A place it felt safe and, if not exactly welcomed, at least comfortable. In truth, I enjoyed its presence that afternoon. It was so natural I couldn't think it anything but comforting.

Perhaps this unassuming feline had it right. Resting—abiding—in a place of peace. The world surrounding this creature was busy. Thirty feet away, cars whizzed past. Birds flitted in the bushes beside it. But the cat had chosen to snuggle in deep in a place it was certain it belonged—a place of comfort, a place of peace.

Lord, when the chaos of our lives surrounds us, and even when it doesn't, may we always find You—our true peace. Help us to abide in You, always and forever, as our true source of comfort and peace. Bless us with heavenly confidence that we belong in Your amazing presence. Amen.

—Heidi Chiavaroli

DECEMBER 19

Birds of Different Feathers

And if one member suffers, all the members suffer with it; or if one member is honored, all the members rejoice with it.

—1 CORINTHIANS 12:26 (NKJV)

MOM, WHAT'S WRONG with that blue jay?" Its squawking had lasted fifteen minutes. One look outside showed the problem.

Stretched across the grass ten feet away lay a four-foot black snake. Hopping around nearby, two blue jays screamed their outrage. Between the birds and the serpent cowered a tiny, down-covered jay. It must have fallen from its nest.

While wondering what to do, I heard the beautiful notes of a towhee. I saw it across the yard, seeming to add its fury at the situation from a safer distance.

Not willing for the jay to get eaten, I hurried outside, and as I had hoped, the snake slithered away. With that threat gone, we watched as the parents kept jumping and twittering encouragement at their offspring. The tiny bird hopped to the hedge between our property and our neighbor's.

We watched it crawl up to the top of the hedge, flex its wings, launch into the air, and . . . fall to the ground. Over and over, it tried.

By now, the towhee had flown. It surprised me to see two cardinals, often considered enemies of the blue jays, fly in to trill their support to the baby jay. Hop up, launch, fall. All four adult birds called in turn, until the little one succeeded in flying a short distance. We cheered and went about our day, knowing the baby would make it.

Every time I think of this, it reminds me of church families. The unity of those three bird species for one helpless soul reflects the way Jesus wants us to surround those in need, regardless of our station, our color, our age.

Whether rejoicing or helping those we meet,
we embody Jesus's hands and feet. —C.M.

—Cathy Mayfield

Forty Red-Winged Angels

And God said, "Let there be lights in the vault of the sky to separate the day from the night, and let them serve as signs to mark sacred times, and days and years."

—GENESIS 1:14 (NIV)

MY ISSUES WITH travel anxiety have always been with me. Every trip to a foreign country, even a simple overnight, brings fears that are unfounded. As an alcoholic needs help and support to stop drinking, I have to leave my inabilities in the hands of God.

My farm sitter is wonderful, so I have no worries as I leave my pets in her care, yet the irrational worry persists.

Recently, a trip to a country I had always wanted to visit was gifted to me. I had time to plan and everything fell into place, but the weight on my chest was palpable. I asked God for signs. My pets all seemed to feel my unrest and clung to me, but I found no peace. The trip was to one of my late father's favorite places, so I talked with him as if he were with me.

I begged for some symbolic token from God that all was well. As I parked my car at the airport, a flock of cardinals appeared out of nowhere. I counted them as they all flew in at once. Forty spots of red, bright and muted, they surrounded me and my vehicle. Their appearance was just the assurance I needed. God delights in signs that He knows are unique to us. Only God knows that I cherish the legend of cardinal visits, and for me it was just the symbol I needed to feel comfort. And it was the trip of a lifetime!

Dear God, thank You for sending me messages to let me know You hear my prayers. Amen.

—Devon O'Day

DECEMBER 21

Calf Burglar

You have persevered and have patience, and have labored for My name's sake and have not become weary.

—REVELATION 2:3 (NKJV)

MY HUSBAND, CRAIG, has brought many calves home from the ranch. Sometimes the mamas just don't take to them, so Craig rubs them down and bottle-feeds them for a few days.

One such calf was Loretta, named for Craig's favorite country singer. The feisty thing would latch onto the bottle and guzzle the milk replacer down. She quickly graduated from our backyard to the corral with other new moms and babies.

Any doubt about how she would fare vanished when Loretta immediately scampered off to cows feeding on hay and latched on to one, then another, then another.

"She's the calf burglar," Craig said one day.

"So, she's going to make it without her silly mom?" I asked.

"Not only is she going to make it—she's putting on weight better than the others," Craig said. "She's got perseverance, that's for sure."

Loretta taught me that a never-quit instinct is important for me too. It's easy to give up when a task or commitment gets hard. I faced that yearly as an English teacher when all my juniors and seniors turned in their research papers a week before Christmas break and I measured my stacks of work in feet.

I was tempted to just let the work slide, but then I would remember Loretta. She grew strength from persisting, and I would too. One paper at a time, and I would always finish the job before my students left for the holiday. Loretta taught me that life-sustaining character is built when I keep trying.

Lord, give me the strength to persevere through whatever challenges lie ahead of me today. Thank You for being my guide. Amen.

—Janet Holm McHenry

DECEMBER 22

Ready, Set, Go!

I wait for the L*ORD*, *my soul waits, and in his word I hope.*

—PSALM 130:5 (ESV)

SEVERAL YEARS AGO, we visited Bandelier National Monument in New Mexico to explore the Anasazi ruins. We arrived very late in the afternoon, planning to enjoy an evening picnic. As we followed the Main Loop Trail, we noticed the ravens. They perched everywhere. As evening approached, the number of ravens increased. They crackled, clucked, and chattered. They seemed excited. Other people noticed the birds too.

"What's going on?" my husband asked. We soon found out as a cloud of bats emerged from a cave above the trail. The ravens swooped in to meet them. For a brief moment, the sky was filled with bats and birds. The lucky bats escaped into the twilight. The lucky ravens took supper home to their nestlings. Their patience had paid off. Their anticipation had been rewarded.

The incident reminded me of Jesus's parable in Matthew 25 about the ten virgins with their lamps. Five of them were foolish, taking no oil for their lamps. The other five wisely filled their lamps, taking extra oil, too, so they would be ready no matter what time of night the bridegroom arrived. The five wise virgins enjoyed the wedding feast. The five foolish ones missed out.

Jesus shared this parable in answer to his disciples' question about when He would come again. Jesus didn't give them an exact time. He merely advised them to be ready. The ravens, like the five wise virgins, eagerly anticipated the good things coming their way. They were prepared. They were excited. I don't know when my Lord will return, but I want to be prepared for Him. I want to be like the ravens—eagerly anticipating the good things to come.

He gives to the beasts their food, and to the young ravens that cry.
—Psalm 147:9 (ESV)

—Shirley Raye Redmond

DECEMBER 23

The Gift

All things were created through Him and for Him.

—COLOSSIANS 1:16 (NKJV)

IT WAS TWO nights before Christmas. My husband, Terry, and I were in the pet store, buying food and toys for our cats. The store was festively decorated. People were roaming the aisles with their dogs. Some of the four-legged shoppers had been freshly coiffed at the in-store pet salon. Christmas was in the air. As we approached the checkout register, I noticed the customer in front of us. A skinny German shepherd with badly matted hair sat at his side. The young man was beaming as he unloaded his purchases. "I found him at the side of the road on my way to work. He's a beauty." The dog looked anything but pretty.

"He's a Christmas gift," announced the dog's rescuer to the clerk, "a special gift from me to me."

This unkempt rescue dog brought to mind the memory of my grandparents. At the edge of their farm property, they had found an abandoned collie. It, too, had been starving like the rescued German shepherd. When they took the collie in, it had looked as rough and bony as this German shepherd. Not only did that rescue collie become a loving pet, but it ended up saving my grandpa's life by barking for help when he fell down a well.

I watched as the young man, carrying bags of dog food and toys and whistling "Joy to the World," left the store. His Christmas gift was at his side, wagging its tail. Indeed, God was still rescuing that day—with His creatures often turning out to be gifts carrying blessings yet unseen.

Walk of Faith: *There are so many unwanted dogs and cats needing homes. This Christmas, consider giving a gift to your local shelter or rescue group.*

—Sandra Clifton

DECEMBER 24

Skittles

God decided in advance to adopt us into his own family by bringing us to himself through Jesus Christ. This is what he wanted to do, and it gave him great pleasure. So we praise God for the glorious grace he has poured out on us who belong to his dear Son.

—EPHESIANS 1:5–6 (NLT)

AS MISSIONARIES, MY family and I find ourselves in places we never dreamed we'd be. While living in Australia on assignment, we often spent Saturdays driving through the wine country.

Stopping for fuel one day, we found a sweet discovery.

A few weeks earlier, the owner of the gas station encountered an orphaned baby kangaroo on the side of the road. He saved the joey from the dingoes by taking the little creature home and nursing him back to health. He told us Skittles had become the store mascot, spending most of his time greeting customers in the aisles or sleeping in a backpack strapped to the owner's chest.

With the owner's permission, I called for the joey. "Skittles, are you awake?"

The furry orphan hopped out of the bag and let me scratch his ears. I picked him up, and he snuggled against my chest, perhaps attempting to recapture the soothing beat of his mother's heart. I was a sad substitute for the real thing, but he settled for any comfort he could get.

I was reminded of my own need for a Savior. I, too, was a helpless, hopeless orphan, bound for death. Thankfully, God sent His Son to rescue me and adopt me, making me His own.

Becoming children of God endows us with all the privileges of His Son, Jesus. Christ's coming to live among us and His work on the cross has strapped us to our Father's chest forever. Like Skittles, let us embrace the adoption of the Rescuer and never look back.

Father, thank You for sending Your Son to us. Thank You for the goodness and protection You provide. May I revel in the glory of Your favor. Draw me ever nearer to You. Amen.

—Tez Brooks

DECEMBER 25

Scarlet Songbirds

Look at the birds of the air.

—MATTHEW 6:26 (NIV)

I LOVE CARDINALS. GROWING up in Pennsylvania, I was blessed to see these scarlet beauties, especially vivid in the snow. Cardinals became synonymous to me with Christmas. The brilliant red males added to the celebration. In flight, or perched on a branch, they were lovely to behold.

During a visit to my hometown, I took a long walk, hoping to spy a cardinal. Like a gift from heaven, a male cardinal flew into a tree along the way. Blessed to see this bird in any season, I took a photograph, capturing that memory to share with my family.

Cardinals are categorized as songbirds. They can sing twenty-four different songs, and it is believed that female cardinals sing a song to relay to their male partners they are hungry. I wonder now if the cardinals were what I had heard singing when I awoke to birdsong as a little girl.

The cardinals in North America were named by colonists because the male's crest reminded settlers of a biretta, a Catholic cardinal's red cap. For Christians, cardinals symbolize both the birth of Christ and His crucifixion—that He came to give us everlasting life through His blood, wash us whiter than snow, and give us songs to sing.

I wish we had cardinals in Oregon. Instead, I must enjoy them as artificial ornaments on my Christmas tree, painted on porcelain plates, or as knickknacks. But the most important cardinals are the ones I can visit in my memory, whenever I choose to reminisce.

Scriptures let us know God is a bird-watcher. He sees every sparrow that falls and reminds us that God cares for us so much that He sent His Son, Jesus, to us in the form of a tiny newborn child. When I look at the cardinal, I thank our Creator for a beautiful bird that reminds us of Christmas and Easter, too, all wrapped up in one.

Dear God, thank You for the gift of Your Son. May the cardinals' bright red remind us of Christmas and Your Son coming to earth as an infant to live among us. Amen.

—Kathleen Ruckman

DECEMBER 26

Leaping for Joy

Then will the lame leap like a deer, and the mute tongue shout for joy. Water will gush forth in the wilderness and streams in the desert.

—ISAIAH 35:6 (NIV)

MY HUSBAND AND I had just moved to a country house. No, it wasn't quite like Downton Abbey. In reality, we had purchased a two-story farmhouse on a cul-de-sac. The nearest Target was almost an hour away. The mall was even farther out. Even our first apartment had been closer to civilization, minutes away from everything I needed.

Growing up in a subdivision with copycat houses, cars parked on narrow streets, and few trees, this was very different for me. Driving home in the dark made me nervous. Where were the comforting streetlights?

Our small acreage backed up to a beautiful border of pine trees surrounding a large field. We could see for miles. One day from the back deck, I saw movement. Grabbing binoculars, I zoomed in to see a herd of deer. They dodged around one another and seemed to tease, running off in giant circles. They looked like children playing on the playground. Gracefully, they seemed to fly around the field. I couldn't guess how high they were leaping. They radiated joy, and I laughed out loud.

Since then, I have endured many periods of loss. Taking steps forward felt impossible most days. Grieving is hard work. Hesitant steps slowly turned into leaping as my heart healed and joy returned. I began to feel ready to drop the hurt and embrace life once again.

I often think about those deer when I look outside from our deck. The trees have grown so tall that we can't see the field anymore, but the gleeful gift those deer gave me will never be far from me.

Lord, I am grateful that You can heal broken hearts and broken spirits. Through dependence on You, I can learn to stand again. Your strength has become my strength. Amen.

—Twila Bennett

DECEMBER 27

Turkey Lookout

Be alert and of sober mind. Your enemy the devil prowls around like a roaring lion looking for someone to devour.

—1 PETER 5:8 (NIV)

IN OCTOBER 2017, wildfires decimated my hometown and surrounding areas in Sonoma County. Smoke from the fires hung in the air for weeks, and humans and animals alike were on edge until the fires were fully extinguished. This was especially evident the day I saw a flock of wild turkeys moving through my neighborhood.

There were nine hens and one tom. The hens calmly grazed. The tom, however, had his head raised to the sky. I've never seen a turkey keep watch like this. I've seen a tom strut attentively nearby, or graze along with the flock, or sometimes impressively spread his tail, but this turkey had stretched his neck out as far as it would go and tipped his head upward, watching the smoky brown sky. Not once as I observed the foraging flock did the tom turkey lower his head. I was impressed with his diligence, even more with its God-given protective instincts. The tom only knew something was desperately wrong and he had to stay alert.

I often feel like something is desperately wrong in the world, but unlike the tom turkey, I'm quick to realize what it is: so many people live their lives without regard for either God or others around them, and if I'm not careful, I can easily fall into the same trap. Through everyday prayer, I can enlist the help of my Father in heaven to be alert. He guards my heart and mind, strengthens me against spiritual attack, and informs me of areas where I'm weak and need to be extra vigilant. My good and gracious God will not let me be overcome.

It is the small temptations which undermine integrity unless we watch and pray and never think them too trivial to be resisted. —Louisa May Alcott

—Marianne Campbell

DECEMBER 28

Not My Load

Therefore I tell you, do not worry about your life, what you will eat or drink; or about your body, what you will wear.

—MATTHEW 6:25 (NIV)

THE MULE STOOD still, as if it didn't even notice the blankets and stuffed bags on its back. Though its muscular legs seemed sturdy and sure, I could understand why pack animals are called the "beasts of burden." How many miles had this strong animal traveled through the mountainous terrain?

Seeing the overloaded mule, I was reminded that my worries can feel like bundles piled high on a pack animal. When my husband lost his job in a corporate restructure, we spent a year roaming through the rocky paths of unemployment. Anxious thoughts about finances weighed heavily on my mind. Month after month, we waited for God's provision. As our savings dwindled, my shoulders slumped under my mounting concerns. Though I knew God wouldn't always rescue us in ways we hoped, I stood amazed when God's people began presenting us with financial gifts, enough to cover that month's bills. He then blessed my husband with a job in time to cover the next month's bills.

Scripture confirms the futility of worrying and assures us God provides for all His creation, from flowers to furry creatures and everything in between. If our loving Father clothes the grass, why wouldn't He care for the people He's made in His image?

These verses remind me that I need not fret over things my Father knows I need. Unlike the mule, I, along with all God's people, never have to carry any burdens for our loving Master. I can experience peace and remain confident in His provision instead of worrying. And when I'm tempted toward anxious thoughts, I can say, "That's not my load."

Faithful Father, thanks for carrying our burdens and caring for our needs. Amen.

—Xochitl E. Dixon

DECEMBER 29

Besties

One who has unreliable friends soon comes to ruin, but there is a friend who sticks closer than a brother.

—PROVERBS 18:24 (NIV)

WHEN I WAS a five-year-old and the youngest in the family, my older brothers didn't want to play with me. If not for my Norwegian elkhound, Dusty, I would often have found myself playing alone.

Dusty was my closest companion. Her patience allowed me to include her in many of my imaginary adventures—from time travel to hide-and-seek. Whether I was dressing her up or pretending she could talk, she never fussed about joining me.

We were best friends.

Lacking athletic prowess, I was bullied and beat up by other kids. Coming home discouraged and hurt, I would head straight for the backyard and Dusty before going inside the house. She was always available for a hug or a lick as we snuggled and I told her about my day. Drying my tears on her thick, soft coat, I would tell her all about my hopes and fears. Those were precious moments.

The Bible tells us God will never leave us or forsake us. He, too, allows us to cling to Him, to share our sorrows and our hopes. One day, He will dry all our tears.

Those years with Dusty taught me about God's character. By the time she died, I was thirteen and learning that Christ was the place to find loyalty and a reliable friendship. The Lord used my dog to help me understand His great love for me. God's been my dearest friend since.

When your spirit feels crushed by the trials of life or you experience loneliness, remember the Lord is near. Embrace His presence, enjoy His friendship.

Real joy comes when we get the right desire met—the desire for God himself.
—Michael W. Smith

—Tez Brooks

DECEMBER 30

The Second Look

Stop judging by mere appearances, but instead judge correctly.

—JOHN 7:24 (NIV)

MY TWO "GRANDGEMS," Sidney and Nicholas, have small pets. A hamster and a betta fish belong to Sidney. Nicholas cares for two baby bettas. I think their parents are giving them opportunities to prove themselves dependable enough to welcome a puppy into the home.

While the family has dogs, I wondered if an unknown dog might frighten one child or both. So, before we attended a birthday tea party in some Victorian gardens, I mentioned the two huge dogs that lived there.

I worried that the first glimpse of Bastian, an old golden retriever, or Dexter, an old Lab, could put my grandgems in a panic. The dogs surrounded one's car upon arrival. Tails wagging, big smiles on their doggie faces, wet noses thrust inside if one tried to open the car door. I was used to their greetings, but to Sidney and Nicholas, the old dears might appear threatening.

Once our group moved to the tea table and began to feast and visit, the grandgems disappeared. Sampling scones and sipping tea with one's little finger raised didn't keep them entertained. But the children of the house—and the dogs—kept them busy. After a while, Nicholas came back to check in. He patted Bastian, declaring, "Little dogs look like fun. But they're actually scary. Big dogs look scary, but really, they're fun!"

I smiled at his newfound wisdom and thought of times I had judged others by their outward appearance. Nicholas's declaration reminded me that, just as I can't judge a book by its cover or determine a dog's good or bad manners by its size, I need to avoid making assumptions about other people based on what they look like.

If you judge people, you have no time to love them. —Mother Teresa

—Cathy Elliott

DECEMBER 31

Diving Deep for the Good

Ask and it will be given to you; seek and you will find; knock and the door will be opened to you.

—MATTHEW 7:7 (NIV)

THE SUN SHONE off the water as I strolled along the Cliff Walk in Newport, Rhode Island, seeking some inspiration for a new story. From the corner of my eye, I caught a loon diving beneath the surface. I kept my gaze on where the creature went under, surprised by how long it could hold its breath.

A moment later, it popped above the surface a short distance away. But not for long. It dived again, and I found myself captivated by its search as I walked along, wondering where it would break the water and forgetting about my story-brainstorming intentions.

I waited. Stopped walking and leaned on the rail that bordered the cliff. I scanned the area. Waited some more. Where could it be?

Finally, the loon popped above the surface. I smiled, wondering if it caught a fish. Later, I would learn that this sleek creature could dive to depths of two hundred feet for as much as five minutes as it searched for its next meal. That's some serious seeking!

As I watched this loon, I noticed how persistent it was in diving back beneath the water. Over and over again. It's simply what it did. Searched.

And in the search, it found.

Isn't that what God promises those who seek? Not only for this beautiful, persistent bird, but for us, for me. Whether I am caught up in despair, in the midst of suffering, or in a place where all is well and peace abounds, I will seek Him. He will give me hope. He will give me ultimate love. He will grow my heart to look more and more like Him.

Jesus, as I look ahead to the new year, help me seek You in every area and aspect of my life, every day. Thank You for the peace You give both in the midst and at the end of the search. Amen.

—Heidi Chiavaroli

About the Authors

JERUSHA AGEN imagines danger around every corner but knows God is there too. So naturally, she writes suspense infused with the hope of salvation in Jesus Christ. With a BA in English and a background in screenwriting, Jerusha is a speaker and the author of the *Fear Warrior* blog, where she writes about fighting against fear in our everyday lives. Jerusha also teaches as an industry professional in Tricia Goyer's Write That Book online club. The daughter of two veterinarians, Jerusha has always shared her life with a menagerie of pets. You'll often find her posting irresistibly adorable photos of her Furry Fear Warriors (three big dogs and two little cats) on social media. Visit Jerusha at www.JerushaAgen.com and connect with her on Facebook, Instagram, Pinterest, and Twitter.

LINDA BARTLETT feels like the most blessed person on the planet. She has been blessed with family, friends, and many furballs during her lifetime. She has also had two of the most fulfilling and fun jobs available: teacher and flight attendant. The cherry on top is the chance to now write for Guideposts. God is good all the time; all the time God is good. Living in the small town of Lindstrom, Minnesota, is another blessing. Linda is pictured with her current fur baby, Cesar.

RANDY BENEDETTO has been writing for more than fifty years. He has a keen interest in God's creations in nature and God's relationship with human beings. He is presently compiling his childhood memories and adventures and stories of his parents and relatives so his memories and his family's history will not be lost in time but available for his children and grandchildren. He also loves to write poetry and about biblical stories and biblical history. Randy shares his writing, artwork, poetry, and just plain funny stuff in get-well packages that he takes to people in hospitals or nursing homes. Even in their weakest moments, people can enjoy the writings and art and have a good laugh with visiting friends. Randy also enjoys creating award-winning wood carvings, sculptures, and wood burnings, as well as charcoal, colored pencil, and pastel drawings, of the animals that have been a part of his life. Retired since 2011, Randy and his wife live in a cabin at a ranch in Colorado, where they enjoy having their children and grandchildren nearby.

TWILA BENNETT was a contributing writer to *The Cat on My Lap* and *The Dog at My Feet*, and has contributed to two *All God's Creatures* devotionals from Guideposts. Currently, Twila is the communications manager for Camp Roger/Camp Scottie in Michigan. As the founder of Monarch Lane Consulting, she helps writers create proposals and establish their unique brand. Previously, Twila was a branding and marketing executive for Revell Books. She loves camping and boating, and sunsets make her swoon. Twila adores her husband, Dan, her son, Zach, and their boxer, Rocky, and lives in Rockford, Michigan. For more information, visit https://MonarchLaneConsulting.com.

TEZ BROOKS loves observing animals to discover biblical truths. With his knack for befriending creatures, he's been called Dr. Doolittle. Whether he's hiking with his dog, rescuing injured wildlife, or writing about nature, his passion for hearing God's voice is evident. As an award-winning author and international speaker, Brooks writes primarily on family issues. His work appears in *The Upper Room*, *Clubhouse*, and *Focus on the Family* magazines and on CBN.com. His editorials are featured regularly on Jesusfilm.org and seen by more than thirty thousand readers each month. Tez serves on the leadership team of Word Weavers International and is a full-time missionary journalist for Jesus Film Project. Brooks lives in Colorado Springs with his family and loves movies, pizza, and the color orange. You can learn more at TezBrooks.com.

Homemaker **MARIANNE CAMPBELL** lives in Sonoma County, California, where she was born, raised, and educated. She developed her love of animals during childhood on her family's Gravenstein apple farm. Her spirit of adventure led her to visit Japan, Thailand, Nepal, Israel, and Egypt in the early 1980s. From 1984 to 1990, she served in the US Navy, where she met her husband, Scott. They have two grown daughters and now live "in town." Marianne tries to bring a little country life to her city living by keeping a small backyard flock of chickens. In her spare time, she enjoys reading, studying history, white-thread crocheting, gardening, hiking local trails, playing *World of Warcraft*, and putting on tea parties for friends and family. She facilitates a small ladies' Bible study group in her home on Tuesdays and serves as a church musician on Sundays.

LUCY CHAMBERS serves Christ Church Cathedral and the downtown Houston community as manager of the historic Cathedral Bookstore. A firm believer in the power of sharing stories to deepen connection and improve lives, she has worked with words for more than thirty-five years as an editor, publisher, teacher and writer. In addition to books and writing, she enjoys making miniature gardens, serving on the altar guild, and volunteering for literary and green organizations. She and her husband, Sam, have two daughters in college and one dog at home.

HEIDI CHIAVAROLI began writing thirteen years ago, just after Jesus had grabbed hold of her heart. She used her two small boys' naptimes to pursue what she thought at the time was a foolish dream. Despite a long road to publication, she hasn't stopped writing since! Heidi writes women's fiction, combining her love of history and literature to write split-time stories. Her debut novel, *Freedom's Ring*, was a Carol Award winner and a Christy Award finalist, a Romantic Times Top Pick, and a Booklist Top Ten Romance Debut. Heidi loves exploring places that whisper of historical secrets, especially with her family. She loves running, hiking, baking, and dates with her high school sweetheart and husband of sixteen years. Heidi makes her home in Massachusetts with her husband and two sons. Visit her at heidichiavaroli.com

LINDA CLARE is the author of seven books, including the novel *The Fence My Father Built* (Abingdon, 2009). Her most recent book, *Prayers for Parents of Prodigals*, released in January 2020, was published by Harvest House Publishers. A frequent contributor to the Chicken Soup for the Soul series and Guideposts, Linda taught creative writing at Lane Community College in Eugene, Oregon, for more than a decade and now serves as an expert writing advisor for doctoral students at George Fox University, Newberg, Oregon. She lives with her family in Eugene, Oregon, where she loves to garden, play with her three "grandorables," and maintain her critter menagerie of cats, bunnies, and the occasional chameleon. Find Linda at lindasclare.com or on Facebook or Twitter.

ASHLEY CLARK writes devotions for Guideposts and romantic dual-time fiction set in the South. Her debut novel *The Dress Shop on King Street* was released December 3, 2020. With a master's degree in creative writing, Ashley teaches literature and writing courses at the University of West Florida in Pensacola. Ashley has been an active member of American Christian Fiction Writers for about a decade. She lives with her husband, son, and two rescued cocker spaniels off Florida's Gulf Coast. When she's not writing, she's rescuing stray animals, dreaming of Charleston, and drinking all the English breakfast tea she can get her hands on. Find her online at ashleyclarkbooks.com or on Facebook at Ashley Clark Books.

SANDRA CLIFTON and her husband, Terry Clifton, recently celebrated their forty-second wedding anniversary, with cats present. They see their pets as family and through the years have gotten so much joy from being around them. "We are always learning so much from them," Sandra shares. Sandra has taught high school honors English and Spanish as well as ESL to immigrants. She has published stories for kids in Sunday school publications. Later in life, as Sandra says, "I finally figured out what I wanted to do when I grew up." Sandra enrolled at Oral Roberts University College of Theology and Ministry in Tulsa, Oklahoma, and graduated with her master of divinity and doctor of ministry degrees. She has worked as a church counselor and has given motivational talks to groups on various empowerment topics, as well as appearing on national TV and radio programs. Sandra has also written books based on her Christian faith. She has been a volunteer for animal rescue and in food and clothing distributions through the church. Sandra and Terry love to take walks and enjoy travel. Sandra's favorite mode of transportation is the train. She was raised in a "Santa Fe railroad" family and rode trains all the time growing up. Together, Sandra and Terry are co-writing cozy mysteries for kids and adults. "This is a joy and an honor to write *All God's Creatures* devotionals," says Sandra. "I feel so happy connecting with the loving family of Guidepost readers who share a love for all God's creatures." Sandra's photo includes her eighteen-year-old Manx cat, Barnie, a rescue featured in her devotion "The Survivor."

TERRY CLIFTON has a background as an actor, having performed around the country in musical theater productions. While working as an associate producer for a popular Los Angeles morning television talk show, he met his wife, Sandra, when he booked her as a guest. They recently celebrated their forty-second wedding anniversary. Terry has spent the last twenty years doing freelance book design, writing, and editing. Terry and his wife have taught adult Sunday school and volunteered in community feeding programs. They make sure to take their daily walks where they often find "fodder" for writing ideas. They love to travel, especially by train, and get excited about exploring new places. They sometimes cowrite fiction and are completing a cozy mystery series for kids and one for adults. Terry considers it an honor to contribute to the *All God's Creatures* devotional.

TRACY CRUMP is a writer, speaker, and editor best known for contributing more than two dozen stories to the *Chicken Soup for the Soul* series and other anthologies. Her course, How to Write for Chicken Soup for the Soul, is one of Serious Writer Academy's top sellers, and she teaches workshops and webinars on writing for the series. She has published approximately sixty devotions, and her articles have been featured in magazines such as *Focus on the Family, Parent Life, Mature Living, Southern Writers Magazine,* and *Woman's World.* As codirector of Write Life Workshops, Tracy encourages others to "Write Better, Write Now." She edits a popular newsletter with story callouts that has inspired many to move forward with their writing, and her love of teaching takes her to conferences where she helps writers hone their craft. She is also a freelance editor and a proofreader for *Farmers' Almanac.* But her most important job is grandma to four adorable grandchildren. Visit Tracy at TracyCrump.com or WriteLifeWorkshops.com or connect at facebook.com/AuthorTracyCrump/, twitter.com/TracyCrumpWrite, or linkedin.com/in/tracycrump/

XOCHITL (SO-CHEEL) E. DIXON is the author of *Waiting for God: Trusting Daily in God's Plan and Pace* and the children's picture book *Different Like Me.* She is also a regular contributor to *Our Daily Bread* and Guideposts' *All God's Creatures.* She equips and encourages others to grow closer to God and others, nurturing spiritual growth through prayerful study and application of Scripture. Sharing God's truth and love to the ends of the earth, she enjoys serving Jesus with her service dog, Callie. She likes singing; art; photography; hanging out with her husband, Alan, and their sons, AJ and Xavier; and connecting with readers at www.xedixon.com.

CATHY ELLIOTT is a full-time writer in Northern California whose cozy mysteries reflect her personal interests, from quilting and antique collecting to playing her fiddle with friends. She also leads music at church and cherishes time with her grandchildren. Cathy's cozy plot twisters include *A Vase of Mistaken Identity, Medals in the Attic,* and *A Stitch in Crime.* She is also a contributing author to Guideposts' *Every Day with Jesus* and *All God's Creatures.* For more information about Cathy, visit her at www.cathyelliottbooks.com.

PEGGY FREZON is an award-winning author of books about the human-animal bond, including *The Dog in the Dentist Chair: and Other True Stories of Animals Who Help, Comfort, and Love Kids* (Paraclete Press, 2019). She's thoroughly enjoyed meeting many of the animals in the book, such as a friendly potbellied pig (and his baby piggy siblings), a gentle 150-pound Newfoundland dog, and Magic, a hero miniature horse. Peggy is a contributing editor of *All Creatures* magazine and a regular writer for *Guideposts* magazine. Her stories also appear in Guideposts' *Angels on Earth* and *Mysterious Ways* and in more than twenty *Chicken Soup for the Soul* books. Peggy and her husband, Mike, rescue senior golden retrievers. Twelve-year-old Ernest (pictured) is a cancer survivor, therapy dog, and special Book Buddy for a first-grade class. Peggy and Mike also share their home with an energetic three-year-old golden retriever, Petey. Look for her new book about miniature therapy horses, available this fall (Revell). Connect with Peggy at peggyfrezon.com, on Instagram at pfrezon, and on Facebook at facebook.com/PeggyFrezonbooks.

JEANETTE HANSCOME has been telling stories since she was three years old and came up with a creative explanation for why the family kittens were missing. She is now the author of five books, including *Suddenly Single Mom: 52 Messages of Hope, Grace, and Promise,* as well as a speaker, freelance editor, writing coach, and proud mom of two sons. Jeanette has contributed to many devotionals, including Guideposts' *Mornings with Jesus 2019, Every Day with Jesus,* and *All God's Creatures,* and to Kathy Ide's Fiction Lover's Devotionals, *21 Days of Grace* and *21 Days of Love.* Much of her recent writing flows from her experience of living with a rare visual impairment (which includes a lack of color vision) since birth. As a member of the West Coast Christian Writers Conference Board, a writing workshop leader, and the official welcomer for the Mount Hermon Christian Writers Conference, she has many opportunities to connect with fellow storytellers and word lovers. She enjoys spending her free time singing at her church and in the Blackhawk Chorus, knitting, crocheting, practicing creative lettering, and making homemade gifts. She and her younger son live in the San Francisco Bay area. Visit her website/blog at Jeanettehanscome.com.

LORI HATCHER is the author of *Refresh Your Faith: Uncommon Devotions from Every Book of the Bible* and *Hungry for God . . . Starving for Time: Five-Minute Devotions for Busy Women.* She shares a love of animals with her four grandchildren, who are always willing to help her turn over rocks, visit a zoo, or hunt for critters so they can study them up close. Everywhere they look, they see the fingerprints of God on His creation. Connect with Lori at LoriHatcher.com.

Out of the abundance of her heart, **TRACY JOY JONES** speaks, blogs, and writes stories that take others on adventures in love and hope. She writes from a heart full of gratitude to her heavenly Father and believes that stories are often the best carriers of truth. Tracy and her husband co-own Jones House Creative, a graphic design firm, where she has the joy of helping other authors tell their stories. In her free time, she reads voraciously, teaches piano, volunteers, gardens, and laughs at every opportunity. Tracy currently lives in Jenks, Oklahoma, where she has the joy of raising three children, Noah, Ava, and Luke, as well as a sweet Holland Lop bunny named Beebo (pictured here), a snarky bearded dragon named Drax, and a darling Maltese named Lucy. She enjoys a rainbow of birds at her feeders, squirrels in her trees, and a family of raccoons under her back porch. She'd love to connect with you through her website, tracyjoyjones.com, or on social media.

A *Publisher's Weekly* bestselling, award-winning author of more than fifty novels and 1.7 million books in print, **DEB KASTNER** enjoys writing contemporary inspirational western stories set in small communities. She feels especially blessed to be able to include faith as a natural and genuine part of her characters' lives. Deb lives in beautiful Colorado with her husband and a pack of miscreant mutts. She is blessed with three adult daughters and two grandchildren. Her favorite hobby is spoiling her grandchildren, but she also enjoys reading, watching movies, listening to music (The Texas Tenors are her fav), singing in the church choir, acting onstage, and exploring the Rocky Mountains on horseback.

LIZ KIMMEL lives in St. Paul, Minnesota, has been married for forty-one years, and is mother to two and grandmother to four. After earning a bachelor's in elementary education at Bethel College in St. Paul, she published two books of Christian poetry/prose and a grammar workbook for middle-school students. She is the communications coordinator for Bethel Christian Fellowship. Her writing is included in all of the *Short and Sweet* books to date, which contain stories written (with a few exceptions) using words of only one syllable. She has also written for several other Guideposts projects, including the Someone Cares greeting cards. Her deepest desire is to be an articulate, beautiful, creative daughter, emerging from God's heart into the jumbled kaleidoscope of lovely mankind and never overlooking people—but quietly and rightly sharing truth; understanding, validating, welcoming; and exalting Yahweh zealously.

ERYN LYNUM is the author of the book *936 Pennies: Discovering the Joy of Intentional Parenting* (Bethany House Publishers). She lives in northern Colorado with her husband, Grayson, their four children, and their black Labrador, Maja. They spend their days hiking, camping, and adventuring through the Rocky Mountains. Eryn grew up exploring the United States with her family and traveling the world throughout high school and college. She and her husband now pass on that insatiable curiosity for creation to their children as they homeschool and travel as a family. One of their top family values is to "do life together," and they seek to do that in work, school, faith, and play. Every chance they get, the Lynums incorporate creation and all God's creatures into their learning approach and life lessons. Eryn has been featured on Focus on the Family, FamilyLife, Proverbs31 Ministries, MOPS International, Bible Gateway, Her View from Home, and For Every Mom. Every opportunity she gets, she is out exploring God's creation with her family and sharing the adventures at ErynLynum.com.

CATHY MAYFIELD thrills to see the wildlife in the forests of central Pennsylvania with her husband, Kevin, and their German shepherd mix, Kenai. She delights in times with her four grandchildren, especially when reading to them or taking them on walks and discovering God's creation with them. Cathy homeschooled their three daughters throughout their thirty-plus years of schooling. She also taught many classes to other homeschool students and held writers' clubs in her home. All three daughters won various writing awards, including the National Scholastic Writing Award for an original play. They also ran a drama troupe from their home for eight years, with one daughter writing most of the plays and musicals. If not reading or writing, Cathy enjoys heirloom crafts, such as tatting, crocheting lace, quilling, and her newest: the revival of redwork embroidery "in whatever color I happen to choose." Anything Christmas brings her special joy! "I've always loved writing devotions but mixing them with my love for all animals gives me extra pleasure."

JANET HOLM MCHENRY is a national speaker and the author of twenty-four books—six of those on prayer, including the bestselling *PrayerWalk: Becoming a Woman of Prayer, Strength, and Discipline* and her newest, *The Complete Guide to the Prayers of Jesus*. She is known for prayer-walking her small town in California's Sierra Valley, where she frequently encounters all kinds of God's creatures. Janet and her rancher husband, Craig, have raised four children and a variety of pets. A journalism graduate of the University of California, Berkeley, Janet formerly worked as a newspaper reporter and a high school English teacher and academic adviser. She serves as the prayer coordinator of The Bridge Church in Reno and fosters an online prayer community through Facebook. Her business name is Looking Up! because she encourages others to pursue a praying life. Janet loves traveling to new places with her husband, kayaking the mountain lakes with him near their home, and spending time with their ten grandchildren. She also loves hearing from readers and speaking at conferences and retreats.

DEVON O'DAY is a career broadcaster with a résumé that includes her most recent position as radio host on *Nashville Today* at 650AM WSM and her former position with *Gerry House and the House Foundation, Mix92.9* in Nashville. Her résumé also includes nationally syndicated shows including *Country Hitmakers, The Saturday Night House Party,* and *America's #1s.* Former Miss Louisiana National Teenager and pioneer of the plus division of the Ford Modeling Agency in New York City, Devon O'Day is also the author of four books published by Thomas Nelson and Zondervan and two books published by Abingdon Press, including *My Southern Food* and *My Angels Wear Fur.* She has been a contributing writer for Guideposts' *All God's Creatures* devotional books and magazines for the past three years. As a songwriter, she has had songs recorded by Lee Ann Womack, Dolly Parton, Hank Williams Jr., Pam Tillis, Neal McCoy, and Trace Adkins. Devon and Gerry House wrote "The Big One," which became a number one hit for George Strait. She is the narrator for more than seventy audiobooks for Thomas Nelson and HarperCollins, and her voice has been heard on every major network for national clients including Hilton Hotels, KFC, and Fellowship of Christians and Jews. Devon was the host of national radio specials for Garth Brooks, the Chicks, Kenny Chesney and Bill Gaither. Devon also hosted Tammy Wynette's biography on the Lifetime network. Her voice welcomes visitors at the Women's Basketball Hall of Fame, narrates the Turtle Sanctuary's Documentary in North Carolina's Outer Banks, and instructs people where to find the nearest Mr. Goodwrench when they call the help center nationwide. She speaks across the country for both corporate and church groups, combining storytelling and humor for motivation and inspiration.

JOY PITNER lives just outside Charleston, South Carolina, on a small homestead a few miles from the beach with her husband, two children, honeybees, chickens, a pig named Penelope, and a horse named Hatch, which is boarded next door. A self-titled "homesteading foodie," Joy has a passion for gospel-centered hospitality. She loves delighting people with food, creating inviting spaces with farmhouse décor, and teaching others simple ways to do the same. Joy and her husband, Brad, own and operate a gourmet kitchenware store, The Coastal Cupboard, where they get to share this passion for entertaining with others. In between working on the homestead, homeschooling her children, and helping with the family business, Joy makes time to pursue her writing . . . and because of everything she has going on, there is no shortage of inspiration! Her big faith in God is woven throughout it all, and she loves to take the stories and experiences from her life and use them to inspire others to a bigger faith of their own.

SHIRLEY RAYE REDMOND has sold articles to such publications as *Focus on the Family, HomeLife,* and *Christian Standard* magazines, and Chicken Soup for the Soul: *Touched by an Angel.* She has written several nonfiction animal books for children, including *Lewis and Clark: A Prairie Dog for the President* (Random House) and *The Dog That Dug for Dinosaurs* (Simon & Schuster). *Pigeon Hero!* (Simon & Schuster) won a national Oppenheim Toy Portfolio Gold Book Award. *Courageous World Changers,* profiles of fifty gutsy Christian women (Harvest House), was released in January 2020. She has been married for forty-two years to her college sweetheart, Bill. They are blessed with two adult children and their spouses, plus four adorable grandchildren. She joyfully serves as prayer chairperson for her community Bible study class in Los Alamos, New Mexico.

AMELIA RHODES lives in a small town in Michigan with her husband and two teenage children. She loves to connect with friends over coffee or while hiking a great trail. She is the author of *Pray A to Z: A Practical Guide to Pray for Your Community.* Amelia's writing has also been featured in Guideposts' *Every Day with Jesus* and previous editions of *All God's Creatures.* Amelia speaks regularly to women's groups on topics of spiritual growth, friendship, and community, offering practical tools for living our faith in the everyday. She would love to connect with you online at www.ameliarhodes.com or on Facebook at www.facebook.com/ameliarhodeswriter/.

LORI STANLEY ROELEVELD is an author, a speaker, and a disturber of hobbits who enjoys making comfortable Christians late for dinner. Biblical, funny, and real, she inspires courage and Christ-centered confidence. She's authored three nonfiction books, *Running from a Crazy Man, Jesus and the Beanstalk,* and *The Art of Hard Conversations,* as well as a novella, *Red Pen Redemption.* Though she has degrees in psychology and biblical studies, she learned the most from studying her Bible in life's trenches. Blogger. Wife. Mother of adults. Part-time giant-slayer. Not available for children's parties. Though she once tried to escape, she adventures with Jesus in a small town in Rhode Island with a host of creatures, great and small.

KATHLEEN RUCKMAN is the author of children's books, poetry, articles, and devotionals in mainstream Christian publications. Her poem and inspirational article were each awarded first place in the national Cascade Writing Contest. Kathleen has taught women's Bible studies for several years. She enjoys reading; hiking with her husband, Tom; and visiting small towns and museums. She is the mother of four adult children, and her seven preschool and baby grandchildren are the love of her life. Kathleen has been writing stories since she was six years old. The desire of her heart is to write for God's glory.

With a heart to encourage, **CRYSTAL STORMS** loves to see women overcome self-doubt and find rest close to His heart as God's beloved. She is a Jesus girl, award-winning author, and artist. Drawing from her personal faith and her love of God's Word, Crystal shares her honest struggles so readers know they're not alone in theirs. She writes on faith and marriage in her blog and in both print and online articles. Crystal serves as a chaplain for the Tampa chapter of Word Weavers International and as a secretary for Stirling Toastmasters. She loves coffee, chocolate, tea, good books, and most of all Jesus. When she's not writing, Crystal loves spending time with her husband, painting flowers, enjoying beach days, having coffee with friends, and reading good books with Minnie on her lap and a cup of tea and piece of chocolate close by. Crystal is married to Tim, her best friend for more than twenty-five years. They live in Florida with their sweet Yorkie, Minnie. Connect with Crystal at CrystalStorms.me.

MISSY TIPPENS is a pastor's wife, mother of three adult children, and an author from near Atlanta, Georgia. She loves being involved in their church through the Happy Sack Ministry (healthy weekend snacks for local elementary and middle-school kids) and their music ministry. She particularly enjoys singing in the choir! Missy has loved many fur children over the years and now looks forward to visits from her granddogs. After more than ten years of pursuing her dream of publication, Missy made her first sale to Harlequin Love Inspired in 2007. Her books have since been nominated for several awards, including the American Christian Fiction Writers Carol Award and the Romance Writers of America RITA Award. Visit Missy at missytippens.com, twitter.com/MissyTippens, and facebook.com/missy.tippens.readers.

KATHY CARLTON WILLIS writes and speaks with a balance of funny and faith, whimsy and wisdom. Not many funny girls also have Bible degrees! Kathy served for thirty years in full-time church ministry with her husband, Russ. She's active as a book-industry pro (she founded WordGirls) while also staying involved in her local church and national speaking ministry. Kathy addresses the issues that hold people back and shines light on their path to freedom. She coaches others to learn how to remove the training wheels and not just risk but also take pleasure in the joyride of a life trusting in God. Even with all the circumstances she's faced, she grins with an expectant hope and contentment in the Lord. She has authored Bible studies such as *The Grin Gal's Guide to Joy* and *Grin with Grace*. She offers speaker advice in *The Ultimate Speaker's Guide: Practical Tips, Tools and Takeaways*. CBN.com features Kathy's popular blog, *Grin and Grow with Kathy*. Kathy shines, whether she's shining the light on God's writers and speakers or reflecting God's light during her speaking programs.

DAVID L. WINTERS is an author, speaker, and humorist from Kensington, Maryland. He writes both fiction and nonfiction, including the award-winning *Taking God to Work* with Pastor Steve Reynolds. The focus of his writing includes bringing a biblical worldview to contemporary problems. His latest release is *The Accidental Missionary: A Gringo's Love Affair with Peru*. In 2016, he retired from the Department of Homeland Security where he served as a division director and policy analyst. His government career also included more than twenty years with the Office of Naval Research, the research and development arm of the US Navy. As a layman, he has served local churches as an elder, deacon, small-group leader, and Sunday school teacher, among many other positions. He also volunteers for various community organizations and charities.

Scripture Reference Index

Acts
17:27, 89
9:15, 129
16:14, 256
15:33, 262
13:38, 272
28:30–31, 306

1 Chronicles
4:40, 43
28:20, 108
16:25, 224
16:27, 224

Colossians
3:1–2, 50
3:12, 80
3:9–10, 160
3:23, 166, 288
3:9–10, 337
3:23–24, 358
1:16, 369
3:1–17, 19

1 Corinthians
12:27, 23
12:12–14, 37
10:23, 135
12:4–6, 150
12:26–27, 222
6:20, 241
13:4, 295
10:24, 330
10:23, 331
12:26, 365

2 Corinthians
5:1–5, 29
1:3–4, 45
8:20, 59
3:17, 64
5:17, 91
5:4, 138
9:8, 151
3:18, 170
4:17, 176
12:10, 194
4:18, 278
6:13, 303
5:20, 308
1:3–4, 327

Deuteronomy
13:4, 7
31:6, 40
10:12–13, 56
1:36, 154
31:6, 183
33:27, 195
1:14, 335

Ecclesiastes
3:11, 39
4:9–10, 139
3:1, 285

Ephesians
2:10, 6, 11
3:17–19, 51
2:8–9, 66
2:10, 74
2:8, 152
4:2, 168
3:16, 169
5:15–16, 248
4:32, 266
1:7, 269
2:1–2, 291
2:4–5, 291
2:12–13, 316
2:19, 342
1:5–6, 370

Exodus
34:14, 14
19:4, 53
20:17, 73
4:10, 102
4:8, 145
33:14, 237
14:14, 339

Ezekiel
12:1–2, 146
34:12, 214
36:26, 338

Galatians
5:15, 26
5:1, 64, 192
6:9, 236
5:1, 246

Genesis
1:20, 55
1:25, 93
1:28, 99
1:20, 155
16:13, 228
1:21, 296
15:6, 325
1:14, 366

Hebrews
12:1–2, 3
6:11–14, 34
11:1, 58
5:12, 77
3:13, 81
12:1–2, 121
1:3, 123
11:1–3, 126
4:13, 191
13:6, 205
12:10, 219
12:11, 220
4:15–16, 261
12:1–2, 264
6:11, 286
10:23, 354
10:36, 354
12:1–2, 359

Isaiah
55:9, 2
43:1, 19
40:1, 21
43:20–21, 48
41:10, 52
30:18–19, 75
41:10, 79
40:31, 82
53:5, 96
41:13, 100
24:14, 107
30:21, 117
54:2, 137
40:31, 140
61:1–3, 161
43:19, 164
45:3, 172
6:5, 180
40:8, 201
60:19, 211
43:19, 244
45:3, 257
41:13, 284
11:6, 287
40:31, 290
2:3, 292
46:10, 299
40:30–31, 304
32:18, 333
42:16, 355
49:18, 361
35:6, 372

James
3:16, 12
2:8, 15
1:5, 97
1:12, 176
5:14, 203
1:17, 210
1:4, 231
1:20, 298
1:17, 329, 340
1:19, 345
3:7–8, 352

Jeremiah
30:17, 96
29:11, 193

Job
12:7–10, 144
12:10, 197
12:7–8, 297
5:19, 349

Joel
2:22, 233

John
10:9, 27
1:4, 41
10:27, 85
11:25, 98
13:34–35, 111
10:27, 116
15:5, 143
14:2, 177
16:33, 178
10:27, 199
15:9, 204
10:5, 208
10:27, 225
1:45, 226
7:24, 234
9:10–11, 235
15:11, 247
4:7, 250
10:10, 265
10:27, 268
15:15, 278
14:16, 279
10:14, 289
16:13–14, 324
7:24, 362
15:4, 364
7:24, 376

1 John
3:19–20, 28
3:18, 65
4:18, 127, 179
4:12, 202

4:10, 209
2:1, 267
1:9, 321

2 John
6, 56, 216

3 John
3, 245

Joshua
1:9, 103
4:7, 142
1:9, 275, 318

Lamentations
3:22–23, 189
3:24–25, 212, 350

Leviticus
19:18, 218

Luke
11:8, 57
15:4, 115
15:10, 184
6:38, 196
24:35, 213
10:36–37, 242
12:6, 244
8:17, 270
10:41–42, 323
12:24, 326
8:18, 334

Mark
6:31, 30
4:39, 149

Matthew
6:26, 5
4:4, 24
24:42, 38
4:4, 72
7:7–8, 113
28:19, 128
4:19, 152
12:34, 163
10:29, 184
25:21, 207
25:40, 215
5:9, 221
5:4, 233
14:31, 239
17:20, 254
6:26, 260
6:27, 300
16:26, 307
5:16, 311
18:14, 313
9:369, 319
25:21, 332, 341
10:29, 343
10:31, 343
6:25, 350
6:26, 371
6:25, 374
7:7, 377

1 Peter
4:10, 23
2:2, 24
4:12–13, 105
3:4, 106
4:8, 280
3:8–9, 281
1:8, 322
5:7, 347, 360
5:8, 373

2 Peter
3:8, 18
1:3, 78
3:9, 162
1:19, 174

Philippians
4:11–13, 10
4:19, 13
4:8, 118
4:13, 133
2:9–11, 172
3:20, 173
3:13–14, 232
4:8, 258, 276
3:20, 353

Proverbs
16:3, 16
16:17, 36
17:22, 46
19:11, 60
3:5–6, 61
16:24, 71
4:5, 83
3:5–6, 104
12:10, 110
16:28, 124
14:30, 147
15:1, 158
6:27–28, 159
4:23, 163
3:5, 175
29:6, 206
30:28, 227
15:13, 230
12:18, 251
15:1, 293
28:25, 312
3:5, 317
3:3–4, 341
13:4, 358
4:25, 359
18:24, 375

Psalms
130:5, 4
121:8, 8
46:10, 9

139:23–24, 17
40:16, 25
3:4, 31
28:6–7, 35
68:19, 42
23:2–3, 44
90:12, 49
37:1, 54
107:8–9, 63
116:12, 63
19:12, 67
121:7–8, 68
86:4, 69
90:17, 70
143:8, 76
121:7–8, 84
77:20, 86
40:2, 87
108:1–2, 88
52:8–9, 92
80:12–13, 112
16:11, 119
91:9–11, 120
91:4, 127
33:5, 130
91:15, 131
8:1, 141
104:24, 144, 148
18:6, 153
16:11, 156
19:14, 158
89:21, 165
34:18, 167
37:7, 182
8:3–4, 186
10:14, 187
6:4, 198
139:13, 200
18:28, 211
27:13–14, 212
96:1, 223
27:14, 229
23:2–3, 237
63:7–8, 238
42:1, 240
121:4–5, 243
23:2–3, 249
104:31, 255
104:24–25, 255
119:50, 259
77:6, 273
119:9–10, 274
30:2, 277
119:143, 282
145:13, 284
91:4, 290
139:16, 294
139:9–10, 301
32:8, 302
144:7, 305
130:6, 309
116:8–9, 310
63:7–8, 320
62:7, 320
38:18, 321
121:1, 326
94:19, 327
32:7, 348
25:20, 349
28:7, 351
141:3, 352
90:11, 356
34:7, 357
121:1–2, 360
130:5, 368
147:9, 368

Revelation
2:17, 109
21:23, 174
21:4, 253
16:13, 263
2:3, 367

Romans
12:11, 22
12:3, 82
11:29, 101
7:15, 114
8:38–39, 134
12:18, 136
8:15, 185
12:18, 190
5:8, 209
12:14, 271
12:18, 287
1:20, 297
15:13, 314
12:4–5, 328
3:3, 363

1 Samuel
16:7, 47, 171, 336, 344

Song of Solomon
2:12, 122
2:15, 181

1 Thessalonians
5:11, 95
5:13, 217

2 Thessalonians
3:3, 20

Titus
3:5, 98

Zechariah
9:9, 90

Zephaniah
3:17, 32, 132

A Note from the Editors

We hope you enjoyed *All God's Creatures 2021*, published by the Books and Inspirational Media Division of Guideposts, a nonprofit organization that touches millions of lives every day through products and services that inspire, encourage, help you grow in your faith, and celebrate God's love.

Thank you for making a difference with your purchase of this book. Your purchase helps support our many outreach programs to military personnel, prisons, hospitals, nursing homes, and educational institutions.

We also create many useful and uplifting online resources. Visit Guideposts.org to read true stories of hope and inspiration, access OurPrayer network, sign up for free newsletters, download free e-books, join our Facebook community, and follow our stimulating blogs.

To learn about other Guideposts publications, including the bestselling devotional *Daily Guideposts*, go to Guideposts.org/Shop, call (800) 932-2145, or write to Guideposts, PO Box 5815, Harlan, Iowa 51593.

***All God's Creatures* Digital Delivery**

Included free with the purchase of this book, you can receive your daily devotions digitally for one year. Simply go to Guideposts.org/AGCdaily, fill in your email address, and enter code: Grasshopper. You will then receive your *All God's Creatures* devotions daily via email–easily viewable on your computer, smartphone, or tablet. Enjoy your daily inspiration, meaningful Scripture, and inspirational quotes anytime, anywhere!